D1742861

G85G0

Deliberation and Democracy: Innovative Processes and Institutions

)

WARSAW STUDIES IN POLITICS AND SOCIETY

Edited by
Radosław Markowski

VOLUME 3

Notes on the quality assurance and peer review of this publication

Prior to publication, the quality of the work published
in this series is reviewed by an external referee
appointed by the editorship.

Stephen Coleman / Anna Przybylska / Yves Sintomer
(eds.)

Deliberation and Democracy: Innovative Processes and Institutions

PETER LANG
EDITION

Bibliographic Information published by the Deutsche Nationalbibliothek
The Deutsche Nationalbibliothek lists this publication in the Deutsche
Nationalbibliografie; detailed bibliographic data is available in the internet
at http://dnb.d-nb.de.

Library of Congress Cataloging-in-Publication Data
Deliberation and democracy : innovative processes and institutions /
Stephen Coleman, Anna Przybylska, Yves Sintomer (eds.). — 1st ed.
pages cm
Includes bibliographical references and index.
ISBN 978-3-631-64826-1
1. Elections. 2. Public opinion polls. 3. Democracy. 4. Political participation. I.
Coleman, Stephen, 1961- editor. II. Przybylska, Anna, 1973- editor. III. Sintomer, Yves,
editor.
JF1001.D435 2015
321.8—dc23   2015020542

This publication was financially supported by the Institute of Sociology
at the University of Warsaw and the University of Warsaw Foundation.

Cover illustration:
Zofia Konarska, Katarzyna Minasowicz, http://www.para-buch.pl

ISSN 2193-3774
ISBN 978-3-631-64826-1 (Print)
E-ISBN 978-3-653-03727-2 (E-Book)
DOI 10.3726/978-3-653-03727-2

© Peter Lang GmbH
Internationaler Verlag der Wissenschaften
Frankfurt am Main 2015
All rights reserved.
Peter Lang Edition is an Imprint of Peter Lang GmbH.

Peter Lang – Frankfurt am Main · Bern · Bruxelles · New York ·
Oxford · Warszawa · Wien

This publication has been peer reviewed.

www.peterlang.com

Contents

Stephen Coleman, Anna Przybylska & Yves Sintomer

Introduction

We inhabit democracies that are radically incomplete and very far from John Rawls' normative model of a "nearly just and nearly democratic society" (Rawls 1971)[1]. Beyond the head-counting rituals of elections, the vital buzz of public disputation that ought to provide a permanent soundtrack to democracy is conspicuously lacking. Forceful and ubiquitous critiques of contemporary politics converge around a common theme: the absence of either an impetus or a space for intelligent, intelligible and inclusive public debate. The mass media are criticised for telling a limited range of stories featuring a predictable cast of "out of touch" political characters. Political parties have turned themselves into marketing organizations, obsessed with clichéd values designed to appeal to "the median voter". Governments are increasingly managerial, speaking to people in a language of spin that constrains political choice and feeds distrust. Last but not least, the impact of the public sphere on real decision making is evanescent; the weight of citizenry in global governance is reduced; and the influence of strong non-democratic global players – principally, the world financial markets – seems to increase relentlessly. At the global level, our societies are becoming ever more unequal (Piketty 2013), a result that contrasts sharply with the normative ideal that all voices deserve recognition and that the force of the strongest arguments should prevail (Habermas 1996).

Largely missing from everyday politics is a culture of deliberation in which citizens are encouraged to share and contrast their preferences and values. Such intersubjective encounters open up a space for people to understand one another and, sometimes, change their original positions under the influence of convincing arguments and evidence. At its best, deliberation gives fluidity to democracy. It saves politics from derailment by disagreements that have escaped the need for convincing elaboration or intelligent public reflection and reduces the narrow meanness that is so often associated with the sordid politics of 'winners' and 'losers'. It opens up a space for the public to think about who it is, what it needs and wants, and how to act collectively in ways that take all actors into account. As John Stuart Mill (1855, 67) put it, deliberation enables the citizen "to feel for and with his fellow citizens, and become consciously a member of a great community".

---

1   The editors would like to thank Lisa-Flor Sintomer for her formal editing work.

Deliberation also helps to clarify the political alternatives among which citizens have to choose in order to determine their own future. It has the potential of confronting the huge obstacles that power structures pose to the aim of realising a nearly just and nearly democratic society. Contrary to what some of the Founding Fathers of modern republics pretended, democratic deliberation has shown that it need not be restricted to the parliamentary arena of elitist circles and that it can thrive within a much wider public sphere. As Marx (1973, 190) put it:

> If the parliamentary regime lives by discussion, how can it forbid discussion? In it all interests and social institutions are transformed into general ideas, and debated in that form. How can any interest or institution then assert itself to be above thought, and impose itself as an article of faith? [...] The deputies, by constantly appealing to the opinion of the people, give the people the right to express their real opinion. [...] When you play the fiddle at the summit of the State, what else is there to expect than that those down below should dance?

However, in passing from closed elite spheres to a wider public, democratic deliberation encounters huge challenges. Whether on a local, national or global scale, it can only take place if certain conditions are met. Firstly, it must be open to all to set the agenda, take part in discussion and determine the outcome, independently of unequal resources and interests. Secondly, there must be an opportunity for all views to be expressed openly, regardless of who happens to hold them or whether they meet with popular approval. Thirdly, there should be no veto on styles or terms of deliberative engagement, allowing for the equal inclusion of vernacular and affective modes of discourse. Fourthly, deliberators should be constrained by no rules but for those to which they have explicitly agreed, and there should be no pre-determined outcome to discussion. Last but not least, democratic deliberation should lead to (or, at the very least, influence) real decisions. It is needless to say that these conditions are not often present in the real world. However, this does not mean that democratic deliberation and deliberative democracy are normative ideals valid only for a society of angels. They inform actual experiments and political dynamics which do take place in our societies, facing strong obstacles, solving old problems, and raising new questions. They constitute "real utopias" – setting horizons that can never be reached, but towards which progress can be made in the present (Fung and Wright 2003).

Towards this end, deliberative mini-publics represent a kind of political laboratory in which the deliberative ideal can be tested and developed, its potential can be demonstrated, and challenges to democracy can be studied. When mini-publics are well-organized, ordinary citizens can be encouraged to approximate the conditions of ideal deliberation. In the course of deliberation, when the depth of a public problem or the scale of support for policy solutions are to be measured, it makes sense that the group reflecting on the issues is representative of the population that will bear the consequences. To avoid the creation of "elites" based on certain socio-economic characteristics, random sampling – or, at least, stratified sampling followed by actions which target the inclusion of underrepresented constituencies – is a powerful tool (Nabatchi et al. 2012). For these reasons, mini-publics differ from other democratic experiments, such as participatory budgeting, that are more embedded in everyday social and political relations and in which the logic of democratic deliberation is compromised by the logic of inclusive participation (Avritzer 2002; Sintomer et al. 2013). These latter methods are more open to empowerment dynamics and therefore can challenge asymmetries of power-relations, but are also often influenced by pressure groups that do not necessarily defend the worst-off. In addition, they are based on self-selection and as such "are likely to attract only strong partisans" (Goodin and Dryzek 2006).

As our experience regarding the practice of deliberation grows, the position from which we evaluate it, and the criteria of this evaluation, change. For the clarity and conclusiveness of studies, our expectations regarding deliberative encounters need to be explicit (Grönlund, Bächtiger and Setälä 2014). Each question concerning the public good needs to reflect carefully on the method of information gathering, taking into account the well-being of the entire community concerned. It is a symptom of the maturity of the subject that in many current publications there is an explicit concern for rigorous empirical evaluation (Geissel and Newton 2012; Geissel and Joas 2013; Nabatchi et al. 2012). This is vital for the development of the theory and practice of deliberation.

Deliberation and participation may be presented as opposed models of democracy, but they do not have to be (Held 2006; Goodin 2008). However, trade-offs are inevitable, and there will always be those who prime the logic of unrestricted participation over deliberation, and vice versa. Most deliberative mini-publics rarely have much impact on the wider public sphere and in the worst cases, democratic deliberation could become an alternative to deliberative democracy (Chambers 2009). In such circumstances deliberative mini-publics could even be implicated in a different kind of elitism, which claims that involvement of lay citizens in politics can only ever take place within the managed arena of mini-publics, other forms of participation being suspect of bringing emotional and non-reasonable elements. This is why some researchers and practitioners explore a path in which their quasi-ideal democratic norms are articulated with a more inclusive and heterogeneous public discourse taking place within the wider public sphere, while others discuss the issue of scaling-up deliberation (Elstub and McLaverty 2014; Grönlund, Bächtiger and Setälä 2014).

Mini-publics often do not meet the expectations of direct influence on policy, and they can be experimental rather than efficacious. Most of them are top-down instruments and because they are not legally institutionalized, they depend upon the good will of political authorities. This is perhaps why the vast majority of them have not produced substantial changes in the real world. However, they can have other kinds of impact (Goodin and Dryzek 2006; Nabatchi et al. 2012). They have been created as a response to the failures in public communication and the inability of the mass media to support a reflexive dialogue. In a number of cases they are grounded in the tradition of social intervention in social sciences and as such they are co-created with participants (Kennis and McTaggart). Although the prominent position of mini-publics in scientific inquiry has been noticed and even criticized (Chambers 2009), the issue of deliberation in elective institutions, in social movements and in referenda has still to be systematically explored (Gastil 2008; Kriesi 2012). Mini-publics do not replace the institutions of representative democracy, nor those of direct democracy; they coexist with other forms of participatory democracy. A next step in their development should be their institutionalization and inclusion in a global perspective (Sintomer 2011).

The present book aims to explore and encourage such articulations; to consider ways in which the high standards of experimental deliberation can be adjusted to the realities of what Coleman and Blumler (2009) have called "a more deliberative democracy". Arising from a conference at the University of Warsaw in June 2012, the chapters in this volume focus upon innovative deliberative processes and institutions. The majority of them contain data collected by researchers in the process of trying to answer questions that are central to the elaboration and evaluation of deliberative practices. Research on deliberation has developed considerably in recent years, giving rise to detailed and robust results. This book presents a synthesis of some of them and contributes to a certain "provincialization" (Chakrabarty 2007) of the usual suspects by opening the panorama beyond West-European and North-American experiments. It comprises four sections. The first concerns contemporary challenges and new approaches to the public sphere. The second focuses upon a specific deliberative technique – the Deliberative Poll – and compares findings emanating from this practice in different political and cultural contexts. The third section addresses the formidable challenge of determining what constitutes deliberative quality. Finally, the fourth section problematizes democratic deliberation and deliberative democracy as they relate to the complex challenges of contemporary politics.

Section I – Innovative Deliberative Devices and the Public Sphere

The public sphere, "in which the public organizes itself as the bearer or public opinion" (Habermas 1989), has always been socially more diverse and politically less argumentative than the somehow idealized and normative version proposed by Habermas. In addition, it is presently a much more complex political space than it was in the era of eighteenth-century coffee-house discussion or even twentieth-century newspaper-driven discourse. It is now mediated through many competing as well as converging channels of public communication. Publicness has changed. As Coleman and Ross (2010) argue,

> As the idea of a singular, potentially univocal public is abandoned, a pluralistic conception of the public as a patchwork of co-existing and overlapping communities has emerged. This fractured public lacks the metaphysical integrity that once gave legitimacy to notions of sovereign nationhood and moral universalism.

Within this new discursive environment – which some are now conceptualising as a "deliberative system" (Parkinson and Mansbridge 2012) – novel techniques of engaging citizens in face-to-face discussions are proposed, experimented with, and sometimes institutionalized. While the mass media remain the primary source of information used by people in keeping up with the fast-changing world and framing their political decisions, digital media open up spaces for direct involvement in agenda-setting and the exchange of opinions. These and other dimensions of the changing public sphere are discussed in the chapters of the first section.

In the opening chapter **Katherine R. Knobloch**, **John Gastil** and **Tyrone Reitman** consider the institutionalization of deliberative mini-publics. Their discussion focuses on the exciting case study of the Oregon Citizens' Initiative Review which brought together twenty-four randomly selected and demographically stratified citizens to deliberate on state-wide initiatives over the course of five days. A most interesting feature of this study is the integration of this deliberative innovation in the official electoral process. The Oregon Citizens' Initiative Review managed to connect the reflections of a deliberative mini-public to the larger public sphere and, subsequently, had the power to impact upon electoral decisions. The authors base their analysis on interviews with organizers, direct observation and archival evidence.

Access to the results of empirical research regarding the use of internet media in democratic and non-democratic countries has substantially grown over the past two decades. It allows researchers to test hypotheses regarding the capacity of digital communication to open up deliberative space, regardless of the more general openness or opacity of political systems. Informal online communication is developing very fast worldwide, and it has become a major dimension of Chinese society. Its impact on official political discourse is discussed by **Fan Yang** in chapter Two. First, the author familiarizes readers with the interrelation of political and judicial institutions. He then presents a case study that explains how the Chinese authorities respond to communication via social media. The empirical focus here is upon Weibo, which is considered in terms of its strengths and weaknesses as a deliberative space, as well as on its role in democratizing public communication in a deeply authoritarian state.

In chapter Three **Weiyu Zhang** addresses the problem of digital divide and its consequences for public participation in deliberative exercises. The fairly optimistic findings she presents suggest that when disenfranchised groups are invited to participate in e-deliberation, the level of their engagement is not much different from the average. There are no substantial differences in the amount of talk and the number of arguments. Contrary to the expectation that the disenfranchised would feel disadvantaged in experiencing e-deliberation, most disenfranchised groups, except for younger people, reported higher satisfaction after participating than their peers.

Mass media, and particularly public broadcasting in its role as a key source of civic information, are considered by **Kees Brants** in chapter Four. He explores the demise of the deliberative dream that seemed to be inherent to the mission statements of public service broadcasting. This chapter characterizes the logic of public broadcasting, its place in the changing media landscape and relationship to a more deliberative public sphere.

Section II – Deliberative Poll: Recent Implementations

The second section of the book turns to empirical studies of Deliberative Polling. This method of public consultation was proposed by James Fishkin in 1988. Subsequently it was developed and implemented with Robert Luskin in a range of political and social contexts in relation to various issues. The Deliberative Poll has become one of the most discussed deliberative mini-publics next to Planning Cells invented in Germany (Dienel 1997), Citizens' Juries in the USA (Crosby 1975), and Consensus Conferences in Denmark (Joss and Durant 1995). Evidence from Hungary, Japan and Poland in Deliberative Polling implementations is considered in this section. As each of these deliberative exercises employed the same methodology, it is possible – at least to some extent – to compare data and draw some general conclusions about the relationship between a universal method of deliberation and the contextual specificity of its implementation. Apart from positive effects of the method's use for the quality of talk of ordinary citizens on policy issues, the authors draw the readers' attention to some challenges that require further investigation, analysis and generalisation of results based on comparative data. First of all, there is a need for empirical evidence on whether, and under what conditions, the positive results of deliberation may go beyond short-time effects upon citizens who were directly involved, and upon the wider public. Other challenges under scrutiny are: the role of experts and the time distribution between them and participants for creating better informed opinions; the inclusion of a broader public in the discussion; and making politicians responsible for explaining the use of the results of public consultations.

In chapter Five **James Fishkin** sets out an argument in favor of Deliberative Polling and reflects on the trend of bringing power to the people through institutional attempts to create inclusive public debates. He responds to arguments of those who perceive an intrinsic conflict between the increased participation of citizens and the level of thoughtfulness with which they provide an input into the democratic process. He sets out to identify the conditions that allow for more inclusion and, at the same time, deep collective reflection. Random sampling and moderated debates are intended to engender evidence-based reflection on policy alternatives by citizens whose social characteristics are representative to a given community. The precise institutional design may well counter such defects of group behaviour as polarization of opinions.

In chapter Six **Anna Przybylska** and **Alice Siu** reflect on the main premises and impact of a Deliberative Poll on the functions and management of the stadium extended for UEFA EURO 2012 in Poznań. They refer to data collected during public consultations and an evaluation study. A particularly interesting feature of this analysis is the educational effect of the Deliberative Poll, at least in the short-term. The research findings presented here confirm the advantages that the careful preparation of public consultations and information materials can bring. Based on empirical evidence the authors consider the issue of time distribution between participants and experts that can best serve deliberation. The principal problem with this exercise does not concern the quality of the consultation process, but the inability or unwillingness of officials to communicate openly and clearly to the public about how its results are to be included in decisions.

In chapter Seven **György Lengyel**, **Borbála Göncz**, and **Éva Vépy-Schlemmer** write about the temporary and lasting effects of a Deliberative Poll organized in the Kaposvár Region of Hungary. The discussion focused on unemployment and its perceived relationship to EU integration. After the deliberative exercise took place participants appeared to be better informed and their opinions became more balanced. The majority were enthusiastic about the event and declared a continuing interest in the topics discussed. However, a follow-up survey conducted a year after the Deliberative Poll showed that the majority of the opinion changes were short-term. The authors investigate the contrasting characteristics of those who changed their mind temporarily and lastingly.

The concern of **Tatsuro Sakano** in chapter Eight is the knowledge gap between members of recruited deliberative mini-publics and society at large. He considers a Japanese Deliberative Poll on energy and demonstrates that its outcomes were forgotten by the general public only six months after the debate. The author reflects on conditions under which the problem might possibly be solved and focuses on the inter-subjectivity which results from communication and mutual learning between the participants in the Deliberative Poll and the broader public. He argues that Deliberative Polls can lead to more representative and thoughtful public discussion than that generated by conventional public meetings.

Section III – Deliberative Quality

The chapters that comprise the third section of the book provide an insight into the crucial question of how far deliberative exercises can be shown to enhance the quality of public expression, reflection and interaction. The meaning of deliberation has been subject to various and rather divergent definitions. While there can be no agreed objective criteria of deliberative quality, it is possible to set out a number of clearly defined and reflexively adopted assumptions about what might contribute to such quality and what would be absent from it, and use it as a tool in robust empirical investigations. The evaluative criteria of deliberative quality set out in these chapters make explicit the observations and judgments that can all too easily be left unstated and under-theorised.

In chapter Nine **André Bächtiger** and **Jürg Steiner** present their discourse quality index (DQI) as a very promising tool for measuring the quality of deliberation in various contexts. One of the most interesting dimensions of their study is that it articulates a theoretical definition of deliberation, largely derived from a critical interpretation of Habermas, and efficient quantitative methods that enable to operationalize the concept. The DQI had previously been applied in various institutional contexts, most notably parliamentary discussions. In this chapter, André Bächtiger and Jürg Steiner apply it to the transcripts of an Australian Citizens' Conference, offering fascinating insight into possible ways of coding for deliberative quality.

What is the relationship between deliberation and direct democracy, which implies a wide public sphere that is specific when compared to electoral debates? This is the question posed by **Marco R. Steenbergen, André Bächtiger, Seraina**

Pedrini and **Thomas Gautschi** in chapter Ten. The authors refer to empirical data from their study preceding a Swiss referendum on the expulsion of foreigners with a criminal record in 2010. They analyze the impact of access to information and deliberation on knowledge that has meaningful consequences for citizens' choices. In their experiment the authors divided participants into three groups, each exposed to different conditions. They found out that although it is difficult to generate meaningful deliberation within a national population, the organisation of well-planned deliberative initiatives can contribute more to the public acquisition of knowledge than mere access to information.

In chapter Eleven **Elżbieta Wesołowska** argues that although numerous authors have recognized the importance of group deliberation processes, their dynamics under real conditions remain understudied. She points to a few attempts to evaluate the quality of deliberation, e.g. through application of self-descriptive measurements filled in by the participants, but considers that limited methods fail to explain which different deliberative criteria are realised in such debates. The method proposed in this chapter is a standardized procedure based on the reconstruction of the theoretical model of deliberative debate set out by Gutmann and Thompson (1996).

In chapter Twelve **Marcin Zgiep** attempts to create an analytical framework inspired by the concept of distributed deliberation (Goodin 2008; Thompson 2008). A key characteristic of distributed deliberation is its emphasis upon a network-based account of a dynamic, pluralistic, multi-phase – rather than static, singular – image of the reason-giving process. He explains how particular discourses are linked to different types of institutions and how these perform diverse functions and contribute to the quality of a deliberative democratic system.

Section IV – Deliberative Democracy: Reflexive Perspectives

In the final section we move from more specific theoretical, empirical and methodological questions, to a consideration of why any of this matters. This leads us to fundamental questions of democratic normativity: What should a healthy, vibrant democracy look like? What minimal features, beyond occasional rights to vote, should democratic citizens possess? What is and could be the meaning of deliberative democracy, and the extension of deliberation much beyond the deliberative mini-publics? In the concluding three chapters these questions are interrogated.

In chapter Thirteen **Stephen Coleman** and **Giles Moss** consider the ontological status of deliberation. The authors argue that the deliberative practice is best thought of as a normative construction, rather than something naturally occurring and given, and that deliberative researchers are complicit in its contemporary enactment. Deliberation is conceived as a normative set of practices to support different conceptions of democracy. Deliberative researchers, claim these authors, privilege certain forms of talk and employ (or even design) particular architectures and technologies of deliberation. Focusing on online deliberation, the chapter concludes with an argument in favor of a politics of deliberation that is normatively explicit.

In chapter Fourteen, **Yves Sintomer** analyses the logic of randomly-selected deliberative mini-publics. He begins by exploring the role of sortation in Renaissance Florence, which implied a Republican logic of self-government, and contrasts it with contemporary mini-publics based on (more or less) representative samples. The author suggests that modern deliberative mechanisms with randomly select participants face a number of challenges. He concludes that there is a potential trade-off between deliberation in the English sense of the term (good discussion), when developed within mini-publics, and deliberation in the senses found in Romance languages (decision of a collective body). The solution to this trade-off must be a combination of deliberative and participatory initiatives in support of democracy.

In the final chapter Fifteen, **Claus Offe** considers the features of contemporary democratic failure and offers corresponding proposals for a reinvigorated democracy. He discusses how public will formation and expression might be improved. Paying particular attention to the effects of deliberation, he scrutinizes possible and desirable functions of deliberation as well as some institutions in which they could be performed.

References

Avritzer, Leonardo. 2002. *Democracy and the Public Space in Latin America*. Princeton/ Oxford: Princeton University Press.

Coleman, Stephen, and Jay G. Blumler. 2009. *The Internet and Democratic Citizenship: Theory, Practice, and Policy*. New York: Cambridge University Press.

Coleman, Stephen, and Karen Ross. 2010. *The Media and the Public: "Them" and "Us" in Media Discourse*. Oxford, England: Wiley-Blackwell.

Crosby, Ned. 1975. *In Search of the Competent Citizen*. Working Paper. Plymouth: Center for New Democratic Processes.

Chakrabarty, Dipesh. 2007. *Provincializing Europe: Postcolonial Thought and Historical Difference*. Princeton/Oxford: Princeton University Press.

Chambers, Simone. 2009. "Rhetoric and the Public Sphere: Has Deliberative Democracy Abandoned Mass Democracy?" *Political Theory* 37/3: 323–350.

Dienel, Peter C. 1997. *Die Planungszelle*. Wiesbaden: Westdeutscher Verlag.

Elstub, Stephen, and Peter McLaverty (eds.). 2014. *Deliberative Democracy. Issues and Cases*. Edinburgh: Edinburgh University Press.

Fung, Archon, and Eric Olin Wright (eds.). 2003. *Deepening Democracy. Institutional Innovations in Empowered Participatory Governance*. London/New York: Verso.

Gastil, John. 2008. *Political Communication and Deliberation*. Los Angeles: SAGE.

Geissel, Brigitte, and Kenneth Newton (eds.). 2012. *Evaluating Democratic Innovations. Curing the Democratic Malaise?* London: Routledge.

Geissel, Brigitte, and Marco Joas (eds.). 2013. *Participatory Democratic Innovations in Europe. Improving the Quality of Democracy?* Opladen: Barbara Budrich Publishers.

Goodin, Robert, and John S. Dryzek. 2006. "Deliberative Impacts: The Macro-Political Uptake of Mini-Publics." *Politics and Society* 34 (2): 219–244.

Goodin, Robert E. 2008. *Innovating Democracy: Democratic Theory and Practice after the Deliberative Turn*. Oxford: Oxford University Press.

Grönlund, Kimmo, André Bächtiger, and Maija Setälä. 2014. *Deliberative Mini-Publics. Involving Citizens in the Democratic Process*. Colchester: ECPR Press.

Gutmann, Amy, and Denis Thompson. 1996. *Democracy and Disagreement*. Cambridge, Mass.: Belknap.

Habermas, Jürgen. 1989. *The Structural Transformation of the Public Sphere*. Cambridge: Polity Press.

Habermas, Jürgen. 1996. *Between Facts and Norms: Contributions to a Discourse Theory of Law and Democracy*. Cambridge, Mass.: MIT Press.

Held, David. 2006. *Models of Democracy*. Cambridge: Polity Press, third edition.

Joss, Simon, and John Durant (eds). 1995. *Public Participation in Science. The Role of Consensus Conferences in Europe*. London: Science Museum.

Kemmis, Stephen, and Robin McTaggart. 2005. "Participatory Action Research: Communicative Action Research: Communicative Action and the Public Sphere." In *The SAGE Handbook of Qualitative Research,* eds. Norman K. Denzin and Yvona S. Lincoln, 559–603. *London*: SAGE Publications.

Kriesi, Hanspeter. 2012. *Political Communication in Direct Democratic Campaigns. Enlightening or Manipulating?* Houndmills: Palgrave Macmillan.

Marx, Karl. 1973. "The Eighteenth Brumaire of Louis Bonaparte," in idem, *Surveys from Exile*. Harmondsworth: Penguin.

Mill, John Stuart. 1855. *Considerations on Representative Government*. London: Longman, Green & Roberts.

Nabatchi, Tina, John Gastil, G. Michael Weiksner, and Matt Leighninger (eds.). 2012. *Democracy in Motion. Evaluating the Practice and Impact of Deliberative Civic Engagement.* Oxford: Oxford University Press.

Parkinson, John, and Jane Mansbridge. 2012. *Deliberative Systems: Deliberative Democracy at the Large Scale.* Cambridge: Cambridge University Press.

Piketty, Thomas. 2013. *Capital in the Twenty-First Century.* Cambridge Mass.: Harvard University Press.

Rawls, John. 1971. *A Theory of Justice.* Cambridge, Mass.: Harvard University Press.

Sintomer, Yves. 2011. *Petite histoire de l'expérimentation démocratie. Tirage au sort et politique d'Athènes à nos jours.* Paris: La Découverte.

Sintomer, Yves, Giovanni Allegretti, and Carsten Herzberg. 2013. *Participatory Budgeting Worldwide,* Bonn: Engagement Global, Dialog Global 25, http://www.service-eine-welt.de/images/text_material-3651.img.

Thompson, Dennis F. 2008. Deliberative Democratic Theory and Empirical Political Science. *Annual Review of Political Science* 11: 497–520.

Section I.
Innovative Deliberative Devices and the Public Sphere

Katherine R. Knobloch, John Gastil & Tyrone Reitman

Chapter One. Connecting Micro-Deliberation to Electoral Decision Making: Institutionalizing the Oregon Citizens' Initiative Review

Introduction: Deliberative Events and (the Lack of) Institutionalization

The theory, practice, and study of public deliberation has undergone expansive growth over the past two decades, and it has given rise to—or theoretically framed—several novel opportunities for community discussion and empowered citizen decision making (Gastil and Levine 2005; Goodin and Dryzek 2006; Nabatchi et al. 2012)[1]. Few of these processes, however, have been institutionalized as formal parts of governing systems and granted official decision-making power or other forms of direct influence. In other words, most such processes are typically disconnected from the very decisions they seek to influence.

The Oregon Citizens' Initiative Review (CIR) is one deliberative event that has been granted governmental legitimacy as a means of public voice, if not authoritative decision making. The CIR was developed to improve the quality of information available to voters regarding state-wide initiatives by connecting small-scale deliberation with electoral decision making. Briefly, CIR organizers convened representative groups of twenty-four registered Oregon voters for five days to study and deliberate on statewide initiatives. At the end of their deliberations, each panel of citizens wrote a page of analysis about their assigned initiative for the official Oregon State Voters' Pamphlet, which the Secretary of State delivered along with mail-in ballots to every registered voter in the state. As many as eighty percent of voters report using the Voters' Pamphlet when making voting decisions

---

1   The research presented in this report was supported by the National Science Foundation (NSF) Directorate for Social, Behavioral and Economic Sciences' Political Science Program (Award #0961774) and a joint learning agreement with the Kettering Foundation. The views expressed in this chapter are solely those of the authors. We are grateful to Ned Crosby and Pat Benn for continuous insight on institutionalizing citizen deliberation, a purpose to which they have devoted many years and considerable energy.

(Gastil and Knobloch 2010). Such widespread use allows the Citizens' Statements produced by the CIR to play a prominent role in voter education and subsequently influence the outcome of binding governmental decisions.

In 2011, the CIR became a permanent part of the Oregon electoral process and a state commission was developed to oversee its implementation. In this chapter, we tell the story of the CIR and describe its journey to becoming a permanent part of state government as well as its prospects for fuller integration into electoral systems nationally and internationally.

The CIR is one variety of mini-publics, small scale deliberative processes drawing on a representative sample of the population, that have proliferated over the past few decades (Dahl 1989; Fung 2003; Goodin 2008). Like the CIR, most mini-publics serve to connect small-group deliberation with macro decision making by feeding the results of deliberative processes into larger public discourse (Goodin 2008). This allows the wider public to use the information and conclusions from such events in their own decision makingand thus promotes "vicarious deliberation" (Gastil, Richards and Knobloch 2012).

Most deliberative mini-publics, however, typically have neither institutionalized authority nor political influence. In short, they are disconnected from the very decisions they aim to influence, as was the case for the Australian Citizens' Parliament (Carson et al. in press). Very few mini-publics have gone so far as to invest real legal authority in a broad cross-section of the public, with prominent exceptions being Canadian Citizens' Assemblies (Lang 2007; Warren and Pearse 2008) and Deliberative Polls in China (Leib and He 2006). More often, these structures provide recommendations that are either distributed through the media without a tangible connection to policy decisions or are passed on to governing officials who may or may not use those recommendations when reaching their own conclusions (Goodin and Dryzek 2006).

Some exceptions that have been granted decision-making authority have addressed quasi-technical issues outside the most contentious political controversies (Einsiedel, Jelsøe and Breck 2001; Warren and Pearse 2008). Juries could count as another contrasting case, but the scope of juries remains narrow, albeit wider when one considers the potential for politically-motivated jury nullification of laws that jurors find unjust (Gastil et al. 2010). In sum, mini-publics have gained traction over the past few decades as a form of community engagement, but they tend to have limited power in influencing politically contentious policy debates.

By contrast, the Oregon CIR was designed to focus on ballot measures voted on by the general public that typically engender passionate debate (Broder 2000; Matsusaka 2008). The Citizens' Statements produced by the CIR panels receive a prominent space in the Voters' Pamphlet, a widely-read platform that can potentially sway a large portion of the electorate (Bowler and Donovan 1998). The United States has produced a plethora of deliberation scholars and practitioners (Ryfe 2007) as well as deliberative forums (Fung 2003; Goodin 2008; Nabatchi et al. 2012), but prior to the Oregon CIR, it had not established by law a deliberative innovation that granted a random sample of the public such substantial political power.

The Creation of the Citizens' Initiative Review

The Case for Reforming the Initiative Process

Before examining the case of the CIR, however, we begin with reflections on the current state of initiative elections, as commonly practiced in the United States. The initiative and referendum process empowers the electorate to vote on the passage of a law or amendment to a constitution. Introduced during the Progressive Era, the initiative was designed to enhance direct democracy. Ballot initiatives were meant to make the government more accountable to the public by circumventing the corrupting powers of entrenched parties and special interest groups (Bowler and Donovan 1998; Guthrie 1912). South Dakota was the first state to write the initiative into their constitution in 1898 (Matsusaka 2008), and in 1902, Oregonians voted on a ballot referred by the legislature that implemented the initiative process and became the second state to adopt the initiative (Oregon State Archives 2013–2014). Oregon was the first state to bring a law before the voters, passing two initiatives, including direct primaries, in 1904 (Matsusaka 2008). Twenty-four states and Washington D.C. now have the initiative (Matsusaka 2008), as well as many Western European countries and former Soviet republics (Lupia and Matsusaka 2004). When one considers municipalities, and other smaller political units that put bonds and other measures to a popular vote, hundreds of political units across the globe practice the initiative or a closely related form of direct democracy.

Though public opinion tends to favor the initiative, scholars and public officials are wary of its usage (Broder 2000; Lupia and Matsusaka 2004; Keown 2010). One of the primary concerns relates to campaign finance. In Oregon, individuals or organizations interested in getting an initiative on the ballot must collect signatures of support from six percent of the voting population—eight percent for constitutional amendments—equating to roughly 85,000 to 120,000 signatures (Oregon Elections Division 2012). Signatures are often gathered by solicitors who are paid for their time. In 2010 one accounting estimated that it cost an average of

$5.32 per signature to get a measure on the ballot in Oregon (Ballotopedia 2013), or between $420,000 and $630,000.

A related concern arises from the complexity of many initiatives. Lacking traditional heuristics, such as simple voting cues from political parties, and without in-depth knowledge about the proposition in question, voters often rely on interest group campaigns and political elites to form preferences (Gerber 1999; Gerber and Lupia 1999). This may be particularly detrimental when either proponents or opponents of an initiative can drastically outspend their competitors. In a state as large and diverse as California, $155,000 can move the vote by as much as 1.1 percent (Stratmann 2006), with the price tag for a percentage swing likely lower in smaller political units. Thus, even though initiative elections may be more beholden to the public will than the legislature (Lupia and Matsusaka 2004; Matsusaka 2008), the complexity of initiative language and the large sums of money used to generate and contest them can undermine their ability to achieve the progressive ideals for which they were adopted.

When faced with initiatives' potential costs, elevating the quality of information provided to voters is even more apparent. In Oregon, half of the increases in expenditures since 1990 stem directly from the passage of initiatives (Keown 2010). Moreover, a longitudinal analysis of the fiscal effects of initiatives found that they were more likely to decentralize governing costs and shift expenses related to government services and infrastructure from state to local governments (Matsusaka 2000). While these fiscal impacts point to the power that initiatives give to citizens, they highlight the need to ensure that voters have the information necessary to make good, and economically sustainable, decisions.

Methods

The Oregon CIR grew out of an interest in correcting some of these problems. In exploring the development and institutionalization of the CIR, we bring together three different perspectives. The first author of this essay interviewed several individuals directly involved in this process, as well as various individuals who have worked closely with the project over the years. The second author has corresponded and collaborated with people advocating this and similar processes over the past decade. The third author served as co-director of Healthy Democracy Oregon (HDO), which lobbied for and ran the panels. The first and second authors directly observed the 2010 and 2012 CIRs, as well as several planning meetings before, during, and after them. In addition, we each took part in legislative hearings aimed at exploring the quality and impact of the panels (Gastil and Knobloch 2010; Knobloch, Gastil, Richards and Feller 2013b), and we have attended several conferences with organizers and observers of the CIR in which we have discussed the growth of the CIR and its impact on the voting public.

We also have archived documents generated during the legislative hearings in which the CIR was discussed, as well as the promotional materials produced by HDO for the purpose of publicizing and building support for the panels. For the remainder of this paper, we rely on our vantage points—as different varieties of participant observer—and the evidence gleaned from our archives and funded research to reflect on this newly institutionalized form of deliberative governance.

Development of the Citizens' Initiative Review

In 2003 Tyrone Reitman and Elliot Shuford met in a public policy graduate pro-gram at the University of Oregon. Reitman had previously worked as an advocate for Oregon initiatives but was growing increasingly frustrated with the mislead-ing tactics used by campaigns both for and against statewide ballot measures. He and Shuford discussed the value of the initiative process, with both agreeing that such attempts at direct democracy were positive but in need of a new approach to reform. Looking for solutions, in 2006 the two contacted Ned Crosby, the founder and president of the Jefferson Center for New Democratic Processes, a Minnesota-based non-profit that focused on improving democracy.

Citizens' Juries

Since the 1970s, Crosby had been working on deliberative democracy projects, in particular developing the Citizens' Jury, a mini-public that gathers a stratified random sample of between 12 and 24 citizens together to discuss public policy issues (Crosby and Hottinger 2011; Crosby and Nethercutt 2005; Smith and Wales 2002). In this process, citizens meet for several days, take part in small and large group discussions, and hear testimony from advocates and witnesses. In the end, a jury develops recommendations that public officials and/or the electorate can use when making decisions. Since their inception, more than three hundred citizens' juries have been run, by the Jefferson Center as well as other organizations, in the U.S., the U.K., Australia, Canada, Japan, and Spain, focusing on political issues like healthcare and education as well as on the policy-proposals and qualifications of candidates for elected office (Crosby and Hottinger 2011).

Hopeful for the prospect of Citizens' Juries but recognizing their lack of insti-tutional authority, the second author of this chapter, John Gastil, imagined the Citizens' Juries restructured as a "citizen panel" process in his book, *By Popular Demand: Revitalizing Representative Democracy through Deliberative Elections* (Gastil 2000). Gastil argued that such panels could serve as a potentially powerful 'deliberative voting cue' that citizens might choose to follow when seeking guidance before voting on an initiative.

Crosby (2003) argued along similar lines, with a specific focus on adapting the Citizens' Jury process. Shortly thereafter, Gastil and Crosby (2005, 2006) sought to bring such panels to the state of Washington, located in the Pacific Northwest region of the United States. Crosby developed a full-fledged proposal, in the form of legally vetted draft legislation, and he asked the state to fund citizens' panels that would review state-wide initiatives. With opponents wary of the cost that an unproven institution may add to an already overburdened state budget, the idea faltered after a hearing in a state legislative committee.

Although Crosby was unsuccessful in implementing the process in the state of Washington, news of his proposal reached that state's southern neighbor, Oregon, when Shuford attended a speech given by Crosby in 2001. The idea stagnated when the Jefferson Center's tax-exempt status was revoked because some of its Citizens' Juries had evaluated candidate positions on political issues (Keown 2010). In 2006, however, Shuford and Reitman returned to the idea while seeking to improve Oregon's initiatives, and they worked together with Crosby and his wife Pat Benn. Reitman and Shuford acted as co-directors of a board that included Crosby and Benn, former secretaries of state from both parties, and legislative and election officials. They called their organization Healthy Democracy Oregon (HDO) with the express intent of establishing the first CIR in the state of Oregon.

Legislative Development

In 2007, HDO introduced House Bill 2911, sponsored by Representative Peter Buckley (D-Ashland).[2] This bill proposed establishing a CIR in a manner similar to the ongoing proposal in Washington state. The bill died in committee (Keown 2010), but it piqued the interest of several legislators and the secretary of state.

After seeking advice from former secretaries of state and current legislators, HDO ran a test of the CIR in 2008 to better establish the credibility of the process. With the help of the League of Women's Voters and private donations, HDO gathered twenty-four voters who had been randomly selected and stratified to match the demographics of the state electorate. For five days, the citizen panelists learned

---

2   In the United States, representatives and senators are commonly denoted by their political party and city of residence within a state. The "D" indicates membership in the Democratic Party, and "R" indicates belonging to the Republican Party. In modern American politics, the Democrats are the more liberal or progressive party, and the Republican Party advocates more conservative social and fiscal policies.

about and deliberated on Measure 58, which would limit the use of English as a second language for K-12 instruction in Oregon. Neutral experts, along with proponents and opponents (hereafter referred to jointly as policy "advocates"), provided testimony to the panelists, who used that information to create a statement identifying key facts and arguments relevant to the initiative. At the end of the week, HDO held a press conference at which the panelists presented their statement outside the state capitol building in Salem. The League of Women Voters independently evaluated the process and found that both panelists and advocates were highly satisfied with the review and did not perceive bias.

After this initial success, Secretary of State Kate Brown suggested that HDO introduce the CIR as a one-year trial run, with the goal of evaluating more extensively its quality and impact. That year HDO promoted House Bill 2895, which would establish the Oregon CIR pilot process. In their earlier attempts at institutionalization, citizen panels faced opposition partly because they required government funding. Based on feedback provided by Oregon legislators, the Oregon CIR would still be housed in government but would be funded by private donations. Soon after, the state legislature considered adopting the process.

Reitman and Shuford, along with some of the panelists from the 2008 test run, began lobbying for the bill. HDO reached out to the public and circulated a statement of support for the CIR, gaining upwards of 30,000 signatures. In addition, they created a short explanatory video of the CIR that provided an easy-to-understand overview of the process' design and purpose. The chair of the House Rules Committee at the time, Representative Arnie Roblan (D-Coos Bay), took up the bill by acting as one of its sponsors, and he helped lobby for its passage. A bi-partisan group of legislators sponsored the bill, with seventeen members of the state House of Representatives and ten state senators signing on as co-sponsors. The bill received its first hearing in the House Rules Committee in March, 2009 (Keown 2010).

According to testimony provided before the House Rules Committee, the CIR was intended to provide informed, non-partisan information that voters could use when deciding how to vote. This was viewed as a supplement to the more narrowly focused explanatory statement and financial impact statements that already appeared in the state's Voters' Pamphlet, while also serving as an alternative to the more inflamed rhetoric that came to voters through paid campaign messages in that same Pamphlet. Alternative means of initiative reform, such as campaign finance laws, faced opposition based on the argument that they limited free speech. By contrast, the CIR provided a means of reforming initiative elections without taking away anyone's rights.

Though some legislators voiced opposition to the CIR, primarily concerned with the cost and it continuing a wider trend of expanding state government, the bill received bi-partisan support. On June 16, 2009, the Oregon legislature approved House Bill 2895 with a vote of 47–7 in favor in the House and 23–7 in the Senate. Both Democrats and Republicans voted in favor of the bill, but all of the "nay" votes came from Republican legislators, an issue we revisit later in the context of the 2011 legislative session.

House Bill 2895 allowed for a pilot run of the process and inclusion of the statements produced by the CIR in the state's voters' guide. Though the bill included a sunset clause requiring evaluation before considering a permanent renewal of the CIR, this marked the first time a consequential, government-sanctioned deliberative project of this scale had been adopted in the United States. On June 26, 2009, Governor Ted Kulongoski signed the bill into law and paved the way for CIR pilot panels in the 2010 statewide general election. Shortly thereafter, the second author of this chapter obtained funding from the National Science Foundation for the evaluation of the event, and a team of researchers was organized for this task.[3]

Implementation and Development

2010 Citizens' Initiative Review Panels

Having successfully conducted a test of the CIR in 2008 and being the primary agent behind the bill's passage, HDO was chosen by the Oregon Secretary of State to implement the 2010 project. Because the bill contained no funding mechanism, however, HDO was responsible for gathering the funds necessary to implement the panels. HDO set about finding private donors and organizations, primarily reaching out to good governance organizations at the state and national level. For the pilot process, each review cost approximately $125,000; thus, the two reviews combined to cost a quarter of a million dollars.

---

3   In 2013, the federal government passed legislation that restricted for one year the National Science Foundation (NSF) funding of political science projects. This is the result of an amendment by U.S. Senator Tom Coburn (R-Oklahoma). In 2015, Congress is considering cutting in half its funds for NSF in the social science, via the "America COMPETES Reauthorization Act of 2015." We mention it here only because a key to the reestablishment of the Oregon CIR was the research conducted in 2010–11 with NSF funds. Without public support for research evaluating deliberative processes like the CIR, it will become more difficult to assess, and consequently design and sustain, such innovations in the future. When we successfully sought a second NSF grant to continue our research in 2014, we applied to the Decision, Risk, and Management Science program, not Political Science.

To create the citizen panels, HDO randomly selected 10,000 Oregon state voters and mailed them an invitation that included a letter of support from Secretary of State Brown. HDO asked recipients whether they would be willing to participate in the CIR and complete a brief demographic survey. From the initial request, 3.5 percent responded to the survey and were then entered into a pool of several hundred voters. From this smaller pool, the HDO staff anonymously selected twenty-four panelists and five alternates for each week to match the demographics of the Oregon electorate in terms of age, gender, ethnicity, education, partisan affiliation and place of residence. The selection process was constructed in consultation with Davis, Hibbitts, and Midghall, Inc. (a survey research firm located in Portland, Oregon) and overseen by the League of Women Voters of Oregon. Panelists who were chosen to attend received a stipend of $150 per day, which approximated the state's average daily wage. HDO also covered panelists' travel and lodging expenses and, in some cases, childcare.

HDO assembled a team to lead the forum. Larry Pennings, who had worked with the Jefferson Center in planning and moderating Citizens' Juries, was tasked with developing the long-form agenda for the five-day event. He and three other experienced moderators were hired to facilitate the CIR, with a different pair of moderators each week. In addition, HDO took on temporary staff members responsible for researching the initiatives, communicating with advocates, experts, and the media, and assisting in logistical planning.

Having secured funding as well as staff and citizen panelists, HDO ran a shortened version of the process in Seattle in mid-June of 2010. This forum was designed to test and debug aspects of the process, including the organization of questions and information when moving from small group discussions to plenary sessions (i.e., those involving all panelists at once), and it also tested the method for panelists to develop their key findings. Members of the HDO staff and board acted as advocates debating Initiative 1098, a Washington State measure that would have established an income tax exclusively for the state's top earners. HDO reached out to a focus group firm, which gathered twenty-four demographically diverse individuals for an abbreviated two-day deliberation. The result was numerous refinements to the CIR process, which likely improved its official sessions in Oregon later that summer.

During the planning process, HDO negotiated with the Oregon Secretary of State about how the Citizens' Statements produced by the CIR would be formatted in the Voters' Pamphlet. Though the statements were given a prominent location, appearing after the explanatory information but before the paid for pro and con arguments, no consensus was reached on what the page should look like. Due to the fact that it would be written by citizens and would be unfamiliar to voters,

HDO sought to differentiate it visually from other sections of the Pamphlet. The Secretary of State rejected all proposed graphics, and the result was a page that retained the two-column format similar to the paid pro and con arguments that already appeared in the Pamphlet.

Finally, with funding for two CIR panels but more measures appearing on the ballot in the fall 2010 election, HDO had to select which ones to review in the summer of that same year. In selecting which initiatives to review, HDO considered the complexity of the initiatives, voters' attitudes towards them, and the availability of both pro and con advocates. Members of the research team assisted with initiative selection by conducting a quick telephone survey of 100 Oregon voters. The survey asked respondents their position on the measures likely to appear on the November ballot as well as a number of related questions. These were used to determine on which initiatives the electorate was most closely divided and those issues that perplexed the public more than others.

During this time, HDO reached out to advocate teams to see if they would be available to participate in the CIR. Though initiative proponents were readily available, finding organized oppositions to the ballot measures proved more difficult. Whereas backers had spent months developing the initiatives and gathering signatures for them, critics were less likely to have developed an organized opposition months before the election.

Based on both voter feedback and the availability of advocates, HDO chose two initiatives to review. The first, Measure 73, would increase mandatory minimum sentences for repeat driving under the influence of intoxicants charges (DUII) and for certain repeat felony sex crimes. The second, Measure 74, would create a regulated system for the production and distribution of medical marijuana. Oregon had already legalized medical marijuana through a previous initiative but had limited mechanisms in place for either its growth or sale. A third initiative, concerning the continuation of a parks tax, was initially chosen but failed to gain the number of signatures needed to qualify for the ballot.

From August 9–13, 2010, panelists met at a conference center in Salem, Oregon for the first official CIR, which reviewed the mandatory sentencing measure. The second CIR, concerning medicinal marijuana, was conducted August 16–20. For each review, the panelists met for five consecutive days from 8 AM to 5 PM. During that time, they learned about the initiative and listened to evidence provided by advocates and neutral witnesses. They engaged in small group discussions and facilitated plenary deliberations to identify important facts about the measure, lingering questions to be answered, and the strongest arguments in support and opposition. At the end of the week, the panelists worked together to write a Citizens' Statement that included Key Findings (information related to the initiative that more than a majority of the panel found both relevant and factually accurate) and Statements in Favor and Opposed, the latter written by the panelists who supported and opposed the measures, respectively (though even the pro and con arguments were reviewed and discussed by the full panel). The panelists voted 21–3 against the mandatory minimum measure and 13–11 in favor of medical marijuana dispensaries. The Statements were included in the official Oregon Voters' Pamphlet, received by every household in Oregon with a registered voter.

Permanent Renewal in 2011

After the pilot test, HDO began advocating for the permanent implementation of the CIR. HDO drafted House Bill 2634, which would renew the CIR in perpetuity and include the Statements' produced by the panel in the Voters' Pamphlet for all future initiative elections. In addition, the bill would set up a state commission responsible for overseeing and, eventually, implementing future reviews. The commission would be comprised of former CIR panelists and moderators as well as the neutral members of the committees that write the explanatory information and fiscal statements in the Pamphlet. The bill also placed stipulations on which measures could be considered for review by requiring that first priority be given to those measures that either altered the state constitution or would have the largest fiscal impact.

In line with the legislature's request for a review of the pilot process, HDO staff, CIR panelists, initiative advocates, and the research team (i.e., the first and second authors of this chapter) were invited to hearings held by the House and Senate Rules Committees in late 2010 and early 2011 to explain the CIR process and provide an assessment of its quality and impact. As part of that testimony, the research team compiled an evaluative report of the CIR, gauging its deliberative quality and impact on the election (Gastil and Knobloch 2010).[4]

Though the report noted specific areas for improvement, the evaluation concluded that the CIR lived up to the deliberative ideals that inspired it, particularly in comparison to the strategic rhetoric it was designed to supplement (Gastil and Knobloch 2010; Knobloch et al. 2013a). Table 1 shows a key element of that report—the "CIR Report Card" that summarized the qualitative assessment of deliberative quality for the 2010 CIR panels. The table included herein also includes equivalent ratings from the 2012 CIR panels (Knobloch et al. 2013b).

---

4   The assessment was completed using the evaluative scheme developed in Gastil, Knobloch and Kelly 2012.

Table 1: Summary Assessment of the Quality of Deliberation in the 2010–2012 Oregon Citizens' Initiative Review Panels

Evaluative category	2010		2012	
	M73 Mandat. Mins.	M74 Marij. Dispens.	M85 Corp. Taxes	M82 Non-Tribal Casinos
Promote analytic rigor				
Learning basic issue information	B+	B+	B+	A–
Examining of underlying values	B–	B	B	A
Considering a range of alternatives	A	B	A	B
Weighing pros/cons of measure	A	A	A	A–
Facilitate a democratic process				
Equality of opportunity to participate	A	A	A	B+
Comprehension of information	B+	B+	A–	B+
Consideration of different views	A	A	A	A–
Mutual respect	A–	A	A	B
Produce a well-reasoned statement				
Informed decision making	A–	A	A	B
Non-coercive process	A	A	A	A–

The 2010 CIR report also found that the Citizens' Statement had a significant impact on the voting decisions of those who read the statements, with as many as twenty-five percent of readers finding new arguments or information regarding the initiatives, and that voters who read the Statement that strongly opposed mandatory minimum sentencing were much more likely to vote against the otherwise highly popular initiative (Gastil and Knobloch 2010).

In their legislative testimony, the panelists also reported high satisfaction with the process and a desire to see the growth of similar processes in other sectors of government. As Ann Bakkensen, a panelist who reviewed mandatory sentencing, noted in her testimony:

Just about the only thing people can agree on in politics right now, is that our system doesn't serve its citizens any more. To reclaim a political system that is of the people, by the people, and for the people, the change has to come from the people. That's why the time is right for the Citizens' Initiative Review. It puts some decision-making power back into the hands of the people.

Not all impressions were so positive. During the first review, proponents of mandatory sentencing, sensing that the panelists were moving toward opposition to the measure, threatened to leave during the CIR deliberations. HDO staff convinced them to remain, in part by making it clear that the review would continue with or without their involvement. By the end of the week, however, the proponents became highly dissatisfied with the process, arguing that the panelists needed many more hours to study the issue and that advocates had insufficient rebuttal time.[5]

In their legislative testimony, these advocates came out against the CIR. They argued that it could not produce a high quality and factually accurate statement and that the process amounted to the government telling the citizens how to vote on initiatives. In addition, they were concerned that the panelists may have pre-developed opinions on a measure under review and that organizations could use donations to the CIR to advance their particular causes and influence the process. These arguments gained little traction in the legislature, though some of these concerns were used to amend the bill by regulating more clearly who could donate to the CIR and what stipulations they could place on their donations.

Ultimately, the bill received bi-partisan sponsorship with initial backing by ten state representatives and five senators. As Representative Vicki Berger (R-Salem) noted, "I wish I had a week to sit with the members of the committee and deliberate about the important things that we talk about" (Public Hearing, House Bill 2634 2011). In early June of 2011, both the House and the Senate approved the bills, with a vote in favor of 36–22 and 22–8 respectively. On June 16, the governor signed the bill into law.

Figure 1 shows the breakdown of the vote across the two parties and in the two chambers. As in 2009, every Democrat in the state legislature supported the CIR, and they were joined by a minority of Republican electeds. Republicans made up over one-quarter of the CIR bill's support in the Senate and one-fifth of the support in the House. Looked at another way, almost one-in-four Republican state representatives (24.1%) supported the CIR, whereas 42.8% of Republican state senators took that position. These figures exclude the two state representatives— one Democrat and one Republican—who did not vote. In sum, the CIR sustained bi-partisan support from 2009–2011, and it managed to pass in a chamber (the House) that was split 50/50 between two parties.

---

5   During its own rebuttal, the opposition to this measure noted the irony: Proponents had placed on the ballot a measure they believed the lay public could not grasp in a full week of deliberation, yet they asked the statewide electorate to judge their initiative while aware that the average voter devotes considerably less effort to deliberation on initiatives.

Figure 1: Vote in the Oregon Senate and House on House Bill 2634 to creates a Citizens'
Initiative Review Commission

House Vote - May 23, 2011		Senate Vote - June 1, 2011	
Yes (36)	**No (22)**	**Yes (22)**	**No (8)**
D D D D D	R R R R R	D D D D D	R R R R R
D D D D D	R R R R R	D D D D D	R R R
D D D D D	R R R R R	D D D D D	
D D D D D	R R R R R	D R R R R	
D D D D D	R R	R R	
D D D D R			
R R R R R	**Not Voting (2)**		
R	D R		

Note. The political party of those voting is indicated by D (Democratic) and R (Republican).

The 2012 Review

The first permanent iteration of the CIR took place in August 2012. Because the newly created CIR commission had not had time to develop adequately by this point, HDO was again tasked with implementing the reviews. House Bill 2634 required that the CIR first consider those measures that changed the state constitution, so this meant selecting for review two particular issues: Measure 82, which would allow non-tribal casinos in the state of Oregon, and Measure 85, which would eliminate a corporate tax refund and divert the money to education funding.

To implement the 2012 reviews, HDO modified the strategy used two years earlier, and they managed to reduce cost per review to approximately $100,000. They again sought funding from "good government" organizations, and they received the bulk of their funds from the Omidyar Network, a "philanthropic investment firm" created by the founder of eBay. Larry Pennings was again chosen to develop the agenda for the process, and four moderators were selected to facilitate the review, three of whom had experience from 2010. Panelist recruitment followed the 2010 protocol, though this time the invitation was stamped with the official state seal and, likely due to its official nature and voters' greater familiarity with the CIR, the survey had a response rate of approximately eight percent, more than twice the result from 2010.

The highest hurdle HDO faced in preparing for the 2012 panels was the advocates. The advocates for corporate tax reform (Our Oregon, a [4] political advocacy organization) backed out of participating one week before the CIR panel convened. In defense of their withdrawal, the communications director of Our Oregon told *The Oregonian* newspaper that "the output of the Citizen's Initiative Review has zero impact on shaping the opinions of voters." In response, former secretaries of state and a former attorney general—members of HDO's board—wrote a rebuttal, arguing that the CIR served Oregon voters and was an important addition to initiative elections (Frohnmayer and Keisling 2012). The second author of this chapter also weighed in by pointing out that the 2010 report did, in fact, show a clear impact on voters' knowledge and preferences on initiatives (Gastil 2012).

Even without the support of the measure's advocates, however, the review would still be held. HDO set about contacting other supporters of the initiative, ultimately creating an advocate team that included tax reform and education advocates. The first review, regarding corporate tax reform, was held from August 6–10, at the conference center in Salem where the 2010 reviews were held. The second review, regarding non-tribal casinos, was held August 20–24, this time in Portland. The move from Salem to Portland allowed for greater visibility of the event, because it was held in the most populous city. In the future, the CIR may be held in different cities across the state to heighten its exposure and allow a wider swath of the public to attend the review as audience members.

The panelists again met for five days, utilizing a similar format to that used in 2010, though slight adjustments were made based on HDO's internal critique and recommendations provided by the research team (Gastil and Knobloch 2010). The 2012 process improved the CIR in many aspects, particularly by permitting more time for feedback on the final statements from the advocates and panelists, the embrace of values-centered discussions, and via the new "Additional Policy Considerations" section to the Citizens' Statement. In 2012, the panelists voted 17–7 against non-tribal casinos and 19–5 in favor of the corporate tax reform. Once again, the CIR showed signs of influencing voters, as measured through panel surveys and an online experiment, and voter awareness of the CIR reached 51 percent (Knobloch et al. 2013b).

Conclusion: Future Prospects

While the CIR develops as a part of state government, the role of the non-governmental organization Healthy Democracy Oregon is changing. In fact, to reflect its broader purpose, the new name of this organization is simply Healthy Democracy, a fact that underscores its potential reach beyond the geographic borders of Oregon.

The bill that permanently implemented the CIR empowered the CIR Commission as an official state agency to take over the process. As the CIR commission plays a greater role in orchestrating the review panels, Healthy Democracy's presence will likely diminish. During this transition, the Healthy Democracy Fund, a charitable organization that grew out of the work of Healthy Democracy Oregon, will provide advice on implementing reviews in other locations and continue to serve as the development arm for the CIR.

The CIR process itself is transforming as well. Though improved compared to 2010, the most recent panels encountered challenges that may further develop as advocates and the public become more aware of the CIR (Oregonian Editorial Board 2012). As the CIR potentially expands its power, entrenched interests are likely to seek its co-optation. The advocates at the 2012 CIR, on private casinos in particular, were better prepared to engage in sustained debate than were their predecessors, and they provided detailed sourcing materials for most of their factual claims. Proponents and opponents brought in their own economists, who offered conflicting budget forecasts and made it difficult for panelists to discern the truth. (In their Statement, the panelists said that the economic data on that issue was equivocal.) Advocates will become even savvier as the process develops, and the robustness of the CIR's deliberative process will be tested further in coming years.

As we noted at the outset, the governmental authority granted to the CIR remains rare. The CIR is the first of its kind, and those deliberative structures that do exist often lack both the ability to influence wider public discourse and the legitimacy granted to the CIR as a state-sanctioned institution. The CIR represents a remarkably important step in the deliberative movement precisely because it has been sanctioned by state government, and such processes have the potential to spread. Participatory budgeting in Brazil has seen such expansion, growing from an experiment in participatory governance to an institutionalized system of budget allocation in Brazil and other countries in South America and Europe (Cabannes 2004) and now even the United States.[6]

---

6   One useful resource for tracking the advance of such programs is the Participedia case repository, which is available online at http://www.participedia.net.

The CIR has similar potential. Non-governmental organizations and elected officials in other states have already expressed interest in bringing Citizens' Initiative Reviews to their communities. Several representatives of such organizations, as well as elected officials, sat in on parts of the 2012 Portland review. During their visit, they learned about the project and its prospects and met with HDO staff and members of the research team to discuss implementation and outcomes. Civic organizations and individual citizens in Arizona, California, Colorado, Washington state, and Switzerland have expressed interest in implementing CIRs. More recently, in 2014 pilot CIR projects were held in the city of Phoenix, Arizona and the State of Colorado. In 2015, legislation to create the CIR was introduced in Washington State, where the bill advanced through multiple committees but did not come to a floor vote, and a bill is now active in the State of Massachusetts legislature.[7]

Though setting up CIRs at the state level will require time and funding, cities and counties with initiatives and referenda may be able to adopt and implement similar processes in shorter time frames and at substantially reduced cost. As with Participatory Budgeting, it will likely take time for widespread uptake of the process, but the CIR has the potential to dramatically alter the way citizens connect with government, and with one another, to reach decisions.

References

Ballotopedia. 2013. *2010 ballot measure petition signature costs.* Accessed January, 2013. http://ballotpedia.org/wiki/index.php/2010_ballot_measure_petition_ signature_costs#cite_ref-5.

Bowler, Shaun, and Todd Donovan. 1998. *Demanding choices: Opinion, Voting, and Direct Democracy.* Ann Arbor: University of Michigan Press.

Broder, David S. 2000. *Democracy derailed: How millionaires and special interest groups have usurped the initiative process and endangered the government the founders envisioned.* San Diego, CA: Harcourt.

Cabannes, Yves. 2004. "Participatory budgeting: A significant contribution to participatory democracy." *Environment and Urbanization* 16 (1): 27–46.

Carson, Lyn, John Gastil, Janette Hartz-Karp, and Ron Lubensky (eds.). 2013. *The Australian Citizens' Parliament and the Future of Deliberative Democracy.* University Park, PA: Pennsylvania State University Press.

---

7   Up-to-date information about these efforts and evaluations of the 2014 CIRs can be accessed online at http://sites.psu.edu/citizensinitiativereview.

Crosby, Ned. 2003. *Healthy democracy: Bringing Trustworthy Information to the Voters of America*. Minneapolis, MN: Beaver's Pond.

Crosby, Ned, and John C. Hottinger. 2011. "The citizens jury process." In *The Book of the States* (chapter 8). http://knowledgecenter.csg.org/kc/content/citizens-jury-process.

Crosby, Ned, and Doug Nethercutt. 2005. "Citizens Juries: Creating a trustworthy voice of the people." In *The Deliberative Democracy Handbook*, eds. John Gastil and Peter Levine, 111–119. San Francisco, CA: Jossey-Bass.

Dahl, Robert. A. 1989. *Democracy and Its Critics*. New Haven, CT: Yale University Press.

Einsiedel, Edna F., Erling Jelsøe, and Thomas Breck. 2001. "Publics at the technology table: The consensus conference in Denmark, Canada, and Australia." *Public Understanding of Science* 10 (1): 83–98.

Frohnmayer, Dave, and Phil Keisling. 2012. "Citizens' Initiative Review problems show improving democracy takes work." http://www.oregonlive.com/opinion/index.ssf/2012/08/citizens_initiative_review_pro.html.

Fung, Archon. 2003. "Survey article: Recipes for public spheres: Eight institutional design choices and their consequences." *Journal of Political Philosophy* 11 (3): 338–367.

Gastil, John. 2000. *By popular demand: Revitalizing Representative Democracy Through Deliberative Elections*. Berkeley: University of California Press.

Gastil, John. 2012. "Citizens' Initiative Review does help voters, study shows". *Oregonian/OregonLive*. http://www.oregonlive.com/opinion/index.ssf/2012/08/citizens_initiative_review_doe.html.

Gastil, John, and Ned Crosby. 2005. "Hey, Washingtonians: Show some initiative!" *Washington Law & Politics*, 14, http://www.lawandpolitics.com/washington/.

Gastil, John, and Ned Crosby. 2006. "Taking the initiative." *Seattle Times*, November 26, Sunday editorial section, http://www.seattletimes.com/opinion/taking-the-initiative/.

Gastil, John, and Katherine Knobloch. 2010. *Evaluation Report to the Oregon State Legislature on the 2010 Oregon Citizens' Initiative Review*. Seattle, WA: University of Washington.

Gastil, John, Katherine Knobloch, and Meghan Kelly. 2012. "Evaluating deliberative public events and projects." In *Democracy in Motion: Evaluating the Practice and Impact of Deliberative Civic Engagement*, eds. Tina Nabatchi, John Gastil, Michael Weiksner and Matt Leighninger, 205–230. New York: Oxford University Press.

Gastil, John, and Peter Levine (eds.). 2005. *The deliberative Democracy Handbook: Strategies for Effective Civic Engagement in the 21ˢᵗ Century*. San Francisco: Jossey-Bass.

Gerber, Elisabeth R. 1999. *The Populist Paradox: Interest Group Influence and the Promise of Direct Legislation*. Princeton, NJ: Princeton University Press.

Gerber, Elisabeth R., and Arthur Lupia. 1999. "Voter competence in direct legislation elections." In *Citizen Competence and Democratic Institutions*, eds. Stephen L. Elkin and Karol E. Sotan, 147–160. University Park, PA: The Pennsylvania State University Press.

Goodin, Robert E. 2008. *Innovating democracy: Democratic Theory and Practice after the Deliberative Turn*. Oxford: Oxford University Press.

Goodin, Robert E., and John S. Dryzek. 2006. "Deliberative impacts: The macro-political uptake of mini-publics." *Politics & Society* 34 (2): 219–244.

Guthrie, George W. 1912. "The initiative, referendum and recall." *Annals of the American Academy of Political and Social Science* 43: 17–31. http://www.jstor.org/stable/1012537.

Keown, Laura B. 2010. *Making policy deliberative: The Case of Citizens' Initiative Review in Oregon*. Master's thesis from the Department of Political Science at the University of Oregon. https://scholarsbank.uoregon.edu/xmlui/handle/1794/10665.

Knobloch, Katherine, John Gastil, Justin Reedy, and Katherine C. Walsh. 2013a. "Did they deliberate? Applying an evaluative model of democratic deliberation to the Oregon Citizens' Initiative Review." *Journal of Applied Communication Research* 41 (2): 105–125.

Knobloch, Katherine, John Gastil, Robert C. Richards, and Traci Feller. 2013b. *Evaluation report on the 2012 Citizens' Initiative Reviews for the Oregon CIR Commission*. State College: Pennsylvania State University.

Lang, Amy. 2007. "But is it for real? The British Columbia Citizens' Assembly as a model of state-sponsored citizen empowerment." *Politics & Society* 35 (1): 35–70.

Leib, Ethan J., and Baogang He (eds.). 2006. *The Search for Deliberative Democracy in China*. New York: Palgrave Macmillan.

Lupia, Arthur, and John G. Matsusaka. 2004. "Direct democracy: New approaches to old questions." *Annual Review of Political Science* 7: 463–482.

Matsusaka, John G. 2000. "Fiscal effects of the voter initiatives in the first half of the twentieth century." *Journal of Law and Economics* 43 (2): 619–650.

Matsusaka, John G. 2008. *For the Many or the Few: The Initiative, Public Policy, and American Democracy*. Chicago: University of Chicago Press.

Nabatchi, Tina, John Gastil, G. Michael Weiksner, and Matt Leighninger (eds.). 2012. *Democracy in Motion. Evaluating the Practice and Impact of Deliberative Civic Engagement*. Oxford: Oxford University Press.

Oregon Elections Division. 2012. *State Initiative and Referendum Manual*. http:// oregonvotes.org/doc/publications/stateI&R.pdf.

Oregon State Archives. 2013–2014. "Initiative, referendum and recall introduction". In *The Oregon Bluebook: Almanac and Factbook*. http://bluebook.state. or.us/state/elections/elections09.htm.

Oregonian Editorial Board. 2012. "The Citizens' Initiative Review's quest for relevance." *Oregonian/OregonLive*. http://www.oregonlive.com/opinion/index. ssf/2012/11/the_citizens_initiative_review.html.

Public Hearing, HB2634: Hearing before the Rules Committee, Oregon State House. 2011. http://www.leg.state.or.us/listn.

Ryfe, David M. 2007. "Toward a sociology of deliberation." *Journal of Public Deliberation* 3 (1). http://www.publicdeliberation.net/jpd/vol3/iss1/art3.

Smith, Graham, and Corinne Wales. 2002. "Citizens' juries and deliberative democracy." *Political Studies* 48 (1): 51–65.

Stratmann, Thomas. 2006. "Is spending more potent for or against a proposition? Evidence from ballot measures." *American Journal of Political Science* 50 (3): 788–801.

Warren, Mark E., and Hilary Pearse (eds.). 2008. *Designing Deliberative Democracy: The British Columbia Citizens' Assembly*. Cambridge: Cambridge University Press.

Fan Yang

Chapter Two. Informal Deliberation over a Highly Publicized Case in Weibo Space of China: Process, Influences and Quality

Introduction

Informal online public deliberation serves as an important factor for China's democratization. In this chapter, its functioning is explained in reference to Weibo (microblogs) and specific discussions that have taken place there. Through case studies, we focus on the role these informal public deliberations that take place on China's Weibo play in political and legal processes and their overall impact.

In China, it is the Chinese Communist Party (CCP), rather than independent judicial courts, that decides on the outcome of the majority of high profile cases in the country. In light of this, internet communities, such as SNS sites and Weibo, become new platforms where hundreds of millions of people gather to form a new political public sphere. Although the central government has imposed cyberspace control, it is unlikely to be an all-pervasive force due to the particularities of new Web 2.0 technologies. Indeed, in recent years, the highly publicized court cases are almost always the most popular topics of discussion among the users of these online communities nationwide – contrary to the wishes of the central government.[1] This is because when people sense injustice or foul-play in these highly publicized trials, they are more willing to express their views on the web, and in the process, engage in extensive and in-depth deliberations with others. Certain well-known lawyers, public intellectuals, and journalists also play important roles in such interactions – it is through them that formidable pressure from public opinion regarding a particular case is exerted. This, in turn has to some extent influenced the final outcomes of the trials themselves. Yet, due to particularities, the judicial system does not respond to the public influences directly, but to

---

1   Since there is a keyword searching function in Sina Weibo, people can see not only the frequency and trend of certain topics, but also the ranking of hot topics. On one's home page, hot topics will be updated instantly. With these tools, I found that the judicial cases are always hot topics in Weibo. For example, the "Wu Ying case" was ranked in the top ten of Weibo hot words list for a long time. About the Weibo data statistics function, see the "micro data" (Wei Shu Ju) website: http://data.weibo.com/.

political pressure that the CCP leadership – out of the need to maintain its own rule – exerts upon it. The central party frequently reacts to pubic pressure after it has accumulated to a certain degree. It analyzes these public deliberations and implements them via the courts as it deems necessary. The performance of the judicial system might also affect the public deliberation in turn.

In a paper focusing on Chinese media-judiciary relations in 2005, Benjamin Liebman (2005) argued that if the public wants to influence the court outcomes, in most cases it has to first influence the party leadership. In the era of new media, nothing changes for this situation. In fact, a particular interactive pattern has emerged between the judicial system, public opinion, and the power system of the CCP.

Figure 1: Interaction between the Judicial System, Public Opinion, and the Power System

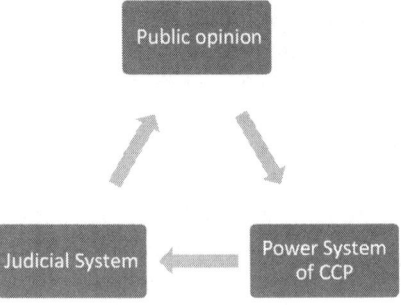

While this framework is at times unilateral and relatively fragile, it describes an important feature of Chinese politics: informal democratic deliberations in the public sphere influence legal outcomes indirectly.

Through the analysis of a specific high-profile trial (the Wu Ying case), in this paper demonstrates how these processes and interactions play out specifically and gives a general evaluation on the public deliberation.

The Rise of Web 2.0 and a New Public Sphere in China

Most of the existing research on the Chinese public sphere is concerned with the role that traditional media, such as newspapers and television, play in transferring public opinions. There are, however, many shortcomings to this approach, the most obvious of which owes to the disparity that exists between conventional media outlets and public opinions due to the government's extensive control over the former.

This situation has changed to some extent since the advent of Web 2.0. With the emergence of internet blogs and other online communities such as Weibo, the ways by which information spreads have profoundly changed – no longer is information dispensed from a single source, and under these conditions public opinion may be created bottom-up, the "true public opinion" emerges.

China has the largest number of Internet users in the world. According to a report by the China Internet Network Information Center (CNNIC), by the end of June 2013, the number of Internet users in China has reached 591 million, with around 464 million people who also access the web via mobiles (CNNIC 2013). Out of China's various social media platforms, Weibo has been at the forefront of this expansion of users and, unsurprisingly, it also exerts the greatest influence. Since 2010, the number of Weibo users in China has increased from only 63.11 million to 195 million by June 2011, and by June 2013, the number has sky-rocketed to 330 million (People's Daily Overseas Edition December 1, 2011). According to CNNIC statistics, the active users account for 56.0%. In China today, these figures change rapidly, and correlate largely with important events that occur in the country. For instance, the number of Weibo users jumped four-fold during 2011. Sina's official statistics (CNNIC 2012) showed that the fastest growth of the number of users dates back to the "Wenzhou EMU Incident" of July 2011 (i.e. a serious railway accident which cost the lives of 40 people and 192 injuries): the user-base grew by almost 20 percent in about half a month (The Telegraph 2014). Indeed, Weibo serves as one of the main forums for the discussion and exchange of information of popular and controversial social and political issues in China.

One should note that China's Weibo is considerably different from a Western social media platform such as Twitter. Firstly, the brevity of the Chinese language allows individuals to use only a third of the space required for Western languages to express the same meaning (An 2012). Secondly, Weibo allows users to publish more than 140 characters. In other words, Weibo can function both as a conventional blog and as a microblog, like twitter. Thirdly, twitter can only display 5 comments and "50+" (which means "more than 50" but not precise) forwarded messages, whereas such limits do not exist on Weibo. Additionally, since April 2013, Weibo further implemented a feature that displays the number of visitors (views) to a publisher's individual tweets. Popular tweets are viewed hundreds of millions times and have hundreds of thousands of forwarded messages and comments, adding to the cohesion and conformation of online discourse. Finally, and also most importantly, the Chinese government prohibits visiting almost all the mainstream foreign social media websites through the Great Firewall technology. This includes Twitter, Facebook, Youtube, etc. China's Weibo remains as one of the few platforms for Chinese "netizens". These important characteristics make it crucial and irreplaceable in China's political public sphere today. To give an example of this: China's top twenty opinion leaders are all registered and active figures on Weibo rather than individual blogs, and each of them has at least a few million followers (Zhao 2012).

There have already been discussions surrounding the role that Weibo plays as a type of political public sphere.[2] For example, DingXin Zhao (2012) believes that Weibo played a very important role in China's political democratization today, but the public discourse that takes place on Weibo is more or less unquestioning and irrational, leading to a problem of populism. K. C. Yang (2013) also thinks that Weibo is the most important political public sphere in China today, and is regarded as one of the most threatening arenas by the government. Similarly, Ya-wen Lei (2011) argued that the development of China's internet, especially the SNS sites, has accelerated the democratization of China. Some well-known Chinese scholars and media persons had also expressed their views on Weibo's influence on Chinese society, such as Ti An (2012), Kaifu Li (2012), Lan Yang (2011) and Zijian Du (2011), believing that it is one of the most important forces transforming Chinese society. The mainstream media in the Western world have also noticed it and frequently bring up the influences of Weibo in China.[3]

In addition to what has already been mentioned, it should be emphasized that two specific features of Weibo have had effects on Chinese politics. Firstly, historically, there has not been any discernible public sphere since the founding of the People's Republic of China. But Weibo, because of its particularform of expression, plays such a role well. In an arrangement where almost all traditional media are firmly under the control of a centralized state power, Weibo enables the Chinese grassroots to suddenly find a channel of expression; such contribution to Chinese political discourse in the past few years has been pivotal. Secondly,

---

2   In China, there are very few journal articles focusing on the online public discussion because the government does not support such studies, and even prohibits them, while foreign researchis rarely deep because of language and information problems. That is why many of this chapter's references are informal speeches, newspaper articles, etc.

3   *Le Monde* has reported the influences of Weibo on Chinese politics and society with a title of "Weibo versus Shibada, la dynamique chinoise" (Weibo versus the 18th Conference of the CCP, the Chinese dynamic, *Le Monde*, September 12th, 2012). There is a blog channel at "lemonde.fr" to report the news on Weibo every day (http://weibo.blog. lemonde.fr). Some media, such as the *Washington Post*, often report news of Weibo space, seehttp://articles.washingtonpost.com/2013-01-03/world/36211710_1_sina-weibo-chinese-internet-users-internet-crackdown.

the CCP itself, recognizing the indispensable position that Weibo now holds in Chinese politics, has tried to appropriate it for their aims. By the end of June 2013, various Chinese governmental sections have established around 79000 official accounts at Sina Weibo (Sina Governmental Weibo Report for the First Half Year of 2013). The governmental sections employ specialized staff for aggregating volumes of data and information that occur on Weibo every day.[4] At the same time, the state authorities are increasingly communicating with citizens through Weibo. For example, information about natural disasters, "the trails of Bo Xilai", and other news worthy of national attention have all been broadcast live on Weibo.

Indeed, Weibo has become the main medium of China's political public sphere which overtime has become more and more active, constituting an important force in Chinese politics.

Public Deliberations on a Judicial Case in the Weibo Space

China's judicial system is unique when compared to its Western counterparts, in that it is referred to in the official discourse as "A socialist judicial system with Chinese characteristics" (Wang 2011). In practice, this simply means that the organs of the CCP exert a more or less direct leadership over the courts. The CCP's unit tasked with controlling the judiciary is called "the Political and Legal Committee of the CCP". It was established from a central to a local level of the Party organization. Within this power hierarchy, the Chief Justice of the Court is just a member in the committee and has less power than, as well as operates under the direct leadership of, the secretary and the deputy secretaries of the Political and Legal Committee. While the power of the Political and Legal Committee is not clearly defined by the current Constitution and laws, in practice, it is responsible for instructing all affairs of justice and social security. Therefore, for the most important judicial cases, the courts are under the direct guidance of the Political and Legal Committees.[5]

Another organization that shares the capacity to affect and restrain a judge's independence is the court's Judicial Committee. According to Chinese law, the Judicial Committee is the highest judicial organization in the court, composed of the Chief Justice of the court, the Vice-President, members of party committee, the President of the Tribunals, and senior judges. It does not directly hear cases

---

4   These people are the so-called "fifty cent party" or "water army" in China. Their official name is "internet security officers" or "internet police" (Rongbin Han 2013).

5   Detailed studies about the institution of Chinese politics and law committee can be seen in Yongkun Zhou (2012).

through courts. In reality, however, the Judicial Committee is the lead agency of a court, subject to the superior leadership of the Political and Legal Committee and entitled to weigh in on important and difficult cases.

Ordinary cases are usually processed independently by the court and the presiding judge in strict adherence to laws and regulations. But when faced with cases of great social and political significance, – that is highly publicized cases – the judges will be deprived of the autonomy of their jurisdiction by their superiors. These authorities will have already determined the outcome of these cases. The judges and the courts maintain a façade of independence. Folk wisdom in China is well adapted to the realities of the judicial system, as the saying goes: "The big cases are dependent on politics; those in the middle on social impacts; and small ones on the laws."

Many reasons account for the existence of this judicial system with Chinese characteristics. On the one hand, it is a representation of the Party-state political system that the CCP has established in the judicial arena; on the other hand, it is related to the thousand-year old political and legal tradition of Imperial China. Executive and judicial powers have intertwined since the Qin Dynasty (221–207, BC) whereby executive and judicial authorities overlapped.

The Wu Ying Case

A trial of a financial fraud case may serve as a good example of the functioning of the system.

Wu Ying was a female entrepreneur in Zhejiang Province. On March 2007 she was arrested on the charge of illegally collecting money from the public. After more than two years of investigations and hearings, on December 2009 the Middle People's Court of Jinhua City sentenced Wu Ying to death on conviction of financial fraud, depriving her of lifelong political rights, and confiscating her personal property. In January 2010 Wu Ying appealed. Her main justification was that the purpose of borrowing money was for her company rather than for squandering it on herself. In April 2011 the Zhejiang Provincial Higher People's Court began the second phase of the Wu Ying trial. On January 18, 2012 the higher court rejected the Wu Ying's appeal and maintained the death sentence.

While the first phase of the trail already attracted widespread public attention, during the second phase it became one of the hottest topics in the online public sphere.[6] During the National People's Congress in March 2012 Prime Minister

---

6 Through the Sina Weibo keyword search function (http://data.weibo.com/), it can be found that the Wu Ying case had been one of the hottest topics in the period from January to February 2012.

Wen Jiabao was asked by a journalist about the case. On April 20, the appeal of Wu Ying's death penalty was rejected by the Supreme People's Court. The Supreme Court stated that Wu Ying should be punished by law, but since she has truthfully confessed the crimes as well as her bribery of some public officials, she should be sentenced to death with a postponement of her execution. The case was returned to the Zhejiang Higher People's Court for a retrial. On May 21, 2012, Zhejiang Provincial Higher People's Court re-heard Wu Ying case, convicting her of financial fraud and sentenced her to a death penalty with a two-year suspension, which means that after two years, if she commits no more crimes, she would receive a life sentence. The final outcome of the case was not in any way different from the conclusion of the review by the Supreme Court, Eventually, Wu Ying was sent to jail.

Public Deliberations on the Case

Next, I will briefly describe the process of public deliberation, and analyze the typical discourses in it in order to show two things: the interaction mechanism between public deliberation and the power system and the rational and irrational factors in the deliberation.

The Wu Ying case lasted more than five years. After her first trial, the case trigged widespread concern among the public, especially among active members on Weibo. Public attention reached its peak after the second phase of her trial that basically reestablished the verdict from the first trial. From the end of January to early February 2012, the Wu Ying case was one of the most discussed topics on Weibo. Every single day witnessed tens of thousands or even hundreds of thousands of messages regarding the case. Until May 22, 2012, there were in total 372 million tweets discussing the case on Weibo, and this figure did not include messages that were deemed "extreme" and deleted by the authorities. Many tweets received a great number of comments and forwards.[7] When the final judgment was handed down on the 21st of May, there were nearly 15 million tweets regarding the

---

7   In the era of new media, the Chinese government still imposes relatively strict controls on the Internet, but these controls have no specific legal basis. The government usually requires internet companies to manage it. If there were a social or political problem, the companies would be punished. In practice, companies have their own censorship rules to abide by the official regulations. For instance, Sina Weibo often deletes some "sensitive" tweets after it has been spread. Even so, the transmission efficiency of new media is much better than the traditional media. For how Chinese officials monitor the Internet, see Yonggang Li (2009).

decision. In the public deliberation surrounding Wu Ying's trial, some "Big V"[8], including scholars, writers, media persons, lawyers, etc., became some of the most leading participants who played the role of "public intellectuals".

In the beginning, deliberations were considerably centered on the issue of guilt and the death penalty as (un)just in regards to the discussed offence. For instance:

Qin Hui, a well-known scholar from Tsinghua University, who in general supports removing the death penalty from the Wu Ying case, expressed his views in the concise and rational manner: "even if Wu Ying was guilty, she should not be sentenced to death for committing such a crime. Though it may not be the time to abolish all death penalties, the principles of 'being cautious with handing down the death sentence' and 'reducing the number of death sentences' should be materialized first in such cases." His views and the way he expressed them were highly appreciated by the online readers, and the tweet received many forwards on Weibo.

During the period of the second trial, the public online discussions became more emotionally charged. While most of them remained rational analyses of the case, there were also some sentimental threads of discourse, even coming from some legal professionals. During the 2012 Chinese New Year a lawyer tried to mobilize the public opinion to action. He openly called users of Weibo to "make comments" on the Supreme Court's website, and to "Save Wu Ying". He made a detailed description of how to help Wu Ying through the online "opinion communication mailbox" of the Supreme People's Court. He wrote: "Wu Ying's head can fall to the ground at any time… Lawyer Li Changqing will appreciate you very much for voicing your opinions… Save Wu Ying!" His discourse was filled with emotional words and contained no justifications, but this tweet was transmitted nearly 8,000 times within a few days.

On January 31, during the Supreme Court review, famous writer Yihe Zhang issued a tweet calling on online celebrities to stand up for Wu Ying. The tweet was entitled: "Save Wu Ying from the guillotine!" She wrote: "Wu Ying, a woman who shouldn't be killed, is meeting the final moment of life judgment. I am openly calling again: keep the women alive from the guillotine! Please! Pop stars, movie stars, sports stars, …let us call together: Keep the woman alive from the guillotine!" This tweet attracted nearly 20,000 forwards and more than six thousand and six hundred comments.

---

8   "Big V" (Da V) is a term used in Chinese internet. It refers to those who have a discourse power in cyberspace. V represents the real-name authentication.

Both Yihe's and Changqing's tweets were very typical emotional calls in public discussions on the Wu Ying case. They just voiced their opinions without any justifications. Yihe Zhang, as a "liberal" female writer, often plays the role of an emotional appellant among public intellectuals in China. This is also evident in the Wu Ying case. Her tweet utilized emotional language in an effort to arouse people's sympathy and attention.

People engaged in the discussion included Wu Ying's family members, netizens moved by the story as well as public figures, which also shows the importance of Weibo. To attract more public attention, Wu Ying's father opened an account on Sina Weibo. By registering himself with his real name as opposed to an alias, he was designated a "V" (verified) user. He used a photo of Wu Ying crying in court as his profile picture. He introduced himself as "I am Wu Ying's father. Wu Ying was sentenced to death by the second instance". In total, he posted less than 80 tweets, but gained more than 65000 followers.

An anonymous user created a Weibo account under the title "A compilation of public opinions on the Wu Ying case". He updated and forwarded the latest Weibo views and opinions on the case every day, and provided a platform for public discussion. His profile picture is a cartoon depicting a weak man who is struggling to hold up an official stamp, the symbol of power. It implied the message of restricting the abuse of power through the pressure of online public opinion, no matter how feeble the netizens think they are.

The few examples above are indicative of the types of public discussions that occurred on Weibo. Such short tweets can be read very fast and spread widely, but is is difficult to use them in a deep deliberation because of their limited of length. For deepening the public deliberation on this issue, the long tweets, analytical articles and seminars are indispensable.

Actually, at the same time of Weibo (short tweets within 140 Chinese Characters) discussions, many longer tweets about the Wu Ying case also continued to appear and were transmitted widely by Weibo. Some of them, written by legal professionals, had analyzed the Wu Ying case in detail; others written by news reporters, university professors and other public intellectuals concerned mainly the social and political impact of the case. These articles were in dialogue with each other, and contributed to the in-depth discussions, and were not limited to simple appeals on Weibo. For instance:

Xianping Lang, a famous economist from Hong Kong, offered a conspiracy theory. He believed that the local police was the wire-puller in the trial. He wrote:

"They [the local police] want to convince people that Wu Ying is a cheater and she does not have money at all. But in fact, more than 100 pieces of real estate and 30 sports cars of this so-called 'cheater' were held in custody by the Dong Yang police. According to the law, a provincial higher court can only conduct a legal review, rather than a fact-based review on the judicial case. So the fact-based review of the case depends on the Dong Yang police. But why were the police so eager to auction off her assets before the final court judgment?! A car worth 16 million RMB was sold for only 3.9 million; a 50-million RMB hotel was sold for only 4.5 million! These facts prove that the Dong Yang police have been a key player pulling the strings in the chain of illegal interests (…)"

Through this speech, we can see that Xianping Lang had made a proper justification, although his point of view was only an assumption. For example, he gave two corresponding pieces of evidence for one judgment, which shows a higher level of argumentation by some standards of deliberative discourse analysis.[9] Before this tweet was deleted, it had already attracted nearly 19,000 forwards and six thousand comments. The reason for deletion is unclear. It may have aroused people's conjecture and inquiry on "power controls judiciary" in a way of rational analysis.

The content of the mainstream media was re-used in Weibo to add to the discussion. For example, an article by He Bing, a law professor from the China University of Politics and Law, proposing the establishment of a citizen jury system for death sentences was quoted by microbloggers and forwarded on Sina Weibo thirty-thousand times. It might have been due to his statement: "the death penalty also exists in foreign countries, but the courts there are rarely subject to such great pressure as our own courts, because citizen participation in judicial trials can effectively reduce pressure on the judges." Professor He analyzed in his article why cases like the Wu Ying case can get such a huge wave of public attention in China. For him the main reason is that the judicial democratic mechanism is imperfect, and the judiciary is easy control by the power system.

The climax of the public deliberations of the Wu Ying case happened on February 6th and 7th 2012, when two unofficial conferences on the case were convened. The Public Policy Research Center at the China University of Politics and Law hosted a conference entitled "On the Rights and Wrongs and the Fate of Wu Ying, On the Civil Financial Environment of China". Among the 19 participants of the seminar, there were Wu Ying's father and her lawyers, six professors of law, seven lawyers, two economists, a journalist, a famous novelist and a businessman from Zhejiang province. Before the conference almost all the speakers had expressed their points of view through Weibo and each garnered numerous followers. The

---

9   For example, in the DQI (Discourse Quality Index) methods of deliberative discourse analysis of Jürg Steiner, André Bächtiger, Markus Spörndli and Marco R. Steenbergen (2004), if one gives two pieces of evidence for one judgment, it shows a high level of deliberation.

four-hour conference was broadcast live on Weibo, and attracted hundreds of thousands of Weibo users to participate in the discussion. The conference followed a strict procedure. First, the father and lawyer of Wu Ying presented the case, then each participant spoke in turn; the host controlled the time and procedure. After the first round, they posed questions and debated on issues where their opinions diverged. Finally, the participants briefly summarized their own points of view. The whole event went relatively smoothly. On a number of legal and financial details, there were still some small differences. But at the end a basic consensus was reached that Wu Ying should not be put to death.

The conference originated from the discussion in Weibo space, and there were also instant interactions between the offline conference and the Weibo online discussions. However, unlike the typical online discussions, this conference followed certain procedures. There were also certain limitations to the participants – most of them were legal scholars and intellectuals. Their discourse was relatively more rational and deeper than the short tweets of Weibo. They reached a rational consensus (that the criminal circumstances of Wu Ying did not warrant a death penalty, that China's financial system should be reformed, etc.) rather than making simple emotional appeals.

The next day, another group of jurists and entrepreneurs attended another conference organized by the Tian Ze Institute of Economic Research in Beijing. The entire conference proceeding was also broadcast to the public through Weibo. In a manner very similar to the previous conference, they also issued appeals to those in power "to be cautious with the death penalty, and to reform the financial system".

At this point, it is possible to draw some preliminary conclusions from the case presented above relevant to the deliberation in Weibo space in general and to the offline deliberation. Leaders of the public deliberation were mainly legal professionals and intellectuals. Their discourse was relatively objective and rational, which is good for the public to recognize the facts of the case and reach a consensus. However, because someone's life hinged on the outcome of the case and perhaps corruption of government officials was involved, many netizens chose to express their anger in an emotional way. All in all, both rational analyses and emotional appeals formed the mainstream discourse in the public deliberations of the Wu Ying case.

The Influence of the Public Deliberation

As people actively discussed the Wu Ying Case in cyberspace, in February 2012 China's official media, the Xinhua News Agency, reported for the first time on the

Wu Ying case and the extensive discussions it had caused. The News Agency interviewed jurists, sociologists, economists and entrepreneurs who had expressed their views on Weibo, and analyzed the phenomenon whereby the court handed down a sentence which differed greatly from the expectations of the public. The deeper reason for the dissatisfaction of the public opinion, as expressed by the report quoting the words of these experts, was that China's financial system has been monopolized, and unofficial financing is very difficult;[10] executing Wu Ying in light of these larger systemic problems will not at all solve the problem. This news report could be seen as the first official response from the power system. It was then widely disseminated through Weibo, and the opinions expressed online became cautiously optimistic to the final outcome of the trial. At the same time, the legal and academic elites were speeding up their agenda online as well, hoping to take this opportunity to promote China's financial reform and legislative reform (VOA 2012).

The large-scale public discussions had aroused the attention of the CCP authorities. It was recognized that if the case was not properly handled, it would cause another ever greater backlash from the public. Therefore during the Chinese National People's Congress in March 2012, Premier Wen Jiabao expressed his views on a court case for the first time.[11] He said:

> "I have noticed that there has been much public attention paid to the Wu Ying case. On this matter, I want to make the following points. First, a thorough study must be conducted concerning the legal aspects of private lending and the principles that should be observed in handling this matter so that there will be clearly defined legal safeguards for private lending. Second, the Wu Ying case must be handled on the basis of real facts and in accordance with the laws (…). Third, the case shows that the development of private finance is not in line with the requirements of social and economic development in China." (Wen 2012).

Wen's remarks indicated that the highest authority of the Communist Party was paying attention to the public opinion expressed online. Additionally, he provided some clear guidance to the judicial system on how to handle the case. From a certain perspective, what Wen said was also a part of the public deliberation. It proved that the informal participatory democracy in the public sphere had forced

---

10 According to Chinese laws, large private lending is prohibited and constitutes a kind of crime.

11 Actually, the Chinese prime minister almost has only one press interview every year and answers about 10 plus questions, which are usually arranged in advance. Generally the questions are all about the most important domestic and foreign issues. The fact that the Wu Ying case was raised during such an interview demonstrates its importance.

the power system to respond and make concessions. And the discourse of Wen was also a rational response to the public. People on Weibo generally agreed that Wen's speech implied that Wu Ying would almost certainly escape the fate of being executed, and that the reforms of the financial system in China would eventually begin.

The subsequent development of the case proved that this expectation was correct. It is noteworthy that on May 21, at the time of the expression of the final judgment in Wu Ying's case, the Zhejiang Provincial High Court held a very rare press conference in response to the concerns of the public. The spokesman of the High Court answered four questions of the official media Xinhua news agency. Almost all of these were related to the topics discussed online by netizens. For two of these questions, the reporter began with the phrase: "Some netizens pointed out that (...)" It is evident that during the entire trial the opinion of internet users played a very important role and the court hoped to ease the pressures from the online public sphere so that it could satisfy the superior authorities.

Wu Ying was imprisoned just one day after the final judgment. Different from the lively discussions online, the judiciary hoped to deal with the case quietly and that people could forget it as soon as possible. They refused all media interviews, except the official media of the central authorities, and even imposed a tough restriction on meetings between Wu Ying and her family. For this reason Wu Ying's father opened a Weibo account. Only the CCP's organs holding power over the court, the Zhejiang Provincial Political and Legal Committee, can impose such a restriction. According to the report of *China Times* (Huaxia Shibao) (2012), after the final judgment, the Political and Legal Committee of Zhejiang Province held a whole-day meeting on the problem of Wu Ying's family meetings. The journalist reported that all meetings between Wu Ying and her family must gain the prior agreement of the provincial Political and Legal Committee, since this case was deemed special and sensitive – and because "Wu Ying's father has a Weibo account."

Conclusion

Wen's response, the press conference of the Zhejiang High Court after the final instance, and the performance of the Zhejiang Province Politics and Law Committee in dealing with this matter, show clearly that public deliberation has really impacted the operations of the power system and that in turn the power system affected the judicial decision. This phenomenon is very common in China. In the era of Weibo, this characteristic is strengthened.

Weibo plays an important role in China. It already, to some extent, has the elements of forms and foundations of deliberative democracy that have been confirmed by several studies. The analysis of the Wu Ying case only confirms this. In today's China, it's very difficult to look for an effective mechanism of civic participation. Scholars have carried out some political experiments of deliberation in China, for example the experiments of Baogang He at Wen Ling (Fishkin, He, Luskin, and Siu 2010) and Tianpeng Yuan's experiments at Nan Tang (Kou and Yuan 2012). But these experiments, under political control of government cannot really play an important role at the national level (Richard 2009). The emergence of new media, like Weibo, is a very good opportunity for the development of legitimate participatory and deliberative democracy. Numerous facts have proven its effectiveness even in some political constraints. Comparing to the standardized form of deliberative democracy, it seems very informal, is maybe not be the "true deliberative democracy", but it has proven that it works in China.

Yet, this informal public deliberation has grave disadvantages. It lacks the necessary procedures and rules. So the consequence is that it is difficult to reach a rational consensus. Many times, the Weibo public sphere is occupied by a variety of powerful discourses. In the analysis of the Wu Ying case, they are also visible. Although the public discussion on the Wu Ying case finally reached a consensus, it may just be because a majority of its participants had converging viewpoints. In the Weibo discussions, the irrational, emotional discourse often prevails, because this kind of discourse is likely to get more positive responses.

On the one hand, it is clear that the Weibo public sphere is an important force in China's democratization. On the other hand, we must also be alert to the populist tendencies. Perhaps, just as Habermas points out, establishing the standardized procedures of deliberative democracy, and continuing to improve them, is the only path to produce a high quality democracy.

References

An, Ti. 2012. "Behind the great firewall." *TED speech*. Accessed August 7, 2013. http://www.ted.com/talks/michael_anti_behind_the_great_firewall_of_china.html.

CNNIC. 2012. "The 29th China Internet Development Statistics Report." Accessed August 7, 2013. http://www.cnnic.net.cn/hlwfzyj/hlwxzbg/hlwtjbg/201206/P020120612484958777344.pdf.

CNNIC. 2013. "The 32th China Internet Development Statistics Report." Accessed August 7, 2013. http://www.cnnic.cn/gywm/xwzx/rdxw/rdxx/201307/t20130717_40663.htm.

Du, Zijian. 2011. *There are no limits for the micro-force (Weili Wubian)*. Shen Yang, Liao Ning: Wan Juan Publishing Company.

Fishkin, James, Baogang He, Robert C. Luskin, and Alice Siu. 2010. "Deliberative democracy in an unlikely place: deliberative polling in China." *British Journal of Political Science* 40 (2): 435–448.

Jiabao, Wen. 2012. "NPC Closing Ceremony, Premier Wen Jiabao Meets the Press." Accessed May 24, 2012. http://www.cctv.com/english/special/Live/wenjiabao/index.shtml.

Kaifu, Li. "Weibo is China's most influential modern media." http://tech2ipo.com/56246.

Lan, Yang. 2011. "The generation that's remarking China." *TED Speech*. http://www.ted.com/talks/yang_lan.html.

Lei, Ya-wen. 2011. "The Political Consequences of the Rise of the Internet: Political Beliefs and Practices of Chinese Netizens." *Political Communication* 28: 291–322.

Liebman, Benjamin. 2005. "Watchdog or Demagogue? The Media in the Chinese Legal System." *Columbia Law Review* 105 (1): 1–157.

Richard, Benoît. 2009. «La dictature délibérative chinoise. Démocratie, crise ou renouveau?» *Sciences humaines* 5: 24.

Rongbin, Han. 2013. "Adaptive Persuasion in Cyberspace: The *Fifty Cents Army* in China." Conference paper for Annual Meeting of America Political Science Association. Chicago, IL, August 29 – September.

Shengjun, Wang. 2011. "Some Opinions on the Socialist Judicial System with Chinese Characteristics." *Qiu Shi* 3 (March): 13–16.

Sina, 2013. "Sina Governmental Weibo Report for the First Half Year of 2013." http://vdisk.weibo.com/s/A-q4TgwJY4hz.

Steiner Jűrg, André Bächtiger, Marcus Spörndli, and Marco R. Steenbergen. 2004. *Deliberative Politics in Action. Analysing Parliamentary Discourse*. Cambridge: Cambridge University Press.

Yanding, Kou, and Tianpeng Yuan. 2012. *Practisable Democracy (Ke Caozuo De Minzhu)*. Hang Zhou, Zhe Jiang: Zhe Jiang University Press.

Yang, Kenneth C. 2013. "Weibo (Microblog), Emerging Civil Society, and the Cyber Public Sphere in China". Paper presented at the conference of the International Association of Media and Communication Research. Dublin.

Yonggang, Li. 2009. *Our Great Fire Wall*. Gui Lin, Guang Xi: Guang Xi Normal University Press.

Yongkun, Zhou. 2012. "The History and Evolution of Politics and Law Committee." *Yan Huang Chun Qiu* 9: 7–14.

VOA. 2012. "The impacts of Wu Ying case." Accessed August 18, 2012. http://
    www.voachinese.com/audio/Audio/66483.html.

Zhao, Dingxin. 2012. "Weibo, Political Space and China Development." Simian
    Humanity Lecture in East China Normal University. http://globalvoicesonline.
    org/2012/05/10/china-political-space-of-the-weibo-blogging-platform/.

Zhang Weiyu

Chapter Three. The Disenfranchised and E-Deliberation: Beyond Access

Introduction

Online deliberation, or eDeliberation, refers to an emerging body of practices that purposely foster open, fair, and rational discussions over the Internet. Websites such as *e-the-people.org* and *e-democracy.org* provide ordinary citizens an online space to have democratic conversations (Dahlgren 2001). Projects such as Deliberative Polling go online to take advantage of its relatively lower cost and longer duration compared to face-to-face deliberation (Luskin et al. 2006). Both types of practices have been found to be able to promote respectful listening, change attitudes, increase knowledge, and so on (Monnoyer-Smith and Talpin 2010). However, the contribution of such practices to democracy in general is contested among scholars (Dryzek 2009; Dahlberg 2001; Graham 2008; Shane 2004). One critique concerns the various inequalities seen in both access to and use of information technology, such as those of racial inequalities (Mossberger et al. 2006) and inequalities in technical capitals (Zhang 2010). Considering the central role information technology plays in eDeliberation, how the disenfranchised engage and experience eDeliberation becomes crucial because the representativeness of participants and their voices directly influence the legitimacy of decisions generated from such deliberative practices (Chang et al. 2014).

The tradition of political participation research provides the basis on which we can project the relationship between eDeliberation and the disenfranchised. Participation in American politics is not universal, and those who do take part are, in important ways, not representative of the public at large (Schlozman et al. 2005). Considering that eDeliberation is an activity that requires time, money, and skills, we expect that the disenfranchised groups would be underrepresented in eDeliberation. Digital divide research highlights the unequal ownership of new technologies since the early stage of the Internet. Recent studies on the digital divide go beyond uneven access and into inequalities among persons with formal access to the Internet by utilizing the concept of "digital inequality" (DiMaggio and Hargittai 1991; Norris 2001). As a democratic practice that takes advantage of online technology, eDeliberation is also exposed to the threats of digital inequality (Zhang 2010).

To what extent this inequality exists and how such inequality manifests itself in eDeliberation are questions that need to be answered.

The purpose of this research is to provide empirical analyses to demonstrate the relationship between the disenfranchised and eDeliberation, which is to see whether certain demographic groups are underrepresented in the process of on-line discussions. The current study is based on two field experiments using the Internet as the tool to deliberate: The *Electronic Dialogue* project was a year-long panel study conducted during the 2000 U. S. presidential election, whereas the *Health Dialogue* project focused on formal policy deliberation on healthcare reform in 2004. Both projects involved multiple groups that deliberated on electoral or healthcare issues in chat rooms for multiple rounds. Following previous research on both political participation and digital divide, five disenfranchised groups are identified in this study: females, racial minorities, younger citizens, and people with lower education and income. Utilizing survey analyses as its main method, this study is interested in one general question: How do the disenfranchised participate and experience eDeliberation?

Political Participation and E-Deliberation

Political Participation and the Disenfranchised

The vitality of democracy is determined by the degree and scope of citizens' participation. Representativeness of the citizens in political activities has been one of the major concerns for political research for a long time. Previous studies show that groups disadvantaged in terms of socio-economic status (SES) are often underrepresented in political activities (Burns, Schlozman, & Verba 2001 for females; Leighley 2001 for racial minorities; Nie et al. 1996 for people with low education; Schlozman et al. 2005 for people with low income; Zukin et al. 2006 for young people). *Education* is a key determinant of civic participation (Hauser 2000). The 2000 presidential election data show that among people who have eight years of education or less, the voting turnout is around 26.8%; for people who have a college degree or higher, the rate is as high as 72.0% (Schlozman et al. 2005). *Age* is second only to education as a predictor of virtually all forms of civic engagement. Schlozman and her colleagues (2005) showed that only 28.4% of the youngest eligible citizens (18 to 20 years old) voted in 2000, whereas 67.6% of those 65 years and older did. *Income* was another determinant of civic engagement. When comparing those with family incomes below $15,000 and those at the top of the income ladder, whose family incomes exceeded $75,000, Schlozman and her colleagues (2005) reported that the poor were markedly less active in the following activities: voting, working in a campaign, making a campaign contribution, getting in touch with a public official, taking part in a protest, march or demonstration, getting involved in an informal effort to solve a community problem, serving as an unpaid volunteer on a local governing board such as a school board or city council, and being affiliated with an organization that takes stands in politics.

Although *gender* differences in voting were slight – 56.2% of females and 53.1% of males voted in the 2000 presidential election (Schlozman et al. 2005), statistically significant disparities were found between women and men in campaign contributions, contacting an official, and political organizational affiliation. In all of these, women tended to do less (Burns et al. 2001, 65). The richest body of research on disenfranchised groups and political participation comes from studies on *racial minorities*. Election data have shown that current turnout rates do not manifest big differences between Whites (56.4% in the 2000 presidential election) and Blacks (53.5%), but a significantly lower proportion of Hispanics voted (27.5%; Schlozman et al. 2005). Asian Americans were situated in between – 44.0% voted in 2000 (Lien et al. 2004).

Since Verba and his colleagues published their classic works on political participation in an American context, many kinds of democratic innovations have come into the horizon (Smith 2009), among them is a theoretically appealing type called deliberation (Dryzek 2000). Deliberation, which emphasizes procedural rationality, has become the most recent fad among participatory acts (Gastil and Keith 2005). Compared to past forms of participation, the difference lies in the norm that requires participation to be deliberative (Habermas 1989). In addition, deliberative participation demands openness to all citizens (i.e., basic and fair opportunity according to Gutmann and Thompson 2004); and as long as their participation is marked by reason (i.e., reciprocity according to Gutmann and Thompson 2004), the decision-making mechanism treats their opinions equally. The importance of deliberation is contested among scholars. One key critique argues that deliberative participation is subject to the threats of participatory inequalities as much as, if not more than, other forms of political participation. Critiques of deliberative democracy (Dryzek 2009; Fraser 1992) argue that deliberative participation faces a serious challenge precisely because of its emphasis on rational argument. The disenfranchised are known to lack resources supporting their involvement in political activities (Verba and Nie 1972). They are even less well equipped with the capabilities that are necessary to function in a political system that runs on rational arguments (Bohman 1997). Deliberative participation could thus be exclusive in "informal norms defining what counts as proper deliberation" (Gutmann and Thompson 2004, 10).

Empirical studies of deliberation provide preliminary evidence regarding the disenfranchised. Many deliberative forums allow self-selection to decide who the participants are (Button and Ryfe 2005), which means that the structural inequalities that hinder minority participation in politics remain untreated. Karpowitz (2006) systematically examined factors that influence attendance at local public meetings and found that older people, lower-income people, less educated people, non-Whites and females are all less likely to attend than others. Research on juries finds that their decision-making process is often dominated by members with high social status (Mendelberg 2002 for a brief review). Female and African-American jurors were found to be less influential than men and Whites on final decisions in certain circumstances. Mendelberg and Oleske (2000) examined town meetings on school desegregation and found that white participants used rhetoric that appeared to be universal, well-reasoned, and focused on the common good, but that, in fact, advanced their group interest, while black participants interpreted such rhetoric as racist and group-interested, which resulted in conflict.

Both the general political participation and the deliberation literature suggest that the disenfranchised would be less likely to participate in deliberation than other groups. Previous research points out that the reasons are three-fold: First, the disenfranchised have fewer resources (e.g., time and money) to support their involvement (Verba and Nie 1972); second, they have fewer opportunities (e.g., being nominated as a candidate) to take part in such activities (Rosenstone and Hansen 1993); third, they might have lower motivation (e.g., lower self-efficacy) to do so (Delli Carpini 2000; Zhang and Chang 2014). Whereas the first two barriers are structural, the lack of motivation could be considered as a long-term result of such structural marginalization. In other words, the disenfranchised are disappointed by the existing system and discouraged to pursue changes through the existing structure, due to their prior experience of dealing with the system. The Internet, as argued in Luskin, Fishkin, and Iyengar's paper (2006), provides an open platform that involves relatively lower cost as compared to face-to-face deliberation. It is also less limited by the time and location that face-to-face deliberation often requires. Moreover, the Internet is believed to transcend some of the existing structural constraints as envisioned by some digital democracy scholars (Benkler 2006). Whether the combination of deliberation and the Internet (i.e., eDeliberation) can overcome participatory inequalities needs to be examined against empirical evidence.

Digital Inequalities and E-Deliberation

The emergence of new technologies such as the Internet is considered one of the drives that revived our interest in deliberation in the 1990s (Gastil and Keith 2005).

Theorists have been debating on the importance of the Internet to serve as a revitalized public sphere. The radical model of democracy, for example, recognizes the value of online discussions in promoting antagonistic pluralism (Mouffe 1999). In line with this model, scholars found that online political discussions can contribute to the range of opinions and the intensity of debate even though the discussions involve severe opinion conflicts and do not always appear to be deliberative (Chadwick 2009; Dahlberg 2001; Papacharissi 2008). The deliberative model of democracy, in contrast, stresses not only online discussions but also the deliberativeness of discussions that may be fostered through the Internet (Held 2006). On the one hand, the Internet seems to be promising because unlike other social institutions, the Internet opens up possibilities for a variety of stakeholders (not just the state or commercial entities) to take advantage of it (Dahlberg 2001). The Internet's institutional characteristics echo Habermas' requirement that the public sphere be an independent social and discursive arena. In addition, the Internet is relatively open compared to other discursive spaces, such as that of mass media (Zhang 2012). The Internet's openness facilitates the universal access that the Habermasian public sphere favors. Finally, the Internet's interactive features foster communication among citizens, including both formal discussions on political issues (Kiousis 2002; Zhang 2013) and informal encounter of such exchanges (Graham 2008; Zhang 2006).

On the other hand, the digital divide literatures continuously remind us of the potential perils of net-public sphere. Research along this line focused on unequal *access* to computers, then to the Internet, and then to broadband. Considerable empirical evidence shows that income, education, age, race, and gender significantly predict access to the Internet (Bucy 2000; Hacker and Steiner 2002; Loges and Jung 2001). When it comes to online deliberation, Price (2009) reported that people who attended his eDeliberation initiatives were significantly more likely to be white than those who did not, significantly older, and better educated. The second-level digital divide that has been proposed (Bonfadelli 2002) is that the divide over skills (i.e., over the quality use of the Internet) exists even as the access gap is closing. The demographic predictors were found to significantly shape users' Internet skills as well (Van Dijk and Hacker 2003). The digital divide research joins with the political participation literature to provide theoretical foundations based on which we can expect the unequal access to eDeliberation. However, beyond access, the engagement and experience of the disenfranchised are not fully explained.

DiMaggio and Hargittai (1991) proposed to expand the digital divide approach to "digital inequality", in order to account for the various unequal attributes (e.g., unequal social support) among persons with access to the Internet. Unequal usage of the Internet was found and discussed in many studies that focus on political discussions naturally occurring online (Davis 2005; Van Zoonen 2005; Wilhelm

2000; Wright 2007). In terms of organized formal online deliberation, Lowndes and colleagues (2006) provided a CLEAR model to explain the relevant attributes that citizen engagement, regardless of its online or offline format, involves. They argued that engagement is most effective when citizens have the resource and knowledge (Can do), the sense of attachment (Like to), the opportunity (Enabled to), the mobilization (Asked to), and chances to get the views considered by policy makers (Responded to). According to this model, even after opportunities are extended to and mobilization is made among the disenfranchised, they seem to have less effective engagement than the rest due to their lack of the others factors such as resource, knowledge, sense of attachment, and influence on policy making. This paper thus generally hypothesizes that the disenfranchised groups, defined as females, racial minorities, younger people, and people with lower education and income, will show fewer positive indicators regarding eDeliberation. Following the suggestion by digital inequalities theorists, this paper will emphasize indicators that go beyond access. Specifically, this paper examines engagement and experience in eDeliberation among persons with formal access to the Internet. First, even when citizens are offered equal opportunity to participate in eDeliberation, they are not equally *engaged* during the procedure.

H1: Disenfranchised group members are less likely than other group members to *talk* and to *argue* in eDeliberation.

Second, after engagement, there is the difference in experience that comes with the engagement in eDeliberation. It is not a coincidence that Besley and McComas (2005) proposed to stress experience in the examination of political participation in general while Burkhalter, Gastil and Kelshaw (2002) made the same proposal when operationalizing deliberation in particular. Participants' subjective perception of their experience has been shown to have important impacts on not only whether participants would accept the decisions generated from the activities but also whether participants would continue engaging in the same activities in the future (Zhang 2015). Again, according to the CLEAR model, the disenfranchised may have less positive experience than the rest due to their lack of the supportive factors to fully take advantage of eDeliberation. Unequal *experience* is thus expected and tested in the second hypothesis.

H2: Disenfranchised group members are less *satisfied* with their experience than other group members.

Method and Results

The data come from the *Electronic Dialogue 2000* project (ED2K) and the *Healthcare Dialogue* project (HCD) in 2004, two multi-wave panel projects each lasting roughly one year. The two projects are distinguished from other deliberation studies and the Internet-based studies in a number of ways. While most deliberation studies examine deliberative practices in a face-to-face setting, the ED2K and HCD take advantage of the unique capacities of the Internet and World Wide Web for circulating information, conveying public discourse, and gathering survey data. Different from most Internet-based studies, which examine asynchronous message boards or less formal and happenstance "chat" experiences on the Web, both projects here created synchronous, real-time, moderated group discussions that were designed specifically to produce useful citizen deliberation. Facilitation/moderation was standardized across both discussions and groups. In addition, neither project relied on a convenience sample of Internet users, as is common in most deliberation studies and Web-based studies. Instead, they began with a broadly representative sample of Americans and attempted to recruit from that sample a set of discussion groups that would be, in their entirety, as nearly representative as possible of U.S. citizens. In order to address the digital divide concern, all the people included in the sample were offered free equipment, free Internet, and free training, if needed.

The core of both projects consisted of groups of citizens who engaged in a series of synchronous electronic discussions about issues facing either the unfolding 2000 presidential campaign or the country's healthcare reform. A set of baseline surveys assessed participants' opinions, communication behaviors, political psychology, political activities, and a variety of demographic, personality, and background variables. Subsequent group deliberations generally included pre- and post-discussion surveys. The full text of all group discussions, which lasted an hour apiece, was recorded. A series of end-of-project surveys were then conducted after the last discussion was finished. This paper utilizes two types of data: surveys and discussion transcripts. The surveys included recruitment, baseline, post-discussion, and end-of-project surveys. Content analysis was carried out on discussion transcripts to measure the amount of talk and arguments during eDeliberation. The details of all the measurements of variables can be found in Appendix A.

Analytical Strategy

Both engagement and experience variables were analyzed using OLS regressions. Variables were added step by step. The first block of variables included the five demographics that define the disenfranchised. In addition, three groups of control variables were included. The first group included variables that were intended to control for available time. The second group included political psychology variables such as political interest and efficacy. The last group of control variables measured traditional forms of civic engagement such as political participation and community involvement. Regressions on the argument variables included one additional control variable, which was amount of talk. The amount of talk was found to be highly correlated with the total number of arguments (ED2K: $r = .57, p < .001$; HCD: $r = .88, p < .001$).

Engagement

Table 1.1 shows that in both projects, non-Whites consistently spoke less than Whites, even after controlling for a series of variables. Females talked more than males in ED2K although the difference was only marginally significant. What seemed to be significant in both projects were political psychology variables such as argument repertoire and political knowledge.

Table 1.1: Regressions predicting amount of talk

	Amount of talk	
	ED2K	HCD
(Constant)	104.443	131.816
Education	25.047	4.946
Male	−90.788+	41.642
Age	−0.630	2.062
Income	0.383	4.051
Whites	134.866*	136.354*
Married	−90.248	18.213
Schedule flexibility	8.862	−1.330
Children under 18	21.693	46.350
Full-time job	26.346	6.450
Student	−230.237	94.277
Argument repertoire	22.358***	26.422***
Political knowledge	440.504*	53.286+
Political interest	−35.007	−120.863*
Political efficacy	−36.342	21.964
Interpersonal trust	70.607	157.448*
Party-ideology index	−8.397	19.709**
Political participation	5.039	31.625*
Community activities	24.639	0.533
News exposure	1.304	−2.425
Political discussions (PD) frequency	−0.279	4.584
PD perceived disagreement	−80.463*	–
PD directly expressed opinions	39.922	–
N	612	541
R-Square	0.37	0.41

+p < .10, *p < .05, **p < .01, ***p < .001

The findings regarding number of arguments showed no difference in the ED2K project. In the HCD project, the differences were also only marginally significant: Non-Whites scored lower than Whites on number of con-arguments. Surprisingly, people who had lower education provided more pro-arguments than those who had higher education. Again, what seemed to be powerful predictors were political psychology variables including argument repertoire and political efficacy.

Table 1.2: Regressions Predicting Number of Arguments

	Number of pro-arguments		Number of con-arguments	
	ED2K total	HCD Discussion4	ED2K total	HCD Discussion4
(Constant)	3.493	5.834	0.913	−8.880+
Education	−0.057	−0.313+	−0.002	−0.076
Male	0.532	0.528	−0.219	−0.177
Age	−0.004	0.053	−0.028	0.037
Income	−0.009	−0.235	0.005	−0.040
Whites	0.253	−1.458	0.378	2.097+
Married	1.920*	−0.652	1.840	1.371
Schedule flexibility	0.096	0.028	0.393*	−0.023
Children under 18	−0.122	0.115	−0.769+	0.706
Full-time job	−0.998	0.137	−0.236	1.490
Student	−1.511	−1.553	0.616	7.164*
Argument repertoire	0.166*	0.290**	0.214*	−0.016
Political knowledge	−0.017	−0.725	−3.890	0.412
Political interest	−0.544	−0.858	−0.064	−0.253
Political efficacy	0.711*	0.614	0.034	1.198*
Interpersonal trust	−0.337	0.751	0.003	1.871
Party-ideology index	−0.210*	0.059	−0.047	−0.045
Political participation	−0.587**	−0.250	−0.657*	0.025
Community activities	−0.100	0.182	0.126	−0.222
News exposure	0.066	0.001	0.155*	−0.030
Political discussions (PD) frequency	−0.015	0.203	0.040	0.091
PD perceived disagreement	−0.007	–	0.780	–
PD directly-expressed opinions	0.136	–	0.477	–
Amount of talk	0.006***	0.039***	0.009***	0.035***
N	539	242	539	242
R-Square	0.56	0.79	0.57	0.78

+p < .10, *p < .05, **p < .01, ***p < .001

The magnitudes of the significant effects show that among the three significant demographics, race, or being Whites, was the most important one. Its effects on amount of talk and number of con-arguments were the largest among all the five demographics. The relatively large effects of race suggest that we should pay special attention to these differences when advocating a deliberative form of political participation in the American context.

H1 was partially accepted (or partially rejected) mainly due to the race inequality. In other words, a significant gap between Whites and non-Whites in talking and arguing contributes to most of the negative findings regarding the disenfranchised at the engagement stage. Interestingly, although with marginal significance, the effects indicate that females and people with lower education occasionally showed stronger engagement compared to males and people with higher education.

Experience

Regression findings suggest that in most cases, positive experience was found for the disenfranchised (see Table 2 for detailed statistics). Experience was measured by an index which shows attendees' satisfaction with various aspects of online deliberation. Rating high in satisfaction was considered as favorable experience. Table 2 shows that people with lower incomes were more satisfied with both projects than those with higher incomes. People with less education were more satisfied with the HCD discussions more than people with better education. Females rated higher satisfaction with the HCD discussions than did males. However, compared to older citizens, younger people were less satisfied with online deliberation consistently across two projects. Race did not make any significant difference.

Zhang Weiyu

Table 2: Regressions Predicting Satisfaction

	ED2K		HCD	
	Discussion3	Discussion4	Total	End-of-Project
(Constant)	4.652***	4.184***	4.480***	3.967***
Education	−0.007	−0.017	−0.037***	−0.030**
Male	0.052	0.023	−0.080	−0.114+
Age	0.001	0.008**	0.004+	0.010**
Income	−0.002*	−0.003***	−0.010	−0.017+
Whites	−0.177	0.103	−0.080	−0.104
Married	−0.082	−0.172+	−0.004	−0.034
Schedule flexibility	−0.010	0.025	0.001	0.005**
Children under 18	−0.067	−0.046	0.013	0.021
Fulltime job	−0.026	0.075	0.063	0.055
Student	−0.734*	−0.318	−0.075	0.004
Argument repertoire	0.011	0.011**	−0.009+	−0.006
Political knowledge	−0.653*	−0.757	−0.102**	−0.055
Political interest	−0.190*	−0.057	0.009	−0.001
Political efficacy	−0.036	0.002	0.016	−0.009
Interpersonal trust	−0.205+	−0.020	−0.068	0.009
Party-ideology index	−0.007	0.002	−0.008	−0.002
Political participation	0.068*	0.030	−0.015	−0.002
Community activities	−0.006	0.016	0.022	0.012
News exposure	0.004	0.000	0.007*	0.008*
Political discussions (PD) frequency	0.025*	0.017+	−0.004	−0.009
PD perceived disagreement	0.120	0.048	--	--
PD opinion expression	−0.028	−0.022	--	--
N	300	447	400	469
R-Square	0.15	0.15	0.15	0.12

+p < .10, *p < .05, **p < .01, ***p < .001

When looking at the magnitudes of coefficients, we can see that demographics carried different weights in different projects. In online deliberation that discusses a widely recognized issue (e.g. the ED2K, which focused on the US presidential election of 2000), the sizes of the effects of the two significant predictors are relatively small. In comparison, in discussions that center on health care issues that may be new to public deliberation, demographics show more significant and stronger effects.

H2 was mainly rejected because favorable experiences were found among the disenfranchised more often than unfavorable experiences. It suggests that contrary to our expectation, the disenfranchised including females, people with lower education and incomes actually had higher satisfaction with the online deliberations than males, people with higher education and incomes. Meanwhile, younger citizens' negative experience with online deliberation should receive critical attention.

Another observation across both engagement and experience analyses is that the ED2K findings sometimes differed from the HCD findings. Females enjoyed the HCD discussions more than males, but not the ED2K disucssions, for instance. These differences between the two projects suggest that the topics to be discussed in online deliberation have different impacts. Females might be more concerned by healthcare topics due to their roles in families, and feel less interested in election topics. A follow-up analysis partially confirms this explanation (see Appendix B for detailed statistics). OLS regressions on the health discussion scale ($M = 6.35$, $SD = 5.56$, Cronbach's $alpha = .75$) and the attention to health news scale ($M = 3.44$, $SD = .89$, Cronbach's $alpha = .92$) demonstrate that, after controlling for the four other demographic and the control variables of available time, females were more likely to discuss health issues and pay attention to health news than males. Future research should examine inequalities when citizens are deliberating other public issues.

Conclusion

This study both confirms and challenges our existing understanding about the disenfranchised and their engagement/experience with participatory initiatives such as eDeliberation. At the engagement stage, only race persisted as a significant factor of inequality. Other demographic variables either showed no difference or in a few cases, manifested a pattern that was against our hypothesis, with a marginal significance. Although it is too early to make conclusive claims, the findings regarding the more active engagement of women and people with lower education do not stand alone. Polletta and Lee (2006) observed that members of disenfranchised groups, including women and people without a college degree, were *not* less likely to make claims during the online discussions after they were included. Moreover, women were more likely to make narrative rather than non-narrative claims, compared to men. Using amount of talk and number of arguments as measurements of engagement in eDeliberation, we conclude that race should be considered as a major obstacle to equality at this stage whereas other inequalities were not severe.

With regards to the evaluation of their experience, the disenfranchised, contrary to our expectation, showed more satisfaction not less in most cases. This finding is particularly encouraging for deliberation practitioners, which suggests that if they are able to overcome the access barrier and get the disenfranchised into the process, these often left-out groups would appreciate their experience more than the others. Recalling the finding that satisfaction can predict one's acceptance of the decisions and intention to participate in future deliberation (Zhang 2015), this finding implies that the disenfranchised may be encouraged to get more involved in such processes as legitimate decision-making mechanisms. However, we should not ignore the persistent negative findings regarding younger citizens. They consistently did not enjoy the discussions as much as older participants, regardless of the discussion topics. Along with the racial inequality finding mentioned above, future research should definitely put more efforts in understanding younger citizens and racial minorities in terms of their engagement and experience with eDeliberation, at least in the context of the US.

Now I attempt to provide some initial explanations regarding the empirical findings. Firstly, I want to tap on the negative findings about racial minorities and youth. I would suggest that racial inequalities in the US are historically deep-seated and despite of years of efforts to equalize different races, the reality is that such inequality has evolved from apparent discrimination to subtle differentiation, which is even more difficult to be addressed even through an ideal process of deliberation. As long as the American society still considers race as politically relevant, no practices, including our eDeliberation initiatives, would be able to be exempted from racial inequality. Youth, in contrast, is an emerging problem rather than a historical issue. It seems that younger people are less interested by traditional politics than older people nowadays. Although our eDeliberation efforts involve new technologies and novel discussion mechanisms, the issues to be discussed, i.e., election and health care reform, may still be too traditional to the youth. In order to attract younger people to join deliberation, we need to allow youth themselves to define what they want to discuss and in which formats.

Secondly, the positive findings with regards to the disenfranchised need explanations too. My take on this is that eDeliberation, or online deliberation, does show the potential to bracket the offline social economic status markers that often serve as barriers for the disenfranchised to fully engage in and experience political participation. Our research design has been intentionally kept blind to pre-existing inequalities such as those in demographics and has encouraged all participants to talk and argue. Considering that the disenfranchised often have fewer resources and opportunities to be involved in political debates and decision-making offline, this eDeliberation practice gives them the rare chances to be heard and to exchange opinions with other people who may come from a more advantaged social position. This explanation implies that eDeliberation, although confined by existing conditions including social inequalities, does have the potential to go beyond such social inequalities and at least temporarily create a relatively more equal discursive space for the disenfranchised.

This study is not without limitations. Although demographics consistently showed significant effects, they rarely provided sufficient explanation of the variance. Some of the model fits were lower than 0.20, such as those of satisfactions. This suggests that a large part of the variance in these variables remains unexplained, and many significant predictors have not yet been discovered. Therefore, it can be concluded that demographic variables do matter, but they might not be the most important factors shaping the experience with online deliberation. However, the engagement variables showed high R-square values. In addition, this paper mainly focuses on testing the possible inequalities in eDeliberation. Discovering a statistical model that can explain most of the variance is, at best, a periphery concern.

Another major limitation regards the age of the data. Both datasets were collected more than ten years ago. There are a few reasons why such data are still worth reporting. First, the quality of the two datasets is still high even using today's standards. Some unique features, including the national random samples, the free access to computers and the Internet, as well as the technical training and support provided, all distinguish these two large-scale projects as those among the most rigorous attempts to test the potential of eDeliberation. If there can be a choice, recent data are definitely preferred. However, considering the demand for resource to re-run such projects, it should be much more cost-efficient to fully utilize what we have already than to start another brand new project. Second, the design of the two studies purposely bridged the digital divide in accessing ICTs. Therefore, the situation was not vastly different from now after the penetration rate increased over years. Lastly, previous research on political participation has shown that inequalities are persistent. The scope or degree of inequalities might change over time but the basic patterns of who are disenfranchised should remain almost the same. Therefore, the age of the data is not very detrimental given the topic examined here. Nevertheless, there should be new research that continues such efforts, if resource allows.

This study has shown that, as a relatively new practice, eDeliberation faces the challenge of participatory inequalities, however to a different extent than older forms of political participation. Previous studies (Price 2009) showed that inequalities still existed at the attendance stage, even after equal opportunity was provided (e.g., random sampling). However, when the disenfranchised were included in eDeliberation, the demanding process of deliberation, which requires a large amount of reasoning, does not necessarily always disadvantage the disenfranchised further, if efforts are made to make the process as fair and easy-to-participate as possible. Meanwhile, deliberation practitioners should pay special attention to eliciting active contribution from racial minorities and younger citizens, at least within the US context. Equal opportunity is a crucial first step but it does not automatically translate to equal engagement and equal experience. In order to make eDeliberation more sustainable and legitimate, a careful examination of the mechanisms through which equal engagement and experience can be improved is the direction both researchers and practitioners should follow.

Acknowlegement

This research is supported by grants to Vincent Price and Joseph N. Cappella, both of professors at Annenberg School for Communication, University of Pennsylvania. For instance, the Healthcare Dialogue (HCD) project was granted by The National Science Foundation (Grant EIA-0306801) and the Annenberg Public Policy Center of the University of Pennsylvania. Views expressed are those of the author alone and do not necessarily reflect opinions of the sponsoring agencies and the principle investigators. The empirical analyses are based on the author's doctoral dissertation.

Appendix A. Measurements of Variables

Measurements of the Independent Variables

Education was measured as year of education (ED2K: $M = 13.30$, $SD = 1.84$; HCD: $M = 14.34$, $SD = 3.10$). A continuous version of *age* was used in analyses (ED2K: $M = 42.19$, $SD = 15.17$; HCD: $M = 46.34$, $SD = 15.53$). *Gender* was a dummy variable, with "1" referring to male and "0" to female. Fifty percent of ED2K recruitment respondents and 48 % of HCD respondents were male. *Income* used an interval version in the HCD project: $M = 64,110$, $SD = 53,660$. The measure was not available for every respondent in the ED2K project (746 out of 2327 respondents answered the income question), but among those who answered this question, the statistics are as follows: $M = 64,150$, $SD = 52,670$. In the ED2K project, 78% of recruitment respondents were Whites, 8% Blacks, 7% Hispanic, 3% Asian, 1% American Indian, and 3% others or do not know. The *race variable* was re-coded into a dummy one, with "1" referring to Whites (78%) and "0" to non-Whites. Not everyone gave us their race information in the HCD project, but among those we know (1949 out of 3134 respondents), it showed almost the same racial composition as ED2K (80% Whites).

Measurements of Engagement

Amount of talk. For the respondents who attended at least one discussion event, the number of words entered into each discussion was tallied electronically (only for substantive sections of the discussion, omitting casual interchanges at the beginning and end of each event). A total word count was summed, for each participant, across all discussions events included in the analyses (ED2K: $M = 828.74$, $SD = 671.95$; HCD: $M = 766.83$, $SD = 583.75$).

Number of arguments. Teams of one to three trained graduate and college students coded discussion transcripts into pro-arguments and con-arguments. In ED2K, the average inter-coder reliability (*Kappa*) of both pro- and con-arguments was .79. The arguments were separated into pro- (ED2K: $M = 10.58$, $SD = 8.21$) and con-arguments (ED2K: $M = 14.53$, $SD = 11.17$). These measures in HCD were only available in discussion 4. Pro-arguments (HCD D4: $M = 11.24$, $SD = 10.24$) and con-arguments (HCD D4: $M = 11.22$, $SD = 9.53$) were separately measured. In HCD, the average inter-coder reliability (Krippendorff's *alpha*) of pro-arguments was .67 and that of con-arguments was .66.

Measurements of Experience

Satisfaction. In the ED2K project, satisfaction was measured only in the post-discussion 3 and 4 surveys. The items that made up the satisfaction scale included (a) "the discussion was interesting," (b) "the moderator was helpful," and (c) "the discussion was enjoyable." Each was measured by a five-point scale from 1 ("totally disagree") to 5 ("totally agree") and averaged (ED2K D3: $M = 4.25$, $SD = .76$, Cronbach's *alpha* = .79; ED2K D4: $M = 4.20$, $SD = .75$, Cronbach's *alpha* = .83).

In the HCD project, measures of satisfaction were available in each post-discussion survey and based on four items: (a) "the discussion was interesting," (b) "the moderator was helpful," (c) "the discussion was enjoyable," and (d) "there was satisfaction with the group decisions." Each was measured by a five-point scale from 1 ("totally disagree") to 5 ("totally agree") and averaged. Reliability of the individual scales (i.e., Cronbach's *alpha*) ranged from .73 to .78. An aggregated measure of HCD enjoyment was calculated and used in the analysis (HCD total:

$M = 3.92$, $SD = .55$). The end-of-project enjoyment had more items, including (e) "there was enough time spent on each topic," (f) "I learned a lot from the discussions," and (g) "I liked the people in my discussion groups" (HCD EOP: $M = 3.77$, $SD = .67$, Cronbach's *alpha* = .89).

Measurements of Control Variables

Available time. Time is an important resource to support online deliberation, and it was observed using several different variables: First, whether one was *married* (ED2K: 64% married; HCD: 64% married). Second was *number of children at home* (ED2K: $M = .35$, $SD = 1.00$; HCD: $M = .59$, $SD = .98$). Third was whether one had a *fulltime job* (ED2K: 57% does; HCD: 56% does). Fourth was whether one was a *student* (ED2K: 4%; HCD: 4%). Finally, how many available time slots one checked indicated one's *schedule flexibility* (ED2K: $M = .67$, $SD = 1.45$; HCD: $M = 34.27$, $SD = 16.63$). The difference between the two projects was due to the available time slots respondents could choose from. In the ED2K project, only 12 choices were provided, whereas in HCD, 71 were available.

Argument repertoire. This is a measure of opinion quality, referring to the relevant reasons that one has for one's own opinions and the relevant reasons that others with opposite opinions might have. The validity and reliability of this measure have been demonstrated (Cappella, Price, and Nir, 2002). The variables used here were measures of total number of arguments obtained in the baseline surveys (ED2K: $M = 6.60$, $SD = 5.44$; HCD: $M = 4.89$, $SD = 4.92$).

Political knowledge. In the ED2K project, items included ten general political and civic knowledge questions (e.g., who has the final responsibility to decide if a law is constitutional or not), seven questions about the personal backgrounds of the presidential candidates (e.g., which one of the Democratic candidates was a professional basketball player), and an additional seven questions about issue positions of candidates in the Democratic and Republican presidential primaries (e.g., which of the Republican candidates supports vouchers). All 24 items were scored 1 for correct answers and 0 for incorrect answers. The items were averaged to create a scale ($M = .62$; $SD = .19$, Cronbach's *alpha* = .82). The baseline survey in the HCD project used a shorter version of such questions, which contained five items that were added up to comprise a scale (HCD: $M = 3.85$, $SD = 1.30$, Cronbach's *alpha* = .62).

Political interest. In the ED2K project, two questionnaire items comprised a political interest scale. The questions, measured on a 4-point ordinal scale, inquired about habitual following of public affairs and caring which party had won in the 2000 elections. The majority of respondents (79%) reported that they followed public affairs either "most" or "some" of the time. About 50% of the respondents replied that they cared "a great deal" which party had won the elections. A scale averaging the two responses was computed ($M = 3.20$, $SD = .71$, Cronbach's *alpha* = .62). In the HCD, two similar items were used, including habitual following of politics (measured in the recruitment survey) and caring which party had won in the 2004 elections. Eighty one percent of respondents reported that they followed public affairs either "most" or "some" of the time. Sixty six percent of respondents replied that they cared "a great deal" which party had won the elections. Averaging them led to a scale ($M = 3.22$, $SD = .84$, Cronbach's *alpha* = .50).

Political efficacy. Efficacy was assessed by asking respondents to register their agreement with the following three items: "People like me don't have any say about what the government does;" "I don't think public officials care much about what people like me think;" and "sometimes politics and government are so complicated that a person like me can't understand what's going on." Responses ranged from 1 = strongly agree to 5 = strongly disagree, where higher disagreement corresponded with a stronger sense of efficacy. Items were averaged to form a scale (ED2K: $M = 2.52$, $SD = .98$, Cronbach's *alpha* = .66; HCD: $M = 2.74$, $SD = 1.00$, Cronbach's *alpha* = .71).

Interpersonal trust. In both projects, three forced-choice items commonly used in the General Social Survey tapped trust in other people (e.g., "Generally speaking, most people can be trusted" versus "You can't be too careful in dealing with people"). Trustful selections were coded "1," and mistrustful selections were coded "0." The scale was the average of the three items (ED2K baseline: $M = .60$, $SD = .39$, Cronbach's *alpha* = .74; HCD Baseline: $M = .57$, $SD = .40$, Cronbach's *alpha* = .74).

Party-ideology index. Participants were asked about their party identification and its strength. They were also asked about their overall ideological leanings, on a continuum from strong liberal to strong conservative. The two components, which were highly correlated, were combined to form an 11-point scale with "strong liberals–strong Democrats" coded as 5, "strong conservatives–strong Republicans" coded as –5, and "moderates-Independents" coded as 0 (ED2K: $M = -0.26$; $SD = 3.18$; HCD: $M = .06$, $SD = 3.29$).

Political participation. To assess political participation, respondents were asked whether or not they had participated in a variety of political activities in the past 12 months. These activities included: contacting a public official, attending a public hearing or town hall meeting, trying to convince some to vote for or against a political candidate, attending political meetings or rallies, doing work for a candidate, donating money to a candidate, wearing a candidate's campaign button or applying a candidate's bumper sticker, contacting a newspaper or TV station about an issue of concern, or trying to get someone to sign a petition. All positive responses were coded as "1" and summed to form a scale (ED2K: $M = .98$, $SD = 1.38$, Cronbach's *alpha* = .62; HCD: Cronbach's *alpha* = .75, $M = 1.81$, $SD = 1.65$).

Community activities. An index of community participation was obtained on the second baseline questionnaire in the ED2K project. Respondents were asked whether or not they had participated in a variety of neighborhood activities in the past 12 months. These activities included adult education classes, exercising at a work out club, self-help group, reading/religious group, organized recreation league, church related activity, neighborhood association, and youth development program. A scale was created by scoring each membership as "1" and adding them up ($M = 2.26$, $SD = 1.72$, Cronbach's *alpha* = .53). In the HCD project, an index including nine items was created ($M = 1.82$, $SD = 1.65$, Cronbach's *alpha* = .56). The activities included most of those asked for the ED2K baseline except for self-help groups. In addition, serving in a jury was included in the HCD measure.

News exposure. In the ED2K project, exposure to mass-mediated current events content was measured by five different items inquiring about the respondents' self-reported media use during the past week (0 to 7 days). Newspaper reading, political talk radio exposure, exposure to television national network news, cable news, and local news were scaled together ($M = 15.50$, $SD = 7.84$, Cronbach's *alpha* = .61). In the HCD project, two more items were added, which were Internet news use and exposure to NPR. Thus the scale in the HCD project has a larger range ($M = 17.82$, $SD = 9.49$, Cronbach's *alpha* = .59).

Political discussions. The ED2K project included a comprehensive measure of everyday political discussions and their features. Respondents were asked to name (by giving initials) up to two close friends or family members with whom they discussed public affairs. They were then asked to identify several features of these discussions, including their relationship to the named person, the typical number of days per week they talked with the person about politics, the extent to which they tended to disagree, and the extent to which they directly expressed their opinions. A second battery asked respondents to name (again by giving initials) two acquaintances, such as "people at work or simply people you see going about your day," with whom they discussed public affairs. The same follow-up questions were used for these named discussants as well. An additive scale was constructed as a count of the potential 0 to 4 discussion partners. Slightly less than 11% did not name any discussion partners, and about 56% named four discussion partners.

Frequency of discussion was measured in the ED2K project. The respondents reported how many days in the past week (0 to 7) they discussed political issues with each of the four named discussion partners. An additive scale of the respondents' answers to the four questions was computed ($M = 5.94$, $SD = 4.93$,

Cronbach's *alpha* = .74), with those who did not name any discussants coded as 0. Disagreement between the discussants was also measured in the ED2K project. For each of the four discussion partners, the respondents reported the extent to which the named discussant tended to disagree with the respondents' own views. Disagreement was measured on a 5-point ordinal scale ranging from "never" to "almost all the time." An average scale was computed since otherwise this measure would be highly correlated with the frequency of discussion measure ($M = 2.49$, $SD = .71$, Cronbach's *alpha* = .49). Those who did not name any discussants were coded as 0. Opinion expression among the discussions was available in the ED2K project. For each of the four discussion partners, the respondents reported the extent to which they directly expressed their opinions when discussing with the named discussant. It was also measured on a 5-point ordinal scale ranging from "never" to "almost all the time." Similarly, an additive scale was computed ($M = 4.19$, $SD = .85$, Cronbach's *alpha* = .82).

A simpler version of political discussion was used in the HCD project. Respondents were asked to report how many days in the past week (0 to 7) they discussed politics with either family/friends or acquaintances/people at work. The items were aggregated to create a scale ($M = 4.28$, $SD = 3.73$, Cronbach's *alpha* = .68).

Appendix B. Regressions, Additional Data

Table 1: Regressions Predicting Health Discussion and Attention to Health News (HCD)

	Discussion on Health Issues	Attention to Health News
(Constant)	−3.542***	1.606***
Education	0.346***	0.057***
Male	−1.468***	−0.090*
Age	0.068	0.019***
Income	0.060	−0.002
Whites	−0.440	−0.071
Married	0.543+	0.051
Schedule flexibility	0.026**	0.005***
Children under 18	−0.085	−0.019
Full-time job	1.386***	0.102*
Student	1.341+	0.035
N	964	1,387
R-Square	0.11	0.17

+p < .10, *p < .05, **p < .01, ***p < .001

References

Benkler, Yochaï. 2006. *The wealth of network: How Social Production Transforms Markets and Freedom*. New Haven and London: Yale University Press.

Besley, John C., and Katherine A. McComas. 2005. "Framing justice: Using the concept of procedural fairness to advance political communication research." *Communication Theory* 15 (4): 414–436.

Bohman, James. 1997. "Deliberative democracy and effective social freedom: Capabilities, resources, and opportunities." In *Deliberative Democracy: Essays on Reason and Politics*, eds. James Bohman and William Rehg, 321–348. Cambridge, MA: The MIT Press.

Bonfadelli, Heinz. 2002. "The Internet and knowledge gaps: A theoretical and empirical investigation." *European Journal of Communication* 17 (1): 65–84.

Bucy, Erik P. 2000. "Social access to the Internet." *Press/Politics* 5 (1): 50–61.

Burkhalter, Stephanie, John Gastil, and Todd Kelshaw. 2002. "A conceptual definition and theoretical model of public deliberation in small face-to-face groups." *Communication Theory* 12 (4): 398–422.

Burns, Nancy, Kay. L. Schlozman, and Sidney Verba. 2001. *The Private Roots of Public Action: Gender, Equality, and Political Participation*. Cambridge, MA: Harvard University Press.

Button, Mark, and David M. Ryfe. 2005. "What can we learn from the practice of deliberative democracy?" In *The Deliberative Democracy Handbook: Strategies for Effective Civic Engagement in the 21st Century*, eds. John Gastil and Peter Levine, 20–36. San Francisco, CA: Jossey-Bass.

Cappella, Joseph N., Vincent Pirce, and Lilach Nir. 2002. "Argument repertoire as a reliable and valid measure of opinion quality: Electronic Dialogue in campaign 2000." *Political Communication* 19: 73–93.

Chadwick, Andrew. 2009. "Web 2.0: New challenges for the study of e-democracy in an era of informational exuberance." *I/S: Journal of Law and Policy for the Information Society* 5 (1): 9–41.

Chang, Leanne, Thomas Jacobson, and Weiyu Zhang. 2013. "A Communicative Action Approach to Evaluating Citizen Support for a Government's Smoking Policies." *Journal of Communication* 63 (6): 1153–1174.

Dahlberg, Lincoln. 2001. "Extending the public sphere through cyberspace: The case of Minnesota E-Democracy." *First Monday* 6 (3). Accessed November 7, 2008. http://www.firstmonday.dk/issues/issue6_3/dahlberg/index.html.

Davis, Richard. 2005. *Politics Online: Blogs, Chatrooms, and Discussion Groups in American Democracy*. New York & London: Routledge.

Delli Carpini, Michael X. 2000. "Gen.com: Youth, civic engagement, and the new information environment." *Political Communication* 17: 341–349.

DiMaggio, Paul, and Estzer Hargittai. 2001. "From the 'digital divide' to 'digital inequality': Studying Internet use as penetration increases." Princeton University Center for Arts and Cultural Policy Studies, Working Paper Series number 15. Accessed November 7, 2008. http://www.princeton.edu/~artspol/workpap/WP15%20-%20DiMaggio%2BHargittai.pdf.

Dryzek, John. 2009. *Deliberative Democracy and Beyond: Liberals, Critics, Contestations.* Oxford: Oxford University Press.

Fraser, Nancy. 1992. "Rethinking the public sphere: A contribution to the critique of actually existing democracy". In *Habermas and the Public Sphere*, ed. Craig J. Calhoun, 109–142. Cambridge, MA: The MIT Press.

Gastil, John, and William M. Keith. 2005. "A nation that (sometimes) likes to talk: A brief history of public deliberation in the United States". In *The deliberative Democracy Handbook: Strategies for Effective Civic Engagement in the 21st Century*, eds. John Gastil and Peter Levine, 3–19. San Francisco, CA: Jossey-Bass.

Graham, Todd. 2008. "Needles in a haystack: A new approach for identifying and assessing political talk in non-political discussion forums." *Javnost-the Public* 15 (2): 17–36.

Gutmann, Amy, and Dennis Thompson. 2004. *Why Deliberative Democracy.* Princeton, NJ: Princeton University Press.

Habermas, Jürgen. 1989. *The Structural Transformation of the Public Sphere: An Inquiry into a Category of Bourgeois Society.* Cambridge: MIT Press.

Hacker, Kenneth L., and Robert Steiner. 2002. "The digital divide for Hispanic Americans." *The Howard Journal of Communication* 13: 267–283.

Hauser, Seth M. 2000. "Education, ability, and civic engagement in the contemporary United States." *Social Science Research* 29: 556–582.

Karpowitz, Christopher F. 2006. "Extremists or good citizens? The political psychology of public meetings and the dark side of civic engagement." Paper presented at the annual meeting of the American Political Science Association, Philadelphia, PA, USA.

Kiousis, Spiro. 2002. "Interactivity: A concept explication." *New Media & Society* 4 (3): 355–383.

Lowndes, Vviven, Laurence Pratchett, and Gary Stoker. 2006. "Diagnosing and remedying the failings of official participation schemes: The CLEAR framework." *Social Policy & Society* 5: 281–91.

Leighley, Jan E. 2001. *Strength in numbers? The political mobilization of racial and ethnic minorities.* New Jersey: Princeton University Press.

Lien, Pei-te, Margret M. Conway, and Janelle Wong. 2004. *The politics of Asian Americans: Diversity and community*. New York: Routledge.

Loges, William E., and Joo-Young Jung. 2001. "Exploring the digital divide: Internet connectedness and age." *Communication Research* 28 (4): 536–562.

Luskin, Robert C., James S. Fishkin, and Santo Iyengar. 2006. "Considered opinions on U.S. foreign policy: Face-to-face versus online Deliberative Polling®." Accessed November 7, 2008. http://cdd.stanford.edu/research/papers/2006/foreign-policy.pdf.

Mendelberg, Tali. 2002. "The deliberative citizen: Theory and evidence." *Political decision making, deliberation and participation* 6 (1): 151–193.

Mendelberg, Tali, and John Oleske, 2000. "Race and public deliberation." *Political Communication* 17: 169–191.

Monnoyer-Smith, Laurence, and Julien Talpin. 2010. "Participatory frames in deliberative devices: The Ideal-EU case study." Paper presented at the 4th Online Deliberation conference. Leeds.

Mossberger, Karen, Caroline J. Tolbert, and Michelle Gilbert. 2006. "Race, place, and information technology." *Urban Affairs Review* 41 (5): 583–602.

Mouffe, Chantal. 1999. "Deliberative democracy or agonistic pluralism?" *Social Research* 66 (3): 745–59.

Nie, Norman H., Jane Junn, and Kenneth Stehlik-Barry. 1996. *Education and democratic citizenship in America*. Chicago: The University of Chicago Press.

Norris, Pippa. 2001. *Digital Divide: Civic Engagement, Information Poverty, and the Internet Worldwide*. Cambridge: Cambridge University Press.

Papacharissi, Zizi. 2008. "Democracy online: Civility, politeness, and the democratic potential of online political discussion groups." *New Media & Society* 6 (2): 259–83.

Polletta, Francesca, and Lee, John. 2006. "Is telling stories good for democracy? Rhetoric in public deliberation after 9/11." *American Sociological Review* 71 (5): 699–723.

Price, Vincent. 2009. "Citizens deliberating online: Theory and some evidence". In *Online deliberation: Design, research, and practice*, eds. Todd Davies, and Seeta Peña Gangadharan, 37–58. CSLI Publications.

Rosenstone, Steven J., and John M. Hansen. 1993. *Mobilization, participation, and democracy in America*. New York: Macmillan Publishing Company.

Schlozman, Kay L., Benjamin I. Page, Sydney Verba, and Morris P. Fiorina. 2005. "Inequalities of political voice." In *Inequality and American democracy*, eds. Lawrence R. Jacobs, and Theda Skocpol, 19–87. New York: Russell Sage Foundation.

Shane, Peter M. 2004. *Democracy online: The prospects for political renewal through the Internet*. New York & London: Routledge.

Smith, Graham. 2009. *Democratic innovations: Designing institutions for citizen participation*. Cambridge: Cambridge University Press.

Van Dijk, Jan, and Kenneth Hacker. 2003. "The digital divide as a complex and dynamic phenomenon." *The Information Society* 19: 315–326.

Van Zoonen, Liesbet. 2005. *Entertaining the citizen: When politics and popular culture converge*. Rowman & Littlefield.

Verba, Sydney, and Nancy H. Nie. 1972. *Participation in America*. New York: Harper and Row.

Wilhelm, Anthony G. 2000. *Democracy in the digital age: Challenges to political life in cyberspace*. New York & London: Routledge.

Wright, Scott. 2007. "A Virtual European Public Sphere? The Futurum Discussion Forum". *Journal of European Public Policy* 14 (8): 1167–85.

Zhang, Weiyu. 2006. "Constructing and disseminating subaltern public discourses in China." *Javnost-The Public* 13 (2): 41–64.

Zhang, Weiyu. 2010. "Technical capital and participatory inequality in eDeliberation: An actor-network analysis." *Information, Communication & Society* 13 (7): 1019–1039.

Zhang, Weiyu. 2012. "Virtual communities as subaltern public spheres: A theoretical development and an application to the Chinese Internet". In *Virtual community participation and motivation: Cross-disciplinary theories*, ed. Honglei Li, 143–161. Hershey, PA: IGI Global.

Zhang, Weiyu, Xiaoxia Cao, and Minh Ngoc Trah. 2013. "The structural features and the deliberative quality of online discussions." *Telematics & Informatics* 30 (2): 74–86.

Zhang, Weiyu and Leanne Chang. 2014. "Perceived Speech Conditions and Disagreement of Everyday Talk: A Proceduralist Perspective of Citizen Deliberation." *Communication Theory* 24 (2): 124–145.

Zhang, Weiyu. 2015. "Perceived Procedural Fairness in Deliberation: Predictors and Effects." *Communication Research* 42 (3), 345–364.

Zukin, Cliff, Scott Keeter, Molly Andolina, Krista Jenkins, and Michael X. Delli Carpini. 2006. *A new engagement?: Political participation, civic life, and the changing American citizen*. Oxford, UK: Oxford University Press.

Kees Brants

Chapter Four. The Demise of a Deliberative Dream? Challenging the Mission of Public Service Broadcasting in Europe

Introduction

Like so many political morality tales, this one is about democracy and how, in a globalized world, with the economy in a state of collapse and citizens more and more distrusting authorities in general and the political elite in particular, a platform for equal and meaningful deliberation seems ever so necessary. The more direct a democracy, the more vital is public deliberation for opinion formation and collective decision making. For individual citizens to actively participate, knowledge through (permanent) education is a precondition, because it allows for an informed citizenry which can engage in synergetic and meaningful discussion. Having equal access to deliberation, sharing arguments on the basis of a critical and rational debate, discussing openly a plurality of points of view with mutual understanding and the common interest in mind, and learning from each other's ideas by being open to them, all these qualities resonate with the ideas of the Enlightenment.

Central to the modern versions of the deliberative model of democracy is often the notion of the public sphere, especially as developed and propagated by Jürgen Habermas in his influential *Strukturwandel der Öffentlichkeit* (1962), which twenty seven years after its German publication was translated as the *Structural Transformation of the Public Sphere* (1989). In the English language, the book and concept went on to conquer the western world, especially because the notion of public sphere, although only focusing on one aspect of the German concept, was much more accessible and user-friendly than Habermas' complex and polysemic *Öffentlichkeit*.

A public sphere or public domain is a social 'space' between the state and civil society, where in a rational, open and pluriform exchange between equals, wants and desires, grievances and ideas can be articulated, problems suggested and solutions proposed, accepted or turned down, compromise reached and, not necessarily, consensus arrived at. Ideally, in that whole process of collective will formation, individuals are transformed, complex issues made sense of, norms challenged and internalized, and identities and social well-being created. And finally, ideas and suggestions in the discursive public sphere could be 'translated' to the decision making sphere. Habermas located that sphere in the 18th century coffee houses in France and the UK, even though they were of a bourgeois nature and originally catered for males only.

Deliberation as a social process, as Dryzek (2000, 1) reiterated, is distinguished from other kinds of communication in that "deliberators are amenable to changing their judgments, preferences and views during the course of their interactions, which involve persuasion rather than coercion, manipulation, or deception." Meaningful deliberation in a modern democratic society cannot exist without the kind of media of communication which, as the European Commission formulated it fifteen years ago, are widely available and accessible; reflect the pluralistic nature of society and are not dominated by any one viewpoint or controlled by any one interest group; make available the information necessary for citizens to make informed choices about their lives and their communities; and provide the means whereby the public debate which underpins free and democratic societies can take place (Oreja et al. 1998, 9). The question is whether such media do exist.

It is in this context that – more than traditional media, such as the press, radio, and television – new information and communication technologies are proposed as the appropriate and effective medicine for democracy in a midlife crisis (Brants 1996). From internet discussion sites, blogs and smart phones to Facebook, YouTube and twitter, ICT-related media are often propagated as easily accessible platforms for political debate, opinion formation and informed participation. Ideally, they provide the building blocks and the infrastructure for truly public, encompassing, equal and open deliberation. The opportunity structure that these new technologies seem to have provided for consciousness raising, debate and action in the Arab spring is often quoted as a case in point (Wolfsfeld et al. 2013).

This very concise overview of the developing concept and changing platforms of deliberation merely serves to place in context what we are inclined to forget. I want to discuss how deliberation lies at the heart of good old West-European public broadcasting – at least in its dominant form until the 1990s and possibly until today. It may seem like a sweeping generalization to put all countries in one basket, but the introduction and underlying mission of public service broadcasting has been quite similar – albeit differently formulated and with a different organizational structure – focusing on the pillars of education, informed citizenry and debate. And although countries may differ in the appreciation of its seriousness and in the solutions proposed, they all seem to agree that public service broadcasting is in a state of flux, if not in crisis. The question is whether these challenges will result in, or have we already witnessed, the demise of an ideal and is the deliberative dream turning into a nightmare? Or is that too somber a picture?

Broadcasting with a Mission

With the notable exception of Luxembourg, where a commercial system has always been in place, the 20th century history of broadcasting in Western Europe is rooted in an idea of public service. As with many contested concepts, there is not one theory or generally accepted notion of what public service broadcasting (PSB) stands for and different organizational structures exist per country. But there has always been agreement that broadcasting had to be based on a belief that the content of its programs was not merely a commodity, but particularly a public or merit good, a universal service for all and guaranteed by the state. One way or the other, the content the broadcasters provide has to be in the public interest, and should be available to all, wherever they live, and accessible for about the same price. As such, the public goods of radio and television had to be produced and distributed by institutions and by mechanisms warranted by the state and other than those familiar in a market economy.

Historically, there had been good reasons for that structure. First, the sky had its limits. After the Second World War there were more demands for terrestrial space than there were frequencies. To have a fair system of their allocation in a situation of scarcity, the state had to be intimately involved, being seen as both the representative and the guarantor of the general interest. At the same time, that did not always sit well with the ideas of freedom *of* expression and *from* government interference. In practice, West European governments uneasily kept their distance with regard to content, while being closely involved in the structure and financing of PSB. Second, with the power to decide who could go on air and who not, and at what price for the audience, programmatic obligations deriving from a sense of public interest had to be defined and set by those who represented the public; in other words by elected political authorities. It usually meant that there was an explicit reference (in a Broadcasting Act or regulatory memorandum) or implicit assumption (within the broadcasting organizations themselves) of the need for programmatic diversity and quality, of catering for all while serving minority interests, and of some programmatic mix of education, information, culture and entertainment. All of those references functioned as both anchor points and programmatic guidelines. Third, public broadcasting began as a pragmatic compromise between the merits of capitalism and the mores of social responsibility, comparable to and in line with the birth of the welfare state in Western Europe. It has been "firmly rooted," Corcoran (1996, 10) has reminded us, "as a belief system and a set of institutional practices, in the optimistic, humanistic Enlightenment idea that the world can be made a human place for all, and that the collective (the nation, the region) is important in order to allow the individual to flourish. Public good and public service converged in broadcasting."

The Enlightenment ideal – but also the welfare state and the social-democratic expectation of the malleability of society – comes back in the mission of public service broadcasting, which consists of three, related elements: a cultural-pedagogic logic, its place in civil society, and its contribution to social cohesion of the nation state (Brants and De Bens 2000). The *cultural-pedagogic logic* refers to public broadcasting's role to provide its audience particularly with what they need as citizens and less with what they may want as consumers. The latter should more or less be left to commercial and profit-driven media. What the public needs, according to theories and practices of direct and participatory democracy, is the cognitive and cultural baggage to understand and perform optimally in a complex world and to participate and contribute qualitatively and rationally to a lively democracy. Consequently, the role of the broadcasters is to educate and broaden people's interests, to inform and confront them with the unexpected, and to enrich the public culturally. Television is also to be enjoyed, of course, as long as its programs are of high quality.

Close to a specification of this logic is the *function of broadcasting in civil society*, its performative contribution to democracy. According to this view, to arrive at rational decision making, one needs an informed citizenry that can take stock of most ideas and views aired, concerning specific issues in society, and ideally form the public opinion or opinions. That way members of the public can make sense of the information and orient themselves in relation to it, and thus be able to sensibly participate in and contribute to the functioning of democracy. In order to arrive at that, public broadcasting (and from a normative democratic theory: the media in general) has to perform a number of functions for society, as an operationalization of their civil role in the public interest.

In the first place, they are to inform about the diversity of facts, views, policies and opinions, relevant for citizens in society, and about the proposed solutions to social problems (Blumler and Gurevitch 1995, 97). Generally, in their news and current affairs programs, they are expected to report those developments that are likely to impinge, positively or negatively, on the welfare of citizens. And they have to do that regardless of political and economic influence and interests and in such a way that justice is done to the plurality of ideas and opinions characteristic for society. In the second place, they have a control function, as watchdogs of power and its misuse. In their informational and documentary programs, they hold elected and unelected officials to account for the fulfillment of their promises and the execution of their decisions. Part of that control can be meaningful agenda setting, when reporters have good reasons to assume that certain issues are ignored or refused entry to the political agenda, or are thwarted in the mist of politico-speak. In the third place, next to these two more educational functions, public broadcasting is expected to provide a platform for articulating wants, desires, ideas and demands expressed in society, for dialogue between citizens and between power holders and mass publics, to communicate such 'voice' to the decision making sphere and the powers that be. This large-scale communicative space for public deliberation can be found in discussion programs, talk shows and in-depth magazines. They form Habermas' public sphere, the modern coffee house, where discussants deliberate and viewers lurk and learn. And all of them ideally form opinions and take up positions based on knowledge, provided through the information and control functions.

Finally, along with the cultural-pedagogic logic and its function for civil society, public broadcasting has a mission towards *social cohesion in society* by contributing to consensus, the protection of a multi-colored and multi-layered national identity and a nation's cultural heritage. Equally, it should support the process whereby alternative, minority identities and sets of values can be put forward. Social cohesion is expected to be the result of participation, loyalty and involvement, three elements which are dynamically related. The idea is that knowledge is a prerequisite for participation, which in itself strengthens loyalty and stronger involvement. The basic premise of the cohesive and consensual function of public broadcasting is that the more individuals participate, the stronger their bond with the system and the more they identify with it, the greater the social cohesion will be. Public broadcasting creates the conditions for participation by informing different groups in society about each other, giving them access and space to articulate equally. As such, PBS is expected to provide the prerequisites for a common frame of reference.

Critique and Challenges, Old...

Until the 1980s, public broadcasting had a more or less total monopoly over the radio and television in most of Western European countries. Although the organizations might differ in emphasis within their mission, the cultural-pedagogic logic and PSB's function for civil society and for social cohesion were an undeniable and almost self-evident matter of fact. The coming of private commercial television some thirty years ago – already before that in the UK (although ITV from its birth in the 1960s had a regulated public obligation), in Italy in the 1970s and in Luxembourg right from the start – changed the landscape and the broadcasting values dramatically. It opened up the market to competition, introduced profit as a steering logic and forced the public monopolists to rethink their remit and their position. Were they to battle it out with their competitors, adapt to the situation or adopt the same logic (Hultén and Brants 1992)?

Opening up the broadcasting market was not the first time that competition and commercialization were criticized as the evils that brought doom to the educational, critical and deliberative role of the media. In his description of the decline of the bourgeois public sphere, towards the end of the 19th century, Habermas had already pointed at the rise of the mass circulation press, which from guardians of the public sphere developed into propagators of private and commercial interests. In short: critical publicity of politicized newspapers dwindled; market-orientation and de-politicizing of content grew; public affairs journalism was replaced by a focus on the sensational and the scandalous; opinion management and manipulation was introduced, fostering passivity and conformity. It sounds familiar.

Similar criticism can be found in the Hutchins Commission on Freedom of the Press in the United States, which shortly after the Second World War formulated answers to, what they saw as, the attack on the libertarian idea of a market place of ideas free from competition and commercially driven media. The commission's concept of a socially responsible press, expected the media to be truthful, comprehensive and intelligent in the account of the day's events; to present and clarify the goals and values of society; to reach every member of society and create a forum for the exchange of comment and criticism; and a means of projecting the opinions and attitudes of the groups in society to one another. This social responsibility theory soon crossed the Atlantic Ocean and also lies – in part *avant la lettre* – at the heart of the mission of PSB. It indicates that in the middle of the 20th century such notions were commonplace, albeit as a critique of and an answer to observed and feared developments. In a way, the ethos of public service broadcasting can also be seen as a response to commercial developments in the press and similar pressures with regard to the organization and financing of the radio first and television later.

As if Habermas' critique of Europe's post-bourgeois public sphere and Hutchins' beating of US commercial media had not sounded loud and clear enough, the opening-up of the broadcasting market and subsequent rise of commercial television in Europe saw a repetition and extension of equally stark warnings. The most outspoken and eloquent critic of commercialization is arguably Jay Blumler – probably not surprisingly an American, living and working most of his life in the UK. He feared that market pressures would jeopardize many features of public broadcasting that West Europeans had previously taken for granted. In his analysis, he formulated seven sets of vulnerable values at stake in liberalized, de-regulated and competitive multi-channel conditions (Blumler 1992, 30ff).

First, quality programming had lost a lot of its priority – both in PSB's readiness to invest in it and in its taking risks for the sake of innovation – and has been replaced by a more calculative approach, in which a frantic search for the right audience-maximizing formula becomes the driving force. Second, there are several indications that principled pluralism of organization and programming of PSB has slowly been shifting to a more pragmatic pluralism, yielding only the amount and those forms of diversity that are likely to pay. Third, instead of insisting on television's role in strengthening identity through national programming and following the internationalization of commercial media, PSB is at risk of subverting to a bland and homogeneous global media culture, also because countries can no longer sustain a strong indigenous production industry. Fourth, program sources of public broadcasting have begun to lose their independence from commercial influences on the structure, scheduling and content of programming, in spite of a general European anti-commercial sentiment and elaborate regulation that were in place until the beginning of the 1990s.

Fifth, the integrity of civic communication is threatened by prioritizing entertainment over information, by short-changing analysis and discussion, by focusing on viewers as consumers and on horse race in political communication, while images and racy soundbites take precedence over substance, information and dialogue. Sixth, the educational aim to educate, inform, stimulate and broaden the horizons of children now has to compete with the commercial drive to please them with what they like and *en passant* exposing them to persuasive and often hidden advertising. Seventh, in more competitive conditions downward pressures are exerted in standards to avoid offence to public sentiments in the fields of violence, sex and the use of bad language.

What Blumler did not mention was that commercial TV introduced programmatic innovations and allowed for more oppositional voices in many a Central and some Western European countries, which had hitherto been ignored or thwarted by the state-controlled "voices of reason." Moreover, part of the structure and programming of PSB runs the risk of creating its own limitations and problems. In spite of its emphasis on equality and on access for minority opinions, the mission and program philosophy had a tendency to paternalism and elitism – 'we know what the public needs' – and to ignore the dissenting voices of agonism and unreason, emotions and irrationality. In their programs, or better: on their platform of Enlightenment, there seemed only room for contributions and deliberations based on ratio and quality "as we know it." Moreover, the question was evaded, whether the public mission needed an organizational (and bureaucratic) structure. Or that a financial guarantee (programmatic subsidy) to make and broadcast programs with a mission, would not suffice.

…and New

Since Blumler formulated his vulnerable values and how they had been threatened, some of the more negative developments surrounding the cognitive, educational and deliberative potential of public broadcasting have intensified in their poignancy, while new emerging trends are popping up. But where on the one hand these trends tend to strengthen the critique, they have also shown a flipside, whereby the new challenges PSB faces are seen as an opportunity.

The more somber picture, however, comes from the *withering of political and public commitment* in many European countries to the organization of public broadcasting. There are several reasons for this. With intensifying competition for audiences, for income, for programs, for star reporters and programmers, the market gets adrift. The financial situation of the public broadcasters is equally problematic. Most of their revenues still come from some form of license fee, but most have to compete for advertising income as well. Without license fees being indexed and with fragmented audiences, the income from both sources declines, while costs (for quality programming, stars, copyright, sports, etc.) rise. Demands for more state subsidy meet at best with raised eyebrows, if only because of the general economic situation. This is strengthened by a kind of legitimacy problem PSB has, as indicated by its waning public support. Why should we, many viewers argue, pay for programs with a mission we did not ask for or do not subscribe to and of a content, genre and format we quite often do not enjoy, while what we like we can get for free? And many a political party (and not only of the populist kind) echoes this anxiety in asking whether we need heavily funded public broadcasting organizations or whether product-subsidies would not suffice. Finally, there seems to exist a crisis of authority and trust, many a public broadcaster in Europe is faced with. Confronted by scandal – and not as reporters this time but as culprits – broadcasting organizations and their professionals inspire less and less trust in their intentions, sincerity, performance, reliability and authority.

A more two-sided picture comes from the *shift of media from a supply to a demand market*. In the wake of growing competition for audiences in a fragmenting market, it is more and more the public who decide what broadcasters should supply and less so the latter who claim that they know what the public needs as citizens in a democracy. On the one hand, this seems to have resulted in a diverse and often complex responsiveness of the media to the versatile wishes of their publics (Brants and De Haan 2010). With more channels, more information and more space for deliberation, there is a professional response to the civic demands of the public for their issue agendas to be taken seriously; an emotional response reflecting a more empathic discourse of bonding with and crusading for the angry public; as well as a commercial response to a volatile consumer who wants to be entertained and pleased. On the other hand, the centrality of the public, their increasing choice and subsequent fragmentation can result in avoidance behavior and declining reach of informative, educational and deliberative programs and equally declining levels of knowledge, especially among the politically less interested (Prior 2007; Van Praag 2012). With the remote control in hand and in a digitized world of plenty they can skip the cultural-pedagogic logic. The effect can be balkanization, whereby publics chose only those kinds and contents of information that fit their preconceived ideas and whereby they are no longer open to conflicting opinions, debate and contestation. This challenges the idea of deliberative democracy, of sharing ideas and views in an open discussion (Koole 2012).

The process of balkanization can be further triggered by the *rise and reach of the internet and mobile technologies*. The picture here – probably the area witnessing the most profound and fundamental change – is again two-sided. On the one hand it has created an immense source for finding and consulting information and extending communication. Social media have created platforms for deliberation that are potentially more interactive than ever, creating opportunities for equal access of more people who can put forward and discuss in a critical-rational way more issues and user-generated content; not limited by time and space, and potentially resulting in a wider and deeper agenda. The *vox populi*, traditionally excluded from the platform of Enlightenment, can present and raise its voice. On the other hand, the tone in many of these discussions can be harsh, angry and intolerant, filled with unsubstantiated one-liners and personal threats, excluding deviant voices and leading to balkanization of discussion sites where one can find the opinions one agrees with. This sometimes results in trial by Twitter of elites, celebrities and suspects of crimes, in wiki-truths or truthiness of rumor and gossip, where the fact-free authenticity of the experience expert can be more credible than the fact-based authority of the learned expert (Bruno 2012).

The internet is also affecting journalism, the traditional news providers, truth finders, sense makers and reality interpreters, whose authority is built on assumed professionalism and reliability (McNair 2013). After the appearance of competition and commercialization, public broadcasting had lost most of its market monopoly. In the past ten years, journalists, particularly those working in PSB, have lost their monopoly on the selection of news, on producing and defining it and its relevance. On the one hand this has rocked the paternalism and the claim of self-evident authority and cultural-pedagogic logic. Traditional media too see in the internet an interactive opportunity structure and an incentive to bond with their publics – although most journalists resent the practical consequence of this bonding. On the other hand, it signals the possible beginning of the end of a professional journalistic culture that was built on a sense of public interest, rules of the game of news gathering and disseminating, and the often implicit codes of practice and ethics that go with that. When everyone can be a journalist, it's everyone's truth (for himself).

Public broadcasting is also challenged by *uncertainty about the place, content and form of politics and political debate* (Brants 2012). It manifests itself, firstly, in a shift from political representation to political performance and the necessity politicians and their advisers feel to brand and sell that performance in a permanent campaign. Secondly, there is a (further) blurring of the distinction between information and propaganda, and the rise of spin, aimed at controlling the interpretative freedom of journalists and persuasively steering the cognitive luggage of what people know and do not know. Thirdly, we witness increasing political mistrust in the aims, practice and power of the media and journalists and an equally cynical attitude of the latter towards power holders, threatening their acclaimed symbiosis and the media's platform function for political and civic deliberation. Fourthly, in many countries there is a shift of TV's platform of representation and deliberation of politics from the genre of news and current affairs to that of talk shows and infotainment – and not with commercial broadcasters alone. They are cheap in format, attractive to a wide audience and they can provide politicians with more air time for discussion and a more friendly, celebrity-oriented environment. At the same time, it is a format that runs the risk of a less critical, truth-finding, knowledge-based and opinion-formation-oriented professional journalism. Finally, these TV-programs with much debate and live interviews also have a tendency towards tribalism: discussion between representatives of two opposing positions, who will, and are expected to, stick to their point and preferably do so loudly, leading to a potential bias of extremities and an amplification of partly organized and partly really existing polarization. Politics between theatre and street-fight.

The socio-political environment of PSB is also witnessing and partly forming *populist tendencies* it has to come to terms with and make sense of, tendencies *in both politics, the media and with the public.* Traditional left-right dimensions and religion, which have characterized cleavages in much of West European society, have begun to be overtaken by a new cultural dimension, characterized by postmodern hedonism on the one hand and new conservatism driven by fears of globalization on the other (Kriesi et al. 2008). Increasingly, protectionist views on immigration and integration have dominated the public agenda and have been voiced on the discussion sites of online and offline media. In most European countries, that sentiment is reflected in the rise of parties with a populist agenda, emphasizing anti-establishment feelings against the "corrupt elite" (Mudde 2004, 543), using an emotional style and "verbal radicalism" (Betz and Immerfall 1998, 2) and propagating nationalistic and anti-immigration policies (Ruzza and Fella 2011). This style and rhetoric begins to emigrate to mainstream parties as well as traditional media, particularly of the tabloid kind, and in popular TV talk shows (Mazzoleni 2003). The question is whether this media populism is the more or less unintended consequence of the selection of news and changes in the media market – negativity and harshness of populist leaders fit professional news values like a glove – or that they are the more intended consequence of populist attitudes of journalists – mistrusting authority and agreeing with anti-establishment and anti-immigration sentiments.

Conclusion

Having sketched these developments – both their threats and opportunities – one is left with the question whether there will be a future for the ideal of public broadcasting. Is there room for its cultural-pedagogic logic steering the informational and educational mission, its civic ideal towards a full, critically informed citizen, open to others and to mutual understanding, and contributing to social cohesion in society? Can public broadcasting provide a platform for and the content of well-argued and substantiated deliberation?

The picture this chapter has drawn of the deliberative potential and reality of public service broadcasting is painted predominantly and increasingly in dark and murky colors. The future of PSB as an organization is, to say the least, uncertain. Competition with other broadcasters and other media for audiences, income, programs and expertise is increasing and, some argue, deadly. Costs of quality programming and program makers, of copy rights and technological and other innovations are rising. Income from taxation, license fees, advertising and other legitimate sources is declining. Audiences are fragmenting, decreasing in size per channel and per program, and in some cases are losing their trust in the professionals. The claim for legitimacy, on the basis of quality and reliability, and for state funding is contested. In a multi-channel, multi-choice reality hit by economic and financial crisis, commitment of political parties and governments for continuous support is waning.

Under these circumstances, the future of PSB's programmatic mission is equally uncertain. What is left of the deliberative dream of public broadcasting, of the cultural-pedagogic logic as a driving force, its function for civil society and for social cohesion? They are still there in most mission statements, but the programmatic practice is ambiguous. Competing with entertainment focused commercial channels has led to a relative decline of expensive watchdog journalism and in the number, variety and depth of informational programs. In several countries talk shows seem to be the exception. These deliberative platforms have become popular and indicative of a more responsive approach of taking the public seriously. We see in this genre often a broader representation of the populace than in news and current affairs programs, a wider range of topics and issues under discussion, and a mix of the serious and the amusing. This makes these shows more attractive and more informative for a wider audience, particularly the politically less interested.

At the same time, the question is whether the aim of the genre to inform and to educate citizens has not been replaced by reaching and pleasing users/consumers. If so, that would affect the style, content and educational value of this format. The attempt to be at once educational, responsive and entertaining, often means that they are usually less about exchanging views and ideas, opinion and will formation and more about performance, contest and who won. Moreover, the confrontational form may well lead to inconclusive dialogue or, better, monologues, with the moderator controlling for time, challenging the contestants and keeping up the fire. That cannot be helpful for sense making nor for social integration.

Are we thus left with a situation of uncertainty, in which the organizational foundation of public service broadcasting is shaking, its future dependent on political commitment, its mission in flux, and its deliberative potential in an uneasy state of ambivalence? Yes we are. At the same time, however, we may in this Age of Internet well be over-preoccupied with yesterday's discussion about a medium, an organizational and programmatic structure that are past their sell-by-date. There are signs, and certainly convictions, that the internet provides a new, wider and more vibrant opportunity structure for public deliberation and a more bottom-up than a top-down cultural-pedagogic logic. It is too early, however, to say that thus public service broadcasting is an unnecessary and obsolete format for the deliberative dream. As the proof of the pudding is in the eating, we first need more empirical ingredients before we discard its alternative.

References

Betz, Hans-Georg, and Stefan Immerfall. 1998. *The New Politics of the Right: Neo-populist Parties and Movements in Established Democracies*. London: MacMillan.

Blumler, Jay. 1992. "Public Service Broadcasting before the Commercial Deluge." In *Television and the Public Interest. Vulnerable Values in West European Broadcasting*, ed. Jay Blumler, 7–22. London: Sage.

Blumler, Jay. 1992. "Vulnerable Values at Stake." In *Television and the Public Interest. Vulnerable Values in West European Broadcasting*, ed. Jay Blumler, 22–43. London: Sage.

Blumler, Jay, and Michael Gurevitch. 1995. *The Crisis of Public Communication.* London: Routledge.

Brants, Kees. 1996. "Policing Democracy: Communication Freedom in the Age of Internet." *Javnost/The Public* 3 (1): 57–71.

Brants, Kees (ed.). 2012. *Journalistiek en Politiek in Onzekere Tijden.* Den Haag: Boom Lemma.

Brants, Kees, and Els De Bens. 2000. "The Status of TV Broadcasting in Europe." In *Television Across Europe. A Comparative Introduction,* ed. Jan Wieten, Graham Murdock and Peter Dahlgren, 7–23. London: Sage.

Brants, Kees, and Yael de Haan. 2010. "Taking the Public Seriously. Three Models of Responsiveness in Media and Journalism." *Media, Culture & Society* 32 (3): 411–428.

Bruno, Nicola. 2012. "Tweet First, Verify Later". Reuter's Institute Fellowship Paper. University of Oxford.

Corcoran, Farrel. 1996. "Arts Council of the Air: Switching Attention from the Service to the Programme." *Javnost/The Public* 3 (2): 9–23.

Dryzek, John. 2000. *Deliberative Democracy and Beyond: Liberals, Critics and Contestations.* Oxford: Oxford University Press.

Habermas, Jürgen. 1962. *Strukturwandel der Öffentlichkeit.* Neuwied & Berlin: Luchterhand Verlag.

Habermas, Jürgen. 1989. *The Structural Transformation of the Public Sphere.* Cambridge: Polity Press.

Hultén, Olof, and Kees Brants. 1992. "Public Service Broadcasting: Reactions to Competition." In *Dynamics of Media Politics. Broadcast and Electronic Media in Western Europe,* ed. Karen Siune and Wolfgang Truetzschler, 116–129. London: Sage.

Koole, Ruud. 2012. "Naar Balkanisering en een Populistisch-Publicitair Complex." In *Journalistiek en Politiek in Onzekere Tijden,* ed. Kees Brants, 93–113. Den Haag: Boom Lemma.

Kriesi, Handpeter, Edgar Grande, Romain Lachat, Martin Dolezal, Simon Bornschier, and Timotheos Frey. 2008. *West European Politics in the Age of Globalization.* Cambridge: Cambridge University Press.

Mazzoleni, Gianpietro. 2003. "The Media and the Growth of Neo-Populism in Contemporary Democracies." In *The Media and Neo-Populism. A Contemporary Comparative Analysis,* eds. Gianpietro Mazzoleni, Julianne Stewart and Bruce Horsfield, 1–20. Westport: Praeger.

McNair, Brian. 2013. "Trust, Truth and Objectivity: Sustaining Quality Journalism in the Era of the Content-Generating User." In *Rethinking Journalism. Trust and*

Participation in a Transformed Media Landscape, eds. Chris Peters and Marcel Broersma, 75–89. London: Routledge.

Mudde, Cas. 2004. "The Populist Zeitgeist." *Government & Opposition* 39 (3): 542–564.

Oreja, Marelino et al. 1998. *The Digital Age: European Audiovisual Policy.* Report from the High Level Group on Audiovisual Policy. Brussels: European Commission.

Prior, Markus. 2007. *Post-Broadcast Democracy. How Media Choice Increases Inequality in Political Involvement and Polarizes Elections.* Cambridge: Cambridge University Press.

Ruzza, Carlo, and Stefano Fella. 2011. "Populism and the Italian Right." *Acta Politica* 46 (2): 158–179.

Van Praag, Philip. 2012. "Fact-Free Politics en de Verantwoordelijkheid van de Overheid." In *Journalistiek en Politiek in Onzekere Tijden,* ed. Kees Brants, 53–71. Den Haag: Boom Lemma.

Wolfsfeld, Gadi, Elad Segev, and Tamir Shaefer. 2013. "Social Media and the Arab Spring: Politics Comes First." *The International Journal of Press/Politics* 18 (1): 1–23.

Section II.
The Deliberative Poll:
Recent Implementations

James Fishkin

Chapter Five. Reviving Deliberative Democracy: Reflections on Recent Experiments

Introduction

A central problem of democratic theory—and practice—has long been how to adapt a certain form of *interpersonal communication— deliberation*—to the large scale nation state: How to bring face to face deliberation both to the public dialogue, and to the decision processes of states or jurisdictions involving many thousands or millions of people. The problem arises because democratic values include not only deliberation, but also another key principle—political equality. And our principal strategies for implementing political equality have, in fact, *undermined* deliberation. The research program I call Deliberative Polling is an empirical investigation into institutional designs that attempt to combine both these values for public consultation.

This problem is really as old as democracy itself. We want to consider the views of all citizens equally—as required by political equality—but we want to do so when they have had good conditions for deliberating about them together—for considering opposing points of view and becoming informed on the issues they are consulted about. The outlines of a promising solution to this problem can be found in a form of democracy practiced in Ancient Athens, which got largely lost in the dust of history for more than two millennia.

Athens

Athens is often thought of as the home of direct democracy, but the *pnyx*, the hill where the Assembly met could only hold, at most, about 6,000 people and there were as many as sixty thousand citizens in fifth century Athens. So, speculations of the American founders to the contrary, Athens was not a place where all the citizens could gather together and make the laws. As time went on, more and more of the crucial decisions were made, not in the Assembly but by deliberative microcosms chosen by lot, citizens juries of 500 or more, the Council of 500, the *nomothetai* (legislative commissions) the *graphe paranomon*, bodies of several hundred up to a thousand persons who would deliberate usually for a day and decide. Uniquely, the Council of 500 met for a year and set the agenda for voting in the Assembly.

This system had some defects: First, the lottery system was imperfect as a form of sampling because for each of ten tribes, people had to first volunteer themselves as willing to serve to be put on the list in the lottery. Second, apart from the Council, which rotated groups of 50, there was no small group discussion. 500 people sat in an amphitheater and heard the arguments on either side in a single day and then voted by a show of hands. But still the basic idea of a deliberative microcosm chosen by lot was practiced in ancient Athens, and maybe for all we know in any of up to one hundred other ancient city states that had some form of democracy, but no written record of their actual institutions.

The modern efforts to revive this ancient idea have had the benefit of employing social science both to study it and improve it. Now there are more than two decades of work with the deliberating mini-public selected by random sampling. These efforts take various forms: Deliberative Polling, the Citizens Assemblies in British Columbia and Ontario as well as less ambitious efforts such as the Citizens Juries, the Citizens Initiative Review in Oregon, the Consensus Conference. Some of these efforts begin with random sampling but have such dramatic non-response that most observers would say that they verge on pure self-selection[1]. Some do not collect any attitudinal data on representativeness so it is difficult, with ample opportunities for self-selection, to know who is putting themselves forward. And some involve microcosms that are so small that evaluating opinion change is not statistically meaningful. However, the basic idea is to form a credible microcosm through random sampling, engage it in good conditions for thinking about an issue and then provide it with an opportunity for expressing its considered judgments. Social science can play a useful role in evaluating the representativeness of the sample and the process for arriving at considered judgments and then expressing them. Having attitudinal data at time of recruitment (and samples of non-participants to compare the participants to) and getting the opinions in confidential questionnaires both facilitate the process. Ideally, the microcosm will start out as a mirror of the public and then it will really think through the issues.

---

1   See for example the Citizens Initiative Review—from 10,000 questionnaires restricted to demographic items, they get 350 responses. From these they select quotas for demographic representation. But there is no way of knowing how the 9,650 differ from the 350 in attitudes. So there is no way of evaluating the motivations for self-selection. The result is a deliberating group of 24 who attempt to reach consensus. But 24 is not a number that is statistically meaningful when there are any real divisions of opinion. A strong majority in favor could actually be a strong majority against.

In that sense, it combines in one institution the conflicting ideas of representation which animated the debate over constitutional design at the American founding. Federalists wanted representatives, as James Madison put it in *Federalist* 10, to "refine and enlarge the public views by passing them through the medium of a chosen body of citizens" (Medison 1987/1788). The refinement used the common metaphor of a filter for deliberation—what Madison called "a strategy of successive filtrations" (Medison 1987, 40). But anti-Federalists wanted representatives to be as close to the people as possible, like them in every way possible. In that sense they should be a "mirror" of the population. The mini-public strategy begins with a mirror and subjects it to the filtration of deliberation. It turns "reflected" opinion to "reflective" opinion.

The central, continuing problem of democratic reform has been to build institutions that realize two fundamental democratic aspirations—*inclusion* and *thoughtfulness*. On the one hand, we need institutions that somehow represent or include all the members of a polity. On the other hand, we need to consult those members under conditions where they are effectively motivated to think about the power they are being asked to exercise. All over the world, democratic reforms bring power to the people through institutions that increasingly emphasize inclusiveness. But the very conditions that allow for more inclusion seem to have undermined collective thoughtfulness. However, this trade-off is not inevitable. Rather it is due to the poverty of the institutional imagination that has guided most modern democratic reforms. This paper explores the rationale for the mini-public effort to expand the democratic tool kit of mechanisms for public consultation. It is aimed at showing that it is indeed possible to combine inclusiveness and thoughtfulness—rather than force us to choose between them.

The Apparent Conflict

Why has it been thought that there is a conflict between the inclusiveness of institutions and the thoughtfulness with which citizens provide an input into the democratic process? Some of the main contentions can be briefly summarized as:

a) Voters may have passions or interests that can motivate dangerous factions.
b) Voters are too ill informed to deal with complex policy or political matters.
c) Voters are incapable of dealing with complex policy or political matters.
d) Voters are subject to mechanisms of group psychology such as "polarization" that undermine the rationality of their choices. These mechanisms arise from group discussion, the very process that would seem most promising to raise the thoughtfulness of democratic inputs.

e) Voters have preferences that are sufficiently heterogeneous that their choices would produce "instability" (cycles violating transitivity) so that the resulting democratic decisions are subject to arbitrariness and manipulation.

Because these contentions are all well-known, I will simply take note of them now in order to frame our review of strategies that might overcome them. Our basic question is whether or not it is possible to avoid these apparent objections and at the same time, succeed in combining the two fundamental democratic aspirations of inclusion and thoughtfulness.

Turning briefly to the first of these objections, American democracy was born in a debate over the founding in which Madison and Hamilton offered a vision of opinion filtered by representatives. The idea was to avoid the passions and interests of the public that might motivate "factions" adverse to the rights of others or the permanent and aggregate interests of the community. Consulting the public directly might be dangerous, it was thought. After all, the people had killed Socrates. The Americans had lived through Shays' rebellion. The founders wanted the cool reflections of deliberative representatives rather than the aroused passions or interests of the mass public. But to do so, they needed to create an elite "republic" that was insulated from the direct input of ordinary citizens. The Senate was selected by state legislatures; the President was selected by an Electoral College that was originally supposed to be a deliberative body (on a state by state basis). The constitution was adopted by a "convention" which was also supposed to be a representative, deliberative body. The resulting system was intended to be high on the thoughtfulness or quality of opinion (filtration or deliberation would serve the public good and protect against tyranny of the majority) but low on elements of inclusion like political equality and participation. The Founders' debate in the US suggests the question for modern democratic reform: is it possible to have a more inclusive system and avoid the problems the Founders envisaged with mass public input? Is the cool reflection of deliberation reserved only for elite representatives, or can it be conducted by the people themselves?

A second line of argument against combining inclusive and thoughtful mass consultation is raised by the whole line of democratic reform that greeted the project of the American founders, beginning with concerns expressed by the Anti-Federalists and moving through populist and progressive reforms right up until our own day. The US now directly elects its Senators; many states conduct referenda and other ballot initiatives; the development of public opinion polling has led to constant informal public consultation. Yet these processes have revealed that the public has little information about the issues it is consulted about. The issue can range from whether or not Iraq had weapons of mass destruction to whether or not, at the height of the Cold War, the Soviet Union was a member of NATO. The public has shockingly little correct knowledge even though educational levels have gone up dramatically since World War II. One widespread explanation for the mass public's low level of information is "rational ignorance." If I have one vote in millions, why should I spend a lot of time investing in more information to make an informed choice. My individual vote or opinion is extraordinarily unlikely to make any difference. Yet our aspirations for public input would seem to depend crucially on citizens being informed. The apparent conflict is that if we aspire to more inclusion, and directly consult a mass public of millions, we find that that it is subject to rational ignorance, undermining the thoughtfulness that can be attributed to the people being consulted.

A third line of argument against the possibility of simultaneously fulfilling the aspirations toward inclusion and thoughtfulness, is the idea that the public may not have the competence to deal with complex policy or political matters. To the extent this is the case, the moves toward more mass participation will bring in people who are incapable of living up to the democratic role assigned to them. Consider Richard Posner's critique of deliberative democracy (Posner 2003). He argues that there is no use consulting the public about substantive policy. All we should expect from democracy is a competitive struggle for the people's vote, along the lines offered previously by Joseph Schumpeter (1942). We get a peaceful decision about the circulation of elites-elites who will take relatively similar positions in order to compete in the same electoral space. But the will of the people is more or less meaningless as the public cannot be expected to have thoughtful or well-formed opinions on any substantive matters. The more we practice inclusiveness and bring the mass public into the process, the more we get away from the competent decisions of elites.

A fourth argument is that even if we brought the public into democratic processes, we would not contribute to the collective thoughtfulness of the process because there are debilitating patterns of group psychology – polarization – that prevent the mass public from dealing with the substantive merits of political or policy questions. Cass Sunstein has argued that the very process that might bring some thoughtfulness to the political process – group discussion – brings pathology. He calls it "polarization" and he means a process whereby groups go to extremes. If there is an issue for which a midpoint can be defined, if the group starts out on one side of the midpoint, it will move after discussion further to that side. If it starts out on the other side, it will move further to that side. The idea is that because of an "imbalance in the argument pool" (more arguments being voiced on one side than another) and because of a "social comparison effect" (people wanting to be publicly identified with the winning viewpoint) this process will replicate itself regardless of content. Sunstein has confirmed his hypothesis with experiments with mock juries (Sunstein 2003).

A fifth argument is that the attempt to take democracy seriously at the level of the mass public (the product of inclusion) is likely to undermine the collective thoughtfulness of democratic results because the public is likely to have such ill thought out preferences that one could get cycles violating transitivity. This embarrassing fact is only covered up by "structure induced equilibrium" that covers up the cycles (either by limiting the alternatives to two so that no cycles are evident, or allowing for agenda manipulation of the choices considered). But the normative conclusion is not affected. The voice of the people, if it were consulted directly on three or more choices, would be arbitrary because pairwise comparisons among the alternatives could yield cycles with preferences of B over A, C over B but A over C. From this perspective it is better not to make any claims about the public will and limit the advantages of democracy to the peaceful circulation of elites.

Responses to the Five Problems

Consider the mini-public or neo-Athenian solution as a response to each of these five problems. While portions of the population may indeed have passions or interests that would motivate factions, in Madison's sense, good random samples of the public will only have those passionate members of factions in their proportion to the population. In moderated discussions, those willing to participate usually abide by the ground rules, contributing, and listening to the dialogue with evident sincerity.

Even in areas of severe conflict it is likely that representative samples of the public will find it easier to discuss contentious issues and find more room for mutual understanding than would the policy elites who speak for those factions. We found this in Northern Ireland with a Deliberative Poll on education reform. There was room for movement on policy and for increases in mutual respect among the mass public, even in the troubled environment of a post conflict situation (Luskin, O'Flynn, Fishkin, Russell 2012). Other projects on highly contentious issues support the same conclusion. The Bulgarian project on policies toward the Roma and the Japanese project on what to do about nuclear power after the Fukushima disaster had intense groups in the public debate, but those in the random sample were more than willing to engage in productive dialogue[2]. The prospects

---

2   See the Bulgaria and Japan tabs at http://cdd.stanford.edu, and the corresponding chapter 8 in the present book.

for mutual civility and productive dialogue in a microcosm can be facilitated by the combination of both factors: who is in the room and what they do once they get there. Random sampling and moderated small group discussions combine to create reason-based and evidence based consideration of policy alternatives.

The second challenge, the low information levels on the part of the mass public, is a real challenge for public consultation. If I have one vote in millions, or one opinion in millions, I may plausibly be subject to incentives for rational ignorance not to invest a great deal of time or effort in becoming informed about the details of policy or politics. However, if I am chosen in a random sample to be part of a deliberating sample of say 300 and a small group of 15, I have far more reason to become informed. Deliberative Polls consistently ask knowledge questions and show significant gains in knowledge in every project. The resulting considered judgments are both representative and informed (Luskin, Fishkin, and Jowell 2002).

Thirdly, there is skepticism as to whether voters are capable of dealing with complex policy choices. Given that they are usually inattentive and uninformed, there is no surprise that many observers have this impression. However, the question of competence would turn on the tasks voters can perform if effectively motivated. The same dynamics for overcoming rational ignorance may also work for facilitating greater voter competence. People pay attention and become more engaged when they think their voice will matter. There is no question that many of the issues faced in Deliberative Polls have been complex and difficult. But there is no easy metric, at least with our data, for measuring the improvement in citizen competence. The microcosms, as they become more informed, appear to change their views for coherent reasons (Fishkin et al. 2011). Regressions show levers of opinion change that appear plausible and coherently connected to the final considered judgments. Such results reinforce our view that the opinion changes are not arbitrary but are motivated by considerations which have been weighed in a balanced and informative context.

But competent at what? I believe the appropriate questions for public deliberation concern collective political will: which policy proposals about what is to be done would the public support or oppose on balance, after considering competing arguments on the basis of reasonably good information? These questions typically concern values and trade-offs about the valued consequences of one path for policy or another. But the questions do not concern the more technical issues of how best to implement a policy direction. We might ask a deliberating microcosm whether or not they wanted the US to have a manned space flight program, but we would not ask them which rocket was the most effective delivery system. While the distinction may, on occasion, be difficult to draw, the basic idea is that there is a difference between the broad direction of policy and the technical expertise required to implement it. The public seems more than competent to deal with the former, under good conditions for getting it engaged, but it should not be expected to become competent about the latter. Years of technical training might well be required.

A fourth concern is that discussion or deliberation may depend on predictable patterns of small group psychology that lead to conclusions regardless of the substantive merits of the issue. So by the so-called law of group polarization, if a group starts on one side of the midpoint it will move further in that direction because of the imbalance in the argument pool and the social comparison effect as people conform to their views of how others are deciding. Cass R. Sunstein has conducted his own experiments with various collaborators and has documented a large literature supporting this finding (Sunstein 2009, 161–168). But as Sunstein has granted, in all his discussions, the Deliberative Poll is the exception to this law. The reasons deserve more extensive empirical investigation. But we think it is because we have elements that restore balance to the argument pool (balanced briefing materials, moderated discussions where both the pros and cons of a given policy are considered, balanced expert panels, etc.) and that mute the social comparison effect (opinions gathered in confidential questionnaires rather than a shared verdict or decision). Hence the critique of deliberative discussion in general needs to be muted by a realization that the precise institutional design may well effect whether defects such as polarization occur. If there is balance and confidential collection of opinion the small group distortions can be avoided, or at least that is the consistent experience of Deliberative Polls and probably other institutional designs that share the same characteristics.

A fifth concern is that public will-formation may be meaningless because of instability in the technical sense of cycles violating transitivity. So the people cannot deliberate democratically because if majority rule were to be exercised in pair-wise comparisons over more than two choices, there could be a cycle from A to B to C and back to A again. The public will becomes incoherent and also open to manipulation by agenda setters. The result could depend on which pair wise comparisons are put on the agenda and in what order. However, there has long been speculation that deliberation could lead to meta-agreement, or a shared understanding of what is at issue, facilitating single-peakedness or an underlying dimension. In an analysis of Deliberative Polls with ranking data applying to multiple options, we found that deliberation increases single peakedness so as to decrease the possibility of cycles. The vulnerability to cycles comes with universal domain and once deliberation limits the preference structures that actually occur the potential vulnerability to cycles disappears. When people deliberate together democratic decision becomes more meaningful (List, Luskin, Fishkin and Mclean 2013).

Overall, the key infirmities in modern democracy can find a constructive response in modern refinements and improvements in the two essential components of the ancient Athenian solution—random sampling and deliberation. Democratic decisions on the basis of reasons considered by the people themselves are entirely practical. The public is capable when effectively motivated. The results are coherent and knowledge driven, competent and collectively consistent. The key challenge is to find the entry points for this kind of democratic innovation in modern systems that primarily value the contest of competitive democracy without any concern for collective will formation. But as our experience and that of the Citizens Assemblies and some other experiments show, there are entry points where this sort of experimentation can thrive and provide data to support further applications and improvements. All we need is for our institutions to continue to be the result of "reflection and choice" rather than "accident and force" in Alexander Hamilton's words in *Federalist* 1 introducing the dialogue that was to follow.

References

Fishkin, James S., Alice Siu, Robert C. Luskin, Nuri Kim, Andreas Katsanevas, and Yushu Zhou. 2011. *What's Next California*. Report. Stanford University. http://cdd.stanford.edu/polls/california/2011/final/nextca-final-report.pdf.

List, Christian, Robert C. Luskin, James Fishkin, and Ian Mclean. 2013. "Deliberation, Single-Peakedness and the Possibility of Meaningful Democracy: Evidence from Deliberative Polls." *The Journal of Politics* 75 (1): 80–95. http://cdd.stanford.edu/research/papers/2013/list-meaningful-democracy.pdf.

Luskin, Robert C., Ian O'Flynn, James Fishkin, and David Russell. 2012. "Deliberating Across Deep Divides." *Political Studies*, http://cdd.stanford.edu/research/papers/2012/deliberating-across-deep-divides.pdf.

Luskin, Robert C., James Fishkin, and Roger Jowell. 2002. "Considered Opinions: Deliberative Polling in Britain." *British Journal of Political Science* 32 (3): 455–487.

Madison, James. 1987 (1787). "The Federalist Number 10." In *The Federalist Papers*, eds. James Madison, Alexander Hamilton and John Jay. New York: Penguin Books.

Madison, James. 1987 (1787). *Notes of Debates in the Federal Convention of 1787*, an introduction by Adrienne Koch. New York: Norton.

Posner, Richard. 2003. *Law, Pragmatism and Democracy*. Cambridge, Mass: Harvard University Press.

Schumpeter, Joseph A. 1942. *Capitalism, Socialism and Democracy*. New York: Harper and Row.

Sunstein, Cass R. 2003. "The Law of Group Polarization." In *Debating Deliberative Democracy*, eds. James S. Fishkin and Peter Laslett. Oxford: Basil Blackwell.

Sunstein, Cass R. 2009. *Going to Extremes: How Like Minds Unite and Divide*. Oxford: Oxford University Press.

Anna Przybylska & Alice Siu

Chapter Six. Long Lasting Effects of the First Deliberative Poll in Poland

Introduction

The aim of this chapter is to present information on the main premises and impact of Deliberative Polling in the specific social and political context of Poland. We refer to data collected during public consultations with the use of Deliberative Polling in Poznań in November 2009 as well as the results of an evaluation study conducted approximately a year later. We also use results of some research on the quality of consultations carried out around that time to provide the relevant background and points of reference for the discussion[1].

New Approach to Public Consultations with Deliberative Polling

When the political system in Poland was being transformed into a democracy, the new model of democracy was taking shape in Western political culture. Deliberative democracy was proposed by those who diagnosed the deficits of liberal democracy in communication within political institutions and, in particular, in communication between politicians and electorates (Held 2006). The results of studies that referred to standards and measures of democratic well-being confirmed the need for democratic renewal (Stoker 2006; Norris 2011).

In the 1990s Poland was a political laboratory. Those who were involved in the debate regarding institutionalization of democracy attest that even though more participatory and deliberative models had been considered, they did not have

---

1   The collaborative partners for the Deliberative Polling* event in Poznań were: the Projekt Społeczny 2012 (Institute of Sociology, University of Warsaw), the Centre for Deliberative Democracy at Stanford University, the City Hall in Poznań, Pentor Poznań. The evaluation of Deliberative Poll was prepared by Anna Przybylska (Institute of Sociology, University of Warsaw). It was financed by Projekt Społeczny 2012. Pentor Poznań conducted the survey. PhD students: Anna Datko and Jacek Kubera (Adam Mickiewicz University in Poznań) helped to conduct interviews with officials and experts.

any impact on politics at the time[2]. It might have been disappointing to many observers from the outside.

Polish politics has undergone a profound transformation, but even 25 years after the democratic breakthrough, Polish democracy is "in flux". This is confirmed by changes in the law, such as institutionalizing the inclusion of lay citizens in decision making, followed by new practices (Olech 2012; Sobiesiak-Penszko 2012). Attempts to codify good practices of participation and deliberation involve the President's office, ministries, local authorties and think tanks. There is public financial support for NGOs to launch, often in cooperation with local authorities, projects that demonstrate, for example, how to conduct consultations in local communities.

Thus, Poland is still a laboratory for democracy. However, it is to be evaluated whether now we are witnessing a deliberative turn, at least in certain domains and activities of public institutions. This judgment will require the preparation of adequate measures and tools to deal not only with institutions or institutionalized procedures, but also with processes of communication involving authorities and citizens. Some attempts have already been made. Among these, the Centre for Deliberation at the Institute of Sociology, University of Warsaw, in 2011, conducted a study based on questionnaires collected from 270 town halls to assess how they had carried out public consultations regarding the most important local investments in the previous four years.

Officials responsible for public consultations were asked questions that demanded reporting facts rather than presenting opinions. The focus was on activities and choices made by representatives of town halls while preparing, conducting and summarizing the results of consultations. Due to the study it was possible to learn among others that:

o public consultations were conducted regarding 27% of the issues that had a profound impact on local community;
o in 54% of the cases, inhabitants had access to relevant information at least 1 day before consultations; the information package did not necessarily present basic facts, constraints, and proposals of actions addressing the problem;
o the consultation results were published in 60% of the cases, and the information on how the citizens' opinions were included in the decisions appeared in 58% of the cases;

---

2   A transcript from the seminar: "Systemic conditions for deliberation" with the participation of politicians, social activists and researchers, organized by the Centre for Deliberation, Institute of Sociology at the University of Warsaw in June 2011.

o the most commonly used IT tool to collect information from inhabitants (14% of town halls used it) was a several-point poll which usually did not bring much information (Przybylska 2011).

In the above study, the number of consultations conducted was not as important as the quality of the consultation processes. If public consultations are to be reflective and meaningful, it is important to point at the deficiencies in the procedure and practice (Geissel and Newton 2012; Nabatchi et al. 2012). But, even if we may want all municipalities to pursue the deliberative model of consultations, there are no sufficient reasons for being too pessimistic about the reported results either. The study was not historically comparative, and if it had been, we might have observed some positive changes in the practices of town halls. Supposedly, Deliberative Polling in Poznań contributed to them.

There are both disagreements and misunderstandings regarding the model of deliberative democracy and its implementation in Poland that we are able to describe based on the empirical data[3]. We may refer to disagreements whenever there is adequate knowledge about models of democracy, democratic institutions and procedures, but there are different opinions regarding their usefulness in a given timeframe or in general. We would speak of misunderstandings whenever there is a mismatch between models of democracy and certain institutions or procedures. An ongoing discussion regarding the place of public consultations in the decision-making process is not always reasoned. In fact, this is a debate on the choice between a representative and a direct model of democracy, but without clear arguments under what conditions to choose one or the other. The stress put on "who decides" takes away the focus from the quality of the procedure that would otherwise assure careful consideration of the choices at hand.

Moreover, there are ambiguities in the interpretation of the law that have consequences for the procedure, and, in turn, for the results of public consultations. This applies, for example, to the understanding of representation and anonymity. Some city halls show a more social-science-based understanding of the statement that all citizens have the right to participate in consultations. This perception allows the selection of participants of public consultations (whenever justified). In other cities, the political (literal) understanding of the same statement makes it impossible to control representativeness of the sample for the given community due to

---

3 We refer here to the data collected by the CD IS UW from representatives of several local governments in 2013 and 2014. Following this, two workshops were organized to clarify some specific issues relevant to the methodology of public consultations within the project: "In Dialogue" http://wdialogu.uw.edu.pl/en/ in 2014.

imposed self-selection. The same goes for anonymity – it can be understood as in social sciences, which allows the organizers to register participants and control data quality, or its interpretation can be literal. For these reasons, while Deliberative Polling was possible in Poznań, it could be contested in Katowice because of random sampling.

The aim of this chapter does not permit us to deal in detail with the issue of the "procedural grey zone" in public consultations in Poland. We would much rather reflect on the contribution of Deliberative Polling to changes in the practice of public consultations with regard to the opinions of Poznań residents, officials, and experts involved. We would like to emphasize that we do not imply that Deliberative Polling in Poznań was the only important innovation in public consultations, or even the most important one in the past years. Nevertheless it has most definitely contributed to the development of practice.

The implementation of the Deliberative Poll in Poland in 2009 may be viewed as an innovation, because it offered a new approach to public consultations. The following elements were particularly important:

1. Including all interested parties in the process of defining problems and preparing information materials;
2. Careful and collaborative preparation of the information package that contained alternative action proposals with clearly stated their advantages and disadvantages;
3. Random sampling of participants, with efforts made to assure that they represented as closely as possible the community affected by the issue;
4. Predictability of the process to all interested parties;
5. A platform for participants to get better informed (due to the access to briefing materials and experts) and express their opinions in moderated discussions;
6. Reporting of the results soon after the consultations.

These points address the problems diagnosed during the case studies or even mirror the postulates of the participants of the field study conducted in the years preceding the use of Deliberative Polling in Poznań (Przybylska 2010).

Two premises for its application as a model method of public consultation deserve special interest. Firstly, although around 2009 it was already politically hazardous to express doubts about citizens' cognitive abilities to tackle problems of public importance, the argument that they lack adequate knowledge to be involved in decision-making processes was present in discussions (Raciborski 2011). The Deliberative Polling method, which highlights the need to provide citizens with relevant information before consultations, weakened this argument.

Additionally, the exchange of contradictory arguments in the open discussion, at least by some members of local community, may be associated with conflict rather than cooperation (Przybylska 2010). Thus, to avoid the effect of developing an artificial affinity of opinions among the consultations' participants, it may be reasonable to use an anonymous questionnaire to collect information on their preferences (Fishkin 2009).

The Subject that Matters

One of the criticisms concerning public consultations, all of which went beyond the scope of subjects required by the law, is that they often concern issues of minor importance. The first Deliberative Polling in Poland put up on the agenda an issue that, at least from the economic point of view, was important to all inhabitants of Poznań. Its objective was to gather data on city residents' preferences about the management of the stadium in Bułgarska St. following the conclusion of the UEFA EURO 2012 tournament.

Four cities in Poland accommodated football teams and their fans during EURO 2012. The stadium in Poznań was modernized, while those in Gdańsk, Warsaw and Wrocław were built from scratch. Host cities had to consider what would happen to the stadiums once the EURO 2012 tournament was over and how to finance these sports facilities.

Apart from the National Stadium, outlays on the construction and maintenance of stadium infrastructure were covered by city budgets. At the stage when politicians had already decided on behalf of residents that the given investment in the stadium would be made, the question concerned benefits for taxpayers. It seemed essential that residents had the opportunity to share their own views on the targeted issue, which was made possible thanks to social consultations.

Until EURO 2012, the stadium in Bulgarska St. belonged to the city and was managed by the Poznań Center for Sports and Recreation (POSiR). The maintenance cost of the stadium was mainly covered by public funds. The principal user of the sports facilities and infrastructure was a private football team named Lech. Maintenance expenditures of the new stadium were to increase roughly fourfold. Without a substantial contribution from the users, it would be a burden on the city budget.

Four scenarios for the future of the stadium in Bułgarska St. were developed for the Deliberative Polling discussion. They differed as to the choice of the operator and management strategy, extent of commercialization of the stadium, and accessibility of its infrastructure for residents' recreational purposes. Each was connected with strengths and weaknesses that were taken into consideration.

It took six months to prepare a set of basic facts and scenarios for discussions that were to be used in the public consultations. The preparatory process included meetings with the representatives of authorities responsible for public communication and sport infrastructure as well as the representatives of football clubs and a regional football association. In addition, workshops were held with the representatives of NGOs and the stadium's architect, while the interviews were conducted with managers of sport arenas in Europe. A preliminary analysis of these workshops, interviews, documents and statistics was provided as well.

The first scenario assumed that the management of the stadium would be entrusted to the Lech football team. The city would continue to support the maintenance of the facility financially. Proponents of this choice stressed the fact that a world-class stadium should have a football club of substantial status as its host to add to its prestige. Without doubt the Lech club is also an element of the promotion strategy of Poznań. This scenario envisaged the location of four training fields in the vicinity of the stadium. The remaining area around the stadium would be used in line with the arrangements between the club and the city. Support for this scenario would trigger substantial outlays from the city coffers.

The second scenario stipulated that the stadium would be managed by the Poznań Center for Sports and Recreation. Under this scenario, apart from the construction and maintenance costs of the stadium, the city would partly cover the expenditure of using sports and recreational infrastructure. City support would ensure participation of residents of different economic status in sports events held in the stadium and in its vicinity. The cost of implementing this scenario would be very high for the city.

The third scenario would have the stadium run by a private enterprise or a public-private consortium. While the use of the stadium would be subject to commercial principles, its vicinity would be an open space for non-commercial sports and recreational purposes. The surface of the stadium building would be leased to the tertiary sector at market prices. This would likewise apply to sports clubs. Lech and other football clubs would not receive financial resources from public funds. This scenario would most likely ensure revenues to cover the maintenance cost of the stadium, but it would not bring a profit.

The implementation of the fourth scenario would offer an opportunity for a commercial use of both the building and the vicinity of the stadium. Shopping and service establishments would be located in the immediate surroundings of the stadium. Space within the entire stadium complex would be leased on market principles. The entire management would be entrusted to a private commercial investor, who would finance the construction of new facilities. This scenario was the most commercial out of the four. It limited access to people of an inadequate income level to the sports and recreational complex. However, the project offered the city a hope for higher revenues and possibly a financial profit.

Procedure and Opinion Formation

Deliberative Polling is a method of public consultations that consists of polls based on random sampling, moderated group discussions and plenary question and answer panel sessions with experts. The participants of the poll in Poznań filled out a questionnaire three times: first during a telephone interview (T1), second upon arriving at the place of the deliberations (T2) and third upon the conclusion of group discussions (T3). The entire event took almost ten hours during one day and included three group discussions and two plenary sessions with city officials and experts. The experts included an architect of the stadium, representatives of two football clubs in Poznań as well as a head of the regional football association and a researcher from the University of Physical Education in Warsaw.

As many as 880 people took part in the first poll (T1) and 148 people participated in the moderated discussions and completed the pre- and post-deliberation questionnaires (T2, T3). In the description of the results that will follow, the term "before deliberation" may refer to measurement T1 or T2.

It is important in Deliberative Polling that participants in deliberations have characteristics that correspond to the characteristics of a population sample. In Poznań, the group of deliberative participants and the group of non-deliberative participants did not significantly differ in their social demographic variables, including sex, educational background and financial status. However, on average, the deliberative participants were slightly younger. In both groups, the vast majority admitted to engaging in some form of physical exercise. Residents of Poznań involved in the deliberations were slightly more active in this respect.

One of the success conditions for deliberations is that its participants be well informed about the issues. There are different sources and categories of knowledge. Before arriving at the venue where discussions took place, the participants had received briefing materials that contained information on the accessibility of sport infrastructure in Poznań, the scale and scope of sport activities of residents, the use and management of some stadiums in Europe, the use of the stadium in Bułgarska St., as well as the alternative scenarios for its future after UEFA EURO 2012. According to our research results, only half of the participants had read the information materials. However, during the group discussions, there was clearly exchange of knowledge derived from the document among them, as evident in the following example: "For me, as a layman, it is surprising that the grass [in the main football pitch] can only be used those few hours a week. But you can cover it. There are modern methods of covering it up, just as it was described in these materials; and, in my opinion, it is very important to protect it" [group 1].

The results of the poll indicated that most of the respondents had been to the stadium at least once, and many visit it regularly. This gave them the advantage of having experiential knowledge. During the deliberations, they would exchange first-hand information on various aspects of the stadium's functions and management: "To be honest with you, the rent that Lech pays per month is very little compared with what Olimpia pays to the Ministry of the Interior. In reality, we pay PLN 150 000 a year for the facility whereas, to the best of my knowledge, Lech pays a rent of PLN 1 500 per month. I would like to find a flat for PLN 1 500 a month as big as the stadium. People pay PLN 1 500 for two rooms" [group 6].

During sessions with experts, the participants could ask questions clarifying some information, like the one above, or filling in some knowledge gaps found during group discussions. The answers were considered and commented on during the meetings that followed, as in this example: "One issue made me think: the president of the Lech club said that he saw no problem in the team financing itself as regards the maintenance of the stadium and all the rest. Thus, a questions arises: why did no one agree to it sooner? Why did they not set up companies which could cooperate with Lech in order to finance the stadium?" [group 2].

In Deliberative Polling the level of knowledge is monitored. The questionnaires that the participants filled in three times included seven questions regarding the stadium, the city and the preparations to UEFA EURO 2012. On average, after the deliberations, the participants' knowledge rose from 68% to 75%. The biggest increase of 14% was observed with respect to the question about the owner of the stadium. It was at the high level of 83% already before deliberations and after them it reached 97%. In general, participants were very well informed about the facilities provided for the European Football Championship 2012, the main uses and users of the stadium in Bułgarska St. and those financially responsible. Quite strikingly, around twice as many people were able to answer any question regarding the stadium correctly, compared with the question on the population of Poznań.

As the deliberations were dedicated to the use of the city stadium and its immediate surroundings, it was necessary to define the area under consideration and the roles that the stadium building and the adjacent area can play. The participants were asked to consider the question of stadium management and sources of its financing. An evaluation of outlays connected with the construction and use of the stadium in the context of the city budget and other public expenses proved a challenge during the debate. It was also difficult to understand whether and when the commercial use of a sports facility is tied with a greater or smaller cost for a single resident.

Nevertheless, the debate made the participants more aware of the question of costs of stadium use. Interestingly, when they came to understand the level of maintenance costs of the stadium, they grew more willing to pay for using its facilities. They indicated that, if the facilities were free of charge, people would not take care of the sports infrastructure, and it would start to fall into disrepair. Rationalizing the use of the entire stadium, deliberations were not limited to football. Participants held lively discussions on the development of other sports and non-sports activities, providing examples from stadiums in other countries. It was also suggested that the city might invest the money raised from payments for the stadium infrastructure in small sports facilities located in various places throughout the city.

The participants had to choose between the option of a wide access to the facilities supported from public funds and a self-financing investment as a commercial enterprise. The responses given between the first and the final poll measurement showed an increase in the support of seeking funds outside the city budget. The percentage of proponents of maintaining the stadium exclusively from city funds dropped from 26% to 7%. The dominant view was that the stadium should be financed by the users, with some support from public funds. Prior to the deliberations, this opinion was shared by 47% respondents, after it by 57%. As a result of the deliberations, the percentage of people believing that the city should not contribute to the financing of the stadium, and on the contrary, it should make money on the lease of commercial space, increased from 19% to 29%. Moreover, responses to other questions showed a greater degree of approval for commercial solutions. The results suggest that after the deliberations the residents understood the possibility or even necessity of commercial uses of the stadium, which would guarantee covering its maintenance costs.

Graph 1: Stadium Financing Options

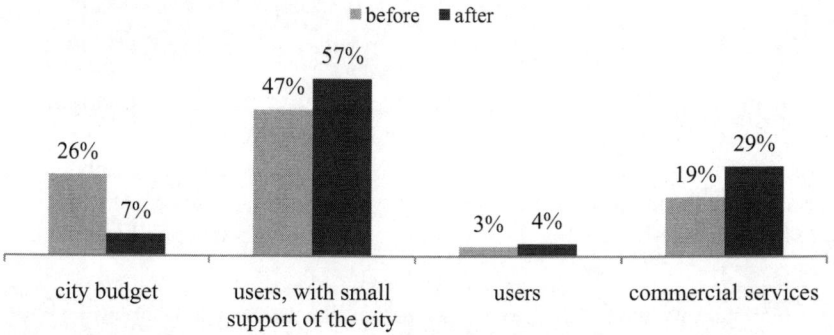

Residents of Poznań tried to strike a balance between the profit-making function of the stadium and its use for open-access recreation. During the deliberations, special emphasis was placed on the fact that the stadium is the property of the city and as such should be accessible to all, irrespective of divisions arising from socio-economic factors. Thus, residents of Poznań did not focus solely on financial criteria. Proposals that aimed at a substantial restriction of access to the sports and recreational facilities for most residents were rejected. Intermediary solutions that reconcile financial profitability with social needs prevailed.

The participants were also presented with four scenarios defining different ideas for the management of the stadium and the surrounding area. Prior to the deliberations, residents favored most the proposal entrusting stadium management to the POSiR. After deliberation, the participants preferred the scenario that opted for a private investor or a public-private partnership that would take commercial action in the stadium, using its vicinity for recreational purposes. Support for it rose from 27% to 49%.

Graph 2: Scenarios of Stadium Management

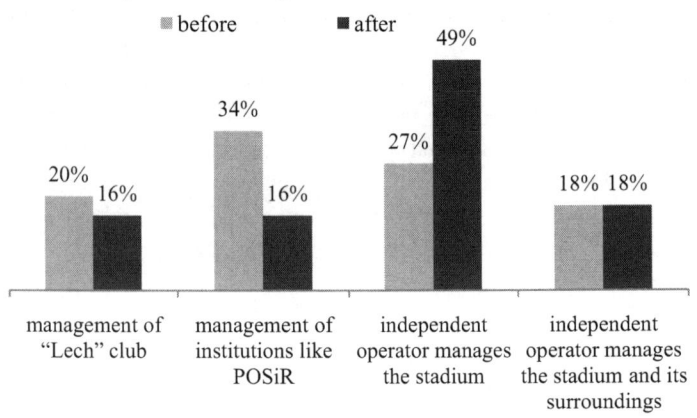

For many, including the representatives of the officials, the weak support for the scenario in which Lech played a role of the stadium's manager was surprising. The poll revealed the false knowledge about the public preferences. Although the Lech football team may have a large group of supporters, the residents of Poznań are not in favor of financing the use of its sports facilities with public money[4].

---

4   More information on the results of Deliberative Poll in Poznań is available in the report: http://cdd.stanford.edu/polls/poland/2010/poznan_EN.pdf.

What We Have Learned from the First Deliberative Polling in Poland?

The quality of public consultations relies on the impartial and reflective process of discussions in groups of people who are representative of the population that is affected by the problem under consideration. In our evaluation, we were particularly sensitive to the opinions of participants of Deliberative Polling: citizens as well as representatives of institutions and organizations. We wanted to know how they perceived the process of public consultations, what were the strengths and weaknesses of the method's application in Poznań, and what was its impact.

The first evaluation was conventionally a part of Deliberative Polling and was based on several questions that were added to the final questionnaire. In January 2011, the participants of Deliberative Polling in Poznań were contacted again and were asked seven questions, including three open-ended questions. Answers were obtained for 96 out of 148 participants. We also conducted eight in-depth interviews with persons representing Deliberative Polling's co-organizers (city hall), experts present during the plenary sessions and observers from social organizations. Additionally, there were four in-depth interviews with the moderators of group discussions. Finally, we posed some questions to journalists representing the local and regional media and analyzed press accounts of public consultations on the use and financing of the stadium in Poznań as compared to news on other public consultations in 2009. The scale of the research was extensive, as we attempted to include many perspectives on Deliberative Polling in Poznań. For the reason of the scarcity of space within the chapter, we will refer to the most important results of this evaluation study.

The answers to questions that participants were asked during Deliberative Polling, as well as one year after it, seemed to suggest the participants' overall positive attitude towards public consultations that concerned the future of the stadium in Poznań. The first indicator may be the mean of 7.2 points, on a 10-point scale, with which the participants evaluated the role of Deliberative Polling in the clarification of their opinions. We may treat the answers to the question regarding the involvement in the potential next Deliberative Polling as another indicator. 58% of the respondents were very positive and further 37% were positive about such a prospect. Only 3% of the respondents would choose not to participate in the consultations. Among the reasons for accepting the would-be invitation were, in the order of importance: overall positive previous experience and, more specifically, orderly discussions and the resulting good ambiance (37%), an opportunity to gain information (25%), the interest in public affairs and impact on public decisions concerning "our" city (17%), a chance to become familiar with the opinions of fellow citizens (15%). For 12% of respondents the participation in Deliberative Polling would rely on the topic. The 3% of the participants, who would reject the invitation, explained their decision by lack of time or by no need to repeat the same, supposedly insufficiently rewarding experience.

It is apparent that the participants enjoyed the small group discussions the most. This is confirmed by answers given in the final questionnaire during Deliberative Polling and questions posed a year after. The mean of 8.4 points on a 10-point scale was the result of the evaluation of the role of group discussions in clarifying the participants' opinions on the future of the stadium in Bułgarska St. The acquisition of knowledge about diverse opinions seems an especially positive aspect of the group deliberations. They took place among people of different ages, educational backgrounds, socio-economic statuses and political views. Conversations within such a diversified group are not frequent. Deliberative Polling gave participants an opportunity to become familiar with arguments that they would not hear under other circumstances.

The respondents seemed certain that during the group discussions they had had free access to adequate and comprehensive information (around 86%). Information included in the briefing materials was generally considered unbiased by three-fourths of the consultations participants. One-fourth said that they failed to support the various scenarios of actions to the same degree. The conviction about the unbiased nature of the information provided was stronger among people who had read all of the briefing materials (around 80%) than in those who had only read some of them (around 67%).

The role of a moderator is the key to a smooth course of the deliberations. Group discussions during Deliberative Polling were a new experience to moderators when compared with focus groups. Moderators were supposed to be transparent as much as possible and, at the same time, to assist participants in the learning process that had two elements: briefing materials and inclusive exchange of information in groups. There were no serious disorders that would put the civility of the discussions at risk. The participants played a role of "ideal citizens" as reported by moderators and as evident from the transcripts. There was just one disruption that was caused by a representative of an NGO who instead of being a neutral observer, tried to pretend to be a tribune of the local community. Undoubtedly, the fact that the debates were anchored in briefing materials presenting basic facts and scenarios of action, which had been read by only a half of the participants, was a challenge. At the same time, it came as a surprise that some participants were able to consider in detail the pros and cons of even minor elements included in the document that they were offered.

The participants were of the opinion that the moderators did not try to influence their views (around 85%) and that they made an effort so that opposing views might be presented (70%). The vast majority of the participants observed that the manner of the discussions allowed each person to voice their own opinions (around 87%). Less conviction was expressed regarding equal contribution of all participants to the debate. One-fourth of the respondents noted the dominant role of some of the group members. Nevertheless, 52% retained their favorable opinion about a balanced participation of all the interested parties. Most participants (around 76%) appreciated the respect shown by the group members to one another. Results of the evaluation of group debates (2009) are presented in the following graph:

Graph 3: Evaluation of Group Debates (2009)

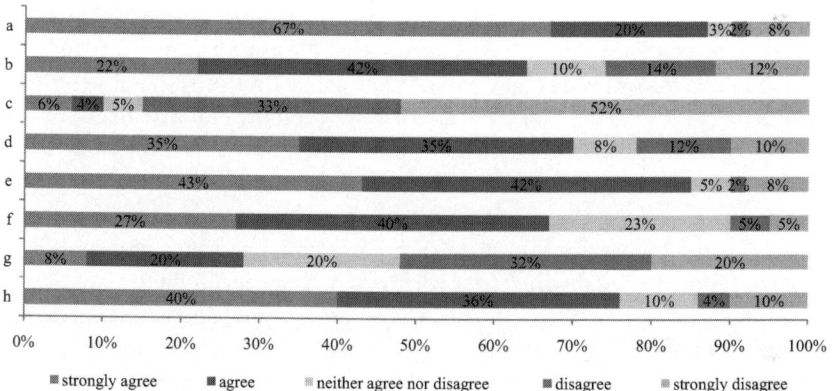

a. the group moderator ensured everyone's participation in the debate
b. members of my group took part in the debate to a relatively equal extent
c. the moderator sometimes tried to win the group to his/her own views
d. the moderator made an effort so that opposing views might be presented during the debate
e. significant aspects of the targeted issue were discussed during the group debates
f. I learned a lot about people who are very different from myself
g. the debate was dominated by several people
h. members of my group respected the views of others

When asked a year after the deliberations about their most vivid memories from group discussions, most of the respondents referred to the subject of discussions: half of them to the management of the stadium and one third to its architectural and/or functional changes. But, interestingly, for 16% of the participants the most vivid memory would be connected with the atmosphere of the meetings or the method of work or the differences in opinions and their change. Only two persons were unable or unwilling to reflect on what happened during the event.

The two plenary sessions that took place between group discussions were slightly less positively assessed by respondents, who gave them 7.2 points on a 10-point scale. A year after the deliberations, 35% of the participants recalled the expert panels through association with different elements of organization, such as who was in the venue, how the experts were prepared, how the questions and answered proceeded. The subjects of discussion that the participants remembered were varied, which could be explained by the fact that each group prepared its specific questions to experts and it tended to focus its attention on them.

The participants of Deliberative Polling also expressed some critical comments regarding the input from experts. These opinions were already present during group sessions and were repeated during the evaluation a year later. The critical opinions did not dominate, but it is worth mentioning them briefly to find their main arguments. The principal criticism was that the information provided by at least some experts was not exhaustive and not sufficiently precise. It was described as "evasive" or "diplomatic", and not a satisfactory resource for a deliberation. In the words of one participant: "We have got more out of what is happening here, in this room [of group debates], than from what happened in the plenary session" [group 2].

There were four to five experts in each panel and ten groups prepared their questions. We adopted the rule that each group had an equal right to ask its questions, unless they evidently overlapped with another's group inquiry. It shortened the time for the experts' answers. But, it is remarkable that there was more criticism, contradictory to the previous one in some of its consequences, saying that the organizers had not allowed representatives of the groups to comment on the experts' answers. Exceptions were made when the group was not satisfied with the answer; nevertheless, if we had allowed for more comments, not all questions could have been asked. Taking into account the time-related constraints of such meetings, there will always be a trade-off between the number of questions and the amount of time for answering them. In the future, we may follow a procedure of a collective decision, taken between groups, on how many questions to ask and which ones specifically. The results of such an experiment may be interesting, as the responsibility for the consequences will be shared with participants to a larger degree.

The city hall's representatives and experts did not have access to the group discussions, but provided us with information on their experience drawn from the plenary sessions. With one exception of a leader of a regional football organization, and previously a politician, all remembered the aim and the content of meetings with residents of Poznań. Although they differed in their anticipations of what such encounter may look like, after Deliberative Polling they all were positive about the event and its results. It is not surprising that each of them approached the issue from the perspective of his specific role, but there were some points in common. Their remarks particularly referred to the rational approach of citizens to the subject, meaningful questions and well thought-out proposals. A person from the city hall team responsible for the stadium's preparation to the EURO UEFA 2012 said: "I was surprised by the rationality of expressed opinions. We were worried, at least I was worried, at the time when scenarios were worked on, that the so called 'social scenario' would win, that there would be a widespread expectation to build the land of happiness where everyone, regardless the costs, would be able to use the stadium". The observation of the stadium's architect was similar: "People were responsible and, actually, there were no such demands, in contrast to what often happens in Poland. Poles like to make demands, whereas these were not made there. There were some very sensible analyses, very specific. I was very surprised by the high level of consciousness of the people at that very moment. Perhaps then after they went on to say something else; but at that time the topic was treated very seriously".

Among the persons interviewed, one representative of NGOs questioned the procedure of public consultations in its aspect of selecting the participants by means of drawing lots. He was of the opinion that citizens selected by a random sample cannot have the sufficient knowledge required for a meaningful discussion. Thus, being an observer of deliberations, he did not obey the role, and tried to convince participants to his point of view. In the interview he denied that there were any information materials that the participants had received, which demonstrated that this element of public consultations was not important to him. Moreover, in the mass media he misinformed the public opinion about the procedure. It could be treated as an element of "politics as usual" where there are many different players with various goals that they attempt to achieve. However, it is worrisome that some NGOs put their opinions over the voice of the citizens and spread information that they did not verify, especially because we are trying to build social trust in democratic procedures. It was also surprising that there was no real watchdog process after Deliberative Polling. Neither from the side of NGOs nor form the side of media. This important issue requires a separate analysis.

In fact, although Deliberative Polling was successful when judged from the point of view of the quality of the process and educational effects, the impact of it on real decisions was mediated by some external factors. The most important factor was the lack of competition among potential investors for a position of the stadium's manager. Thus, the stadium is now managed by the consortium of the football club Lech and a private retail company set up in 2008. The activities of this consortium are supposed to be commercial, so that the city does not have to co-sponsor the stadium. Along with the scenario chosen by the participants, two main football clubs in Poznań use the stadium, not only Lech. There are some elements of social use of the surrounding area, but – as the stadium's architect confirmed – not as many as there could be, taking into consideration the good ideas generated during the deliberations. However, in 2012 there were new consultations on the use of the area adjacent to the stadium, carried out after our interviews and the UEFA EURO 2012, which require a separate study.

Conclusion

Deliberative Polling in Poznań concerned the future of the stadium in Bułgarska St., a major investment connected with the city's preparation to the EURO 2012 European Football Championship. While the city's participation in an international sports event adds to its prestige, the extension of the stadium and its upkeep in the future is cost-intensive. Therefore, a decision was made to subject the long-term strategy of managing and financing the facility to social consultations.

A representative group of city residents took part in Deliberative Polling. After becoming acquainted with the briefing materials, having exchanged considered arguments within groups and after engaging in question-and-answer sessions with representatives of the authorities and experts, they aired their final preferences. With respect to some of the questions, the participants changed their mind during the deliberation and with regard to others, their opinions remained unchanged. Most importantly, in each case the opinions resulted from the deliberation and consideration of the downsides and upsides of different options.

Equipped with the knowledge of the facts and opinions other than their own, residents saw the future of the stadium in a broader perspective. The participants demonstrated that they think about the stadium in the context of the city and the local community. The targeted issue was scrutinized from the point of view of various needs, alternative actions, their advantages and disadvantages. A consultation process built respect for opposing views. The analysis of empirical material collected during and after Deliberative Polling confirms that the effort put into the careful preparation of consultations has consequences for the quality of deliberations, respect among participants as well as between participants and organizers. It brings about satisfaction from being a part of a task team.

The Deliberative Polling event had an important input into developing the know-how of public consultations in Poznań, and possibly, also in Poland, taking into account the feedback from scholars and practitioners. The awareness of some important elements of the consultations procedure is higher, e.g. regarding the form and a role of information materials that participants receive before discussions. The declaration of the officials that the practice follows the guidelines has been archived in the empirical material. More evidence from further research is needed to learn of the performance characteristics.

In the future, to strengthen social legitimacy of the process itself, it is worth putting more stress and effort into building a communication strategy together with different social partners and the media. There should be publicly accessible information on what is being done at each stage of a long preparatory process. It could take a form of a blog in which there are notes on who is invited to participate, who does what, and with what effects. It would also be important to propose a letter of intent signed by officials in which they state how they are going to treat the outcomes of public consultations and what the deadlines for publishing the information about the opinions collected from residents and decisions made in reference to them will be. It is a mistake to assume that there will always be responsible social watchdogs. Considering the procedure, it would be interesting and important to involve participants in decisions on scenarios to be discussed as well as time distribution during the expert panel. The ICT can make it work well from the technocratic point of view.

Since our study was an applied one, its conclusions are oriented toward practice. But, it would be useful and reasonable to complement it with an even more systematic analysis of the content of deliberations based on the transcripts that we have. It will require operationalization of relevant values of openness, mutuality, reflectiveness and rationality beyond what we have done so far. For this task, the texts of our colleagues who publish in this volume will be valuable.

References

Fishkin, James. 2009. *When the People Speak. Deliberative Democracy and Public Consultation.* Oxford: Oxford University Press.

Geissel, Brigitte, and Kenneth Newton (eds.). 2012. *Evaluating Democratic Innovations. Curing the Democratic Malaise?* London: Routledge.

Goodin, Robert, and John S. Dryzek. 2006. Deliberative Impacts: The Macro-Political Uptake of Mini-Publics. *Politics and Society* 34: 219–244.

Held, David. 2006. *Models of Democracy.* Cambridge: Polity.

Marody, Mirosława, Anna Giza-Poleszczuk. 2004. *Przemiany więzi społecznych: zarys teorii zmiany społecznej.* Warszawa: Scholar.

Nabatchi, Tina, John Gastil, G. Michael Weiksner, Matt Leighninger (eds.). 2012. *Democracy in Motion. Evaluating the Practice and Impact of Deliberative Civic Engagement.* Oxford: Oxford University Press.

Norris, Pippa. 2011. *Democratic Deficit: Critical Citizens Revisited.* Cambridge: Cambridge University Press.

Olech, Anna. 2012. *Dyktat czy uczestnictwo? Diagnoza partycypacji publicznej w Polsce.* Warszawa: Instytut Spraw Publicznych.

Przybylska, Anna. 2010. *Internet i komunikowanie we wspólnocie lokalnej.* Warszawa: WUW.

Przybylska, Anna. 2011. *Konsultacje w naszym mieście.* Research report. Warszawa: UW.

Raciborski, Jacek. 2011. *Obywatelstwo w perspektywie socjologicznej.* Warszawa: PWN.

Sobiesiak-Penszko, Paulina. 2012. Prawo a partycypacja publiczna. Warszawa: Instytut Spraw Publicznych.

Stoker, Gerry. 2006. "Explaining Political Disenchantment: Finding Pathways to Democratic Renewal." *The Political Quarterly* 77: 184–194.

György Lengyel, Borbála Göncz & Éva Vépy-Schlemmer

Chapter Seven. Temporary and Lasting Effects of a Deliberative Event: the Kaposvár Experience

Introduction

In June 2008 a deliberative study was organized in the South-West Hungarian Kaposvár district. The participants were residents of Kaposvár and the surrounding 53 villages[1]. The study was conducted by the Institute of Sociology and Social Policy of Corvinus University of Budapest. It was part of a broader comparative project which dealt with different aspects of European integration. One of its objectives was increasing citizen participation and mobilizing the public opinion[2]. Previous field studies had revealed that the greatest immediate problems for the local society in Kaposvár were unemployment and related issues of the local economy. In this way then, two topics were addressed in the study: questions of economy and employment on the one hand, and European integration on the other. This reflects on the European character of the broader subject of the study.

Deliberative Polling (DP) is a technique which combines traditional random-sampling public opinion polls with deliberation in group discussions. This research method had been applied in Hungary only once before this study, but having been conceived in 1988, the method may be considered new also at the international level. In this way, the main objective of the study was experimental. Beside the general objectives of such a study, i.e. assessment of changes in people's of knowledge and opinions upon deliberation, an important objective was to

---

1 Previous versions of the paper have been presented at the Workshop on "Frontiers of Deliberation", ECPR Joint Sessions, University of St. Gallen (April 13–16, 2011), at the Workshop on "Social Resources of Local Development", Corvinus University of Budapest (June 10–11, 2011) and at the Workshop on "Deliberation: Values, Processes, Institutions", University of Warsaw (June 4–5, 2012). The research was supported by the IntUne FP6 project and by TÁMOP-4.2.1/B-09/1/KMR-2010-0005.
2 The IntUne (Integrated and United? A Quest for Citizenship in an Ever Closer Europe) project was an FP6 research project financed by the European Union. The core issues of the research were different aspects of the perception of the European integration: identity formation, scope of governance and representation, It was based on elite and public opinion surveys, interviews and media analysis.

see how this research method can be applied in Hungary. It turned out that the participants changed their mind significantly on several questions. They proved to be better informed on average after the event and their opinions became more balanced in the evaluation of unemployment. Attitudes concerning economic competitiveness became more open, while solidarity and tolerance towards the unemployed also increased. We detected some paradoxical effects as well: support for the EU increased after the event despite the fact that a decreasing proportion of participants felt that EU integration had had an impact on their life. As for the evaluation, the majority of participants were enthusiastic after the event and declared future interest in the topics covered and in participation in public debates (Lengyel 2009).

One year later, as part of a follow-up survey we once again visited the participants and a control sample of non-participants. We measured the stability and change of their knowledge, and their opinions and evaluation of the event. If deliberation is able to enhance knowledge in the long run, it could be an especially useful instrument of collective decision making. If it makes people more circumspect in their opinions, taking into account the positions of others, it may help to decrease social tensions. To see how lasting the effect of deliberation is on knowledge and opinion change, it is useful to measure the effect of a Deliberative Poll, not only immediately after the event. Nevertheless, such follow-up surveys are conducted relatively rarely. This paper summarizes some results of the follow-up survey. We argue that on the majority of the issues addressed, the opinion changes proved to be temporary after the event, and only some of the changes proved to be lasting ones. The paper also investigates the social characteristics of those who changed their mind temporarily and the ones who did so more permanently.

The subsequent sections of this paper are organized as follows: first we provide an overview of the theoretical issues deliberative models and methods address. Then we proceed to discuss some problematic areas within the subject. This is followed by a presentation of the methodology and design of our project. Then we show a summary of the changes in opinions, attitudes, and knowledge that occurred after the deliberation, and whether the changes persisted for one year. Finally, we will try to describe the socio-demographic characteristics of the short- and long-term changes using regression models.

Models and Methods of Deliberation

Deliberation is discussed in two ways in the literature: as a *social model* of collective decision-making, and as a *method* based on organized discussions of smaller or larger groups. While there is a common core of them – discussion of relevant public issues in order to reach the ideal type of properly informed and involved citizens – it seems reasonable to distinguish between models and methods.

Models of Deliberation

The deliberative *social model* belongs to the family of normative thinking that conceives participative forms of collective decision making as being able to substitute for (or correct) the model of representative democracy. While representative democracy refers to a form of government in which citizens vote to elect the leaders, in participative models citizens have an active role in governance. Even so, the border between the two types is somewhat vague: deliberation as a method of communication is present in both forms. The difference lies in the fact that in the representative form, deliberation is mostly a privilege of the selected elites, while in the participative model in principle it directly reaches all participating citizens.

Cohen and Sabel (1997) suggest that the model of directly-deliberative polyarchy is "an attractive kind of radical, participatory democracy with problem-solving capacities useful under current conditions and unavailable to representative systems. In directly-deliberative polyarchy, collective decisions are made through public deliberation in arenas open to citizens who use public services, or who are otherwise regulated by public decisions." In addition, ideally "directly-deliberative polyarchy combines the advantages of local learning and self-government with the advantages (and discipline) of wider social learning and heightened political accountability". They argue that the above aspects of polyarchy strengthen participatory forms and explain the advantages of directly-deliberative decision making as against representative-aggregative one (Cohen and Sabel 1997, 313–317).

Forms of participative democracy – such as deliberative or associative – overlap in many respects. Associative democracy, emphasizing the values of voluntarism, self-government and cooperation, as Piotr Perczynski put it, "could provide concrete arenas of deliberation, and, in fact, the overall associative system could also be seen as an arena of negotiating, competing and cooperating associations" (Perczynski 1999, 13).

The common characteristics of deliberative and associative models are that they put emphasis on direct deliberation among citizens in collective decision making. In the representative model of democracy the emphasis is on the sequence of selection, deliberation among the selected few and voting. It is normally accompanied by asymmetric communication within the media and ex post deliberation among the cognitively mobilized groups of the society. This model is criticized mostly on the ground of failures of the sequence's steps. That leads to a situation in which people are under-informed about and not interested in public affairs. They become alienated from the selected elites, care less about the public good and the very selection may lead to suboptimal results. Selection of representative elites happens in circumstances where people know little about the program of the selected and about the major social problems these programs are supposed to deal with. Public opinion formation relies upon similar conditions.

Deliberative Methods

Deliberative *methods* on the other hand are not normative social models, but refer to *different* forms of civic discussions aiming at involving citizens in public discourse. There are different types within the family of discursive methods. While the aim of the Deliberative Poll is deliberation itself (that is, information for and involvement of stakeholders), other methods emphasize consent-seeking and forming suggestions. Another important distinction within deliberative methods concerns the very aim of the action: at one end of the scale the aim is pure research, on the other the aim is triggering social action. Most frequently the Deliberative Poll lies between the two: research which combines the aims of triggering and studying social action. The participants of deliberative events, in a quest for the public good, argue and debate freely. The arguments may change individual preferences, and raise the level of knowledge of the participants. Deliberation is a learning process, during which citizens gather relevant information, reflect on arguments, and exchange opinions with mutual respect of each other (Fishkin and Farrar 2005). The participants take into consideration balanced and adequate information, and articulate and weigh arguments pro and contra. The very essence of deliberation is consideration of and competition between arguments. The Deliberative Poll as Fishkin put it "attempts to model what the public would think, had it a better opportunity to consider the questions at issue" (1997, 162). It seeks to promote awareness, reflection and responsibility, to build *better citizens*, to increase the decision making competence of citizens, to create a more transparent public life, to increase the participation of the people in public matters, and to support well-grounded public opinion forming through information and discourse (Luskin and Fishkin 2002).

The method of Deliberative Polls tries to provide answers to problems related to public opinion and its measurement (Ackerman and Fishkin 2003). The main question addressed by Deliberative Polling relates to the problem of rational ignorance (Downs 1956) which applies to the social phenomenon when it is not felt to be worthwhile or of importance for people to devote time and effort to gather the necessary information in order to elaborate a well-grounded opinion. However, the lack of information or elaborated opinion does not prevent the interviewee to formulate an opinion when asked, during a public opinion research. One may argue that citizens are rarely well-informed enough on public issues; therefore, public opinion polls represent a superficial reality. Another problem of public opinion is that as information and cognitive skills are not equally distributed, not everyone has an elaborate opinion on every public issue (Zaller 1993) and this problem raises the question of the equivalency of opinions (Bourdieu 1997). Less elaborate opinions or attitudes may also be less stable over time, more prone to change, furthermore, less consistent – even contradictory opinions can coexist in one person's mind (Zaller-Feldman 1992).

Beside the problem with public opinion itself, there are several other technical issues related to its measurement. Some have criticised not only attempts at measuring public opinion, but even generating it by means of presenting issues, formulating and phrasing the relevant questions, and arranging them in a specific order (Zaller-Feldman, 1992). Beside the inconsistency of opinions at the individual level, another problem of public opinion polls is whether a collective decision can be reached by a simple aggregation of individual opinions (Hardin 2003). Opinions that are still consistent at the individual level do not necessarily lead to a consistent opinion at the collective level (Pettit 2003). Those who deal with collective rationality argue that deliberation may help to rationalize collective decisions. If deliberation precedes collective decisions it may help realize the collective good and may help to find a trade-off between the different particular interests. This is why they are often more rational from the perspective of the common good than those decisions which are obtained by simple aggregation of individual opinions.

As the main aim of the Deliberative Poll is to produce an informed public opinion, it is interesting to analyze the changes that occur in the level of knowledge and in the attitudes of the participants of the deliberative event. In order to achieve this, survey data before and after deliberation is to be analyzed. To see whether these changes are a product of a cognitive process of elaboration of opinions it is very useful to measure the long-term effect of Deliberative Poll, however this kind of follow-up research is conducted in relatively few cases (Luskin-Fishkin 1998, Attitudes to Crime 2002; Hansen-Andersen 2004). Furthermore, opinions and attitudes can change due to impacts other than the deliberative event itself – in order to control for the effect of other factors with simultaneous influence the use of control groups is needed.

Research Design and Samples

As mentioned above, in May 2008 a representative sample of the inhabitants of the Kaposvár Small Area was polled (n=1514) on the themes of unemployment, economy and the European Union (T1). The respondents of the survey were invited to participate in the deliberative weekend. A briefing booklet containing information about employment, economy and the EU, pros and cons about the possible measures and policies that could facilitate the discussion, was sent out for all of the 435 persons who declared their readiness to attend. In the end, 108 persons participated in the event held at Kaposvár University on the 21–22 of June 2008. During this weekend the participants discussed the themes with each other in small groups of 5–10 and with invited experts during plenary sessions. They were asked to complete a questionnaire, similar to the first one immediately before (T2) and after the event (T3). A year later, in August 2009 we went back into the field (T4)[3] and interviewed both the participants and a control group. This way we ended up with a sample of 90 persons who have participated in the deliberative event and had taken part in all surveys measuring both short and long term effects of the deliberation, and a control group of 96 persons. People in the control group were selected from those participants of the initial representative survey (T1) who were interested in the event, but did not show up for one reason or another. Everyone involved had completed the initial survey (T1) and the one conducted a year later (T4). This chapter deals with these two groups (see Table 1). One has to keep in mind that village-dwellers and younger people were slightly underrepresented among the participants of the deliberative event.

---

3   In the following tables and graphs T1 will refer to the original representative survey, T3 to the survey after the deliberative event done with its participants and T4 to the survey done a year later among participants and the control group (T2 refers to the survey done at the very beginning of the deliberative event, but this won't be addressed in the current paper.)

Table 1: Socio-demographic Characteristics of the Sample (%)

		Representative sample	Participants	Control group
N		1514	90	96
		100.0	100.0	100.0
Gender	Male	43.2	46.7	43.8
	Female	56.8	53.3	56.3
Education	Primary or less	27.1	23.3	19.8
	Vocational	28.5	31.1	26.0
	High school	32.0	33.3	38.5
	College/university	12.5	12.2	15.6
Age	–44	37.0	25.6	29.2
	45–	63.0	74.4	70.8
Settlement	Kaposvár	66.9	77.8	70.8
	Other	33.1	22.2	29.2
Present occupation	Employee	34.0	24.4	37.5
	Entrepreneur, own business	4.8	2.2	5.2
	Doing casual work	.8	1.1	2.1
	Unemployed	9.8	17.8	8.3
	Pensioner	40.1	47.8	37.5
	On maternity leave	5.3	4.4	3.1
	Student	3.8	2.2	5.2
	Other	1.4	.0	1.0

Cramer's V measures: Gender: n.s., Education: n.s., Age: 0.07^{***}, Settlement: 0.06^{**}, Occupation: n.s. Statistical significance: $^{***} < 0.01$, $^{**} < 0.05$, $^{*} < 0.1$

Temporary and Lasting Changes

We present here the changes in opinion, attitudes and levels of knowledge that occurred immediately after the deliberative event and consider whether these endured a year later. One of the main aims of the Deliberative Poll is to produce an informed public opinion. One possible measure of its success, therefore, is the gain in the participants' knowledge. Before such an event, the participants are sent an information booklet where they are provided with material covering the topics to be discussed. Many of them will also have gained further information from each other in small group discussions as well as from the experts during plenary sessions. Our questionnaire contained nine multiple-choice knowledge questions, out of which five were related to actual numerical data, such as the unemployment rate in the region, nationwide, and in the EU. Four other questions were referred to legal rules, such as eligibility for social welfare benefits and were more textual in character, rather than numerical. Overall, it can be said that the knowledge index[4] was significantly higher both after the deliberation and a year later than before the event. Although there was a slight drop in levels of knowledge a year later, we can still talk about both short-term and lasting changes in information gain. The qualitative and quantitative questions did not follow similar trends: information about numbers did not increase significantly, whereas it did so more clearly at the higher level of knowledge, in terms of qualitative information about the industrial profile of the area and the prevailing legal rules (see Graph 1).

Graph 1: Knowledge Gain of Participants of the DP, Immediate and Lasting Effects (T1–T3–T4) (n=90) (average number of correct answers concerning textual and numerical items)

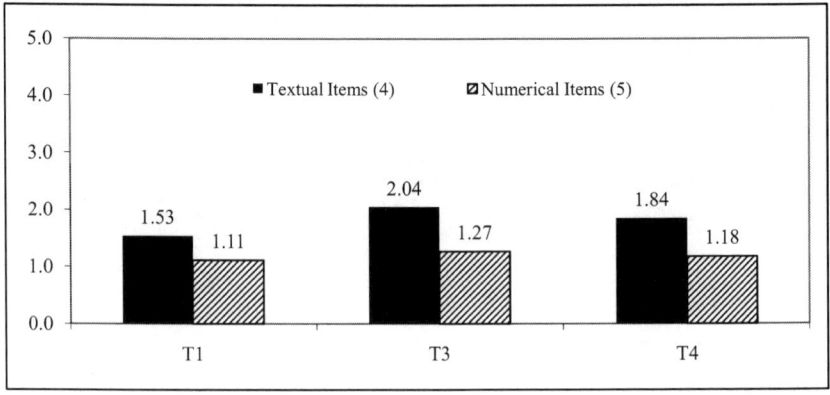

T-tests: Textual Items: T1T3 t= 3.29***, T1T4 t= 2.15**, Numerical Items: T1T3 t= n.s., T1T4 t= n.s.

Interestingly, however, when we look at the control group, a similar trend is detectable: there was a significant increase of knowledge during the year between the pre-deliberation survey (T1) and the follow-up survey (T4), but in their case the change related to knowledge of numerical facts. As no significant differences existed between the participants and the control group in the long term regarding knowledge level, we cannot say that the changes in information gain were clearly due to the deliberative event. Deliberation resulted in a short- and long-term

---

4   Additive indices were created from the nine knowledge items.

knowledge gain in terms of *qualitative* information. This knowledge gain however is contingent, since in the meantime members of the control group also became more knowledgeable about facts and especially figures of unemployment, that is about *quantitative* information. In the long run, therefore, according to our results, deliberation affects the type and not the level of knowledge gain.

Regarding changes of attitudes and opinion, two themes were addressed in our questionnaire: attitudes towards (1) unemployment with related issues of the economy (market, foreign investments, the role of the government and personal responsibility in providing jobs, etc.) and (2) European integration processes. Changes in opinion and attitudes showed different patterns in the case of the different questions[5]. Regarding attitudes towards unemployment issues (see Graph 2) the share of those who thought that 'it's the government's duty to provide jobs for everyone' (as opposed to one's own responsibility) significantly decreased in the short term (from 38% to 17%), but increased over the original level a year later (43%). A similar pattern could be detected regarding opinions about allowances that should be paid to everyone in need: solidarity increased after the deliberation (from 53% to 80%), but it did not persist a year later (59%). In both cases the control group showed very similar attitudes before the deliberation and a year later which means that both the increased solidarity and the increased self-responsibility were an effect of the deliberative event and only a temporary change was generated. Nevertheless, long-term effects could be detected in opinions about the government's increased role, even if this were at the cost of increased taxes. Positive opinion increased from 28% to 34% and was 42% a year later. A similar trend could be detected in the issue of the governments' role in the regulation of the second economy.

Overall, among the 7 questions concerning employment issues, in the case of 4 there were significant short term changes, and there were long term changes in the case of 2 questions.

---

5   Only significant changes (at the p<0.1 or higher level) will be reported in the statistics. The different questions were asked on different scales (1–5, 1–7, 0–10). In order to make them comparable all scales were recoded into a 0–1 scale.

Graph 2: Changes in Attitudes towards Employment Issues (T1–T3–T4, 0–1 average)

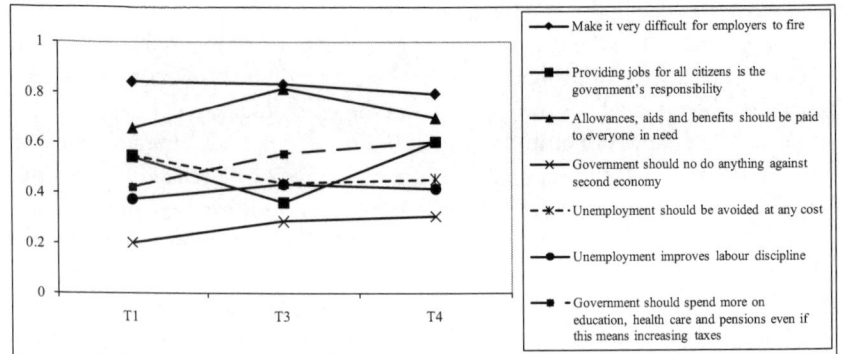

Significant changes:

Providing jobs for all citizens is the government's responsibility: T1T3 t = −4.429***, T3T4 t = 6.286***

Allowances, aid and benefits should be paid to everyone in need: T1T3 t = 3.503***, T3T4 t = −3.628***

Government should not do anything against the second economy: T1T4 t = 1.872*

Unemployment should be avoided at any cost: T1T3 t = −1.989*

Government should spend more: T1T3 t = 2.632***, T1T4 t = 3.569***

In terms of attitudes towards the market economy, participants became more positive towards the idea of an open market immediately after the deliberation, but this change did not have a significant lasting effect a year later according to the average of the answers (see Graph 3). However, when looking at the distribution of the answers there was some realignment over time.

Attitudes towards foreign investments showed a different pattern: a slight positive change after the deliberation and a significant drop a year later. Initially 24% of the participants of the deliberation were against encouraging foreign investments (1–2 answers on a 1–5 scale) that decreased somewhat to 13% after the deliberation but grew again to 38% a year later. In parallel with this trend, initially 48% thought that foreign investments help Hungarian economic development that increased somewhat to 56% after the deliberation and dropped back to 39% a year later.

Among the seven questions concerning economic issues, there was significant short term (T1T3) change in case of one question, and there was no significant long term (T1T4) change in this respect.

Graph 3: Changes in Attitudes towards Market Economy (T1–T3–T4, 0–1 average)

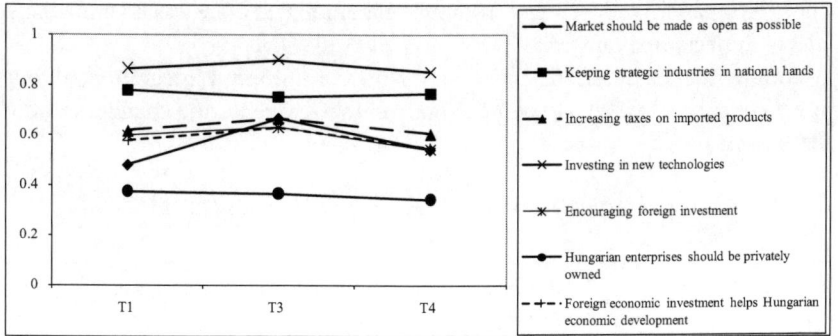

Significant changes:
The market should be made as open as possible: T1T3 change t = 3.864***
Investing in new technologies: T3T4 t = –1.858*
Encouraging foreign investment: T3T4 t = –2.187**
Foreign economic investment helps Hungarian economic development: T3T4 t = –3.046***

Regarding perception of the European integration project, attitudes were more changeable over time, which could be a sign that opinions or attitudes on this subject were not yet crystallized due to the distant, abstract and complicated character of the subject and the low level of public interest (see Graph 4). There was only a short-term change in opinions on the question of strengthening integration, on the perception of the benefits of the EU for Hungary and on the need to make the the EU more competitive in world markets. The pattern of the answers before the deliberation and a year later was very similar among the participants of the deliberation and the control group, which means that in the case of these questions the temporary changes are also to be drawn back to the deliberative event itself.

There were, however, some long-lasting changes, in terms of the increased tax level to be distributed at the EU level and the decreased share of people believing that what happens at the EU level has consequences for their life. In terms of tax redistribution, the initial 10% to be attributed to the EU level has increased to 23% and a year later, despite a slight decrease, it was still at 19%. Regarding the perceived consequences on people's lives, there was an important decrease due to the deliberation among the participants (from 28% to 8%) which went back to some extent a year later, but still represents a drop of 20%. In terms of opinions before the deliberation and a year after, the general trends of the participants' opinions are in line with the control group, where there was a significant decrease as well (from 28% to 15%).

Besides these trends, better social security as the main aim for the EU showed a changing pattern independent from the deliberation, as there was no immediate effect – it decreased only after it.

Among the six questions concerning issues of European integration, all but one were affected by short-term change and there were lasting changes in only three cases.

Graph 4:   Changes in Attitudes towards the European Integration (T1–T3–T4, 0–1 average)

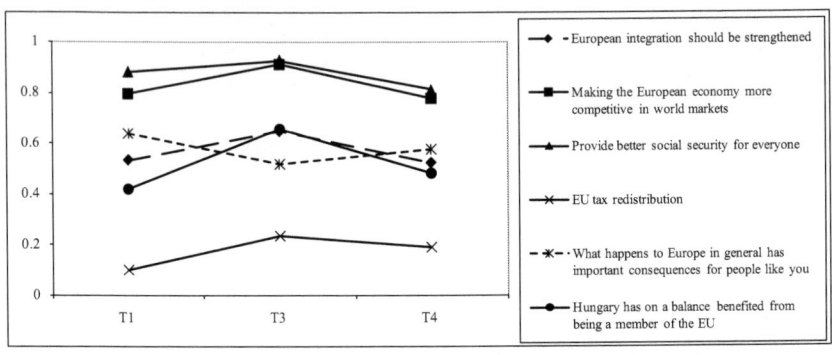

Significant changes:
European integration should be strengthened: T1T3 change t = 2.458**, T3T4 t = -2.324**
Making the European economy more competitive: T1T3 change t = 3.191***, T3T4 t = -4.021***
Provide better social security for everyone: T3T4 change t = -3.66***, T1T4 t = -2.14***
EU tax redistribution: T1T3 change t = 3.005***, T1T4 t = 2.707***
What happens to Europe in general has important consequences for people like me: T1T3 change t = -2.901***, T1T4 t = -2.135**
On balance Hungary has benefited: T1T3 change t = 2.634**, T3T4 t = -2.304**

Overall there were short-term changes in half of the investigated 20 attitude/opinion items and long-term changes in a quarter of them.

To set up a *typology*, four patterns of attitude and opinion change can be discerned. Due to partial overlapping between short- and long-term changes there was *no significant change* whatsoever in the case of eight questions (such as keeping strategic industries in national hands, increasing taxes on imported products, investing in new technologies, that Hungarian enterprises should be privately owned, that it should be made very difficult for employers to fire staff, that unemployment should be avoided at any cost, that unemployment improves labor discipline and that government should not do anything against illegal work). In the case of six questions the deliberation had an immediate effect on opinions but this was *not lasting* and opinions went back close to their initial levels a year later. This was the case of the attitudes towards an open market, that 'it's the government's duty to provide jobs for everyone', 'allowances should be paid to everyone in need', European integration should be strengthened', 'the EU should become more competitive', and that 'Hungary has benefited from its EU membership'. In most of these cases the control group confirmed that the changes were only temporary as there was no change among them and the differences between the participants and the control group were not significant.

In three further questions, however, a lasting change could be detected. Attitudes towards increased government spending with increased taxes, increased EU redistribution and decreased consequences of the EU in one's life all showed a durable change. In these questions it is interesting to see whether the effects can be attributed to the deliberation or to an overall change in the opinion climate (see Graph 5). In the case of government spending and the consequences on EU events on people's lives, the changes were in line with those occurring among the control group, which suggests that these changes cannot be directly associated with the deliberation, but rather with a change in the overall context. As opposed to these trends, responses to the question about EU tax redistribution showed a different pattern. There was an initial gap between the participants and the control group which decreased to some extent after the deliberation. Before the deliberation, the participants were significantly less open to the EU level redistribution than the control group (10% vs. 15%) – by this change the participants did exceed the level of the control group where the opinions on the matter remained unchanged after the deliberation (19% vs. 16%).

Graph 5: Lasting Changes among Participants and the Control Group (T1–T4, 0–1 average)

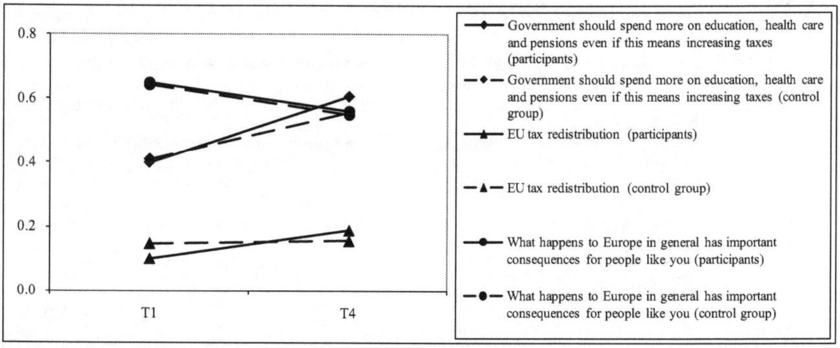

Significant changes among the control group:
The government should spend more: T1T4 change t = 3.146 ***
What happens to Europe in general has important consequences for people like me: T1T4 change t = −2.249**

The last group of changing patterns is where the deliberation had no immediate effect, but opinions had changed a year later; that is, *only long term change* could be detected. This happened for three questions: on encouraging foreign investment, the benefits of foreign investments to Hungary and the need for the EU to promote improved social security. In these cases comparison with the pattern followed by the control group is also important, for it can provide an explanation why these changes happened, whether it was due to a change in the overall opinion climate or the national/ international environment. The spring of 2009 was especially difficult in Hungary due to both the world financial crisis and the Hungarian economic crisis and people's attitudes towards the foreign investments and social security might have changed. Attitudes towards encouraging foreign investments showed a very similar trend among the participants and the control group, with only a slight decline over one year, which was not statistically significant (see Graph 6). So, in this case we might talk about this being an effect of the changing environment. Regarding opinions about how helpful foreign investments are for the Hungarian economy, there was an initial gap between the participants and the control group, with participants being more positive in this respect. A year later, the opinion of the two groups became closer. However, regarding these two latter questions, the slight increase followed by the significant decline in the support for foreign investment among the participants mentioned earlier might be the effect of the deliberation. Regarding the wish for a social Europe, the opinions remained unchanged in the control group, while the participants experienced a decrease during the year after the deliberation – they followed a different trend in this respect, but still, there was no significant difference between the participants' opinion and the control group's opinion.

Graph 6: A Comparison of the Participants and the Control Group (T1–T4, 0–1 average)

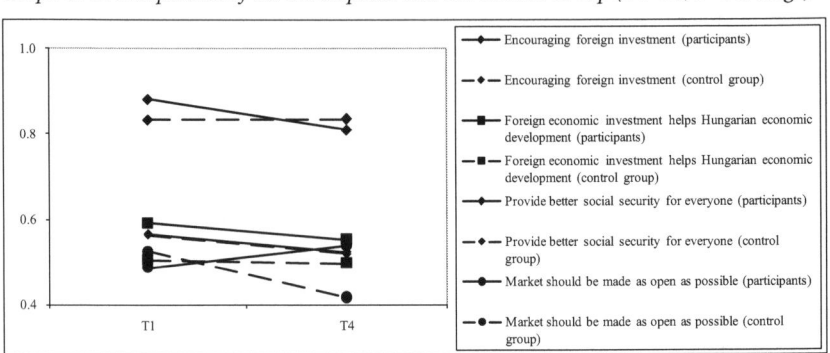

Significant change within the control group:
The market should be made as open as possible: T1T4 change t = –2.145**

Another interesting case concerns attitudes toward the open market, where there was immediate change after the Deliberative Poll, but no lasting effects of the deliberation. However, comparing this trend to the control group, it seems that while no significant change occurred in the long term among the participants (in terms of the average answers), the control group became significantly more reluctant to support the open market. While there was no significant difference between the groups at the beginning, a year later the participants of the Deliberative Poll were more positive towards the idea of an open market than the control group. In this sense, we might hypothesize that after a short positive change followed by a decline in support, the stability of participants' opinions over the long-term could be attributed to their experience of deliberation – without this, opinions would have changed negatively.

Taking all the changes between both groups into account, it can be said that for two questions the significant change was probably due to deliberation itself, although with a different pattern. In the case of the share of tax to be allocated to the EU, the initial opinion of the participants was significantly different from that of the control group; however, a year later, with no changes in the control group, the participants' opinion on the matter became more enthusiastic. As for the question on the open market, there was no significant difference at the beginning between the two groups, but the gap became significant a year later, with the opinion of the control group showing a significant decline while the opinion of the participants remained relatively unchanged.

A Reflective View

Evaluation of the Event

Another interesting result of the deliberative event is the evaluation of its effects and efficiency by the participants themselves. In terms of skills or knowledge that they considered were improved by the event, the participants mentioned first of all an increased motivation to participate actively in public debate (75%), and also to communicate more with other people and better understand their attitudes and behavior (68–69%). A lower number of participants mentioned that the event helped them to comprehend the public debate on employment or to improve their knowledge on employment issues in the EU. A year later, a significantly lower number of participants mentioned that the event served to improve their factual knowledge on the EU or employment issues, as well as their ability to understand and participate in public debate on these issues (see Graph 7).

Graph 7: Evaluation of the Deliberative Event – Perceived Improvement of Knowledge/ skills (T3–T4) (average on a 0–10 scale)

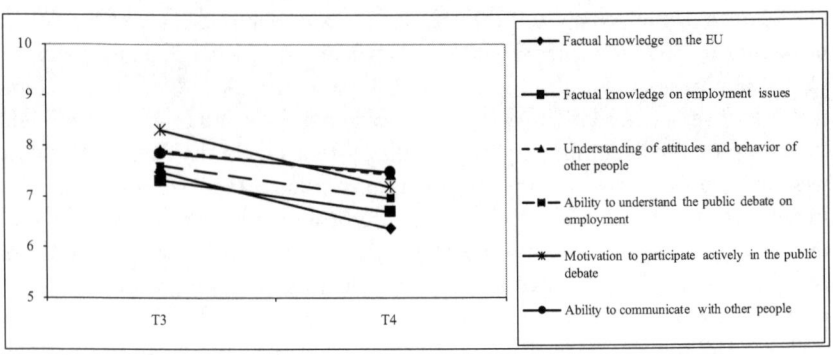

Significant changes:
Factual knowledge on the EU: t = –3.328***
Factual knowledge on employment issues: t = –1.967*
Ability to understand the public debate on employment: t = –2.067**
Motivation to participate actively in the public debate: t = –3.302***

As for their motivation to participate in the event, learning about employment issues was mentioned significantly less frequently a year later than immediately after the event – and they placed more importance on the financial incentive they gained from agreeing to participate (see Graph 8).

Graph 8: Evaluation of the Deliberative Event – Motivation for Participation (T3–T4) (average on a 0–10 scale)

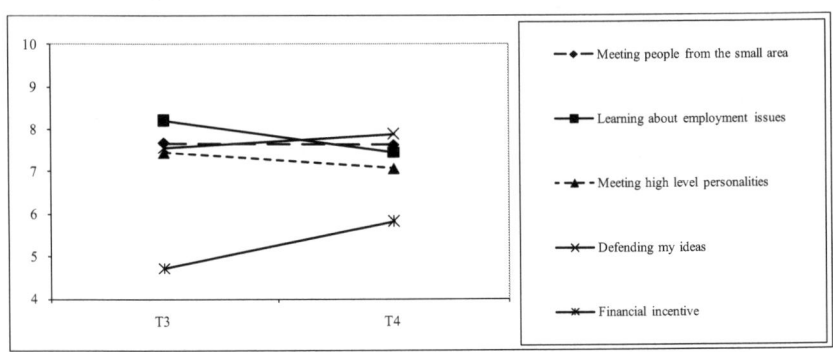

Significant changes:
Learning about employment issues: t = –2.246**
Financial incentive: t = 2.300**

Factors Influencing the Changes

We have seen how different aspects of opinions and attitudes changed after the deliberation and whether these changes were lasting. This raises the question of what factors affected the overall changes in opinions and attitudes. In order to analyze this, linear regression models are used, testing the effect of information and social-demographic factors on opinion and attitude changes. The dependent variables are opinion-change indices where first the opinion changes are calculated from the pre-and post deliberation answers (T1T3) and from the pre-deliberation answers and the answers given a year after the deliberation (T1T4) to the set of twenty questions described previously. Then the absolute value of these variables is summed up in two additive indices that stand for the short- and long-term changes. These indices sum up the intensity of opinion change; however, they contain no information on the direction of these changes.

We have included several socio-demographic variables such as gender, age, education. In order to include information on the respondents' material resources, we used a proxy measuring the quality of the neighborhood recorded by the interviewer. Besides these variables, knowledge change indices were used in our models as a more substantial determinant of the opinion change based on the assumption that opinion change occurs due to increased level of information and knowledge gain.

Four regression models were built: three among the participants of the deliberative event, measuring short-term and lasting changes, and one model where the control group was also included in order to measure the effect of the deliberation itself on the long-term opinion changes (see Table 2).

Regression models show that men were more open to change their opinion than women (see Model 1), however, this is only true of short term opinion changes – it doesn't determine lasting effects of the deliberation. The unemployed changed their mind less frequently than the employed. When these impacts were controlled for other variables (education, knowledge gain, and material conditions) both gender and being unemployed had significant effects on the short term. If we take into account the general trends of opinion change *during the deliberation*, that *solidarity has overall increased*, it is not surprising that the unemployed changed their opinions less than non-unemployed, who might have become more socially sensitive on the matter. On the other hand, the other main trend of the opinion changes, the increased level of self-responsibility regarding finding a job, should have affected the unemployed themselves. Regarding why men are more affected by opinion change, a possible explanation can be that men participate more in public debate and they are also more likely to hold extreme opinions than women – but these explanations cannot be directly verified here. At the same time, those who changed their opinion more also found the event as a whole more valuable in helping them clarify their position on the issues and they felt more active during the informal and social parts of the event. In parallel with this, men were also more likely to find the event more valuable in this sense than women, with an average of 7.51 vs. 5.96 on a 0–10 scale.

In the longer run, there is a similar trend, but this connection is not significant (see Model 2). People with a university degrees were less likely to change their opinions, which could be explained by the fact that their opinions were more established and they had more developed cognitive mobilization skills.

If we include the immediate (T1T3) impact of the deliberative event into the explanation of the long-run (T1T4) opinion changes of the participants (see Model 3) it proves to be the single most important explanatory factor; it overwrites the effects of gender and education as well. Even the impact of knowledge change proves to be unimportant when investigated together with the short-run opinion change index.

If we investigate the long-term impact of participation in the Deliberative Poll on opinion change (see Model 4) it proves to be insignificant. None of the explanatory variables prove to be significant, except for education which counter-indicates opinion change. Interestingly there was no significant difference between the participant group and the control group in terms of the intensity of opinion change. In this sense, it seems that in the long term, the Deliberative Poll had no lasting effect – opinions that changed did so regardless and could not be ascribed to participation in the event. Overall, this is the most important – negative – finding of our paper.

Table 2: Linear Regression Models of Temporary and Lasting Effects (Unstandardized Regression Coefficients)

	Model 1		Model 2		Model 3		Model 4	
Dependent:	**T1T3 opinion change**		**T1T4 opinion change**		**T1T4 opinion change**		**T1T4 opinion change**	
Constant	5.044	***	5.579	***	3.019	***	6.021	***
Male	.790	**	.611		.220		.205	
Unemployed	−.870	*	−.116		.313		−.146	
University	−.693		−1.022	*	−.659		−.712	*
Wealthy neighbourhood	−.010		.233		.248		−.156	
T1T3/T1T4 knowledge change	−.058		−.089		−.076		−.037	
T1T3 opinion change					.509	***		
Participated to the deliberation							−.183	
R Square	.094	n.s.	.062	n.s.	.249	***	.028	n.s.
n =	90		90		90		186	

Statistical significance: *** < 0.01, ** < 0.05, * < 0.1

However, the models presented here are not significant ones, with the exception of the one where previous opinion change is included among the explaining factors. This means that the variables included are not the ones determining the intensity of opinion change. The included variables explain 9% in the case of the immediate opinion change, but only 3–6% of the long term changes.

Besides technical issues concerning the low sample size and the construction of the additive opinion change index, the inclusion of other substantial explanatory variables could be considered. It seems that age, activity/inactivity or media usage do not have a significant impact on opinion change either. On the other hand, when trying to build models on the opinion change in separate questions without any aggregation, the results are similarly insignificant. The opinion change concerning a question is mostly defined by the previous opinion on that matter – without any effects of the mentioned socio-demographic or substantial variables. Level of education had a negative effect on opinion change in the first models, but other basic socio-demographic characteristics did not influence it significantly.

Conclusion

In the literature there is much criticism on the applicability of the deliberative social *model* and it therefore makes sense for the debate on this kind of deliberation to be tested empirically. Deliberative *methods* may offer many advantages, but they also face several problems. Reviewing the empirical studies on deliberation, there are relatively few quantitative and reliable analyses of how deliberation really works. While opinions do frequently change, 'most empirical analyses do not explain the patterns of opinion change or lack of change' (Barbaras 2004, 688).

Proponents of Deliberative Polling suggest the need for follow–up research to determine if the opinion changes brought about by their method are temporary or lasting. The control sample surveyed in this study allows for an assessment to be made of the effect of deliberation and the effect of other factors e.g. public discourse or crisis. Similarly to the Kaposvár Deliberative Poll, participants in follow-up study conducted in Denmark 'reverted somewhat to their initial opinion position' and measured persisted 'increase among the participants in the level of knowledge' (Hansen and Andersen 2004, 271–276). As for knowledge change after the deliberation, the Kaposvár experience shows significant and lasting gains, with two important qualifications. First, this is true only in the case of the textual items, because knowledge of numerical items did not grow in the short run. Qualitative and quantitative information had different chances to influence the knowledge of Deliberative Poll participants (Fishkin et al. 2009). Second, in the long run knowledge levels grew within the control group as well. While the impact of Deliberative Polling mostly had to do with textual knowledge, in the control group of the local population the knowledge about quantitative information grew. It might be thought that it was the impact of the crisis: information about the numerical data concerning unemployment became known. However, in this case the growth should have been detected among the Deliberative Poll participants as well. The difference may have to do with the Deliberative Poll discussions and with the age composition of the samples. Due to the self-selection of the Deliberative Poll sample, the elderly were over-represented among the participants.

In terms of attitude change, in two out of five items there was no change at all. In every third item the changes were temporary only. In two cases out of the twenty the changes were lasting due to the effect of the Deliberative Poll. The two items were ideologically sensitive ones: the higher proportion of tax redistribution on the EU-level and the open market.

The empirical results of the Kaposvár follow-up survey show that the Deliberative Poll had a minor lasting effect on people's thinking. In the short term, immediately after the event, the knowledge of the participants grew significantly;

they changed their mind on several issues; they became more tolerant towards the unemployed; and their opinions became more circumspect and less extreme. They evaluated the event enthusiastically and they felt that they would be ready to participate in further public debates. One year later, most of these effects had disappeared: the level of knowledge and most of the opinion changes did not differ from those of the control group, while the evaluation of the event – although remaining positive in most of the dimensions – became less enthusiastic.

Our findings suggest that Deliberative Polling does not change people's views permanently. For those who want to experiment with forms of participative democracy, this might sound like bad news. But it could also contribute to an improvement in the methods of decision-making. Even if temporarily, it can efficiently contribute to providing better information for citizens and it can enhance the confidence and ability of lay citizens to participate in public affairs in the short run. Prior to important collective decisions it may help to counterbalance the two major problems of voting practices and other forms of decision making: ignorance and disinterest. Better-informed and motivated citizens will be more likely ready to participate in collective decisions shortly after these types of deliberative events.

There is one additional aspect of these findings which is worthy of further study. Deliberative Polls are not only about knowledge gain and arguing. Emotions and stories count as well. In our case, the side effects of the emotional dynamics of the event were mostly positive: tolerance and trust grew (even if temporarily). More evidence is needed to discover whether this is always (or typically) the case. It looks likely that arguing and being informed helps to form balanced opinions. But how emotional dynamics of these events influence the passions of the majority and of opinion leaders in the short and in the long run is a matter for further research.

References

Ackerman, Bruce, and James S. Fishkin. 2003. "Deliberation Day." In *Debating Deliberative Democracy*, edited by James Fishkin, and Peter Laslett, 7–30. Malden: Blackwell.

Esmée Fairbairn Foundation. 2002. "Attitudes to Crime and Punishment: the Results of a Deliberative Poll of Public Opinion." Accessed June 1, 2015. http://www.rethinking.org.uk/latest/pdf/briefing2.pdf.

Barbaras, Jason. 2004. "How Deliberation Affects Policy Opinions." *American Political Science Review* 98: 687–701.

Bourdieu, Pierre. 1984. «L'opinion publique n'existe pas.» In *Questions de sociologie*, Pierre Bourdieu, 222–235. Paris: Les Éditions de Minuit.

Cohen, Joshua, and Charles Sabel. 1997. "Directly–deliberative Polyarchy." *European Law Journal* 3: 313–343.

Downs, Anthony. 1956. *An Economic Theory of Democracy*. New York: Harper–Row.

Fishkin, James S. 1997. *The Voice of the People. Public Opinion and Democracy*. New Haven: Yale University Press.

Fishkin, James S., and Cynthia Farrar. 2005. "Deliberative Polling: From Experiment to Community Resource." In *The Deliberative Democracy Handbook*, eds. John Gastil and Peter Levine, 68–79. San Francisco: Jossey – Bass.

Fishkin, James S., György Lengyel, Robert C. Luskin, and Alice Siu. 2009. "The Kaposvár Deliberative Poll: considered opinions on unemployment". In *Deliberative Methods in Local Society Research. The Kaposvár Experiences*, ed. György Lengyel, 141–147. Budapest: Új Mandátum.

Hansen, Kasper M., and Vibeke N. Andersen. 2004. "Deliberative Democracy and the Deliberative Poll on the Euro." *Scandinavian Political Studies* 27: 261–286.

Hardin, Russell. 2003. "Street–level Epistemology and Democratic Participation". In *Debating Deliberative Democracy*, eds. James Fishkin and Peter Laslett, 163–181. Malden: Blackwell.

Hirst, Paul. 1994. *Associative Democracy. New Forms of Economic and Social Governance*. Oxford: Oxford Polity Press.

Hirst, Paul, and Veit Bader. 2001. *Associative Democracy: the Real Third Way*. London: Frank Cass Publishers.

Lengyel, György (ed.). 2009. *Deliberative Methods in Local Society Research. The Kaposvar Experiences*. Budapest. http://www.uni-corvinus.hu/index.php?id=23241.

Luskin, Robert C., and James S. Fishkin. 1998. "Deliberative Polling, Public Opinion, and Democracy: The Case of the National Issues Convention." Paper presented at the annual meeting of the American Political Science Association. Boston (ms.).

Luskin, Robert C., and James S. Fishkin. 2002. *Deliberation and "Better Citizens."* Accessed June 1, 2015. http://cdd.stanford.edu/research/papers/2002/better-citizens.pdf.

Perczynski, Piotr. 1999. *Citizenship and Associative Democracy. Innovation in Democratic Theory*. Accessed June 1, 2015. http://ecpr.eu/filestore/paperproposal/ecbcec11-f81d-400b-af0e-f75e97a78d48.pdf.

Pettit, Philip. 2003. "Deliberative Democracy, the Discursive Dilemma, and Republican Theory." In *Debating Deliberative Democracy*, eds. James Fishkin and Peter Laslett, 138–162. Malden: Blackwell.

Zaller, John, and Stanley Feldman. 1992. "A simple theory of the survey response." *American Journal of Political Science* 36: 579–616.

Zaller, John. 1993. *The Nature and Origins of Mass Opinions*. Cambridge: Cambridge University Press.

Tatsuro Sakano

Chapter Eight. To What Extent Do Deliberative Polls Promote Discursive Rationality? Some Evidence from a Deliberative Poll on Reframing Regional Governments in the Prefecture of Kanagawa, Japan

Introduction

Japan is known for its strong bureaucracy. Formally the legislative and budgeting power is vested in elected officials and their assemblies. However, the elected officials depend on bureaucrats when they formulate policies. Thus most policies and ordinances are understood to be practically made by bureaucrats. While the fundamental nature of the government has not changed for many years, citizen participation in administrative planning has been institutionalized gradually since the 1970's. Town meetings and public comments are now common at all levels of government, from the nationwide to municipal. Some local governments have taken a step further to enact basic ordinances in order to stipulate their citizens' right to participate in policy making. Kanagawa prefecture, lying south-west of Tokyo, is one of such leading local governments. Out of forty-seven prefecture-level governments, the Kanagawa Prefectural Government (KPG) was third to enact such ordinances in the year 2009. In the same year the first DP in Japan was held by the KPG (Sakano 2012, 24–29).

Along with the trends of expanding citizen participation, social experiments using mini-publics started in the late 1990s. The first Japanese Consensus Conference was held in 1998 by STS (Science, Technology and Society) in a group concerned with gene therapy. It is reported that at least 10 Consensus Conferences had been held by 2012 (Mikami 2012, 44–46). In 2005, the first Japanese version of Planning Cell, called Citizen Deliberative Meeting, was held in Mitaka city, Tokyo. Since the Junior Chamber International Japan (JCI-Japan), with its 704 local branches and close to 36000 members, decided to make a formal commitment to spread Citizen Deliberative Meeting, the number of projects mostly at municipal level has skyrocketted, totaling 156 by the end of 2011 (Shinoto 2012, 101–110).

The first DP was held at this timing just when interest in mini-publics began to arise. However, the bureaucrats have been and continue to be cautious about

using mini-publics. Due to the mindsets nurtured in a paternalistic culture, they habitually think that their role is to formulate best policies, and citizen participation gives them an opportunity to explain their policies to the citizens or at best the last chance for making some final adjustments. Typical responses of bureaucrats towards mini-publics are lined with fears and doubts: the fears concern the possibility that randomly selected citizens may turn down their proposals; the doubts relate to the capacity of randomly selected citizens to deliberate.

Although the KPG claim to be a frontrunner of citizen participation, they also harbored such fears and doubts. They were afraid that ordinary citizens in Japan are too reserved and too shy to accept invitation to attend DP. It was believed that even if they did attend a deliberation meeting, they would not talk freely, as they were not accustomed to expressing their opinions in public. Payment to participants was another contentious issue. As the participants in ordinary town meetings are not usually paid, no justification was found for distinguishing DP participants. These fears and doubts did not go away before the project was implemented. So it was decided to carry out the DP as an experiment first, in order to evaluate and understand its usability, instead of deciding how to reflect the result of the DP in policy making beforehand.

The issue was the Do-Shu-system, a proposal to consolidate the present forty-seven prefectures into about ten larger administrative units, called Do-Shus. Under the Do-Shu system, the most of legislative, budgeting and taxation power now held by the state government was to be delegated to the newly established regional governments, thus creating autonomous regions. The plan was prepared under the Minister specially appointed for this job as a cure for structural problems such as monopole regional growth concentration to Tokyo, rapidly aging population, inefficiency of centralized bureaucracy, and growing fiscal deficit[1]. Although the issue

---

1   An advisory meeting was set under the cabinet to discuss the Do-Shu system. An interim report was generated. But before completing the final report, the government changed from the LDP to the Democratic Party. Then the meeting was terminated. The interim report can be downloaded from the web site (Cabinet Secretariat, 2008. The Interim Report on Do-Shu-sysytem. Accessed June 15, 2015. http://www.cas.go.jp/jp/seisaku/doushuu/080324honbun.pdf.) For the concept of the Do-Shu system, see the report "A Proposal for a Wide-Area Local Government System – Revitalization of the Nation and its Regions" prepared by the National Institute for Research Advancement. The summary is uploaded on the web site (Ntional Institute for Research Advancement. 2005. A Proposal for a Wide-Area Local Government System- Revitalization of the Nation and Its Regions. Accessed June 15, 2015. http://www.nira.or.jp/past/publ/houko/i0502.html.).

was nationwide, Mr. Matsuzawa, the governor of the KPG at that time, thought it should be discussed by citizens and therefore was an appropriate topic for the first DP in Japan to be experimentally implemented by the KPG.

Despite the long and keen interest among Japanese academics, DP was not realized for many years. After the first DP, five other DPs have since been carried out, mainly by university researchers [2]. Among these six DPs, the latest one has gained special attention since the theme was the long term energy plan in response to the Fukushima nuclear power plant accident in March 2011 and it was hosted by the National Policy Unit of Japan (NPU), a division set up within the Cabinet Secretariat to advise the prime minister directly on strategic issues .

In the following part of this chapter, I will evaluate the DP projects in Japan, mainly focusing on the Kanagawa DP, the first DP held in Japan, since I organized it in cooperation with the Kanagawa prefectural government and therefore the data for analysis are easily accessible. In particular, I would like to show how to measure intersubjective understandability and demonstrate that the level of intersubjective understandability was increased in the case of the Kanagawa DP. Then I will discuss how representativeness and quality of deliberation are mutually dependent.

Discursive Representativeness and Intersubjective Understandability

The idea of using randomly selected citizen groups, called "mini-publics," in collective will-formation has inspired various democratic innovations since the late 20th century (Smith 2012, 102). The idea of mini-publics has brought with it the hope that deliberative democracy is a reachable goal. At the root of these hopes lie two assumptions on how mini-publics work. Firstly, a group of randomly selected citizens can achieve better representativeness than elected representatives, in the sense that the former includes a diversity of opinions better than the latter. Secondly, it is possible to create a deliberative microcosm sufficiently close to the ideal speech situation using randomly selected citizens. Smith (2012, 110) expresses these assumptions in his book that "Random selection – with or without stratification – generates the diversity amongst participants that is a precondition for realizing the goods of inclusiveness and considered judgment." "Inclusion" and "thoughtfulness" in James Fishkin's words, are the basic components to be realized

---

2   The first DP was directed by Sakano Lab. of Tokyo Institute of Technology, the fifth DP by Hokkaido University, and the rest of four DPs by the Center for Deliberative Poll of Keio University.

by deliberative democracy (Fishkin 2009, 32). The two assumptions, the one on representativeness and the other on deliberation quality, are derived by reversing two deficiencies of representative democracy, which Cohen and Sabel (1997, 316) identified as lack of "direct participation" and "deliberation". In other words, they are the functional basis to overcome the deficiency of representative democracy. There are two possibilities to regain directness and deliberation. For Habermas (1996), Cohen and Sabel (ibid.), and Dryzek (2001), the informal public sphere or informal network in civil society are the solution. But as Fishkin (2009, 179) pointed out, the public sphere is not necessarily a deliberative communicative system. After all, to function as the place for inclusive deliberation, a voluntary network has to face Olson's collective action problem. The remaining possibility resides in randomly selected citizens. However, the actual functioning of mini-publics depends on various factors. It should be empirically verified to what extent representativeness and deliberation quality have been achieved for each project.

If you focus on DP, James Fishkin (2009) overviewed all the DP projects of the past fifteen years in his book. There is abundant direct and indirect evidencethat DP has been achieving good representativeness and deliberative quality, even under the difficult conditions. However, his evaluations about representativeness concern demographic representativeness, rather than discursive representative-ness explicitly. On deliberation quality of DP, he gave the following evidence: 1) in many cases statistically significant changes of policy attitudes were observed, 2) participants gained significant information, 3) the changes in policy attitudes and the information gains were related, and 4) the participants' subjective evalu-ation and qualitative text analysis showed that the deliberation processes were normatively desirable (Fishkin, 2009, Fishkin and Luskin 2005). But this evidence is indirect. It does not show directly to what extent the opinions were actually im-proved. To deal with discursive representativeness and improvement of opinions more explicitly and directly, we need to reconsider opinions as relational entities. The reasons to do so are as follows.

Statistically speaking, random selection is a method to avoid selection bias. Demographic characteristics can be used as clues to check selection bias. From a political point of view on the other hand, random selection is considered a method to avoid systematic exclusion of certain opinion groups. In late modernity where individualization proceeds so that individuals are required to construct their own lives, collective identity based on socio-economic status does not necessarily cor-respond to policy attitudes as much as it used to. Demographic representativeness does not necessarily guarantee inclusiveness of opinions any more. It is necessary to check inclusiveness of opinions directly rather than indirectly by demographic characteristics. The problem here is that opinions are subjective and relational entities. Opinions are not mere policy attitudes or beliefs. They appear as relationships among policy attitudes, beliefs, and norms. It is not sufficient to measure the distribution of attitudes, beliefs, and norms separately, since meanings appear in their relationships. To measure inclusiveness of opinions is to identify the understandable relationships, which Dryzek and Niemeyer (2008) called "discourses" or "story lines" (Hobson and Niemeyer 2011, 960).

Besides that, as Hobson and Niemeyer (ibid) showed, opinions reflected in these relationships, in their words discourses, will change through the deliberation. If those opinion changes are free from psychological biases and strategic maneuvering, inclusiveness matters more than the initial distribution of opinions. Here we face another problem. We cannot know all the opinions perfectly before the deliberation and neither can we even after the deliberation. This problem of indeterminacy of inclusiveness cannot be avoided as long as our cognitive capacity is limited. It is just like we cannot eradicate selection bias completely without institutional obligation to enforce participation. But as selection bias can be avoided, not perfectly but to a satisfactory level in practice, the problem of indeterminacy of inclusiveness can be solved at the practical level.

Since opinions are subjective and relational, inclusiveness of opinions is to be judged by intersubjective understandability and meaningfulness of the relationships, which are identified as discourses. Dryzek and Berejikian (1993) showed how to identify discourses by applying Q-methodology. Hobson and Niemeyer (ibid) succeeded in analyzing the transformation of discourses through deliberation with the same method. As will be discussed later, their method is not the only one for identifying discourses. Instead of their method, I will propose a method to identify policy judgment framework using SEM (Structure Equation Modeling). In any way meaningful relationships can be identified as discourses. And if they are intersubjectively understandable and meaningful, then non-participants will also use them for their own policy judgments so that the outcome of Mini-publics will link to the collective will formation at the macro level. In fact, discursive representativeness is closely related with intersubjective rationality. I will also discuss this point later. Before that, let us see briefly demographic representativeness and deliberative quality of the Kanagawa DP to compare with the results reported by Fishkin (ibid).

A Preliminary Evaluation of Representativeness and Deliberation Quality of the Kanagawa DP

On December 5, 2009, 152 randomly selected citizens of Kanagawa prefecture assembled together to discuss about the Do-Shu system in Yokohama, the capital city of the prefecture. Despite worries of the bureaucrats, it eventually turned out that almost the same level of representativeness and deliberation quality was replicated as in other previous DPs.

Looking at representativeness in terms of demographic characteristics, the representation of men and the elderly was slightly higher than in the normal population. Although the participants' awareness about the Do-Shu system was higher than that of non-participants, the attitudes towards Do-Shu system were not statistically different. While the political efficacy of the participants was higher than that of non-participants, 90 percent of the participants had not had attended any citizen participation opportunities such as town meetings ever before. Because DP does not have institutional power to enforce participation, selection bias cannot be eradicated completely. However, as Fishkin (ibid.) reported, the randomly selected citizens in the previous DP projects were much closer to the population than self-selection. So did the Kanagawa DP. Furthermore, similar demographic representativeness has also been observed in all other Japanese DPs. Random sampling can work to assemble relatively well balanced citizen representatives in Japan too.

There is one difference concerning Japanese DP in relation to representativeness. That is the low acceptance rate to attend deliberation meeting. In the Kanagawa DP, out of the 3000 randomly selected citizens to whom letters of invitation were mailed 535 answered to T1 questionnaire and 174 agreed to participate in the deliberation meeting. From 174 the actual participants were reduced to 152. The participant rate was only 5%. The participant rates in other Japanese DPs, which are somewhat lower than the acceptance rates, were almost at the same level, ranging from 4.2% to 8.6%, on average 5.2%. In most Japanese DP, mailing was commonly used. The energy DP by the NPU was the exception, where RDD was used, as in the U.S. Despite using a different survey method, the participant rate was 4.3% almost equal to the average. These facts show that differences between survey methods, whether RDD or mailing, are not a crucial in determining participant rate. The comparative data for all previous DPs in other countries are not available. So it is not certain exactly how low the Japanese participant rates are. But it is certainly a challenge for Japanese DP to raise this rate.

On deliberation quality of DP, in the Kanagawa DP almost the same results were reproduced as in Fishkin's 2009 report. The number of participants who agreed to the Do-Shu system increased by 5 percent. It is not a statistically significant change, but significant knowledge gains were observed and also positive correlation between knowledge gains and attitude change was observed. Table 1 shows the relationship between the initial knowledge level and the knowledge gains. There were seven knowledge-related questions. The participants were divided into two groups, depending on the number of correct answers. Levels of knowledge gains were categorized into three groups, depending on the increased number of correct answers. The result shows clearly that the group with low initial knowledge learned more than the high initial knowledge group.

Table 1: Initial Knowledge and Knowledge Gain

	Low Gain 0	Medium Gain 1 to 2	High Gain 3	Total
Initial Knowledge Low <=3	11 (12.6%)	35 (40.2%)	41 (47.1%)	87 (100%)
Initial Knowledge High >=4	24 (40.0%)	35 (58.3%)	1 (1.7%)	60 (100%)

Graph 1 shows the relationship between knowledge gains and changes in policy attitude. The participants were divided into 6 groups corresponding to the cells of Table 1. For example, LL corresponds to the cell of low initial knowledge and low knowledge gain. The first letter indicates the initial knowledge level and the second letter for the level of knowledge gains. Since the HH contains only one observation, this group is omitted in the graph. The vertical axis shows the percentage of those who changed their policy attitudes. The graph shows that the policy attitudes of the high initial knowledge groups were more stable than those of the low initial knowledge groups. And the more knowledge the participants gained, the more frequently their policy attitudes changed except for the LL group. The LL group showed the highest attitude change among all the groups. The result implies that the attitude change of the LL group occurred due to a different reason from other groups. For most participants, the attitude change seems to be information-driven but for the LL group it presumably occurred due to non-attitude. Fortunately, the number of participants classified as LL was small. However, it should not be forgotten that there always will be chances that such a group will remain. The significance of their existence should also be considered further since it might be a sign of a different discourse, not necessarily a sign of irrationality. Their patterns of attitude change might not be random, which should be examined further.

Graph 1: Knowledge Gain and Attitude Change

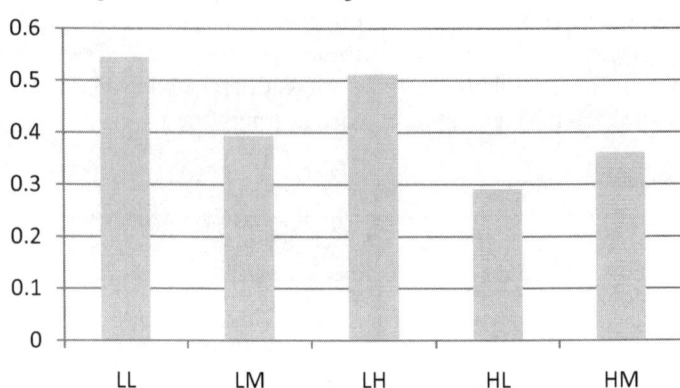

To evaluate the quality of the deliberation process, the questions common to the previous DPs were asked in the Kanagawa DP. As in the previous DPs, the participants of the Kanagawa DP also perceived the process relatively well. 72.9% of them answered that they were able to find out good different opinions. 81.5% found other opinions helpful. 72.9% thought that the opportunity to speak in a discussion group was given equally. 9.9% believed that the facilitator was not neutral (reverse question). 78.0% thought the DP was helpful in policy selection. On the whole, DP has been positively accepted by the majority of the participants in Japan as well. The only exception is the question of satisfaction. Only 62.2% of the participants declared their satisfaction with the discussion. Compared to the previous DPs, we have to admit that the satisfaction level was low. It seems strange that those who perceived the process as equal, neutral, and informative, were not satisfied with it. This contradictory response suggests that the subjective evaluation may not reflect the objective quality of deliberation.

Table 2: Subjective Process Evaluation

Questions concerning deliberative process quality	% of those who agree
1. Equal opportunities to speak in the discussion group were given	72.9%
2. I was satisfied with the discussion	62.2%
3. Others' opinions were helpful	81.5%
4. The facilitator was not neutral (reverse question)	9.9%
5. I was able to find good different opinions	72.9%
6. The DP was helpful in policy selection	78.0%

For objective evaluation of the deliberation process, qualitative text analysis such as "the Discourse Quality Index (DQI)" developed by Steiner et al. (2004) is necessary. Unfortunately, text analysis has not been commonly performed for the evaluation of DP so far except Siu's (2009) study. Through the text analysis of an online DP held in the U.S. she has shown that the opportunity to speak is equally distributed regardless of genders, ages, and ethnicities, and that socio-economic status does not influence discussion. In effect, discourse ethics prevails in minipublics created by DP. The text analysis of the Kanagawa DP has not yet been done. In its stead here let me introduce a preliminary analysis on the distribution of speech opportunities among the participants.

Table 3 shows the gender difference in speech quantity. Quantity of speech is calculated by two indices, one by counting characters and the other by counting the number of speeches par person for one session. It turned out that there was a surprisingly large difference between male and female participants. The male participants talked almost twice as much as the females, measured by the number of characters. On the other hand, the difference in the average number of speeches was not as large as the based on the character count. This means that the men tended to talk longer than the women once they got a chance to speak.

Table 3: Gender Comparison about Opportunity to Speak

Measurement	Male	Female
Number of characters/person	1068.5	510.6
Number of speeches/person	4.0	3.2

Table 4 shows the tendency of speech domination. To evaluate speech domination, three indices are used; the ratio of speech quantity spoken by the most talkative speaker, the ratio spoken by the two most talkative speakers together, and the dominance index. In all indices, the quantity of speech is counted by the number of characters. Domination index is calculated as skewing of the speech accumulation curve. As shown in Graph 2, when the participants are ranked on the horizontal axis according to their speech quantity and their accumulated percentages of speech quantity are plotted on the vertical axis, then a convex curve is derived. If opportunities to speak are equally distributed, the curve becomes a straight line. The more unequally distributed, the area surrounded by the convex curve and the straight line becomes larger. The surrounded area reaches its maximum when the most talkative speaker dominates all of the speeches, which corresponds to the triangle area. Dominance index is defined as the ratio of the surrounded area to the triangle area.

Table 4: Tendency of Speech Domination

Group	Size	Dominance Index	Top 1	Top 1 & 2
A	13	58.0%	21.5%	39.9%
B	14	42.4%	15.9%	28.5%
C	13	62.0%	32.3%	46.4%
E	15	58.7%	15.8%	31.5%
F	13	48.0%	17.7%	34.1%
G	14	74.5%	28.2%	56.1%
H	10	43.6%	18.1%	35.0%
J	13	76.9%	51.9%	65.0%
K	10	53.4%	24.0%	44.8%
avarage		57.5%	25.0%	42.4%

Graph 2: Dominance Index

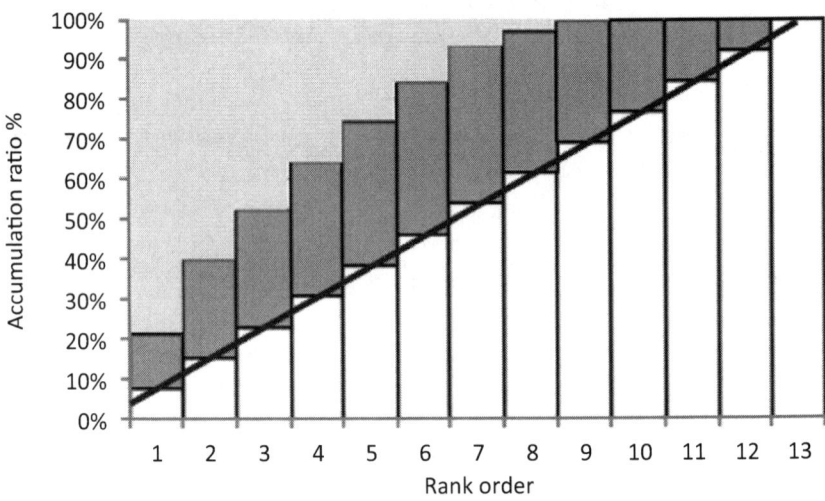

There were eight discussion groups in Kanagawa DP, the size of which was 10 to 15 participants. Table 4 shows the tendency of domination for each group. On average, the most talkative participants talked 25.0% alone and surprisingly the most and the second talkative participants altogether covered 42.4% of all the speeches in the group discussions. In one group, 51.9% of speeches were dominated only by one participant. The objective distribution of speech opportunities turned out to be quite different from the subjective evaluation. I myself attended the discussion groups and got an impression that the discussions were active and well balanced. I observed that one participant moderately controlled another talkative participant trying to keep the chances to speak equal. I thought it was good evidence of discourse ethics. However, my impression was quite different from the objective speech opportunity. Similar impressions might have been held by the other participants. In assessing the quality of the process, relying on only subjective evaluation is risky. It should be complemented by objective evaluation. It will bring about deeper understanding if this speech domination index are checked with other quality indices such as DQI and diversity of opinions.

One of the reasons for the skewed distribution of speech opportunities particularly in group J was considered to be a failure of moderation. Fortunately, most of the moderators trained in the Kanagawa DP project belong to Japan Facilitator Association. They continue to work in all other DPs in Japan and their moderation skill is much improved. Besides that, the longer the participants stay together, the shorter their psychological distance and the smoother their communication. As a matter of fact, in the fourth DP, which was a two night and three day DP organized by Keio University in 2011, it is confirmed by our onsite observation that gender and age influence became smaller than in the Kanagawa DP.

Since speech patterns are culturally sensitive, it may be reflected in the deliberation process. In Japan, men, older, and educated people tend to talk more. However, the fourth case mentioned above indicates that it is possible to make participants immune to such cultural influence if deliberation proceeds in a small groups with trained moderators, even in a country of high context culture, such as Japan.

Furthermore, the contradiction of subjective and objective evaluations hints at the relationship between speech opportunities and learning. When subjective and objective evaluations contradict each other, we tend to think the latter is reliable. But it might be hasty to conclude so. In a paternalistic culture, for example, dominance by an authoritative person may be acceptable because acceptable levels of inequality in speech opportunities depend on reference points and the reference point is probably set high in such a society. If the reference point is set high, subjective evaluation will undervalue the objective level of inequality. Although subjective evaluation deviates from objective reality, it indicates the relative improvement of the process compared to the standard level of each society. In the Kanagawa DP, the opportunities to speak were distributed unequally, but the level of equality might be much improved if compared to the conventional meetings in Japan.

Besides that, our learning capability has some robustness against adverse learning conditions. Unequal speech opportunity is itself normatively undesirable. But under different levels of inequality in terms of speech opportunities, if inequality levels are within a certain threshold, learning through deliberation will occur, which will bring about better judgments. If robustness of our learning capability is high, the threshold for allowing learning is expected to be high. Most participants of the Kanagawa DP thought that the opinions of others were helpful and opportunities were equally given, even though approximately 40% of the discussions were dominated by two participants. This contradiction of objective and subjective evaluation makes sense if the reference point of speech opportunity is set high and learning is robust. However, this explanation is not sufficient to interpret why they showed relatively low satisfaction with the discussions. This is probably because there are some other intervening variables, such as the perceived efficacy of own opinions, at work. In effect, despite the relatively low satisfaction, the level of inequality of speech opportunities can be considered smaller than in conventional meetings and the participants actually learned from other's opinions in a speech situation created by the guidelines of the DP.

However, the quality of deliberation process does not necessarily guarantee the quality of its outcome. So the next question is to what extent the opinions were actually improved? As in the case of representativeness discussed above, opinions are subjective and relational entities. If we cannot identify opinions as intersubjectively understandable relationships among policy attitudes, beliefs, and values, it is difficult for the general public, who do not attend deliberation meetings, to judge whether outcome opinions are meaningful to them or not. When the outcome opinions are more meaningful than the initial ones, we can say opinions are refined. There is supportive evidence of learning as shown in Table 1 and Graph 1. This evidence is not persuasive enough for non-participants to use the outcome opinions for their own policy judgments with confidence. Neither are the subjective evaluations by the participants sufficient for it. We need to develop a method of identifying such meaningful relationships and to check if they are shared by the participants.

Evaluation of Intersubjective Understandability

As Dryzek, Niemeyer, and their group showed (Dryzek and Berejikian 2008; Niemeyer et al. 2005), "Q-methodology" can be used for such a purpose. When applying Q-methodology to identify discourses, any structures among measurement variables are not presupposed. They believe discourses should be identified from subjective responses to measurement variables. To do so, any preconceptions to describe discourses are not necessary. However, thinking about policy judgments, a weak structure can be introduced regardless of the issues to be discussed. It is natural to suppose that policy attitudes are made based on factual judgments and value judgments. Here policy attitude (PA) can be defined as a preference on policy alternatives, value judgment (VJ) as a preference on states of society, factual judgment (FJ) as a forecast of policy influence on states of society, and policy judgment (PJ) as a function which maps a set of factual judgments and value judgments to a policy attitude. If we presuppose such a structure of judgment, then a specific structure can be identified from subjective responses to measurement variables by using Structural Equation Modeling (SEM). Moreover, fitness indicators can be used to evaluate to what extent the judgment structure thus identified is shared by participants intersubjectively. I would like to introduce how to apply SEM to the data obtained at the Kanagawa DP. Before that let me discuss the meaning and the identifiability of an intersubjectively shared structure of judgment.

Following Habermas' argument on discursive rationality (1984, 278), we, as reasonable agents, are supposed to arrive at a universal consensus on truth and moral claims in an ideal speech situation. This assumption is the basis for the belief that through deliberation, unforced collective will formation can be realized. In contrast to other deliberative methods using mini-publics, it is a unique feature of DP that group consensus is not required as an output of deliberation. But as other deliberative methods, DP depends on discursive rationality as a basis of its modus operandi. To require group consensus as an output of deliberation and to presuppose the possibility of universal consensus of judgment are two different things. Without the former requirement, the latter is possible. But without the latter condition, deliberation becomes meaningless, since there is no possibility of mutual learning through communicative action.

Thinking about the degree of discursive rationality in a policy judgment situation, convergence of FJ, VJ, and accordingly PA seems to be a clue of universality, and therefore rationality, achieved through deliberation. However, using the convergence of participants' responses as an indicator of discursive rationality has two problems. Firstly, the convergence might be a result of psychological biases such as group pressure or group polarization. It is difficult to distinguish them from matured opinions. Secondly, we are equipped with only bounded rationality and the ideal speech situation is approachable but never realizable in a real speech situation. On that condition, convergence of participants' responses is not always expected. In fact, such convergence has not been observed in the Kanagawa DP.

In Table 5, the measurement variables of the Kanagawa DP are listed. There are ten variables categorized as FJ, seven variables as VJ, and two variables as PA. To check the convergence of judgments, the variances of pre- and post-deliberation are compared for each FJ and VJ in Table 5. As a result of statistical test of variance, no significant difference has been observed for all the variables at 0.05 level of significance.

Table 5: Measurement Variables of the Kanagawa DP

Category	Measurement variables	
FJ	x1	Positive impacts on regional economy
	x2	Negative impacts on attachment and local identity
	x3	Positive impacts on the efficiency of local governments
	x4	Positive impacts on the employment in overall Japan
	x5	Positive impacts on the government flexibility to local needs
	x6	Positive impacts on Japan's competitively
	x7	Positive impacts on the level of citizen participation
	x8	Disparity expansion in terms of educational quality among regions
	x9	Disparity expansion in terms of economy quality among regions
	x10	Intra region disparity expansion
VJ	x11	Job opportunity
	x12	Preservation of traditional and local industry
	x13	Narrowing gap between rich and poor
	x14	Economic growth
	x15	Japan's economic competitively
	x16	Equal opportunity of education
	x17	Attachment and local place identity
PA	x18	Local autonomy on taxation
	x19	Regional Governments wider than existing prefecture

Table 6: Comparison of Variances between Pre (T2) and Post (T3) Deliberation

FJ	x1	x2	x3	x4	x5	x6	x7	x8	x9	x10
σ T2	0.98	1.05	1.11	0.61	0.88	0.76	1.03	4.81	4.79	4.94
σ T3	0.83	1.00	0.96	0.46	0.99	0.75	1.05	5.41	5.01	4.03
p-value	0.36	0.74	0.40	0.12	0.51	0.94	0.89	0.48	0.79	0.23

VJ	x11	x12	x13	x14	x15	x16	x16
σ T2	3.21	4.09	5.72	4.20	3.88	3.72	4.89
σ T3	4.18	4.08	4.15	4.37	4.02	4.28	4.64

Does the result imply that the Kanagawa DP did not improve its participants' opinions? The answer is no because there remains a possibility that some policy judgment framework was shared by the participants while the participants keep holding different judgments for each FJ and VJ. When such a framework is shared, it is possible for the participants to understand mutually the difference of policy attitudes.

Social construction of subjectively shared framework of judgment is an important aspect of discursive rationality. The possibility of such a framework is discussed by Niemeyer and Dryzek (2007) under the concept of "intersubjective rationality".

Figure 1 shows the structural change of FJ. Firstly, using ten variables of FJ, exploratory factor analysis was done. It is confirmed that there were three groups of variables. The first group was composed of the judgments to predict positive impacts of the Do-Shu system on the regional economy and government efficiency. The second group was composed of the negative predictions for the Do-Shu system, such as expansion of inter and intra-regional disparity in terms of economy and public services. The third group concerned loss of local identity, and contained only one variable.

Based on this result, introducing two latent variables which explain the first two groups, explanatory factor analysis (EFA) was done to compare pre and post judgment structures. The result shows that the coefficients from the latent variables to their corresponding observed variables remained at the same level of positive values and that the correlation between the two latent variables was also kept at the same level of negative value. It is known that the participants perceived there three groups of issues related to FJ at the beginning and kept the same perception after the deliberation. The participants who predicted positive economic impacts and public services tended to disagree with the prediction of disparity expansions. This tendency did not change after the deliberation. However, one change was observed. The correlation between the second latent variable and the prediction of local identity loss changed from non-significant to significantly positive. This parameter change indicates that before the deliberation, local identity loss had been considered separately but after the deliberation the participants began to link it to the other issues of negative impacts.

Figure 1: Comparison of Structures of FJ between Pro (T2) and Post (T3) Deliberation

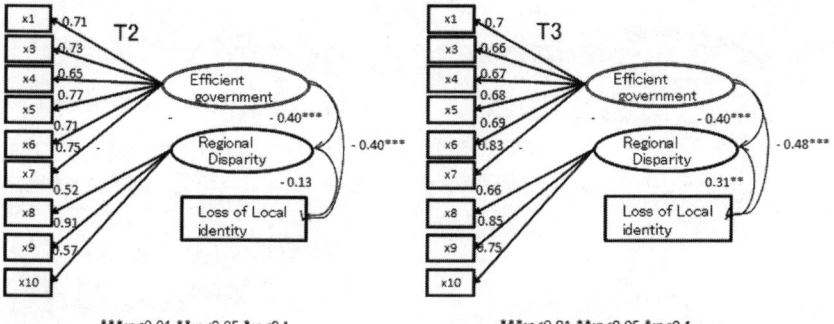

***;p<0.01,**;p<0.05,*;p<0.1   ***;p<0.01,**;p<0.05,*;p<0.1

Next, SEM was conducted to identify the relationship between FJ and PA, using the structure of FJ identified above. Two variables listed as PA in Table 5 were used as dependent variables. The first dependent variable is a preference for the policy to increase local autonomy in legislation and taxation. A preference for the policy to widen the administrative area of the regional government is the second dependent variable. Both are the two important aspects of the Do-Shu system. To support these two policies means to support the Do-Shu System. The result was shown in Figure 2. First of all, all of the fitness indicators were improved after the deliberation. Fitness indicators show how well the model structure explains the observed data. The improvement of fitness indicators suggests that the number of participants who shared the structure of policy judgment increased. Both stable and unstable relationships between FJ and PA were observed. The coefficients of the first latent variable to explain the two dependent variables remained positive, which indicates that those who believe positive impacts kept supporting the Do-Shu system. If one looks at the coefficient values in more detail, one can see an interesting difference. The coefficient to explain the second policy attitude, the preference for widening the administrative area, was larger than the one to explain the first policy attitude, the preference for local autonomy. After the deliberation, the latter became much smaller. During the discussion, there appeared the opinions that to keep the national minimum is a matter of citizens' right not the matter of efficiency and that local autonomy may violate this right. It is highly probable that many participants came to believe that some standards of public services such as quality of compulsory education and labor standards should be guaranteed by the state government. They realized the complexity of the autonomy issue and did not support it simply because it might bring about efficient governments.

Figure 2: Comparison of Policy Judgment Structure

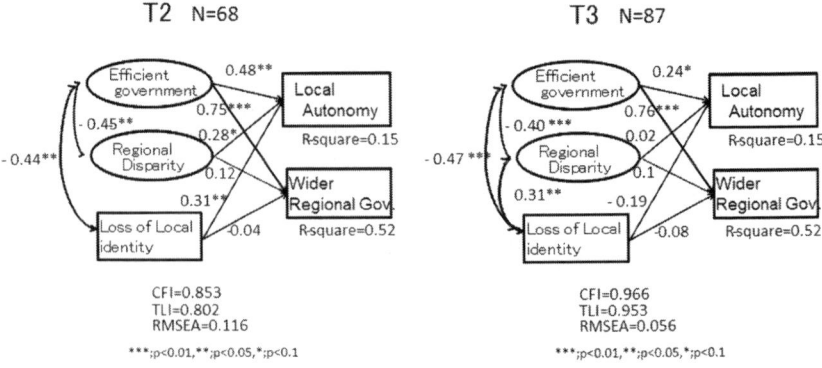

Logically strange relationships were also observed in pre-deliberation. The coefficients from the second latent variable and the prediction of local identity loss to the first policy attitude, the preference for local autonomy, had been positive. The positive coefficients indicate that the participants who predicted negative impacts, i.e. disparity in expansion and local identity loss, supported local autonomy. It did not make sense because if they predicted negative impacts, they would not have supported the Do-Shu system. However, these relationships disappeared after the deliberation. Thus judgments became consistent after the deliberation. Some participants chose the Do-Shu system without considering intricate relationships among the positive and the negative impacts at the start of the deliberation, but after the deliberation they chose policies based on deeper understanding of them. Such participants' learning is considered to be reflected in this structural change of judgment.

SEM can be used to identify intersubjectively shared framework and to evaluate the degree of its sharing. The convergence of participants' judgments for each policy-related issues and sharing framework of judgment are different. Using SEM, it was shown that the participants of the Kanagawa DP did not come to a consensus for each judgment but they shared the policy judgment framework so that they could understand different policy attitudes according to the same framework. Even in an adverse speech situation, where the 40% of the speech opportunities were dominated by several contributors, the participants still learned from one another. There is a possibility that the learning was influenced by the few speech dominators. But if their influences were strong, the convergence of opinions for each judgment should have been observed. Another question is that if facilitation was improved so that less talkative participants had more chances to talk, what would be the opinions after deliberation? Many questions remain to be answered but the analytical technique I have shown here will be helpful to identify opinions as subjective and relational entities.

Conclusion

The success of DP, broadly speaking that of mini-publics, depends on how to create a deliberation space sufficiently close to the ideal speech situation. Since mini-publics are composed of randomly selected citizens, its representativeness is expected higher than other conventional chambers of discourse. Since the size of mini-publics is kept relatively small, it is easier to create a quasi-experimental setting close enough to ideal speech situation. In this chapter, it is shown that DP can achieve better representativeness and deliberation quality compared to the conventional meetings. There remain some problems such as low acceptance rate to take part in the deliberation meeting but DP works in Japan as well. Cultural influence on the deliberation process may differ from one society to another. Nonetheless, it is still possible to make the participants immune to such cultural influences if deliberation proceeds in small groups with trained moderators, even in a country of high context culture. As a result, the participants share the policy judgment framework so that they can understand different policy attitudes under the same framework.

However, the success at a micro level does not necessary lead to the success at the macro level. Although Goodin and Dryzek (2006) sorted out the possible "macro political impacts", they admitted that "large questions remain unresolved concerning how citizen deliberation can be consequential in democratic practice." In fact, the result of the Japanese energy DP held by the NPU was already forgotten by the general public even though it had gained nationwide attention only six months before. The micro-macro gap reflects the gap between the few selected participants and the rest of society at large. The usability of mini-publics for the rest is inevitably "trust based" (Warren 2009). How to design the interface between mini-publics and the larger society for increasing trust is not clear yet. The key to bridge the gap is understandability of the outcome opinions. If they are intersubjectively understandable and meaningful, then non-participants as well as participants will use them for their own policy judgments, so that the outcome of mini-publics will link to the collective will formation at the macro level. In this chapter, it is shown how SEM can be used to identify intersubjectively shared framework. When SEM is applied, it is supposed that opinions are subjective and relational entities, whose structure should be identified from the subjective responses. In this sense, the idea behind this method is same as Q-methodology.

However, our method differs in three respects from Q-methodology. Firstly, a weak causal structure among FJ, VJ, and PA is presupposed in our method. Secondly, Q-methodology is used only for identifying discourses but we use SEM for evaluating a degree of how judgment framework is shared intersubjectively by DP participants. Thirdly, while Q-methodology employs a systematic questionnaire design, in which vast amount of discourse related texts information are collected as corpus, we followed a conventional questionnaire design procedure. The systematic collection of corpus can lower arbitrariness in the process of questionnaire design but the cost of data collection and text analysis is large. As a next step, we are exploring the possibility to apply text processing technology to lower the cost. Aside from these differences, both methodologies have a common problem. Statistical analysis is an effective tool to find latent structures behind data. But it is ordinary citizens who judge whether the identified structure of opinions is understandable/meaningful or not. For ordinary citizens, it is difficult to understand the technical detail of the statistical analysis. The structure of opinions identified using advanced statistics should be explained or presented in understandable formats.

References

Cohen, Joshua, and Charles Sabel. 1997. "Directly Deliberative Polyarchy." *European Law Journal* 3 (4): 312–342.

Dryzek, John S. 2001. "Legitimacy and Economy in Deliberative Democracy." *Political Theory* 29 (5): 651–669.

Dryzek, John S., and Jeffrey Berejikian. 1993. "Reconstructive Democracy." *American Political Science Review* 87 (1): 48–60.

Dryzek, John S., and Simon Niemeyer. 2008. "Discursive Representation." *American Political Science Review* 102 (4): 481–493.

Fishkin, James S. 2009. *When the People Speak.* Oxford: Oxford University Press.

Fishkin, James S., and Robert C. Luskin. 2005. "Experimenting with a Democratic Ideal: Deliberative Polling and Public Opinion." *Acta Politica* 40: 284–298.

Habermas, Jürgen. 1984. *The Theory of Communicative Action. Vol. I: Reason and the Rationalization of Society.* Boston, M. A.: Beacon.

Habermas, Jürgen. 1996. "Three Normative Models of Democracy." In *Democracy and Difference*, ed. Seyla Benhabib, 21–30. Princeton, NJ: Princeton University Press.

Hobson, Kersty, and Simon Niemeyer. 2011. "Public responses to climate change: The role of deliberation in building capacity for adaptive action." *Global Environmental Change* 21 (3): 957–971.

Mikami, Naoyuki. 2012. "Consensus Conference." In *Challenge to Deliberative Democracy,* ed. Hajime Shinohara, 33–60. Tokyo: Iwanami Publishing Company. (三上直之. 2012. コンセンサス会議:市民による科学技術のコントロール. In 討議デモクラシーの挑戦, 篠原一編, 33–60. 東京:岩波書店).

Niemeyer, Simon, and John S. Dryzek. 2007. "The Ends of Deliberation: Meta-consensus and Intersubjective Rationality as Ideal Outcomes." *Swiss Political Science Review* 13 (4) (Winter): 497–526.

Niemeyer, Simon, Judith Petts, and Kersty Hobson. 2005. "Rapid Climate Change and Society: Assessing Responses and Thresholds." *Risk Analysis* 25 (6) (December): 1443–1456.

Sakano, Tatsuro. 2012. "Deliberative Poll". In *Challenge to Deliberative Democracy,* ed. Hajime Shinohara, 3–31. Tokyo: Iwanami Publishing Company. (坂野達郎. 2012. 討議型世論調査DP:民意の変容を世論調査で確かめる. In 討議デモクラシーの挑戦岩波書店, 篠原一編, 3–31. 東京: 岩波書店).

Shinoto, Akinori. 2012. "Citizens' Deliberation". In *Challenge to Deliberative Democracy,* ed. Hajime Shinohara, 99–115. Tokyo: Iwanami Publishing Company. (篠藤明徳. 2012. 市民討議会：日本の政治文化を拓く In 討議デモクラシーの挑戦, 篠原一編, 99–115. 東京：岩波書店).

Siu, Alice. 2009. *Look Who's Talking.* Ph.D. Dissertation. Stanford: Dept. of Communication, Stanford University.

Smith, Graham. 2012. "Deliberative democracy and mini-publics." In *Evaluating Democratic Innovations: Curing the Democratic Malaise?*, eds. Kenneth Newton and Brigitte Geissel, 102–123. London, GB: Routledge.

Steiner, Jürg, André Bächtiger, Markus Spörndli, and Marco R. Steenbergen. 2004. *Deliberative Politics in Action: Analyzing Parliamentary Discourse.* Cambridge: Cambridge University Press.

Warren, Mark E. 2009. "Two Trust-Based Uses of Mini-publics in Democracy." Paper presented at the conference of the American Political Science Association Annual Meeting on Democracy and the Deliberative Society. Toronto. Accessed June 15, 2005. http://papers.ssrn.com/sol3/papers.cfm?abstract_id=1449781.

Section III.
Deliberative Quality

André Bächtiger & Jürg Steiner

Chapter Nine. How to Measure the Quality of Deliberation? The Discourse Quality Index (DQI) as a Possible Tool

Introduction

In everyday language, deliberation is often used as a synonym for any kind of political talk. In the scholarly literature, the concept of deliberation has a more specific meaning. There are several elements to the concept. First, arguments must be justified with reasons that may also be supported by appropriate stories. Second, arguments must be framed in terms of the common good, which does not exclude that self-interests come into play, if they are shown to be compatible with the common good. Third, arguments of others must be treated with respect. Fourth, actors must be willing to yield to the force of the better argument. Fifth, all actors must have the opportunity to speak up in a free and unconstrained way. While in principle these five deliberative elements can be measured in an empirical way, a sixth element is hard if not impossible to measure, namely the truthfulness with which arguments are articulated (Steiner 2011).

How do we get an empirical handle at the five deliberative elements that in principle can be measured? One often used research strategy is to assemble groups of citizens and to encourage them to behave in a deliberative way. One encouragement is to procure participants with briefing material on the issues to be discussed. Another encouragement is to train moderators so that they are able to stimulate a high level of deliberation. The best known research based on this approach is Deliberative Polling (Fishkin 2009). We have no fundamental objection to this approach. It is fitting, when the goal is to investigate whether a high level of deliberation helps to change opinions. Such changes could indeed be demonstrated, when Deliberative Polling was done in many parts of the world (Fishkin 2011). We acknowledge that encouragement as done in Deliberative Polling can indeed help to reach a high level of deliberation.

The problem is, however, that we do not know how high this level actually is and how much it varies from group to group and from individual to individual. This is precisely what we need to know, if we want to investigate how variation in the level of deliberation can be explained in its antecedents and consequences. The theoretically crucial questions are what factors contribute to a high level of deliberation both at group and individual levels and how variation in the level of deliberation influences the outcomes of the discussions. To answer these questions we must have an instrument to measure the level of deliberation. In our research group we have developed such an instrument with the *Discourse Quality Index (DQI)* (Steiner et al. 2005).

The Deliberative Quality Index

What are the main features of the DQI? The units of analysis are individual speech acts. Whenever an actor speaks up, this is considered a speech act. It does not matter whether the actor utters only a few words or gives a long speech. When an actor speaks up again later in the discussion, this is treated as another speech act since its level of deliberation may differ from the earlier speech act. The codebook contains categories for the individual deliberative elements, for the aspect of listening, for example:

1. The speaker ignores arguments and questions addressed to him or her by other participants.
2. The speaker does not ignore arguments and questions addressed to him or her by other participants but distorts these arguments and questions.
3. The speaker does not ignore arguments and questions addressed to him or her by other participants and engages these arguments and questions in a correct and undistorted way.
4. No arguments and questions addressed to speaker.

For the coding it is important that the overall context of the discussion is considered. For the above coding categories, one would have to determine, for example, whether arguments and questions are truly distorted. When a statistical figure mentioned by a previous speaker is not exactly repeated by a later speaker, this may indeed be a significant distortion, or it may be an inadvertent error without significance in the given context. A computer program could not take account of such subtleties of interpretation. To work with the DQI in a competent way, we need well trained coders, who are able to immerse themselves into all the complexities of an ongoing debate. The debates are always audio-taped and if possible also video-taped. At least two coders go through the same material. In our research group, we have used the DQI both for parliamentary debates (Steiner et al. 2005) and more recently also for ordinary citizens (Steiner 2012). Reliability tests are usually of a sufficiently high level. The DQI has now been used by colleagues in different parts of the world both at the elite level and the level of ordinary citizens.

The purpose of this chapter is to illustrate with the transcripts of the Australian Citizens' Conference how the DQI is applied (Carson and Gastil 2013). Thereby, we also want to show problems that may arise using the DQI. It is a flexible instrument that needs to be adjusted for specific research projects. For our illustrative coding we have randomly chosen a debate, and this happened to be the second debate on the second day, September 4, 2009. Of this debate we code the beginning. The moderator was Stuart who by way of introduction asked participants to indicate what they like most about Australian democracy. The two key words coming up were security and freedom. After this warm-up introduction the real debate began. Stuart asked of how Australian democracy could be made better. The first sequence was short with only three speech acts. The topic was education. Alisa spoke first (to make the paper reader-friendly, we put the transcripts in bold letters).

Alisa: I think our local MPs, I mean we put them in, should do a little more, make themselves a little more available to the education of the children. In my era, we used to have them come around and introduce themselves. I don't think that's being done as much, it might be in some, but I don't think overall it's being done enough.

What should be done in education according to Alisa? Members of Parliament should make themselves more available to the education of children. She does not give any reason how this would help education. She only offers a personal story to support her claim. When she was a school child herself, MP's used to visit schools, which nowadays happens rarely if at all. How do we code this speech act according to the level of justification? Here are the corresponding coding categories:

1. The speaker does not present any arguments (asks, for example, merely for additional information)
2. The speaker only says that X should or should not be done, that it is a wonderful or a terrible idea, etc. But no reason is given for why X should or should not be done.
3. The speaker justifies only with illustrations why X should or should not be done.
4. The speaker gives a reason Y why X should or should not be done. But no linkage is made why Y will contribute to X.
5. The speaker gives a reason Y why X should or should not be done, and a linkage is made why Y will contribute to X.
6. The speaker gives at least two reasons why X should be done and for at least two reasons a linkage is made with X.

The speech act of Alisa falls under category 3. In the initial Habermasian version of deliberation, stories had no deliberative quality; in recent years, however, there is increasing recognition that some stories may contribute to a deliberative atmosphere (Steiner 2012). They must be relevant, however, to the issue under discussion. Does the story of Alisa fulfill this criterion? We do not think so. She does not say how the visits of MP's helped the education of children. After all, one could also imagine that these visits merely disturbed the normal school day. Alisa does not give any hints of how the visits helped with her own education or the education of other children. For further developments of the DQI we have to come to terms with how to distinguish stories with regard to their relevance for the issue under discussion. This will not be an easy task and has certainly to be done within the overall context of the discussion. For the case of Alisa, it is easy to determine that her story was not relevant, but there are many other cases where classification will not be so easy.

Let us continue for this initial speech act with the other deliberative elements. Did Alisa refer to the common good? Here are the coding categories:

1. The speaker refers to benefits and costs for all groups represented in the experiment.
2. The speaker does not refer to benefits and costs for all groups represented in the experiment.

Code 1 is used if a speaker considers the implications of a proposal for all groups represented in the experiment, which reveals a common good orientation. Alisa does not make any such references so that code 2 applies. To get at the aspect of the common good, we also used coding categories tapping at whether the speaker refers to abstract principles such as social justice, quality of life and peace. Since Alisa does not make any such references, she gets code 2 for the following categories:

1. The speaker refers to abstract principles, for example social justice, quality of life, and peace.
2. The speaker does not refer to any abstract principles

With regard to respect, we want to know whether a speaker uses any foul language. Alisa does not, so that she gets code 3 for these categories:

1. The speaker uses foul language to attack other participants on a personal level. Include also mild foul language, not only statements such as "you are a liar" but also statements such as "you seem a little confused." Code the names of the participants attacked in this way and give the exact quote of the foul language.
2. The speaker uses foul language to attack the arguments of other participants but abstains from personal attacks. Here again include also mild foul language, not only statements such as "this argument is stupid" but also statements such as "this argument is a little weak." Code the names of the participants whose arguments are attacked in this way and give the exact quote of the foul language.
3. No foul language.

Alisa also does not use any explicit respectful language, so that code 2 applies to the following categories:

1. The speaker uses explicit respectful language towards other participants and/or their arguments. Include also moderately respectful language, not only statements such as "your argument is truly brilliant" but also statements such as "your argument is not bad."
2. No explicit respectful language used.

For listening, we gave the coding categories already earlier in the paper. As the first speaker in the debate, Alisa had not yet had to deal with arguments and questions addressed to her, so code 4 applies. We also investigated whether a speaker changed his or her position. As first speaker, Alisa could not yet react to other positions so code 5 applies to the following categories.

1. The speaker indicates a change of position. Gives as reason for change arguments heard during the experiment.
2. The speaker indicates a change of position. Does not refer to arguments heard during the experiment.
3. The speaker does not indicate a change of position. But does acknowledge the value of other positions heard during the experiment.
4. The speaker does not indicate a change of position and does not acknowledge the value of other positions heard during the experiment
5. As yet no other position articulated

Finally, Alisa could speak in an unconstrained way, which gives her code 2 for these categories:

1. The speaker indicates verbally or by body language that he or she is constrained by the behavior of other participants (interruptions, private conversations, body language such as making faces, yawning, etc.).
2. The speaker can speak in an unconstrained way.

After Alisa spoke, Basil asks the following question:

Basil: Has anyone here emailed their local member and had a response?

Although Basil asks only a brief question, she must be coded according to all categories of the DQI. Her summary coding reads as follows:

Level of justification: 1
Common good: 2
Abstract principles: 2

Foul language: 3
Respectful language: 2
Listening: 3
Force of better argument: 5
Constraints: 2

This coding means that Basil did not take or change his position, did not refer to the common good or abstract principles; he neither used foul nor respectful language, he did listen to the previous speaker without distortions and could speak in an unconstrained way. The answer of Alisa to Basil reads as follows:

Alisa: I've emailed him and haven't got an answer.

For this short answer, she gets exactly the same coding as for Basil above. What is the overall deliberative quality of this short sequence on education? It is quite low. First of all, the level of participation is low with only two actors speaking up. Then the proposal under discussion is not justified and not even debated. There are no references to the common good or abstract principles, and no explicit respectful language is used. The sequence is deliberative, however, in the sense that the actors can speak up in an unconstrained way, do not use foul language and listen to each other.

The next sequence in the debate is much longer and is introduced by Peter:

Peter: Well one of the things that we thought was good was the House (of Parliament), sometimes you get a degree of bipartisanship of working together and it only seems to happen during crisis times so that would be good is if we could have a system where some of the best and brightest from both sides of politics tended to work more collaboratively. If we could encourage that somehow, get them to put the best and brightest in, rather than being always picking at each other for political reasons. If we can try and have them conversing in a way which tries to get a better idea rather than ...

Peter is not very articulate in what he proposes to better Australian democracy. Basically, he suggests more bipartisanship with the best and brightest, which would better Australian democracy. With regard to justification we give him code 2; he makes a proposal without further justification. His summary coding reads as follows:

Level of Justification: 2
Common good: 2
Abstract principles: 2
Foul Language: 3

Respectful language: 2
Listening: 4
Force of better argument: 5
Constraints: 2

We were somewhat hesitant of how to code Peter with regard to the common good. In referring to bipartisanship and collaboration of the best and brightest, he seems to have the common good of the whole country in mind, but he makes this claim only in a vague and implicit way. In order to stimulate further deliberative discussion, Peter should have said in an explicit way how his proposal serves the common good, so he gets code 2. For the other categories, our coding for Peter is straight forward and does not need comments.

Alisa: Tearing each other apart, yeah.

For the remainder of the paper we will mention only codes that are noteworthy one way or another. For Alisa in this speech act it is noteworthy that she listened to Peter without distorting what he said (code 3 for listening). She does not like that politicians tear each other apart and thus, given the context, supports bipartisanship but without giving any reason, so that she gets code 2 for level of justification.

Peter: Rather than tearing each other apart, work together to try and …
Alisa: Yes, strengthen.
Peter: The thing is that they often have fixed ideas, fixed ideology, which are diametrically opposed. That era is slowly going now. We've got problems, we need to have people working together to get better solutions so the more they can do that the better.

These three speech acts are very interactive with Alisa and Peter listening to each other without distorting what the other says (code 3 for listening for all three speech acts). They interrupt each other, which does not seem to bother them so that we give code 2 for constraints for all three speech acts. Peter and Alisa stick with their position that Australia needs more bipartisanship. At first, they still do not give any reason why more bipartisanship will be good for Australian democracy (thus code 2 for level of justification for the first two speech acts). Peter, however, in the last speech act, begins to articulate as reason that bipartisanship leads to better solutions, but he does not make a linkage between bipartisanship and better solutions (thus, code 4 for justification).

Marc: As a follow on from that, we're more likely to have a better democracy if MP's tend to affect the wishes of the electorate rather than the wishes of the party.

Marc brings a new argument into the discussion; democracy would be improved if MP's would follow the wishes of the electorate and not of their party. But he does not give a reason why this would improve democracy (code 2 for justification).

Peter: Yes, a good point.

Peter supports the proposal of Marc, but without further justification (code 2 for justification). For explicit respect toward other participants he gets code 1.

Allan: And just to follow on from what you were saying, I think the party machines of all parties have got to start realizing, instead of trying to control the parties with their own people in the right positions they've got to have the best people in the positions of the people.

This is quite an incoherent statement. Allan seems to argue that political parties should support the best people rather than their own people. Since this suggestion is not justified in any way, Allan gets code 2 for justification.

Peter: Yes, that's a good one.

Peter claims to understand what Allan said, but since Peter does not elaborate in any way, it is unclear what is going on in this exchange, certainly nothing at a high level of deliberation. But for respectful language Peter still gets code 1.

Allan: Because people are getting a bit sick of it, you know. Like I'm only using this, I am only using this for an example. Now some of the people that they've had in the positions there is only through the left or the right wanting to keep control of the people, they haven't had an idea, have they?

This speech act is a continuation of what Allan said before, but since Peter said something in between, it is considered a new speech act. This time, Allan offers additional information that people are sick of politics and that in order to get a political position one must be a political hack of the left or the right. This makes code 1 for justification because he offers merely new information

Marc: That's sort of illustrated back few days ago, you don't have members of the opposition in cabinet.

Marco adds more information, thus code 1 for justification.

Peter: That's right in America. Obama has just put in a Republican as one of his people.

Peter still adds more information (code 1 for justification)

Basil: That's the interesting difference, they pick the best person. I mean hopefully they aren't just doing favors and expecting paybacks, that's always possible but really they should actually put the best person qualified rather than just using the position as payback or finding a job for a mate. They should put someone that's got some intellect, someone who's got some qualifications, some experience in the portfolio, in the area.

Basil argues that people with intellect, qualifications, and experience should get political positions. This is formulated more specifically than was done by other actors earlier in the discussion, but Basil still does not formulate in an explicit way how this would help Australian democracy. Therefore he still gets only code 2 for justification.

Marc: And he just gave his opponent one of the top jobs.

Marc gives more information on the Obama Administration (code 1 for justification).

Basil: Yeah.

The discussion continues to be interactive with participants listening to each other without distortions (code 3 for listening here and for previous speakers).

Allan: But I can't see too, what's wrong with a government, for example, just say treasury, now treasury's an important job and law. Alright now if they haven't got someone with that expertise why can't they have somebody out like academic or something like that and say, we want you to look after that department.

Taking the Treasury as an example, Allan suggests that an academic should run such a department if there is lack of expertise. No reason is given for this argument, so that code 2 for justification.

Alisa: Like an assembly
Allan: … but before they can …
Basil: They do, they have secretaries.

Here the actors interrupt each other, but they do not complain, which is why we used code 2 for constraints.

Allan: … yeah, but why can't they ask another, like an academic to act, someone that they want, but that person has to go before, because they have to go before the Senate committee and the Senate has to ask them questions to make sure their interest aren't conflicting.

Allan repeats his argument that sometimes academics need to step in, but he offers now a reason why this would not be a problem since hearings in the Senate would make sure that there are no conflicts of interest. This linkage, however, is not further justified, so code 4 was applied to the justification.

Marc: **There's one problem with that, you end up with a situation where you have somebody like Condoleezza Rice who is not elected by the people, running the country.**

With this speech act a new dynamic comes into play because Marc is the first to object to what the previous actor has proposed. Using the example of Condoleezza Rice, he objects to the idea that academics should be appointed to high level political positions. He gives a reason for this position, namely that academics are not elected by the people, but does not justify the linkage (code 4 for justification).

Allan: **Yeah, true.**

With the response of Allan the categories of the force of the better argument come into play. Is Allan convinced by the argument of Marc and changes his position with regard to academics in high political positions? It is not clear to what Allan is referring to when he says "true". Does he only acknowledge that Rice was not elected by the people, or does he go a step further in accepting the position of Marc? Given this uncertainty of how to interpret this speech act of Allan, we give no code at all rather forcing a coding decision that we cannot justify in good conscience.

Peter: **Yeah, that's right. Basically you want somebody elected but the people should choose somebody who's qualified. Actually, well, the people don't choose who goes in the portfolio, it's simply the responsibility of the Prime Minister to make sure that the person who goes in the portfolio is not just to pay back to a mate or pay back to a faction. It should be the best person qualified for the job.**

At first, Peter argues that people should elect high level officials, but then he remembers that cabinet members are appointed by the Prime Minister. All the while he repeats that the best qualified persons should be chosen. He does not give any reasons for anything that he suggests (code 2 for justification).

Marc: **That's only the case in the Liberal party. Quite often for example at the State level the corpus selects the government ministers.**

Marc challenges the information given by Peter. The DQI does not have categories to take account of such differences on factual matters. For the further development of the index we have to think of how to add the epistemic dimension of information entering the discussion. How accurate is the information? How contested is the information? It will not be easy to find corresponding categories that will lead to reliable and valid coding.

Allan: **But if you have an elected government, like who using that particular person, just say for example like the Labour party, now there's a lot of people been elected in the Labour party and just say if the treasurer wasn't doing a good job and he never had anybody else to step into the position why can't he say, well, I propose for this academic or whatever to take over the treasury department but has to go through …**

Allan sticks with his position that academics should be appointed if nobody else is qualified. He acknowledges, however, the value of the position of Marc so that code 3 for the force of the better argument.

Marc: **I think as the two of us here responded already to the question in saying that we really need the top person elected by the people.**

This is code 4 for force of the better argument since Marc also sticks to his position but does not acknowledge the value of what Allan said.

Conclusion

There are still eight other speech acts in this sequence on the issue of who should be appointed to high level political positions. Since the nature of the discussion remains the same, we stop here and attempt a summary evaluation of the deliberative quality of this sequence. This is done in a new, 'holistic' way: instead of simply aggregating all individual speech acts (as with the original version of the DQI), we now perform a so-called 'constitutive' evaluation, by highlighting whether certain quality standards of the DQI are present or absent during the whole debate (Gerber et al. 2011).

1. The discussion was deliberative in the sense that nobody complained to be constrained.
2. The discussion was also deliberative in the sense that no foul language was used.
3. With regard to listening the discussion was also deliberative. There was not a single instance where someone ignored questions or arguments addressed to him or her. There was also no case where someone distorted what previous speakers had said. All in all, the discussion was very interactive

4. There were occasional instances where explicit respectful language was used toward other participants.
5. The lowest aspect with regard to deliberation was in how arguments were justified. There was not a single situation where a reason was linked in a coherent way to a conclusion. This low level of justification may have to do with the topic of this sequence of the discussion. How political positions should be filled goes into deep issues of democratic theory, and one can hardly expect that ordinary citizens are able to put forward well justified arguments in this respect. Therefore, for the interpretation of the level of justification one has to take account of the complexity of the issue under discussion.
6. There were no cases where someone in an explicit way referred to the common good or abstract principles
7. With regard to the force of the better argument, there was only one situation of disagreement about a proposal, and no side changed its position.

With these coding illustrations, we wished to show that it is feasible to code speech acts with the Discourse Quality Index (DQI). We also wished to show, however, that it is sometimes not very easy to make coding decisions. Coding, after all, is always a question of interpretation. Despite all the coding difficulties, we generally reach quite high reliability when different persons code the same speech acts (Steiner et al. 2005, 71–72). We also wished to show that the DQI is a flexible measuring instrument that can and should be further developed and improved.

References

Carson, Lyn, and John Gastil. 2013. *The Australian Citizens' Parliament and the Future of Deliberative Democracy.* Pennsylvania: Pennsylvania State University Press.

Converse, Philip E. 1994. "Ideology and Discontent." In *The Nature of Belief Systems in Mass Publics.* Edited by Philip E. Converse. New York: Free Press.

Druckman, James N., and Kjersten R. Nelson. 2003. "Framing and deliberation: How citizens' conversations limit elite influence." *American Journal of Political Science* 47: 729–745.

Fishkin, James S. 2009. *When the People Speak. Deliberative Democracy and Public Consulting.* Oxford: Oxford University Press.

Fishkin, James S. 2011. "Deliberative Democracy in Context: Reflections on Theory and Practice." Paper Presented at the Conference on Epistemic Democracy in Practice, October 20–22.

Gerber, Marlène, André Bächtiger, Susumu Shikano, Simon Reber and Samuel Rohr. 2011. "How Deliberative are Deliberative Opinion Polls? Measurement Issues and Evidence from Europolis." Paper presented at the Joint Sessions of the ECPR Workshops, April 12–17.

Steiner, Jürg. 2011. "Truthfulness (Wahrhaftigkeit) in the deliberative model of democracy." Paper Presented at the Conference on Epistemic Democracy in Practice, October 20–22.

Steiner, Jürg. 2012. *The Foundations of Deliberative Democracy. Empirical Research and Normative Implications.* Cambridge: Cambridge University Press.

Steiner Jürg, André Bächtiger, Markus Spörndli, and Marco R. Steenbergen. 2004. *Deliberative Politics in Action: Analyzing Parliamentary Discourse.* Cambridge: Cambridge University Press.

Marco R. Steenbergen, André Bächtiger,
Seraina Pedrini & Thomas Gautschi

Chapter Ten. Information, Deliberation, and Direct Democracy: Evidence from the Swiss Expulsion Initiative

Introduction

Democratic political theory has taken a clear deliberative turn over the past decade and democratic practice has followed a parallel development[1]. Through deliberative polls, citizen assemblies and juries, as well as other formats, a deliberative niche has been created, which is still small in most places but gaining in prominence. Deliberation, however, is nowhere the dominant form of democracy. It co-exists with other models, namely the direct and representative democratic forms. This raises important empirical and theoretical questions about the interplay between deliberation, on one hand, and these other models of democracy, on the other.

Not much has been written about the interplay between deliberative and direct democracy but from the scant extant literature one immediately gleans that the relationship is complex. Chambers (2001) seems pessimistic about the deliberative potential in direct democratic processes. In contrast, Gastil and Richards (2012) persuasively argue that deliberative processes may be essential for direct democracy, not least because they can help to create informed public opinion (Fishkin 1997). Given the rather immediate policy implications of direct democratic votes, the need for an informed mass public looms rather large in initiatives and referendums. Direct democracy may thus need deliberative democracy at the same time that its very design undermines the latter.

In this chapter, we explore the relationship between deliberation and direct democracy in Switzerland, focusing on a prominent vote in 2010, which concerned the expulsion of foreigners with a criminal record, and analyze to what extent meaningful deliberation could be organized around the expulsion initiative. We find disappointing results, in line with Chamber's expectations. Despite the relatively poor levels of deliberation, however, meaningful knowledge gains could be

---

1   The results presented in this paper were made possible through generous funding of the Swiss National Science Foundation (SNF) through the second phase of NCCR Democracy.

observed among those who deliberated. Moreover, these gains appear to have been permanent, whereas the mere provision of information produced more ephemeral effects on knowledge. The results of our study have interesting implications for our understanding of the interplay between direct and deliberative democracy.

Linking Deliberative and Direct Democracy

What is the relationship between deliberative and direct democracy? This question is not just of theoretical importance but also has important practical implications because both forms are being pursued in a number of countries as means of greater engagement of citizens in political decisions. Why would direct democracy need deliberation? Why would it hamper deliberation? In this section, we take theoretical stock of these questions.

The Deliberative Purpose in a Direct Democracy

Most democratic theorists would probably agree that a politically aware citizenry is an important precondition for a functioning democratic polity. Without knowledge, citizens cannot effectively steer policy or hold elites accountable (Berelson 1952; Luskin 2003). Three quarters of a century of public opinion research, however, have made it quite clear that citizens may not be as well-informed as democratic theorists would like. The levels of factual political knowledge among citizens are frequently very low (Delli-Carpini and Keeter 1996). Perceptions of party positions and performance are often well off the mark (Bartels 2002; Granberg 1993; Lavine, Johnston and Steenbergen 2012; Nyhan and Reifer 2010). And expressed opinions frequently reflect little thought; instead, they are products of non-attitudes (Converse 1964).

Not all agree that this state of affairs is a cause for pessimism. At the micro-level, some have proposed the notion of low-information rationality. Through the reliance on a few simple heuristics or information shortcuts, citizens can make judgments and choices as good as if they had full information (for a cogent statement of this thesis see Lupia and McCubbins 1998). In keeping with this view, Kriesi (2005) has shown for direct democratic votes in Switzerland that less competent citizens rely on heuristics such as partisanship, which allow them to arrive at reasonable decisions. Earlier, Lupia (1994) had come to a similar conclusion for initiative voting in California (Matsusaka 2004).

There is a danger, however, in placing too much stock in heuristics. First, there is now considerable evidence that heuristics do not help those low on information but, instead, help political sophisticates (Lau and Redlawsk 2001). Moreover, heuristics can result in serious biases (Bartels 2002; Kuklinski and Hurley 1994;

Kuklinski et al. 2000; Lau and Redlawsk 2001). This is particularly true of the heuristic of partisanship, which has received considerable attention in the direct democratic choice literature (Kriesi 2005) and can easily lead citizens astray in forming correct impressions of the political world. For example, Lavine, Johnston and Steenbergen (2012) observed that partisans tend to see policy performance through rosy glasses when their party is in power, and overly pessimistically when another party rules. They also observed that partisans can form incorrect perceptions of where parties are located on the issues when all they do is rely on their partisanship. Even their own policy preferences may be dominated by partisanship more than would be prudent (Cohen 2003).

In this context, we can understand the claim of Gastil and Richards (2012) that, despite many virtues, direct democratic votes have often been problematic, for example by producing long-term unintended consequences or by violating constitutional principles. Moreover, ballot measures are often formulated so complexly that there is a real question whether the reliance on shortcuts can really produce an optimal decision, or what some have referred to as a "correct vote" (Lau and Redlawsk 1997; Milic 2012).

Low information rationality, then, is no panacea. Under ideal circumstances, one would like a mass public that is sufficiently well-informed so that it does not need to (exclusively) rely on heuristics and, therefore, will not be misled by them. The question is how best to accomplish this task. Some might argue that the everyday media environment should suffice.[2] When we think of an informed public, we probably think first and primarily of a citizenry that possesses factual knowledge of the alternatives that need to be decided. Such information would seem readily available and in large quantities, especially in the current age of Internet and social media. However, we are less optimistic in our assessment, for there is good evidence that citizens selectively expose themselves to certain arguments and facts (Ditto and Lopez 1992; Frey 1986; Iyengar and Hahn 2009; Taber and Lodge 2006). The pressure to do so increases with the amount of information available. And the process is often geared at the protection of prior beliefs, i.e., the avoidance of disagreeable information. Through selectivity, then, citizens may fail to grasp certain relevant facts and arguments, which may then produce suboptimal decisions.[3]

---

2   On the role of the media in producing deliberative outcomes see Page (1996).

3   Another problem is the quality of media reporting and analysis, which has been widely criticized (Postman 1985; Patterson 1993).

If the provision of information is insufficient for developing an informed public opinion, then what is? Fishkin (1997) and Gastil and Richards (2012) have made a persuasive case that deliberation can and should play a critical role in this process. A properly constructed deliberation, avoids, the problem of selective exposure. As long as the full spectrum of opinions is represented in the group, it is at least in theory impossible to shun certain arguments and facts merely because they are disagreeable.[4] Just as important, however, is the fact that proper deliberation forces individuals to under-gird their positions with arguments and evidence. The idea that one should justify each claim is a central tenet of deliberative theory (Habermas 1992). This ensures that citizens do not just observe different view points but also come to understand why others may disagree with them on issues. It is the combination of diversity and argumentation that should improve citizens' knowledge of the initiatives and proposals that are being voted on.[5]

We conclude, then, that there is a clear deliberative purpose in direct democracy. Unless one places a great deal of confidence in low-information rationality, deliberative processes offer a number of advantages that can help citizens to form informed decisions in referendums and initiatives. The question now is whether direct democracy creates an environment conducive for deliberation.

The Deliberative Hurdles in a Direct Democracy

Chambers (2001) has expressed considerable doubt whether deliberation can flourish in a direct democracy. Her analysis focuses on the specific case of constitutional referendums, but we believe her arguments apply more generally. They revolve around two core ideas, those of irreversibility and deliberative accountability. The problem of irreversibility comes about because the deliberation is interrupted by a vote. The deliberative process may require further discussion but the timing of a vote may foreclose this possibility. Once the vote has been held, further deliberation becomes irrelevant, unless it now pertains to the newly created policy regime. Not only do direct democratic votes foreclose deliberation, but they may also change the dynamic. An open-ended deliberation may encourage

---

4   There are several hidden assumptions here. First, it is assumed that all opinions are expressed, which may not always happen. Second, the willingness to participate in a deliberation may itself be correlated with willingness to entertain alternative views. Put differently, we may only get those individuals involved in a deliberation who are anyways not too protective of their own views.

5   Other important effects of deliberation are the insertion of alternative frames into the discourse (Druckman and Nelson 2003; Niemeyer 2004) and the facilitation of reasoned choice because arguments are connected to political claims (Niemeyer 2007).

an open mind, whereas deliberation in the shadow of a direct democratic vote may close the mind, perhaps prematurely.

The second problem, that of deliberative accountability, is even more serious in our opinion. It pertains to the effect of voting procedures on deliberation (Steiner et al. 2004; Van Mill 1996). Because direct democratic votes work on a majoritarian principle, the voting public is divided into two clear camps: the majority and the minority. The anticipation of such a division undermines proper deliberation. If the majority anticipates that it will win the vote, it can safely ignore the arguments and ideas of the minority. If it is not certain of its success, it will have to pay closer attention to the minority but will probably use its discourse only as a persuasive device and only until the winning margin has been secured. From its position, the minority also stands to gain little from open discussion and is better served by vociferously defending its own position, in order to minimize the impending loss, instead of entertaining the ideas of the majority. In sum, there is little incentive to yield to the force of the better argument.

If one takes Chambers' arguments seriously—and we think one should—then the prospects for deliberation in direct democratic institutions is bleak. However, it is an open empirical question *how* bleak they are. Moreover, even if deliberation does not completely live up to normative standards, it is still possible that some positive benefits may be reaped. Thus, it is time to start considering some evidence.

The Study

Case Selection

We explore direct democratic deliberative potential in the context of a highly controversial initiative vote in Switzerland. On November 28, 2010, the Swiss went to the polls to decide between the expulsion initiative (*Ausschaffungsinitiative*) and a counter-proposal. The expulsion initiative was the brain child of the rightist Swiss People's Party (SVP) and foresaw in the semi-automatic expulsion of foreigners who had committed certain designated crimes. The counter-proposal was sponsored by the government. It contained several elements, which included systematizing the list of crimes that could result in expulsion, making expulsion contingent on the severity of the crime, and aligning expulsion with basic and international law. The counter-proposal also emphasized the integration of foreigners.[6] The

---

6   In addition, Swiss citizens could indicate which proposal they preferred in case both the initiative and the counter-proposal would be accepted.

initiative prevailed with 52.9 percent of the votes, whereas the counter-proposal received 45.8 percent of the votes.[7]

By studying this specific vote, we set the bar high for finding meaningful deliberation. The expulsion initiative was an emotionally charged issue and, as such, perhaps not well suited for reasoned discussion. At the same time, it is precisely this kind of direct democratic vote where deliberation is perhaps most needed, since careful reflection may help to moderate the effects of gut instincts such as a distaste for crime or foreigners. Two other observations speak to this point. First, the public debate was dominated by supporters of the initiative, whose emotionally evocative campaign posters could be found all over Switzerland. In this kind of lopsided campaign environment, exposure to alternative viewpoints is particularly important (Niemeyer 2004). Second, the counter-proposal was relatively complex, as it stressed multiple dimensions: integration, being tough on crime, proportionality, and compliance with basic and international law. To process such complex details, one might need the benefit of deliberation.

Design

To observe the effects of deliberation, we designed an experiment in the real-world context of the vote on the expulsion initiative. This allowed for a more naturalistic experiment, as the decision in the end had real consequences. Such an experimental design carries greater external validity than typical laboratory experiments, which is why we chose to do it this way. However, there may be risks in terms of the internal validity: there was a real campaign going on, which might have differentially affected the treatment and control groups. To minimize this risk, we tried to conduct the study before the campaign rose to its full intensity.

Our experiment consisted of three conditions—one treatment and two controls. The treatment group first received information and then deliberated, whereas the first control group only received information, and the second control group neither received information nor deliberated. The contrast between the treatment and the first control group allows us to disentangle the effects of information and deliberation on outcomes such as knowledge.[8]

Participants were selected through a two-stage procedure. In a first step, we randomly sampled 1670 Swiss citizens who were eligible to vote on the initiative

---

7   The participation rate was 53.1 percent, which is high by Swiss standards.
8   In most Deliberative Polls, the deliberative treatment is confounded with the provision of information.

and the counter-proposal.[9] These individuals participated in a survey (T1), which was conducted approximately two months prior to the vote. At the end of the survey, respondents were asked if they would be willing to participate in an online discussion about the expulsion initiative. The treatment and control groups were created through random assignment from all of those who expressed willingness to do so, which was only 15 percent of the sample.[10] By creating the treatment and control groups from the same subset of individuals who showed an interest in deliberation, we hoped to control for a variety of differences that might have existed if the control participants had been recruited from those unwilling to participate.

Table 1: Experimental Design

		Oct. 1–7		Oct. 25–29			Nov. 29–Dec. 6
Group		T1	I	T2	D	T3	T4
Omitted		√					
Treatment	T	√	√	√	√	√	√
Control 1	C1	√	√	√			√
Control 2	C2	√		√			√

Note: I = information treatment; D = deliberation treatment. The omitted group was unwilling to partake in the deliberation. Data collected in 2010.

The respondents who were unwilling to participate in deliberation were not interviewed again and are not further considered in our analysis. The remaining respondents were interviewed two or three times more. All of these respondents were interviewed again at the end of October, 2010 (T2), upon completion of the information treatment in the treatment and first control group, and after the vote had been taken (T4). The treatment group was also interviewed immediately after deliberating (T3). The timing of the information and deliberation treatments was chosen so that they would occur before the campaign would get underway. Table 1 shows the experimental flow.

The information package for the information treatment consisted of the main arguments of proponents and opponents of the initiative and counter-proposal. We solicited these arguments from all of the political parties, then crafted the

---

9   The sampling and surveying was done by the LINK Institute, a reputable survey house with a great deal of experience in running academic surveys.

10   The respondents were told they would receive financial compensation for the online deliberation. Those who were assigned to the control groups were told that there was no more capacity in the online discussion. However, they still received full compensation.

information materials, and asked the parties for feedback. We followed this procedure to ensure that the participants would receive balanced information that accurately reflected the main arguments in the public discourse.

The deliberation occurred in an online chat room. We opted for this format mostly to reduce the costs of the experiment. However, a secondary consideration was that the chat room format may be easier to scale up than face-to-face deliberation. The chats lasted about an hour and were minimally moderated, in the sense of keeping the deliberations on target and giving everyone a fair chance to participate. The chats covered the general issues of immigration and crime, and then moved to the initiative and the counter-proposal.

An important aspect of the chats was that we created relatively small groups (around 6 people) who represented a broad range of opinions. Based on the responses of the T1 survey, we attempted to maximize the variation of opinions about the expulsion initiative in each group. This was done to stimulate deliberation, which might otherwise have been stilted by a lack of disagreement.

Results

Earlier, we argued that deliberation may play an important role in creating well-informed direct democratic choices. We also argued, however, that direct democracy may not be well-suited for stimulating high-level deliberation. We now turn to the evidence from our experiment.

Did the Expulsion Initiative Leave Room for Deliberation?

To determine the level of deliberation, we employ the Discourse Quality Index developed by Steenbergen et al. (2003). This index assesses deliberative quality based on a set of criteria derived from Habermassian ideas (Habermas 1992). It is generally characterized by a high inter-coder reliability (Steiner et al. 2004) and also appears to have strong validity (Thompson 2008). Here, we code four aspects of the chats: (1) level of justification; (2) respect toward groups (i.e., foreigners); (3) respect toward demands (i.e., the initiative and counter-proposal); and (4) respect toward the arguments of other participants.

Graph 1: Indicators of Discourse Quality

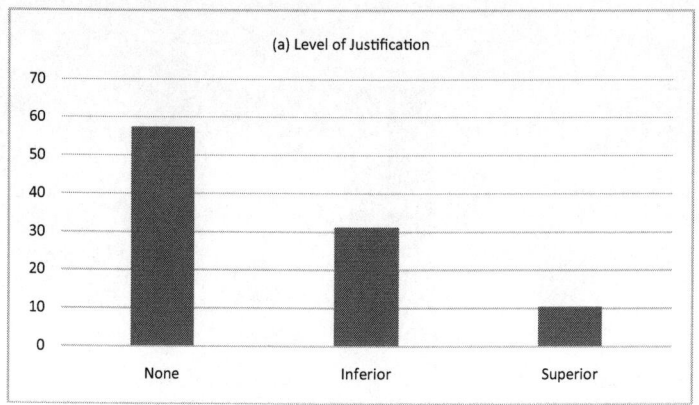

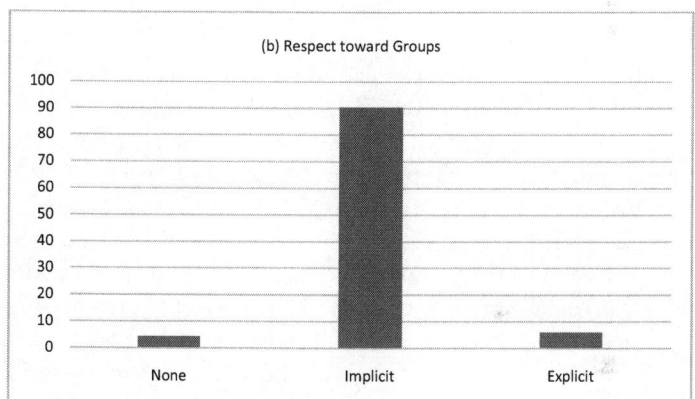

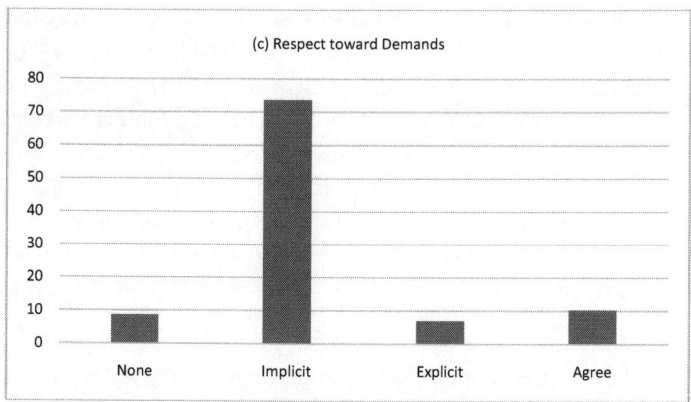

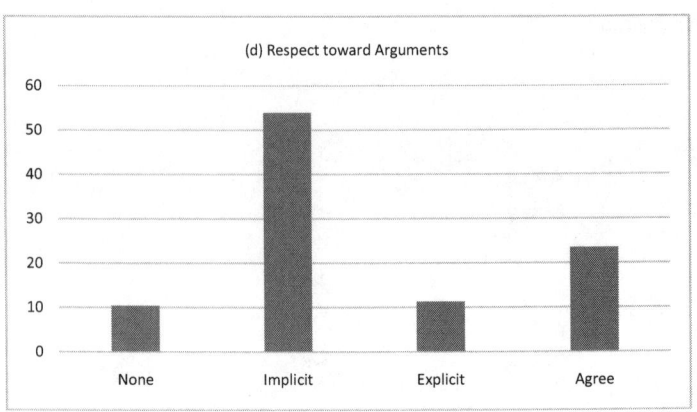

The level of justification refers to the use of arguments in support of a particular position, e.g., in favor or against the initiative. The lowest level ("none") arises when a speaker only states that something should be done (or should not be done) without providing any reasons. The next lowest level ("inferior" justification) involves the use of a reason, but no linkage between the reason and the demand is being made. The highest level of justification in the present coding is that of "superior" justification, in which at least one reason is given and explicitly linked to the demand.[11] When we code speech acts in the chats, what does the level of justification look like? Panel A of Graph 1 reveals that the median speech act contained no justifications whatsoever, with superior justifications occurring in only about 10 percent of the cases, and inferior justifications in some 32 percent of the cases. This level of justification is far from impressive, especially not if we keep in mind that those who deliberated had been exposed to relevant arguments through the information package.

For respect toward groups, we coded whether there were only negative references to the group ("none"), neither negative nor positive references ("implicit" respect), or at least one positive reference ("explicit" respect). As panel B in Graph 1 reveals, respect was almost exclusively implicit, with some 4 percent of the speech acts not being respectful and some 6 percent being explicitly respectful. This is neither a particularly good nor a very bad score.

Respect toward demands was coded using a similar coding scheme, with the addition of one additional category: "agreement." A speech act was assigned to this category if the speaker indicated his or her explicit agreement with the position of

---

11 In the original DQI, this is further differentiated into qualified and sophisticated justifications. We refrain from making this distinction here.

another speaker. As is shown in Panel C of Graph 1, implicit respect again characterizes the median speech act. Negative references to demands occurred in some nine
percent of the speech acts, with positive references occurring in about seven percent
of the cases, and agreement in about ten percent. These results are somewhat more
encouraging, perhaps, as they suggest that an emotionally charged issue does not
have to produce disrespectful discourse.

A similarly encouraging picture emerges for respect toward other speakers'
arguments. Here, disrespectful comments occurred in ten percent of the speech
acts (Panel D of Graph 1). This is offset, however, by explicitly respectful comments, which occurred in about eleven percent of the speech acts, and explicit
agreement with arguments, which occurred in almost 24 percent of the speech
acts. The median speech act was again characterized by implicit respect.

How should we assess the totality of these results? Our sense is that the level
of deliberation in our experiment was not particularly good. Especially in terms
of the level of justification, arguably the most central component of Habermassian discourse, the deliberations fell well short of normative standards. In terms
of respect, things looked better. However, even here the dominance of implicit
respect gives pause for thought. After all, this could indicate that the majority
of the participants did not really pay close attention to the arguments of others.

Was Chambers (2001) right, then, when she expressed skepticism over the
deliberative potential in a direct democracy? We lean towards this conclusion
but should note an important caveat that prevents us from fully embracing it.
The mediocre levels of deliberation in our experiment may have been due to
the format of the deliberation. First, the deliberation may have been too short to
allow the participants, for example, to engage in complex justifications. Second,
and perhaps more important, the online format of the deliberation may not have
been ideal. We say this, in part, because we have seen higher levels of discourse
quality in face-to-face deliberations, for example, in the Europolis Deliberative
Poll from 2009. The chat format may be particularly problematic because it requires participants to type their responses, which requires effort and may cause
their inputs to be abbreviated. Thus, we express cautious pessimism about the
deliberative potential in a direct democracy. At least based on our experiment,
but keeping its limitations in mind, we believe that proper deliberation does not
come easy in the context of direct democratic votes.

Did Deliberation Improve Knowledge?

In spite of the disappointing DQI results, we find significant knowledge gains,
which depend on an interaction between information and deliberation. In our

survey, we asked four factual questions about the expulsion initiative and the counter-proposal. Specifically, we asked if the following statements were true or false: (1) the counter-proposal came from the SVP (false); (2) integration is part of the expulsion initiative (false); (3) foreigners convicted of economic crimes will be expelled under the expulsion initiative (false); and (4) adoption of the expulsion initiative will result in the harmonization of cantonal expulsion practices (true). We coded what proportion of study participants improved their factual knowledge from T1 to T2 (after information provision to the tratement and first control group) and from T1 to T4. The results are shown in Graph 2.

Graph 2: Knowledge Gains about the Vote

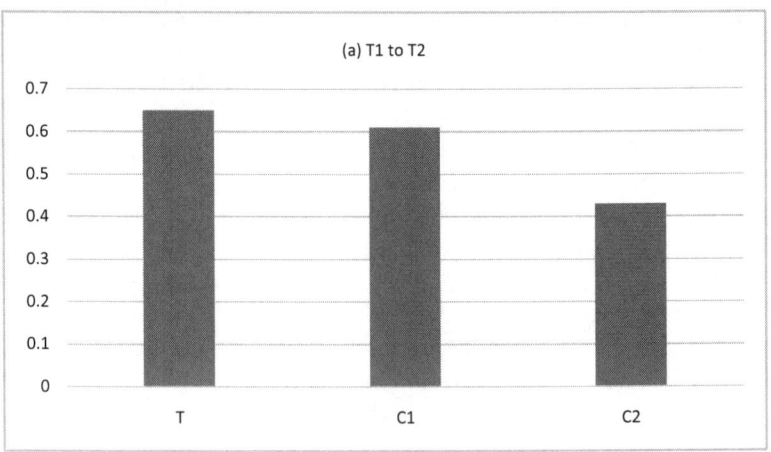

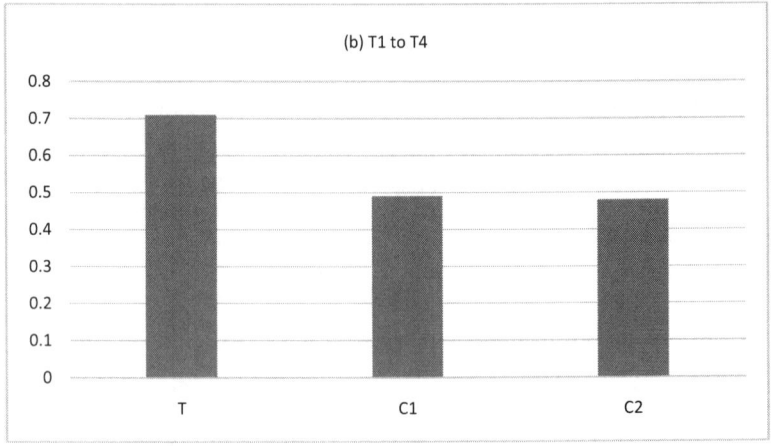

The graph presents an interesting picture. Panel A shows that the treatment and first control group, both of which received information, showed much larger knowledge gains from T1 to T2 than the second control group, which was not exposed to our information stimulus. The difference between the treatment and first control groups is .039 and not statistically significant. The difference between the treatment and second control group is .214 and significant ($p < .01$), whereas the difference between the first and second treatment groups is .175 and also significant ($p < .05$).[12] This points to a clear information treatment effect.

To ascertain the role of deliberation, we consider knowledge gains from T1 to T4, as the fourth wave took place after deliberation in the treatment group. Panel B of Graph 2 shows the proportion of participants who improved their factual knowledge over this time span. The contrast that emerges here is that between the treatment group and the two control groups. The proportion of treated participants showing knowledge gains at T4 is around .0.7 but in the control groups this figure is below .5. The difference between the treatment and first control groups is .215, which is statistically significant ($p < .05$). The difference between the treatment and second control groups is .231, which is again significant ($p < .01$). By contrast, the difference between the two control groups is .017 and not significant. It appears that the knowledge gains in the treatment group persist but that they vanish for the first control group.

Further insight into the empirical patterns can be obtained by performing tests on the difference in proportions from T1–T2 and T1–T4. Using Cochran's test procedure, we observe that the differences in the proportions are not statistically significant (by an exact test) for the treatment and the second control group; Cochran's chi-square statistics are 0.50 and 0.39, respectively. This means that the knowledge gain from T1 to T2 is statistically indistinguishable from that from T1 to T4. The story for the first control group is very different: here Cochran's chi-square statistic is 6.25 with $p < .05$. The implication is that the proportion of participants who improved their knowledge from T1 to T2 is clearly distinguishable from the proportion with knowledge gains from T1 to T4 or, in other words, that the drop seen in Graph 2 is significant.

---

12 For the non-statistical minded, p stands for the p-value, which is the probability of observing a between-group difference as extreme or more extreme as that observed when, in fact, there is no difference. As the p-value drops below a certain level (e.g., .05 or .01) we would be inclined to reject the null hypothesis of no difference.

The results suggest an important conclusion. The provision of information produced, not surprisingly, sizable gains in factual knowledge about the initiative and its counter-proposal. However, it appears that these knowledge gains persist only upon deliberation. The knowledge gains in the information-only group dissipated, so that this group became indistinguishable from those who had not received our information stimulus. Such dissipation did not occur for the participants who deliberated so that, in the end, this group clearly stood out from the two control groups.

Conclusion: Of Glasses Half Empty or Half Full

Direct democracy is gaining ground everywhere around the world (LeDuc 2002). To proponents, it presents an ideal means for including citizens in political decisions and for bridging the gap between the mass public and policy makers. For opponents, it presents an innovation that is neither necessary nor helpful because, they feel, existing representative institutions perform well enough and citizens may not always be the best judges of good public policy. Where one is positioned in this debate depends in no small part on how one answers the following question: how competent is the mass public?

Some have argued that ordinary citizens can make wise direct democratic choices even if they posses relatively little information (Kriesi 2005; Lupia 1994; Matsusaka 2004). Others have argued that the mass public frequently falters when it comes to ballot initiatives (Gastil and Richards 2012). The former would see little need for a deliberative process geared at better informing citizens about their direct democratic choice. The latter tend to see an important role for deliberative processes as a means of improving direct democratic outcomes. We tend to believe that low-information rationality has serious potential shortfalls, which are increasingly recognized in the literature, and that deliberation may thus be important for informed decision making in referendums and initiatives. This is not to say that we believe most citizens to be incompetent but only that their decision making may be improved through a deliberative process.

As we draw this conclusion, however, the question arises whether direct democracy is well suited for deliberation. This question is front and center in the essay of Chambers (2001) who reaches a rather sobering conclusion: direct democracy is not the fertile soil in which deliberation could flourish. At the same time that direct democracy may need deliberation it thus appears to hamper it.

It is against this theoretical background that we commenced our study of deliberation in the context of the expulsion initiative in Switzerland. While it is obvious that no grand generalizations can be derived from such a study, which considers only one vote, at one particular time point, and in one country, we nevertheless believe it presents important clues.[13] These clues leave us in a state of ambivalence: when it comes to the prospects of deliberation in direct democracy, we can either argue that the glass is half empty or half full. Consistent with Chambers (2001), we find that it is difficult to get a real deliberation going on a initiative as important as the expulsion initiative that we studied. In particular, when we think of one of deliberation's central mechanisms for informing public opinion, namely reason-giving, the results are outright disappointing—the glass is half-empty, at best. Nevertheless, we observed significant knowledge gains in our experiment, and these seem to hinge in no small part on the deliberative process itself. This finding leads to a far more optimistic conclusion: the glass seems half full, if not better.

How do we reconcile these seemingly conflicting conclusions? The key is to clearly separate the roles of information and deliberation in shaping political knowledge. The provision of information seems to have been the catalyst in boosting factual knowledge about the initiative. The opportunity to deliberate, however, seems to have been critical in preserving these knowledge gains. Whereas those who only received information gained and then lost knowledge, those who received information and then deliberated gained and preserved knowledge. Reason-giving was not critical for knowledge consolidation. Indeed, we surmise that the mere opportunity to discuss the initiative once more was sufficient for consolidation to set in.

This finding has enormous implications both for the theoretical literature and for empirical practice. Deliberative Polls as envisioned by Fishkin (1997) and others have always had two components: information provision and deliberation. Our results suggest that these components may play very different roles, which have hitherto not been recognized in the theoretical literature: information produces knowledge gains, whereas deliberation consolidates these. The practical implication is that one should separate these components, at a minimum by inserting an intermediate measurement between them but ideally by designing an experiment along our lines.[14] More importantly, if one seeks to establish

---

13 The design, we believe, has general applicability. In particular, we would argue that the use of real control groups (not just controls that consist of people who decided not to participate in deliberation) and the separation of information from deliberation treatments are methodological advantages of our design that can be easily transported to other contexts.

14 In fact, our experimental design could be improved upon by also considering a situation of deliberation without information, i.e., by fully crossing the information and deliberation treatments.

something like a random assembly in the foreground of a direct democratic vote, as Gastil and Richards (2012) propose, then it is important to understand how deliberation interacts with information.

Does direct democracy need deliberation? We believe it can benefit, at a minimum by conveying information that helps to create knowledge. Does it hamper deliberation? It may well have that effect. But even imperfect deliberation appears to bear fruits, as it helps citizens to consolidate their knowledge. The imperfect need not be the enemy of the good and so, perhaps, the glass is not as empty as we at first thought. Deliberative direct democracy, to coin a new term, may thus have a real future. It certainly seems worth exploring it further.

References

Druckman, James N., and Kjersten R. Nelson. 2003. "Framing and deliberation: How citizens' conversations limit elite influence." *American Journal of Political Science* 47: 729–745.

Fishkin, James S. 1997. *The Voice of the People: Public Opinion and Democracy.* New Haven CT: Yale University Press.

Gastil, John, and Robert Richards. 2012. "Making direct democracy deliberative through random assemblies." In *2012 Annual Meeting of the American Sociological Society*, ed. the American Sociological Society. Denver CO: American Sociological Association.

Habermas, Jürgen. 1992. *Faktizität und Geltung: Beiträge zur Diskurstheorie des Rechts und des demokratischen Rechtsstaats.* Frankfurt a.M.: Suhrkamp.

Kriesi, Hanspeter. 2005. *Direct Democratic Choice: The Swiss Experience.* Lanham MD: Lexington Books.

Lau, Richard R., and David P. Redlawsk. 1997. "Voting correctly." *American Political Science Review* 91 (3): 585–598.

Lau, Richard R., and David P. Redlawsk. 2001. "Advantages and disadvantages of cognitive heuristics in political decision making." *American Journal of Political Science* 45: 951–971.

Lavine, Howard G., Christopher D. Johnston, and Marco R. Steenbergen. 2012. *The Ambivalent Partisan: How Critical Loyalty Promotes Democracy.* Oxford UK: Oxford University Press.

Lupia, Arthur. 1994. Shortcuts versus encyclopedias: Information and voting behavior in California insurance reform elections. *American Political Science Review* 88: 63–76.

Matsusaka, John G. 2004. *For the Many or the Few: The Initiative, Public Policy, and American Democracy.* Chicago: University of Chicago Press.

Milic, Thomas. 2012. "Correct voting in direct legislation." *Swiss Political Science Review* 18 (4): 399–427.

Niemeyer, Simon J. 2004. "Deliberation in the wilderness: Displacing symbolic politics." *Environmental Politics* 13: 347–372.

Niemeyer, Simon J. 2007. "The ends of deliberation: Meta-consensus and inter-subjective rationality as ideal outcomes." *Swiss Political Science Review* 13: 497–526.

Page Benjamin I. 1996. *Who Deliberates? Mass Media in Modern Democracy.* Chicago: University of Chicago Press.

Steenbergen, Marco R., André Bächtiger, Markus Spörndli, and Jürg Steiner. 2003. "Measuring political deliberation: A discourse quality index." *Comparative European Politics*, 1: 21–48.

Steiner Jürg, André Bächtiger, Markus Spörndli, and Marco R. Steenbergen. 2004. *Deliberative Politics in Action: Analyzing Parliamentary Discourse.* Cambridge: Cambridge University Press.

Thompson, Dennis F. 2008. "Deliberative democratic theory and empirical political science." *Annual Review of Political Science* 11: 497–520.

Elżbieta Wesołowska

Chapter Eleven. Group Processes in Deliberative Setting. Qualitative Analysis

Introduction

Numerous authors have recognized the importance of group dynamics within the process of deliberation. Wiliamson and Fung (2004, 4) reported "huge variation in the quality of deliberation within the venues that aim to produce it." Mendelberg (2002) remarks that group level forces may stimulate or work against deliberation. Sunstein (2002) speculates that different group dynamics might result in the polarization in some of the deliberating groups, but not in others. Ryfe (2002) postulates that deliberation processes deserve careful investigation and should not be treated as a "black box." However, the dynamics of the deliberation process under real conditions remains an understudied phenomenon. The reason for this might be that a methodology for such a study has not been sufficiently developed.

The most common approach found in empirical research on deliberation is focused on preconditions of deliberation (sometimes called 'inputs'), such as the socio-demographic characteristics of participants; the characteristics of deliberative institutions, such as parliaments or chambers (Steiner et al. 2004); institutional arrangements aimed at fostering deliberative social interactions (Landwehr and Holzinger 2010); or organizational arrangements (such as the kind of facilitation or experimental conditions).

The group process of deliberation itself is often taken for granted. It is expected that within some favourable conditions deliberation will take place. Researchers adopting this approach mostly study the outcomes of the deliberative process at the individual level, such as changes in the participants' political knowledge (Fishkin 1995), attitudes and opinions (among numerous examples Gastil and Dillard 1999, Gastil et al. 2008) or future political participation (Gastil, Deess and Weiser 2002). There is also wide interest in the extent to which consensus might be the result of deliberation (Niemeyer and Dryzek 2007), as well as the quality and acceptance of decisions made by deliberating groups (Schakade, Sunstein and Kahneman 2000).

But do we know if people really deliberate within these 'favourable' conditions? How do people come to an agreement under conditions presumed to foster effective deliberation? In order to answer such questions, we need an analytical methodology to study group dynamics and processes.

Prevailing Methods of Investigating Group Processes of Deliberation

There have been few attempts to empirically evaluate the quality of deliberation. Steiner et al. developed a procedure for studying parliamentary discussions on the basis of Habermasian criteria of discourse ethics (Steiner et al. 2004). The Discourse Quality Index (DQI) includes the dimensions of open participation, mutual respect, logical and rational justification, common good perspective, discussion of values and normative assumptions, the principle of universalism and rationally motivated consensus. It is designed to analyze the content of pre-prepared (sometimes written) speeches articulated in a public forum (to large audiences, such as plenary parliamentary sessions). These speech acts may significantly differ from statements made by citizens in the informal environment of a small group setting.

Rosenberg (2007) attempted to investigate citizen deliberation by evaluating them on the basis of a theoretical typology of discourses that he developed. He described three different forms of discursive practices that might emerge in deliberative settings: conventional, cooperative and collaborative. Each of these forms has a distinctive communication structure and rules of social interaction that correspond to normative demands of different political theories. The first in Rosenberg's typology is the conventional discourse oriented by concrete, situated goals such as determining the nature of a problem and how to solve it effectively. This "involves identifying the specific attributes of the problem, establishing the specific causes and effects and considering possible interventions (…) little attempt is made to integrate the different aspects of the problem or (…) to consider its larger socio-political context" (Rosenberg 2007, 7). Claims of specific facts or preferences are linked to each other in casual, categorical or normative ways that reflect conventional rules of association and common experience.

The second type – called cooperative discourse – reflects the mainstream of deliberative democracy (classical liberal conceptions such as the ideas of Rawls). It is organized around a general subject rather than a particular topic, aims at a better understanding of the problem which would be shared by the participants. It involves considering relationships both between different aspects of a problem and the larger context in which it emerges. Attempts of integration are made. The basic units of cooperative discourse are the presentations of perspectives which should be "explained, justified and challenged by presenting related claims (reasons) and evidence in a manner that follows the rules of logic and reliable observations" (Rosenberg 2007, 8).

The third and most advanced and demanding mode, called collaborative discourse, reflects radical democratic theory as represented by Habermas. "While addressing particular problems it aims to develop psychological and socio-cultural resources of the participants. (…) The discussion of a problem becomes an opportunity to consider the social and political processes whereby rules of argumentation (…) as well as basic assumptions regarding nature, society and individuals are formulated and institutionalized. (…) The goal is transformation, both personal and collective. (…) It is oriented to managing difference in respectful and productive ways" (Rosenberg 2007, 9).

This typology was used to guide the analysis of citizen discussions that were convened under conditions highly favourable to deliberations in terms of participant selection, topic and arrangements. Namely, college-educated volunteers from the area with history of high levels of participation in community politics discussed a topic of personal importance for them (the quality of education of their children). They met several times in small groups led by facilitators trained in deliberation procedures. Despite such favourable deliberative preconditions it turned out that the majority of the discussions could be qualified as the "conventional" type, with social interactions between participants regulated by rules of civility and politeness.

Only two instances of cooperative exchanges were identified out of 210 coded segments. These two instances lasted for a mere 14 minutes out of 14 hours of discussions. Before drawing a pessimistic conclusion from these findings, we should explore the analytical procedure more closely. Rosenberg's analytical procedure included three broad categories for the classification of group functioning. If the discussions analysed did not meet all criteria specific for the higher rank (collaborative), they were classified within the lower (conventional). There are no middle categories. This procedure offers no possibilities for explaining how ordinary citizens search for and manage to find solutions to differences of opinion between them or which of the deliberative normative criteria are most difficult to implement in real life, and therefore require a more planned intervention. Such information has important implications for understanding the practical dynamics of group deliberation.

Stromer-Galley (2007) designed a coding schema for evaluating group discussions that incorporated the following six dimensions of analysis: expression of reasoned opinion, reference to external sources when articulating opinions, expressions of disagreement, equal levels of participation during deliberation, coherence with regard to the structure and topic of deliberation, and engagement of the participants with each other. This coding schema was used to analyse discussions in an experiment called The Virtual Agora Project, which brought together 568 Pittsburgh residents to discuss problems facing public schools (Muhlberger 2005). Stromer-Galley noticed that in the existing literature there is no consensus about what deliberation means and attempted to combine the crucial elements of various definitions. The analytical tool that resulted is not based on a consistent theoretical construction, but on selected elements from different models of communication.

There have also been attempts by some researchers to capture the group deliberation processes by using self-descriptive measurements provided by participants (Morell and Kanter 2005). This is problematic because there may be considerable differences between what is observed by a non-involved external person and what is experienced by involved participants. Experiences concerning the same deliberative debate may be very different for those participants whose views were in the minority, whose views were challenged or contested, and whose opinions were supported by the group majority. Combining such different individual perspectives into several aggregate indicators evaluating the entire discussion may be misleading.

A common shortcoming to all the methods discussed above is that they do not allow one to explain (i) how deliberative a citizen discussion could be if its circumstances were made favourable to deliberation, and (ii) the extent to which different deliberative criteria need to be met in such discussions.

A New Method

Theoretical Foundations of the Analytical Method

What kind of analytical tool do we need for the study of group dynamics? First, it should be a standardized procedure so that any researcher can use it and verify the results of its application. Second, it should be based on the reconstruction of the theoretical model of a deliberative debate (and not on any general model of communication). Third, it should allow for investigation as to which of the particular normative criteria of a deliberative debate were met in the discussion and which were not met (or even violated). Fourth, it should allow for independent investigation of the ways in which the group dealt with discrepancies that were sequentially articulated in its forum. This is because the group may function differently during different stages of its existence, or depending on the issue that is discussed (whether ideological or not). And finally, the evaluation of the group process should be conducted by external non-involved observers (and not on the basis of self-descriptive measures provided by the participants).

The model of a deliberative debate by Gutmann and Thompson (1996) was chosen as the theoretical frame for the construction of the analytical procedure, because it sets the normative framework for citizen discussion within a real-life encounter. Deliberation is defined as a group process of searching for an agreement through a discussion which should be characterized by the following requirements:

1. Individuals take part in the discussion free from any external pressures and their status in the discussion is equal.
2. Participants treat opponents and their views with respect.
3. The controversial issue is collectively analyzed.
4. During the analysis the participants openly express their positions on the issue, make proposals, and present their justifications.
5. While justifying their proposals the participants should obey two principles: the reciprocity principle and the publicity principle.
5a. The reciprocity principle means that the participants should refer to reasons and regulations which the other disputants are able to understand and possibly accept.
5b. The publicity principle assumes that the debate takes place in an open forum and so the speakers should employ reasons which can potentially be accepted by a pluralistic audience. It excludes the use of justifications which are discriminating or offensive.

The deliberative search for an agreement should employ:

6a. The consideration of a controversial issue from the 'public good' perspective.
6b. The disclosure of basic assumptions, convictions, values or concerns underlying the proposals.

Empirical Data

The analytical tool was tested in a research project called 'Psychological prerequisites and consequences of deliberative functioning in political groups' which was carried out by a team of psychologists in the Warsaw School for Social Psychology (SWPS) between the years 2003 and 2007. The research followed a quasi-experimental design. The empirical data comprised 20 small-group discussions.

The groups consisted of 6 to 10 parents of school-aged children (n=185). Participants were asked to devise an outline for a sex-education program for Polish public schools. Some of the topics considered were highly controversial in Poland, such as how to tell young people about contraceptives and abortion. Opinions on these issues are clearly divided within the Polish population and represent underlying worldviews. Some individuals advocate the Catholic Church teaching which stands strongly against the use of contraception and treats abortion as murder of an unborn human. Some social groups adhere to a liberal perspective which accepts the usage of all types of contraception and allows for abortion under specific circumstances. It is called the 'pro-choice view'.

The discussions were facilitated by a trained psychologist who followed a prepared script. In order to foster deliberation within our groups, the following measures were undertaken.

1. We tried to create a social group among the parents by asking them to work on a common task: to formulate group recommendations concerning the education of children in Polish public schools. We informed our participants that the group recommendations would be included in a report for the Ministry of Education, thereby indicating the importance of this collective task.

2. In order to reconstruct the theoretical model of deliberative debates, we worked out a set of norms to regulate group behaviour and these were outlined at the outset by the facilitator. We tried to formulate norms in a way that, on the one hand, would motivate group members to cooperate and look for agreement, but, on the other hand, would not suppress any diversity of opinions.

3. In order to stimulate the disputants toward intensive intellectual effort, we asked them to analyze the problematic issue in a rational way and to attempt to understand how their opinions differ and what they have in common.

More details of the project and its procedures can be found in the literature already published (Reykowski 2006; Wesołowska 2007). The discussions were video-recorded and then transcribed. Altogether it produced more than 30 hours of footage and almost 1100 pages of transcripts. The analytical procedure developed by the author was applied to the analysis of these materials.

Analytical Procedure

The deliberative debate model by Gutmann and Thompson was reconstructed into a set of observable individual behaviours. They were arranged in a table so that coders could easily mark which ones they observed in the course of a group discussion. The core idea of this analytical tool is that if representatives of all sides involved in the discussion of a controversy display behaviours representing all the categories listed, this will mean that a problem is being solved through an ideal deliberative process.

The unit of empirical material to be analyzed was the group trying to cope with a controversy articulated in its forum. The analysis would begin at the moment different positions on a discussed issue were voiced, and conclude when some recommendation concerning it was written down by the facilitator and none of the disputants objected.

The first step was identification of "positions" in the analyzed controversy – individuals who voiced different opinions. In order to code a given speech it had to be analyzed in the context of previous statements in the discussion (for example to code a statement by one person as fulfilling the reciprocity principle, the coder had to look back in the discussion to check the opposite stances, views or ideas that were articulated.

Reliability testing for this procedure was conducted. Two researchers independently rendered 250 statements taken from the transcriptions of different groups. They agreed in 74% of cases on the first codings.

Table 1 presents an example of coding a part of a discussion with the application of this procedure.

Table 1: *Coding Example of a Group Dealing with Discrepancy of Opinions*

Analytical categories	Controversy: how to present the problem of abortion at school?	
	Abortion is murder (person D)	Abortion is a difficult woman's decision (persons E, F)
1a. Disputant articulates his/her own position on a discussed issue.	+	+
1b. Disputant provides a practical reason to support his/her position.	+	+
1c. Disputant provides an ideological justification for his/her position.	+	+
2. Disputant asks a question concerning his/her opponent's position.	0	0
3. Disputant presents counterarguments to his/her opponent's position.	0	+
4. Disputant presents his/her argumentation following 'the reciprocity principle.'	0	0
5. Disputant attempts to analyze the problem and/or proposals of its solutions.	0	0
6. Disputant obeys the principle of respect towards opponents and their ideas.	+	+
7. Disputant encourages other persons to cooperate.	0	– (minus)
8. Disputant accepts analysis of a controversy from a common good perspective.	– (minus)	0
9a. Disputant accepts equal status of different ideological options.	0	0
9b. Disputant accepts individual freedom of choice of a worldview.	0	– (minus)
10. Disputant modifies his/her initial position.	0	0
11. Disputant looks for a superior (or more general) perspective of looking at ideological controversy.	0	0

In Table 1 we see an account of a group discussing how to present the issue of abortion to children. The view that 'abortion should be presented as murder' was advocated by person A. An opposite opinion that 'abortion should be presented as a woman's choice' was represented in the discussion by persons E and F. The pluses in the first three rows indicate that both sides voiced their opinions and presented both practical and ideological justifications. The zeros indicate that the parties did not ask each other questions to learn more details of the opposing view. They did not cooperate in looking for a commonly accepted solution either. The minuses indicate that a given criterion of a deliberative debate was violated – namely one side openly discouraged further discussion of a controversy (by saying 'it makes no sense to talk – we will not come to any agreement on that').

Research Results

How did the citizens deal with ideological controversies under conditions meant to bring about deliberation?

The analytical tool I constructed and applied to the analysis of the data accounted for the classification of the majority of observable behaviours by participants which could be classified as either fulfilling or violating deliberative criteria. Moments when the groups' functioning was close to a deliberative debate ideal were very rare – only 8 of 99 cases when the group dealt with opinion differences could be termed deliberation. In all the remaining situations the groups employed different strategies of coping with differences of opinions, involving various configurations of behaviours derived from the theoretical model. On the basis of the kind and number of criteria that were fulfilled in the group discussion, three main types of group strategies could be distinguished: (i) conflict avoidance, (ii) enforced solution and (iii) conflict resolution. Each of these strategies appeared in several manifestations, as summarized in Table 2.

Table 2: Group Strategies of Dealing with Opinion Discrepancy. Summary of Deliberative Debate Criteria

Group strategies and their forms	Deliberative debate criteria
1. CONFLICT AVOIDANCE:	• presentation of both sides opinions • no or limited justifications • respect
Tolerating the differences	discussion of socially acceptable topics
Muffling the differences	open discouragement/refusal of discussing controversy
Looking for similarities	narratives, story telling
2. ENFORCING A SOLUTION:	• presentation of both sides opinions • argumentation for at least one side's position • analytical approach to controversy • no or limited cooperation
Persuasion	one side domination over discussion
Polemics	elaborate justification of both sides views
Fight	open disrespect for opponents and their views
3. CONFLICT RESOLUTION	• presentation of both sides opinions • argumentation for both side's positions • sometimes reciprocity principle • analytical approach to controversy • cooperation • acceptance of common good perspective • respect
Negotiation	looking for solution through exchange of concession
Common consideration	looking for solution through integration of different views or coordination of organizational options

Conflict Avoidance

The first type of group strategy utilized very few normative criteria described by the model. Participants presented their opinions on a controversial issue and obeyed the principle of respect towards others and their views. There were no instances of insulting behaviour. But justification for taking a particular position were not given. This could hardly be described as a rational, argumentation-based approach to a controversial issue. The core of the controversy was tackled only on its very surface. In this strategy of conflict avoidance the group attempted to avoid articulated opinion differences.

In our material I could observe three ways in which groups tried to avoid conflict. Firstly, some groups simply tolerated differences of position refusing to discuss controversial matters of disagreement and smoothly moving on to another topic. Substitutive topics generally concerned socially acceptable matters which hardly ever evoke any objection, or they involved trivial questions marginal to the main controversy. Secondly, groups attempted to muffle differences by not allowing expressed conflicts of opinion to escalate into an open confrontation. This was done through suggestions to finish the discussion, citing time pressure, warning that continuation of a discussion may result in a quarrel, or indicating that the problem is beyond possible resolution. In some instances the group minority was openly discouraged to elaborate on its stance. Thirdly, some groups endeavoured to look for similarities and find common ground, shared identity among all the participants in the hope of formulating a group stance. Quite often this was done through storytelling. Participants would take turns in relating their personal experiences connected in some way with the controversy under duacussion. The main characters in the stories were the participants themselves or members of their families. In addition to recounting a course of events, the narrator would reveal personal emotions which accompanied them. A story told by one person triggered another story told by one of the listeners, recounting an event in some ways similar to the first story. Thus, a chain of stories developed in the group. Quite frequently such storytelling ended with a statement of commonality of experiences, concerns, needs or motives in the group. It sometimes led to the acknowledgement of a common social category that all the disputants belonged to.

Enforced Solutions

The strategy of enforcing a solution involved situations when one or more positions within a conflict of views tried to promote their own point of view as the whole group recommendation. Various positions were openly articulated in a group forum. Supporters of one position made an effort to elaborate on justifications of their stance, explaining why it outweighed the other positions. They did not cooperate in looking for a commonly accepted recommendation nor did they not analyze the issue from a common-good perspective.

The strategy of enforcing a solution was manifested in three forms: persuasion, polemic and fighting. Persuasion referred to situations in which one side of the conflict was much more active than the other in trying to make its own point of view seem to be the whole group's recommendation. This was done through the presentation of arguments to support a given point of view, emphasising and the advantages and benefits of its implementation. The persuaders often pointed to disadvantages and potential threats of implementing any alternative solution. Representatives of the persuading position supported each other and elaborated on each other's statements. The rest of the group were restrained to only signalling a difference of opinions (without presenting its details). This meant that some (although biased) analysis of a controversial issue was presented in a group forum, but the criteria of reciprocity and cooperation were not met at all.

In polemics more than one set of position-takers tried to persuade each other to accept their own solution through communication and argumentation. They presented justifications for their own proposals, pointed to their respective advantages and the benefits of accepting their position. Position-takers asked each other questions and learnt an alternative point of view in detail. Different points of view underwent analysis in a group forum. Disputants indicated disadvantages, difficulties with the implementation and potentially harmful results of the implementation of solutions differing from their own. Sometimes they applied the reciprocity principle in argumentation. But they did not cooperate in finding a commonly accepted solution. The discussion relied on mutual attempts to convince opponents that 'our' solution was better than theirs.

The last strategy for enforcing a solution deserved the name of 'fight' because after noticing a significant discrepancy of opinions, the holders of one position attempted to diminish the value and legitimacy of the opposite worldview. The attacking side referred to its opponents' views as morally wrong, socially detrimental or removed from real life. At least one group of position-takers we observed used discriminating, insulting or diminishing expressions referring to the other side. The deliberative debate criteria of respect and equal status of alternative worldviews were violated in the group forum. The use of insulting expressions evoked negative emotions in position-takers who felt offended.

Conflict Resolution

The strategy of conflict resolution met many of the deliberative debate criteria: presentation of both sides' opinions, proposals together with their justifications, respect, analytical approach, acceptance of a common good perspective and cooperation in working out an agreement which would address the expectations of both sides.

Conflict resolution was displayed in two ways: 'negotiation' and 'common consideration'. Negotiations involved situations in which rival position-holders tried to work out a solution through a mutual exchange of concessions. They presented their points of views and learnt their opponents' stances. Having become acquainted with opposing views, they tried to argue using their opponents' ideas (employing the reciprocity principle) and looked for a compromise solution which would not violate the values of individuals with different worldviews. Different ideological options were considered as having equal status, but clearly differentiated. Groups applying this strategy managed to devise a common recommendation if at least one set of position-takers decided to modify its initial stance or to propose an innovative solution. No attempt was made to integrate different ideological options.

'Common consideration' was the type of strategy closest to the deliberative ideal. It relied on different position-takers cooperating in working out a common recommendation through the analysis of different proposals and the ideas behind them. Analysis was applied to other people's ideas as well as to one's own, along with their justifications. Some controversial issues were formulated as open questions and posed in a group forum for thorough consideration. Position-takers learnt stances different from their own and justifications for them. They searched for similarities between them or for superior values that might embrace all of them. Different ideological options based on these values were articulated in a group forum. The group applying this type of strategy was able to work out a common recommendation if supporters of at least one position exhibited the cognitive capacity to detect similarities and common ideas in divergent stances.

Conclusion

What have we learnt about citizen deliberation as a result of the application of this analytical procedure? There are two points that could be made in the discussion of the empirical results.

The first is the feasibility of deliberative debates under real-life conditions. If we compare our project discussion of controversial issues concerning contraceptives and abortion with other discussions of these issues that could be observed in Poland – in the streets, the media and public discourse – we might say that the introduction of a deliberative normative context improved the quality of group discussion. More deliberative group functioning requires a careful arrangement of the context of the discussion, formulation of the task, setting the rules of discussion as well as skilful facilitation. Even then, however, the quality of group discussion fluctuates and very rarely approaches the deliberative debate ideal.

The analysis of the group process with the application of the procedure that allows for independent investigation of particular normative assumptions of the model leads to the conclusion that some of the normative criteria of deliberation could be more easily implemented than others. In the data presented above, we saw how it was most difficult to induce group cooperation and an analytical approach to a controversial issue. Problems with group cooperation can be explained by the low levels of interpersonal trust repeatedly reported as characteristic of Polish society. In European Value Survey 2000 Poland appeared in one of the lowest positions among European countries. Convictions such as 'one cannot trust most people' and 'one should be very cautious in contacts with other people' might prove dysfunctional when it comes to cooperation with members of an out-group.

The problems with an analytical approach to a controversial issue might be due to the quite significant authoritarianism still reported as present in Polish society, despite the democratization that took place in the 1990s (Korzeniowski 2006). Authoritarianism – now a classical social psychology concept – is defined as the hierarchical image of social reality consisting of three components: authoritarian submission to authority regarded as appointed and lawful in the society in which the individual lives, authoritarian aggression (perceived to be sanctioned by the appointed authority) and conventionalism (commitment to social conventions) (Altemeyer 1996). Adherence to such deeply rooted attitudes might constitute a barrier to an individual, independent and creative manner of solving problems that require social coordination. Speaking in more general terms, the feasibility of particular deliberative normative requirements might be culture specific.

The second point in the discussion concerns resolving conflicts of values and worldviews by the method of deliberation. The analysis presented in this chapter indicates that the narrative mode of communication may play an important function in solving ideological controversies. It might be either a mode of searching for agreement or an important precondition fostering a deliberative approach to ideological controversies. A personal story is not an argument in the deliberative sense. There is no place for it in the radical vision of discourse as advocated by Jürgen Habermas. Other theoretical conceptualizations of deliberation allow for story telling in discussions as examples or illustrations (Sanders 1997; Young 2001). The empirical research into citizen deliberation suggests that the narrative mode of communication might be a common thing and play important function of promoting further dialog (Black 2008). It might help in reaching agreement through overcoming barriers of interpersonal distrust even in deeply divided societies. Such observation is reported in the most recent work by Jaramillo and Ugarriza (Nussio 2011) with Columbian ex-combatants of the civil war in Colombia. Representatives of leftist guerrillas Farc (Fuezas Armadas Revolucionarias de Colombia) and the extreme right were brought together to discuss the future of Columbia. The underlying psychological mechanism might be that of building common identity on the basis of life experience. Most recent empirical research indicates that in small groups a social identity can operate as a contextual given, which shapes the behaviour of individuals (in a deductive top-down process), as much as the behaviour of individuals within the group can shape social identity (in an inductive bottom-up path). There is also evidence that the process of identity formation can play a key role in decision making, productive collaboration, integrative negotiations and the development of shared cognitions (Postmes, Swaab and Haslam 2005).

A comprehension of the dynamics of group deliberation may contribute to polemics among political philosophers in which three kinds of stances on deliberation are voiced. Advocates of deliberative democracy hope that deliberative debates will produce numerous positive outcomes for participating individuals, social groups and the democratic system. Sceptics fear that deliberative debates are impossible to conduct because they pose high cognitive, emotional and social requirements for the participants. Critics warn that deliberative debates might produce detrimental results, such as exaggerating existing conflicts and open confrontation of adversaries.

The application of the procedure presented in this chapter indicates that the results of discussions carried out under deliberative conditions depend on the group dynamics that occur within them, sometimes sending deliberative debates off the rails and at other times contributing to their success. As Mendelberg (2002, 180) puts it 'group level forces may often work against the kind of conversation that deliberative advocates wish to see'. The analytical procedure of group processes presented in this chapter can be a useful tool for studying group dynamics and identifying appropriate conditions for successful deliberative debate.

References

Altemeyer, Robert. 1996. *The Authoritarian Specter*. Cambridge: Harvard University Press.

Black, Laura W. 2008. "Deliberation, Storytelling, and Dialogic Moments." *Communication Theory* 18 (1): 93–116.

Fishkin, James. 1995. *The Voice of The People: Public Opinion and Democracy*. New Haven, CT: Yale University Press.

Gastil, John, Laura Black and Kara Moscovitz. 2008. "A Study of Ideology, Attitude Change and Deliberation in Small Face-to-face groups." *Political Communication* 25 (1): 23–46.

Gastil, John, Pierre E. Deess and Philip Weiser. 2002. "Civic Awakening in the Jury Room: a Test of the Connection between Jury Deliberation and Political Participation." *The Journal of Politics* 64 (2): 585–595.

Gastil, John and James P Dillard. 1999. "Increasing Political Sophistication Through Public Deliberation" *Political Communication* 16 (1): 3–23.

Gutmann, Amy and Denis Thompson. 1996. *Democracy and Disagreement.* Cambridge, Mass.: Belknap.

Korzeniowski, Krzysztof. 2006. "Authoritarianism in Poland in the Days of System Transformation." In *Understanding Social Change. Political psychology in Poland,* eds. Agnieszka Golec de Zavala and Krystyna Skarżyńska, 71–84. New York: Nova Science Publishers.

Landwehr, Claudia and Catharina Holzinger. 2010. "Institutional determinants of deliberative interaction." *European Political Science Review* 2 (3): 373–400.

Mendelberg, Tali. 2002. "The deliberative citizen: theory and evidence." In *Political Decision-making, Deliberation and Participation: Research in Micropolitics,* (vol. 6), eds. Michael X. Delli Carpini, Leoni Huddy and Robert Shapiro, 151–93. Amsterdam: Elsevier.

Morell, Michael and Adam Kanter. 2005. "The Effects of Group Empathy Levels on Citizens' Perception of Democratic Deliberation." Paper presented at Annual Meeting of International Society of Political Psychology, Toronto.

Muhlberger, Peter. 2005. "The Virtual Agora Project: a Research Design for Studying Democratic Deliberation." *Journal of Public Deliberation* 1 (1): 1–12.

Niemeyer, Simon and John Dryzek. 2007. "The Ends of Deliberation: Meta-consensus and Inter-subjective Rationality as Ideal Outcomes." *Swiss Political Science Review* 13 (4): 497–527.

Nussio, Enzo. 2011. "How Ex-combatants Talk about Personal Security. Narratives of Former Paramilitaries in Colombia." *Conflict, Security and Development* 11 (1): 579–606.

Postmes Tom, Roderick I. Swaab and Alexander S Haslam. 2005. "Social Influence in Small Groups: an Interactive Model of Social Identity Formation." *European Review of Social Psychology* 16 (1): 1–42.

Reykowski, Janusz. 2006. "Deliberation and 'Human Nature': an Empirical Approach." *Political Psychology* 27 (3): 323–346.

Rosenberg, Shawn. 2007. "Ways of Talking, Types of Democratic Deliberation and the Limits of Citizen Participation." Manuscript.

Ryfe, David M. 2002. "Study of 16 Deliberative Organizations." *Political Communication* 19 (3): 359–377.

Sanders, Lynn. 1997. "Against Deliberation." *Political Theory* 25 (3): 347–76.

Schakade David, Cass Sunstein and Daniel Kahneman. 2000. "Deliberating about the Dollars." *Columbia Law Review* 100 (3): 1139–75.

Steiner Jürg, André Bächtiger, Marcus Spörndli and Marco R. Steenbergen. 2004. *Deliberative Politics in Action. Analysing Parliamentary Discourse.* Cambridge: Cambridge University Press.

Sunstein, Cass R. 2002. "The Law of Group Polarization." *The Journal of Political Philosophy* 10 (2): 175–195.

Stromer-Galley, Jennifer. 2007. "Measuring Deliberation's Content: A Coding Scheme." *Journal of Public Deliberation* 3 (1): article 12.

Wesołowska, Elżbieta. 2007. "Social Processes of Antagonism and Synergy in Deliberating Groups." *Swiss Political Science Review* 13 (4): 663–681.

Williamson, Abby and Fung, Archon. 2004. "Public Deliberation: Where We Are and Where Can We Go." *National Civic Review*, 93 (4): 3–15.

Young, Iris M. 2001. "Activists Challenges to Deliberative Democracy." *Political Theory* 29 (5): 670–90.

Marcin Zgiep

Chapter Twelve. Assessing Deliberative Potential. Evaluative Dimensions of Discursive Interaction in Contemporary Democracy

Introduction

One of the major dilemmas in current democratic theory is the relation between representation and participation (Urbinati 2000; Przeworski 2009). Even though there are countries with deep-rooted traditions of direct participation (such as Switzerland, individual states/cities in the USA), all contemporary democracies are representative ones. As direct rule is not possible in the long run, the quality of democratic systems relies mainly upon the functioning of indirect arrangements based on election (voting) mechanisms. In light of observed waning relations between representatives and citizenry, we face two divergent yet parallel challenges: democratic minimalism and democratic radicalism. Either democracy in a broader sense than merely electoral is unattainable, or it constitutes an ideal detached from current political patterns. However, there seems to be a more plausible solution to this problem, which comes with a different image of democracy, one that is described in terms of discursive interaction between various actors. This brings us closer to the deliberative paradigm which became in the last two decades a sound alternative not only to the practice of democracy, but also to its theory.

Although much has been done to clarify some of its basic assumptions and claims, the concept of deliberative democracy still remains an enigma (especially to its critics, who include on the one hand proponents of traditional liberal democracy, and on the other radical democrats inspired by Marxism and critical theory). One of the most puzzling issues concerns the status of deliberation. What are its boundaries? To put it differently, where does it start, and where does it end? Until the whole idea remained within the realm of political philosophy and theory, these questions seemed unambiguous. Yet when the empirical researchers started investigating it, this issue became much more complicated and vague, though many of the assumptions/claims have been tested and verified/falsified (Chambers 2003; Thompson 2008; Mutz 2008).

The goal of this chapter is to link normative assumptions and empirical reality in order to create an approach to deliberative politics which is on the one hand *critical* in pointing towards aspects of the socio-political realm that are problem-atic and thus should be dealt with, and on the other hand *constructive* in pointing towards the socio-political realm as the fundamental background. Whereas the latter lends us tools for observing, describing and explaining politics in general and democratic politics in particular, the former enables us to assess politics from a specific angle, that is from a perspective of deliberation as one of the key ele-ments of contemporary democratic systems[1]. This kind of "constructive criticism" characterizes the approach I intend to elaborate here. Eventually it leads me to what I call "a network-based theory of deliberation", a mutation of the "distributed deliberation" perspective – paired with "deliberative systems" approach – both of which have provided me with inspiration and guidelines in the complex world of discursive interaction.

Distributed Deliberation Perspective

Decentralizing Deliberation

In its first theoretical phase, deliberative democracy has been perceived as a co-herent concept of legitimate democratic decision-making, based on the process of reason-giving between free and equal citizens[2]. However, results of empirical analy-ses proved that this standpoint is not necessarily true in every context (Jackson and Sniderman 2006). The prevalence and quality of deliberation varies over discursive settings, which means that there is no universal principle guiding political behavior and institutions. Thus deliberation remains a part of the more general public life and as such it is unlikely to gain superiority over other mechanisms, e.g. voting, bargaining, and coercion (Walzer 1999). Furthermore if deliberation is dependent on certain features of discursive setting (place, time, formal rules, participants) then evaluation of empirical cases cannot proceed according to the same default set of normative standards. Thus observable situations embody only some features of deliberation – certainly not all of them (Thompson 2008).

---

1 See *The Oxford Handbook of Deliberative Democracy* (2005) for numerous examples of applying deliberative institutions and practices in social and political realm.
2 Although different accounts of deliberation treat this idea in numerous ways (Rawls 1999; Habermas 1996; Cohen 1997), they all have in common the central feature, which is exchange of reasons between at least two actors (or reason-giving). Therefore deliberation can be defined as public reasoning (Richardson 2002) where *public* means that reasons are somehow communicated by different actors (not being kept private), and *reasoning* means searching for arguments that can be shared by all because the positions are oriented towards common ground (not being merely subjective).

Considering now this dyadic dilemma[3], can deliberative democracy be still perceived as a coherent concept? I argue that it can but the coherency must be reconstructed at a certain level of analysis embracing democratic theory and practice (gold standard). Hence two standpoints are in need of modification (Chambers 2003; Goodin 2008; Gastil 2010). First, the top-down approach, which operates at the macro-level, is too abstract to grasp the differences of concrete actions which may lack what the deliberative theory circumscribes as (good, ideal) deliberation. Second, the bottom-up approach, which operates at the micro-level, is too concrete to grasp the commonality of different actions which are part of the bigger picture. Paradoxically what both approaches have in common is that they undermine the opportunity to create a robust alternative to the mainstream liberal paradigm of democratic politics and to its radical visions. Instead of these perspectives, a new approach towards deliberative democracy ought to be designed, one that is at the same time normative and empirical, general and concrete, encompassing all diverse discursive settings and distinguishing them according to certain categories and criteria. Neither does it neglect the essence of institutions rooted in actual liberal democracies nor does it take them at face value. By operating at the meso-level, this approach establishes a framework for studying what has been called recently the "deliberative system" (Mansbridge 1999; Mansbridge and Parkinson 2012), a network of institutions operating in a multi-level environment.

A general outline of this perspective was initially put forth by Robert Goodin in his article "Sequencing deliberative moments," which later became part of the book *Innovating Democracy* (2008), which was an attempt to reconcile the micro and macro levels of deliberative democracy. There he coined the term "distributed (or delegated) deliberation" which lies at the core of my proposal to decentralize (or deconstruct, disaggregate) the notion of "deliberative democracy" in order to make it more useful for describing and assessing real-world politics (Mutz 2008). Unlike ordinary readings, I intend to perceive it not as a clearly defined object of study but rather as a loose yet inter-connected set of "political arrangements" (e.g. institutions) in which individual and collective actors interact with

---

3   In short we may speak of internal and external boundaries of deliberation (who, when and where and how can say something to whom). Internal boundaries are those pointed out by D. Thompson and they refer to various forms of discourse which impose certain restrictions on deliberation. Conversely, external boundaries are those signaled by M. Walzer and they refer to non-discursive forms which also circumscribe the potential and the limits of public reasoning but they are not part of the communication itself.

each other in a variety of ways. The heterogeneity of action leads to plurality of discursive contexts/settings. Therefore the goal of a political scientist concerned with linking theory and practice of deliberation is to find how he/she can analyze the potential of these many different contexts/settings in creating favorable conditions for deliberation.

Extending and Reshaping the Perspective: Deliberative System as the Locus and Context of Discursive Interaction

The path indicated by Goodin is surely an adequate one, but it needs extension and modification. Before I turn to this issue, I would like to critically evaluate his account of DDP named "deliberative Schumpeterianism" (a mixture of deliberative democracy and minimal democracy). As he put it, "What I have been describing is a model of political deliberation, where parties propose and electors dispose" (Goodin 2008, 202). First and foremost, he exposes only part of the entire deliberative system, the one centered on the modern liberal-democratic state based on cyclical and competitive elections during which different parties struggle to procure the votes by presenting arguments for and against certain policy proposals. In this case, evaluation concerns only the behavior of the political elite, mostly elected and to representative a certain degree. Deliberation is brought about by party leaders so that ordinary citizens are excluded and treated as mere spectators. Nevertheless these discussions are genuinely public and thereby they may be judged as more or less deliberative. Even though such talks proceed in partisan (party meetings) and state institutions (parliaments), the other parts of the society are involved in many ways. Apart from horizontal connections between political institutions and parties, it is possible to distinguish certain vertical ones too, that is ones which tie political discourse to meta-political and non-political ones. Basically there are three typical venues of deliberation and three actors pursing it: 1) local and mass media with journalists disseminating information about the content of elite deliberations in order to critically review politicians and shape citizens' opinions; 2) social movements and organizations engaging in making decisions/policies and intervening in particular cases with the support of the broader public; and 3) individuals/groups of citizens gathering occasionally in certain places forming deliberative *demoi* trying to affect elite deliberations and broader public discourse.

The point is that although political elites tend to hide their intentions and act covertly, there is enough pressure to expose these intentions/actions – this pressure has internal as well as external sources. It is caused by a struggle within the political elite (ruling elite vs. opposition parties) to persuade the citizens to support their policy proposals[4]. Furthermore pressure to expose elite actions is also caused by external initiatives: journalists (local and mass media), social activists (e.g. associations, trade unions) and finally ordinary citizens themselves. This is why the discourse of the political elite tends to be public – even though at certain stages of the political process it is hidden from the public, it never happens in absolute isolation. It is clear that the shape and dynamic of deliberation is quite often framed by the actual agenda set out by politicians: the government in the first place. Nevertheless, it is not that common, especially in the case of intelligent journalism, strong civil society and relatively large groups of public-spirited and knowledgeable citizens. Therefore the incentive to deliberate on a certain issue in public may come from different sides, not only and not always from the top of the polity (parliaments, party conventions). The framing effect caused by elites and at the beginning of discussions is unavoidable in many cases but it can be successfully contested, so that the entire discourse is likely to be re-framed eventually. Furthermore, at later stages different individual or collective actors may be effectively engaged, and the degree of this engagement varies from just being heard to being decisive and influential.

As we see above, a "deliberative system" accounts for a network structure resembling at the same time representative party (elite) democracy, and direct participatory (mass) democracy. Without privileging and emphasizing the importance of either of them, it forms the locus and context of discursive interaction among various actors situated in many segments of the polity. Primarily, it is the locus of discursive interaction because through certain symbolic (linguistic) practices people are capable of talking with each other (directly as well as indirectly)[5], exchanging ideas and recognizing the perspectives of others (Schütz 1967; Habermas 1984). Secondarily, it provides the context of discursive interaction because these practices are part of the general structure of ongoing discourses and they are bounded by the physical, non-discursive world. In sum, deliberation is limited by: 1) the form of discursive interaction (formal and informal rules of the game), 2) the interplay of discursive interactions (coordinated or clashing) and 3) the relation between discursive and non-discursive interactions (deliberation vs. aggregation/coercion/violence). Ultimately the deliberative potential of a particular

---

4   Insofar as persuasion refers not only to bare interests and ideology but also to workable ideas and sound arguments as warrants of attaining specific goals, deliberation is present in political discourse.

5   These practices encompass various forms of social interaction: from family disputes to public debates. As far as their participants refer to talking while resolving problems that arise during interaction, this interaction is discursive and might be potentially deliberative.

discursive interaction under scrutiny and the stability of entire democratic system is tied to these three conditions.

In order to properly understand how the deliberative system works one must take into consideration developments of democracy in the post-war period. In short they are linked to trilateral functional transformation of the structure of democratic systems discussed above. In consequence the deliberative system operates within the framework of the three emerging components: the state, the media and society, between which certain ties are established and different actors play certain roles. The state is the locus of power exerted by elected politicians and officials. The media are the locus of information diffused by journalists. Society is the locus of citizens' engagement. The external pluralism and thereby the exogenous contextualization of every component is supplemented by the internal pluralism and thereby the endogenous contextualization. The state provides context for discourse in the media and society, while opposition parties provide context for discourse produced inside and generated outside the government. The media provide context for discourse in the state and society, while left-leaning newspapers become opposition to liberal and conservative ones. Finally society provides context for discourse in the state and the media, while social movements and trade unions become opposition to employer organizations and global corporations. I contend that this picture is far more realistic than those depicted by some proponents of deliberative democracy who do not take seriously the dimension of conflict (partisanship, self-interest, emotion, ideology, polarization, power) in their conceptualizations (Mansbridge et al. 2010). By ignoring these circumstances, they in the end become an easy target of reasonable criticism undertaken mostly by the radical left (Mouffe 2000; Young 2001; Sanders 1997) but also by liberal thinkers (Shapiro 1999; Przeworski 1998).

Assessing Deliberation Systematically: Functions of Discourse in Contemporary Democracy

The extended and reshaped perspective focusing on the constellation of discursive interactions within the democratic system needs some clarification as regards the potential of these practices to generate "deliberative goods", that is symbolic/material preconditions and effects of deliberation, e.g. free and equal participation or consideration of the common good. Hence, according to the above division, we may now introduce six broad evaluative dimensions. Externally, the state is deliberative to the extent that the power exerted by elected politicians and high officials is publicly justified to the society or at least to those concerned/affected by particular decisions. Internally, the state is deliberative to the extent that the power exerted by the ruling elite is justified to the opposition elites and thus controllable and contestable by them. Externally, the media are deliberative to the extent that the information is diffused widely, covering the vast majority of opinions in the society about the actions of the political elite. Internally, the media are deliberative to the extent that information from one source is complemented by information from other sources and thus controllable and contestable by them. Externally, society is deliberative to the extent that engagement in public affairs is large enough to include the vast majority of groups or at least their representatives in forming opinions and political will. Internally, society is deliberative to the extent that engagement in public affairs by one group is complemented by other groups and thus controllable and contestable by them[6]. Regardless of these differences, in each case (justification of power/policy, information about power/policy, participation in power/policymaking) the quality of action matters. It is vital not only to count how many actions (understood as the number of explained decisions, the amount of diffused data, the number of engaged people) were taken during a certain period but also how many of them fulfilled the criteria of what can be called *authentic action*: authentic justification, authentic information and authentic engagement. By this "authenticity principle" I mean that actors taking a specific action put much effort in explaining thoroughly why they made the decision, describing accurately what it means or expressing rightly their feelings and thoughts related to the decision. The idea embodied in this proposal refers to an equilibrium of actions that are either functional, sustaining and developing the deliberative system, or dysfunctional, contributing to the erosion of any meaningful discourse and action.

---

6   Here I refer to the concept of deliberation presented by J. Dryzek in his books about "discursive democracy" (1994, 2002), especially to his idea of "contestation of discourses" which was greatly influenced by the French thinker and social historian Michel Foucault.

Table 1: Discursive Interaction in Contemporary Democracy. Broad Evaluative Dimensions

Evaluative dimension	Structure of the democratic system		
	The state	The media	Society
Content of action (ontology of deliberation)	public justification of power exerted by the political elite	diffusion of information about power by journalists	engagement in public affairs by groups of people
External pluralism (exo-context)	decisions/policies justified to members of the society	information diffused from diverse sources	wide participation in opinion- and will-formation
Internal pluralism (endo-context)	decisions/policies justified to the parties in opposition to the ruling elite	information covering a vast majority of opinions	participation of diverse groups of people
Quality of action (deontology of deliberation = "authenticity principle")	scale of justification: no justification[7] ↓ complete justification	scale of information: no information[8] ↓ unbiased information	scale of engagement: no engagement[9] ↓ reflective engagement

Source: own elaboration.

Having outlined the idea of my own approach towards deliberative analysis, I can look more closely at particular institutions or practices observable in each of the three segments. Goodin has convincingly explained how a party democracy works but – as mentioned above – he rather deliberately overlooked other elements of the modern liberal-democratic state, and he only applied the criteria worked out by Steiner's group. The four discursive forms distinguished above need to be slightly reinterpreted. First, party caucuses/meetings are expected not only to be the venues of sincere partisan talk but also the place where policies are elaborated to address the most vital challenges of the community and where policy options are representative to opinions of the electorate of specific parties. Second, parliamentary debates are expected not only to be the way in which MPs

---

7   "No justification" means that the only reason for making a decision (or introducing a policy) is the sheer will of the government or another administrative agency/body to take certain steps without any reference to principles, data or possible consequences.

8   "No information" means that the quantity of facts in the diffused information is negligible and the presented material is based on negative emotions and/or subjective viewpoints.

9   "No engagement" means that either there are no (or too few) people engaged or the engagement is based on intolerable behavior, such as aggression or violence.

exchange arguments reciprocally, but also the place where MPs from opposition parties can hold the government accountable by questioning and critically examining the activity of high officials. Moreover the role of the speaker in sustaining the exchange of high-quality arguments between mutually respecting MPs should not be easily neglected. Third, the election campaign is not only the moment when everyone can speak on free and equal terms about the well-being of the community but it is also the time when public discourse has enormous impact on the composition of the elected body and indirectly on the subsequent political process. Finally, post-election arguing and bargaining is not only a stage when parties reach rational compromise on government structure but it is also a period when the policy agenda (e.g. the exposé) is formulated under public scrutiny as a reference point for possible critical evaluation of actions taken by the government.

In addition, three other institutions ought to be considered in order to grasp the significance of deliberation within the state. One of them is the judiciary, embodied by constitutional and administrative courts, the other – technocracy, materialized in various permanent or *ad hoc* consultative bodies, research institutes and political think-tanks. Both refer to the use of expertise: professional judges, intellectuals and experts. The role of constitutional courts is to limit power seized by elected politicians through assessment of law-making with reference to procedure and/or content of particular normative acts (Zurn 2007; Rawls 1971). Parallel to this, the role of the administrative courts is to control officials in their particular decisions concerning execution of enacted law. The purpose of technocratic institutions is to advise politicians through assessment of alternative solutions in the process of decision-making. In both cases the idea is to rationalize or justify power in terms of more objective (impartial?) – rather than merely political – motivations as *ratios* supporting legal acts or concrete decisions. Next to this is the executive branch which also has a role to play in the deliberative system. Although it may seem less obvious, local and central administration should refer to or even engage public opinion, particularly when decisions concern sensitive and polarizing issues and deal with a variety of interests and parties. Finally, the head of the state (president or monarch), as an institution designed to represent the entire nation, has an arbitrage function to perform based on its capability to mediate in conflicts between institutions and find a bipartisan solution to impasses or gridlocks.

Constitutional courts are deliberative to the extent they feature several aspects: 1) consider all available possibilities, 2) apply the perspective of common good in their considerations and 3) argue to establish a wider consensus. Consultative bodies are deliberative if they reflect on diverse options and weigh the reasons supporting different alternatives. Administrative actions may be assessed using two criteria: 1) to what degree does it include reflective opinions of citizenry (e.g. through public consultations or public surveys) and 2) how does it respond to social problems stemming from conflict of interests. Conversely, head of the state should attempt to bring diverse opinions together, thus laying the ground for compromise among conflicted parties, similarly to a constitutional court. To sum it up, these discursive abilities paired with institutional guarantees of power division and party competition all form a kind of "deliberative *checks and balances* mechanism" located within the actual political system.

Turning to the media as an essential element of a deliberative system, their nature is twofold. On the one hand, journalists gather and spread information so that they become sources of data essential for any kind of deliberators, be it politicians or ordinary citizens. On the other hand, journalists also invent and create news either by themselves (speculation) or with the help of other public actors: politicians, intellectuals, experts, activists etc. (citation). In both cases they are "triggers" of issues which are then widely debated in public. The point is that it seems virtually impossible to draw a sharp line between these two situations: there is much tension among journalists between their inclination to disclose facts (information) and their propensity to add meanings to the disclosed facts (interpretation). The media provide citizens with information by framing the is-sues under discussion, pointing at some issues or their aspects and marginalizing others, forcing citizens to think in a certain way. However journalists do not only incessantly distribute information about what is happening on the political scene and on its backstage. In fact, by doing it they tend to control the power. Politicians, high officials and other public figures are compelled to speak in public about their actions thus affecting their current and future behavior. Not only is the sphere of their discretion automatically limited, but also citizens' opinions on particular issues and policies are indirectly influenced by the capacity of media discourse to generate political judgments.

Taking all this into account, we may now distinguish several types of discourse within the media segment. First of all, information and public affairs programs are aimed at spreading information about actual events across certain areas (local, na-tional, regional, global) thereby providing people with knowledge they otherwise would not be able to do gain on their own due to costs (Downs 1957). Without sufficient data at their disposal, citizens would make their choices unconsciously (randomly), based only on their natural wisdom and mentality. Regardless of any impact it might have, providing information remains necessary in opinion formation which is tightly connected with deliberation as the latter cannot suc-ceed in any reasonable way if there are too few facts to think through and talk about. Second, press articles are crucial in interpreting past or present events in order to render them comprehensible within the larger context of public life. These interpretations go (sometimes far) beyond pure information about existing facts. Instead of this, their purpose is to help people understand what is going on or what has happened. It is as necessary as in the previous case, because with a more fine-grained, thoroughly-examined information, citizens are better able to shape their opinions and make proper decisions. Furthermore well-crafted articles have enough potential to frame ongoing public debates thus affecting the current course of the political process. Third, interviews with public figures (TV/ radio, newspapers) are designed to expose how the latter were involved in making decisions and what is their responsibility for or link to those decisions. It is the basic structure of an interview – the interviewer asking questions, the interviewee answering them, the audience listening or, in some contexts (e.g. in the studio during talk-shows), responding actively to what was said – that allows controlling the behavior of both the journalist and, to a greater extent, the interlocutor. The audience plays an important role of "an invisible observer" who can alter the communicative exchange through a mechanism of introjection[10]. Fourth, public discussions/debates (on TV/radio, rarely in newspapers) are communication settings in which at least two persons and a moderator gather to address issues by talking to one another. Basically the underlying purpose is to display the existing opinions on given issues and the reasons supporting diverse standpoints. The complexity of relations makes the entire dialogical (tri-logical) structure less rigid, more spontaneous and thus less manipulable by any of the participants.

The Internet as a discursive form is somewhat specific in comparison to the ones described above. Besides professional journalists, it can be used by ordinary citizens to inform about certain facts (e.g. Facebook, Twitter), write about them (e.g. blogs) and talk about them (e.g. chats, forums). Due to its intrinsic egalitarian nature, it becomes a powerful tool in the hands of almost everyone who has the necessary skills[11]. The Internet is the space of convergence of different forms of discourse, "on-line" as well as "off-line" ones. By significantly extending

---

10 This is an important modifier of the discussion since the former may appeal to public opinion in order to put pressure on the latter who has to balance between his own viewpoint and the viewpoint of the people. However the moderator is not absolutely free in his/her communicative behavior because he/she also has to balance between respect towards the interlocutor and inquiry about the issue(s) under discussion.

11 There is, however, a big problem with the so-called "digital divide" weakening the inherent equality principle. As in the case of "off-line" democracy, electronic leadership (elitism) is inevitable. The question is how this leadership is performed and how people react to enunciations of the cyber-leaders.

and enlarging the public sphere, it creates opportunities for mass participation in exchanging opinions and reasons in a spontaneuos and institutionalized way (Coleman and Blumler 2009; Davies and Gangadharan 2009). In combination with real-world action the Internet becomes more and more useful provided people are capable and effective in demanding respect towards their rights or supporting implementation of certain policies.

The evaluative dimensions concerning media discourse are the following. In case of information and public affairs programs the content and form of information comes under assessment. The more comprehensive and relatively unbiased it is, and the more it balances different aspects of an issue, the more it resembles deliberative opinion-formation process. It does not need to tend toward the objective, impartial truth mutually shared by all, but it should not be deceptive, stigmatizing or exclusionary towards certain viewpoints and interests. As far as press articles are concerned, the content and form of interpretation comes under assessment. To the extent that it contains consideration of different arguments and frames public debate with the use of persuasive arguments, it resembles deliberative meta-political control. In interviews and television/radio debates with public actors, the content and form of discussion is under assessment. If the interviewers/moderators guarantee free and equal conditions of participation and induce the interviewees to justify and explain their actions, deliberative meta-political control is likely to prevail. Additional standards for public debates (e.g. campaign debates with candidates standing for public offices) should embrace pluralism in discussion and understanding the positions of others. Finally, the Internet as a convergent device encompasses all of these evaluative dimensions. Furthermore, access to certain electronic forums should be open and unconstrained so as to include as many people as possible.

In contrastto the state and the media, the role of society in the deliberative democracy is stressed by a variety of forms of genuine civic participation such as Deliberative Polls®, Consensus Conferences, Citizens' Juries, voluntary associations or interest groups. Some scholars contend that this enumeration can and should be extended to the grassroots of political life (Walzer and Mansbridge 1999). The most evident practices are by far the institutionalized forms of participatory deliberation (Cohen and Sabel 1997). The reason is that they are all linked to formal decision/policy-making, thus the connection between opinion- and will-formation is tighter. Despite putting emphasis on free and equal access, and participation in public forums, reason-giving among participants and impact on political process and outcome, they all differ to large extent. Traditional public consultations deployed by administration are based on self-selection procedures and do not include the feature of representative participation. It is crucial in such contemporary devices as Deliberative Opinion Polls* (Fishkin 2009), 21ˢᵗ Century Town Meetings (Lukensmeyer et al. 2005), Citizen Assemblies (Warren and Pearse 2008, Carson, Gastil et al. 2013) or Citizen Panels (Gastil 2000) in order to create a microcosm community capable of reasoning on particular local, national or even transnational issues and thereby coming to a thoughtful conclusion on behalf of the members of the wider non-participating community[12]. Furthermore, these institutions require a well-trained moderator who is able to ensure respectful and thorough debate as well as briefing materials covering all options that will be subsequently discussed by participants. However, in principle, they are not aimed at creating even a vague consensus or shared opinion among the participants (in most cases they are based on aggregative voting instead) which would be expected e.g. in Consensus Conferences and Citizens' Juries. This means that mutual respect and trust is more valuable in the latter than in the former. Equally essential is the internal and external efficacy factor. Its importance increases with the scale of the event, degree of engagement, debated issue and expected results of deliberations. Citizens taking part in deliberation with high costs of participation are more likely to search for benefits, such as personal and collective gains.

On the other hand, there is an example of participatory budgeting centered on restoring or maintaining social justice at the expense of proportional inclusion of all interests present in a given community (Baiocchi 2003). In this case material outcome understood in terms of the weak egalitarian principle (Rawls 1971; Steiner et al. 2004) is the most crucial issue. Regardless of any differences, such institutions are deliberative to the extent that the outcome benefits the entire society, not just a particular group, such as the high classes.

The second group of institutionalized participatory deliberation includes those who are part of the state machinery or are somehow involved in decision/policy-making. Social dialogue embodied in bilateral or trilateral commissions is the example of sectoral discourse, that is discourse limited to a specific issue-area, in this case labor relations which structure citizens' life in the most basic sense (Baccaro 2003). This kind of discourse is undertaken among parties to social dialogue, with the government acting as supervisor. Discussions within a particular organization are vital for crafting its position prior to formal debate. As in the case of party

---

12 Yet this representativeness is different than the one observed in democratic elections. It is based on statistical measurements, structuring the population according to such features as age, sex, education, income etc. This kind of representation appears when politics meets science.

meetings, the members should talk the issue over, unveiling their true beliefs so the final position expresses also the attitude of each group member. Moreover the goal here is to develop the best possible standpoint supported by solid arguments. Formal discussions become the testing ground for each organization in its negotiations over labor regulations (e.g. minimal wage), and also for the government in its ability to balance economic productivity (interests of employers) and social security (interests of workers). Hence, the quality of social dialogue depends on the quality of arguments from both sides, acknowledgment of the position of others, consideration of social welfare, and reaching rational compromise on the debated issue. The government is expected to supervise these meetings taking an impartial, balanced position towards all participating sides.

Public hearings account for inclusive law-making open to citizen input. As parliaments are the nominal space of elite negotiations, they also constitute the territory penetrated by interest groups and lobbies, that is well-organized citizens seeking to ensure their private businesses. A public hearing changes the context of this discourse because it establishes formal guarantees on the procedure of drafting a bill in order to make the process more transparent (less prone to corruption). By inviting various groups to public reasoning, decision-makers can no longer stick to their initial viewpoints on a given matter but they must take into account the other viewpoints before making a decision. This practice cannot guarantee a substantial change of minds once the hearing is over unless the participating parties monitor the legislative process afterwards. Yet if the parties represent the major interests and opinions of the society and use sound arguments to convince decision-makers, while the latter have provided enough room for free and relevant discussions, then deliberation can flourish.

Lastly, there are non-governmental organizations (NGO), as a form of bottom-up engagement of citizens in public affairs. They deal with certain issues and may even carry out tasks commissioned by the government or local authorities. Their purpose is to legitimize political power through distribution of responsibility for specific issue-areas among many entities (power-sharing). However, there are cases in which this may turn into a strategy of the government avoiding any responsibility whatsoever. NGOs can counteract this strategy by drawing attention of the public to unresolved issues, erroneous decisions or procedural obstruction. As we can see, citizens organized in such enterprises have different ways of communication: they may cooperate harmoniously with governing bodies but they may also fiercely oppose them. In the former case the likelihood of solving the problem is higher than in the latter, and the same concerns the prospects of reaching some kind of agreement. However, contestation is necessary whenever the government is impervious to justified claims, especially made by groups affected by a particular decision. In both cases it is important that the organization speak on behalf of the people it represents and defend their true interests.

Another group of societal forms of discourse is the non-institutionalized, unconventional, spontaneous forms of deliberation. We can distinguish two types here. First, there are non-discursive settings, such as street manifestations or strikes in workplaces, etc. Although they feature adversarial or agonistic patterns of action (Mouffe 2000) it is possible to uncover here a kind of public talk among participants referring to some sense of value and interest community or at least appealing to the common good (Wood 2012). Expressing preferences publicly can be treated as exposing social injustice in order to make the other side (i.e. government, private sector) more responsive to legitimate demands. Secondly, even if deliberation takes place in discursive contexts, it is regarded rather as a form of public discussion or private conversation. Whereas the former means fostering public reasoning on social problems that ought to be solved, the latter is oriented towards maintaining communication between people on issues relevant to their social life[13]. Discussing issues in public venues (other than political and mediated ones) gives opportunity for anyone to participate in and contribute to current debates, thereby shaping their opinion as well as those of others. In private conversations the deliberative potential is attached rather to interpersonal relations that should be based on sincerity and understanding of other positions than on expressing rational opinions (arguments) on a given issue. Moreover emotions play an important role within private, less-structured patterns of communication provided they include respect towards one another (Krause 2008). Reaching meta-consensus[14] in these discursive settings is more likely than reaching consensus *per se*. In the end, strengthening social bonds through deliberation brings about a more robust political community.

---

13 I refer here to Goffman's idea that social order is maintained due to interactions based on repeatable gestures (dual structure of conversation: questions and answers). If there are no (or too few) interactions, there can be no social order (society) or it is weak and unstable (see 1982).

14 This term was coined by J. Dryzek and S. Niemeyer to name a less demanding form of consensus based upon agreement on the set of values, beliefs and preferences. See Dryzek, Niemeyer 2006, 634–649.

Table 2: Discursive Interaction in Contemporary Democracy. Specification of Evaluative Dimensions

Structure of democratic system	Institution/ practice (discursive form)	Function (role)	Evaluative dimension – aspect(s) under assessment
The state = power (political elite)	party meetings	policy-elaboration	sincerity: trustworthy speech
			public justification: quality of arguments prior to discussions
	parliamentary debates	law-making, executive control	public justification: quality of arguments prior to voting
			meta-communication: ability of the speaker to ensure well-ordered discussions
			mutual understanding: recognition of counterarguments
			impact on process: ability to hold government accountable for decisions
	election campaigns	policy-presentation	participation: free and equal discussion
			common good: consideration of the well-being of others
			impact on process: ability to influence parliament structure
	post-election arguing and bargaining	government-formation, policy-negotiation	mutual respect: recognition of demands and social diversity
			(weak) consensus-building: attempt to reach rational compromise on government structure
	constitutional courts	judicial review	public justification: quality of law-making
			(strong) consensus-building: attempt to reach agreement on general principles
	public administration	policy-making, decision-making	common good: consideration of public opinion input to policies/decisions
			impact on outcome: ability to solve social problems
	head of the state (president/ monarch)	arbitrage (political and social mediation)	conflict-resolution: ability to reconcile conflicting parties
			common good: consideration of the well-being of others
	administrative courts	judicial review	public justification: quality of decision-making
	consultative bodies	(advisory) opinion-formation	public justification: quality of decision-making

Structure of democratic system	Institution/ practice (discursive form)	Function (role)	Evaluative dimension – aspect(s) under assessment
The media = information (symbolic elite)	information programs, public affairs programs	information-pooling	balanced information: information based on facts relevant to the described case
	public interviews	policy-presentation, policy-analysis, meta-political control	meta-communication: ability to question the interrogated person on basis of merit
			public justification: explanation of actions by the interrogated person
	public debates	policy-presentation, policy-analysis, meta-political control	meta-communication: ability to sustain meaningful discussions
			public justification: quality of arguments on the discussed issue
			respect: recognition of counterarguments
	press articles	opinion-formation, policy-analysis	balanced information: information based on facts relevant to the described case
			rational persuasion: consideration of alternative interpretations of the issue
			impact on process: attempt to (re)frame the debate
	Internet (convergence of the media above)	information-pooling, opinion-formation, policy-analysis, meta-political control	criteria applied according to particular discursive form
			participation: free and equal discussion
	public consultations, social dialogue	decision-making	participation: free and equal discussion
			meta-communication: government supervision based on impartiality
			impact on process: ability to influence decision-makers
	public hearings	law-making	participation: free and equal discussion
			impact on process: ability to influence law-makers
	participatory budgeting	decision-making, justice-sensitizing	participation: free and equal discussion
			representation: inclusion of handicapped parties
			impact on outcome: ability to improve social justice

Structure of democratic system	Institution/ practice (discursive form)	Function (role)	Evaluative dimension – aspect(s) under assessment
Society = engagement (citizens, citizen representatives)	deliberative polls*, 21st Century town meetings	information-pooling, opinion-formation	participation: free and equal discussion
			representation: inclusion of all relevant parties
			balanced information: briefing materials covering all options prior to discussions
			meta-communication: ability of the moderator to sustain meaningful discussions
			opinion/attitude transformation: significant change of viewpoints/behavior
			impact on process: ability to influence public opinion and decision-makers
			internal efficacy: sense of being politically competent
	consensus conferences, citizen panels, citizen juries, planning cells	decision-making, opinion-formation	participation: free and equal discussion
			meta-communication: ability of the moderator to sustain meaningful discussions
			impact on process: ability to influence decision-makers
			internal efficacy: sense of being politically competent
			(weak) consensus-building: attempt to find shared opinion on discussed issues
	non-governmental organizations	decision-making, contestation	representation: interests of people realized by the organization
			impact on process: ability to cooperate with/ oppose decision-makers
	social movements, group/mass protests	contestation, justice-sensitizing	sincerity: trustworthy speech
			impact on process: ability to render the political elite responsive to justified demands
	public discussions	opinion-formation	participation: free and equal discussion
			impact on process: ability to shape public opinion
	private conversations	opinion-formation, community-building	sincerity: trustworthy speech
			mutual respect: recognition of other's viewpoints

Source: own elaboration.

Conclusion: from Distributed Deliberation to Network-based Deliberation

The proposal elaborated in this chapter is oriented towards network structures and functioning of overlapping and inter-locking discursive interactions (Hajer and Wagenaar 2003). Instead of concentrating entirely on institutions and practices as objects of analysis and centers of discourse, it widens the perspective, to include the relations between institutions and practices present in multi-layered processes. This idea captures pretty well how each type of institution/practice contributes to the functioning/stability of a deliberative system according to stipulated criteria and what are the connections between specific institutions/practices. Since deliberation resembles a decentralized network (Habermas; Benhabib), we cannot specify precisely where it begins or ends, and thus no real existing democratic institution/practice is *a priori* deliberative unless it scores high on one or more dimensions. The link between deliberation and democracy is more subtle and indirect, which has been illustrated in Tables 1 and 2. Virtually it means a more in-depth analysis. If a particular case is an example of deliberative failure/success, critical attention should be drawn to the surrounding context. The task of the researcher is to look more closely into the appearing trade-offs and elucidate substantial "in-flows" and "out-flows" of deliberative potential.

The final claim I would like to make is that this approach is not intended to create a very precise research design aimed at operationalizing the notion of deliberation. It is rather aimed at clearing the path toward such operationalization. Its major goal is to bridge normative theory with empirical political science so that deliberative democracy might be perceived as a theoretically relevant project as well as a practically viable alternative. Furthermore, this chapter provides evidence for the gap between micro- and macro-deliberation, indicating the direction in which further research might proceed. I argue that creating a "network-based" account of deliberation is a step towards integration of the mini-*demoi* and macro-*demos* levels, thus finding empirical groundwork for the ideal of large-scale deliberative democracy. Only by proving that this integration is feasible are we once again able to understand and regard the latter as a coherent political concept.

References

Baccaro, Lucio. 2003. "What is Alive and What is Dead in the Theory of Corporatism." *British Journal of Industrial Relations* 41 (4) (December): 683–706.

Baiocchi, Gianpaolo. 2003. "Participation, Activism, and Politics: The Porto Allegre Experiment". In *Deepening Democracy: Institutional Innovations Empowered Participatory Governance*. eds. Archon Fung and Erik O. Wright, 45–76. London-New York: Verso.

Carson, Lyn, Gastil, John, Hartz-Karp Janette, and Lubensky, Ron (eds.). 2013. *The Australian Citizens' Parliament and the Future of Deliberative Democracy*. Pennsylvania: Pennsylvania State University Press.

Chambers, Simone. 2003. "Deliberative Democratic Theory." *Annual Review of Political Science* 6 (June): 307–326.

Cohen, Joshua. 1997. "Deliberation and Democratic Legitimacy". In *Deliberative Democracy: Essays on Reason and Politics* 67–91. Cambridge, Mass.: MIT Press.

Cohen, Joshua and Sabel, Charles. 1997. "Directly-Deliberative Polyarchy." *European Law Journal* 3 (4) (December): 313–342.

Coleman, Stephen and Blumler, Jay G. 2009. *The Internet and Democratic Citizenship: Theory, Practice and Policy*. New York: Cambridge University Press.

Davies, Todd and Gangadharan, Seeta P. (eds.). 2009. *Online Deliberation: Design, Research and Practice*. CSLI Publications.

Downs, Anthony. 1957. *An Economic Theory of Democracy*. New York: Harper.

Dryzek, John S. 2002. *Deliberative Democracy and Beyond: Liberals, Critics, Contestations*. Oxford: Oxford University Press.

Dryzek, John S. 1994. *Discursive Democracy: Politics, Policy, and Political Science*. Cambridge: Cambridge University Press.

Dryzek, John S. and Niemeyer, Simon. 2006. "Reconciling Pluralism and Consensus as Political Ideals." *American Journal of Political Science* 50 (3) (July): 634–649.

Fishkin, James. 2009. *When the People Speak*. New York: Oxford University Press.

Gastil, John. 2000. *By Popular Demand: Revitalizing Representative Democracy through Deliberative Elections*. Berkeley-Los Angeles: University of California Press.

Goffman, Erving. 1982. *Interaction Ritual*. Pantheon.

Goodin, Robert E. 2008. *Innovating Democracy: Democratic Theory and Practice after the Deliberative Turn*. New York: Oxford University Press.

Habermas, Jürgen. 1984. *Theory of Communicative Action*, vol. 1: *Reason and Rationalization of Society*. Boston, Mass.: Beacon Press.

Habermas, Jürgen. 1996. *Between Facts and Norms: Contributions to a Discourse Theory of Law and Democracy*. Cambridge, Mass.: MIT Press.

Hajer, Marten A. and Wagenaar Henrik. 2003. *Deliberative Policy Analysis: Understanding Governance in the Network Society*. Cambridge: Cambridge University Press.

Jackson, Simon and Sniderman, Paul. 2006. "The Limits of Deliberative Discussion: A Model of Everyday Political Arguments." *The Journal of Politics* 68 (2) (May): 272–283.

Krause, Sharon. 2008. *Civil Passions: Moral Sentiment and Democratic Deliberation*. Princeton: Princeton University Press.

Lukensmeyer, Carolyn J., Goldman, Joe and Brigham, Steven. 2005. "A Town Meeting for the Twenty-First Century". In *The Deliberative Democracy Handbook: Strategies for Effective Civic Engagement in the Twenty-First Century*, eds. John Gastil and Peter Levine, 154–163. San Francisco: Jossey-Bass.

Mansbridge, Jane. 1999. "Everyday Talk in the Deliberative System". In *Deliberative Politics: Essays on Democracy and Disagreement*, ed. Stephen Macedo, 211–239. New York: Oxford University Press.

Mansbridge et al. 2010. "The Place of Self-Interest and the Role of Power in Deliberative Democracy." *The Journal of Political Philosophy* 18 (1) (March): 64–100.

Mouffe, Chantal. 2000. *The Paradox of Democracy*. London-New York: Verso.

Mutz, Diana. 2008. "Is Deliberative Democracy a Falsifiable Theory?" *Annual Review of Political Science* 11 (June): 521–538.

Parkinson, John and Mansbridge, Jane. 2012. *Deliberative Systems: Deliberative Democracy at the Large Scale*. Cambridge: Cambridge University Press.

Przeworski, Adam. 1998. "Deliberation and Ideological Domination". In *Deliberative Democracy*, ed. Jon Elster, 140–160. Cambridge: Cambridge University Press.

Przeworski, Adam. 2009. "Self-Government in Our Times." *Annual Review of Political Science* 12 (June): 71–92.

Rawls, John. 1971. *A Theory of Justice*. Cambridge, Mass.: Harvard University Press.

Rawls, John. 1999. *The Law of Peoples*. Cambridge, Mass.: Harvard University Press.

Richardson, Henry S. 2002. *Democratic Autonomy: Public Reasoning about the Ends of Policy*. New York: Oxford University Press.

Sanders, Lynn. 1997. "Against Deliberation". *Political Theory* 25 (3) (June): 347–376.

Schütz, Alfred. 1967. *The Phenomenology of the Social World*. Evanston: Northwestern University Press.

Shapiro, Ian. 1999. "Enough of Deliberation: Politics Is about Interests and Power." In *Deliberative Politics: Essays on Democracy and Disagreement*, ed. Stephen Macedo, 28–38. New York: Oxford University Press.

Steiner, Jürg et al. 2004. *Deliberative Politics in Action: Analyzing Parliamentary Discourse*. Cambridge: Cambridge University Press.

Thompson, Dennis. 2008. "Deliberative Democratic Theory and Empirical Political Science." *Annual Review of Political Science* 11 (June): 497–520.

Urbinati, Nadia. 2000. "Representation as Advocacy: A Study of Democratic Deliberation." *Political Theory* 28 (6) (December): 758–786.

Walzer, Michael. 1999. "Deliberation, and What Else?". In *Deliberative Politics: Essays on Democracy and Disagreement*, ed. Stephen Macedo, 58–69. New York: Oxford University Press.

Warren, Mark E. and Pearse, Hilary. 2008. *Designing Deliberative Democracy: The British Columbia Citizens' Assembly*. New York: Cambridge University Press.

Wood, Leslie. 2012. *Direct Action, Deliberation and Diffusion: Collective Action after the WTO Protests in Seattle*. Cambridge: Cambridge University Press.

Young, Iris M. 2001. "Activist Challenges to Deliberative Democracy." *Political Theory* 29 (5) (October): 670–690.

Zürn, Christian F. 2007. *Deliberative Democracy and the Institutions of Judicial Review*. Cambridge: Cambridge University Press.

Section IV.
Deliberative Democracy:
Reflexive Perspectives

Stephen Coleman & Giles Moss

Chapter Thirteen. Under Construction: The Field of Online Deliberation Research[1]

Introduction

How might we describe the development of online deliberation as a field of research and practice? How should we interpret its significance? In this chapter, we argue that deliberative citizenship is best thought of as a construction, rather than something naturally occurring and given, and that the modest field of online deliberation has contributed to its contemporary enactment. Researchers and practitioners of online deliberation tend to deny their hand in constituting deliberative citizenship, since they continue to assume, if only implicitly, that the deliberative citizen is a natural and universal phenomenon, not a constructed one. We argue instead that the deliberative citizen is a construction all the way down, a contingent product of a particular set of discourses and practices, and that online deliberation research plays an important role in enacting as well as studying deliberative citizenship (Cruikshank 1999; Law and Urry 2004; Osborne and Rose 1999; Olson 2008).

In arguing that the deliberative citizen is constructed, and that the field of online deliberation is implicated in its construction, we do not want to suggest that these efforts are not desirable and should be discouraged. We do, however, want to underscore the contingent and 'effectively contestable' (Freeden 2004) nature of any particular form of citizenship and to invite serious reflection, in the absence of any metaphysical certainties, on the political and normative consequences of different discourses and practices of citizenship (Pykett, Saward and Schaefer 2010; Saward 2003).

How then might we evaluate the ways in which deliberative citizenship has tended to be enacted in online deliberation research and practice? After all, while citizenship is always a constructed notion, not all processes of citizen formation are the same. We shall conclude this introductory essay by arguing for online deliberative research and practice to be normatively driven by an effort to produce democratically reflexive citizens; to align our work with the less powerful rather

---

1   The chapter is a reprint of a part of the article under the same title that was published in the *Journal of Information Technology & Politics* 9 (3) 2012.

than reproducing the power of the already dominant; and to pay more attention to the power-mediated relationship between citizen inputs and institutional
outputs. Regardless of whether others share our normative commitment, our
epistemological argument is that one cannot separate discursive constructions of
terms such as citizenship, democracy, and deliberation from attempts to measure
or evaluate their existence.

Our argument proceeds as follows. In Section 1 we outline competing conceptions of citizenship and explain the historical emergence of deliberation as a
prominent idea amongst democratic theorists and reformers. We argue that citizenship is a constructed and contested concept and we consider four of the most
common constructions of citizenship, concluding with the deliberative citizen. In
Section 2 we explore the development of online deliberation as a field of research
and practice and how it entails the construction of a particular conception of deliberative citizenship. In Section 3 we reflect upon the implications of our analysis
and offer some ideas for a future research agenda.

Deliberative Citizenship

The question of civic competence is usually left to lurk in what Robert Dahl (1989)
calls the 'shadow theory of democracy'. Discussions about democratic participation tend to assume, if only implicitly, that the capacities and types of conduct
required for active citizenship are natural and universal. Indeed, to think otherwise seems to threaten to put the central democratic ideal of political equality in
question. It risks siding with those, from Plato to Schumpeter, who have argued
against greater citizen participation in politics and in favor of rule by elites. Insofar
as democratic citizenship presupposes certain forms of often quite demanding
conduct, however, the question of what capacities and traits citizens require, and
how these competencies are developed, cannot be so easily avoided. The ability
of individuals to make the most of their rights and exercise them in a responsible
manner is not natural and does not emerge spontaneously. It has to be learned,
developed, and practiced through processes of socialization, both primary and
secondary (Easton and Dennis 1967; Conover 1994; Torney-Purta 2000; Shah and
McLeod 2009). The various ways in which the idea of citizenship is constructed
reflect these assumptions about the potential for civic competency, confounding
what has been learned with what is natural.

Our aim in what follows is to recognize and typologize four of the most common constructions of citizenships that online theorists and practitioners have
inherited as part of their conceptual repertoire for thinking about the relationship between the Internet and democracy. Like any typology, some features will

overlap the boundaries of each category and there will be an inevitable empirical variance between normative descriptions and applied models.

We begin by acknowledging the self-styled realistic model of citizenship, which tends to place minimal responsibilities upon citizens, believing them to be too busy, insufficiently attentive, and, perhaps, cognitively incapable of doing more than observe political affairs from a distance and voting occasionally for whichever leader or party seems to be most worthy of their support. As Schumpeter (1976, 284) put it, 'Democracy means only that the people have the opportunity of accepting or refusing the men who are to rule them.' Dismissing in the name of 'realism' the capacity of citizens to play a significant or permanent role in public decision-making, proponents of this conception of citizenship have emphasized a more relaxed, monitorial function for the citizenry. As Schudson (2000, 3) has described, monitorial citizens

> should be informed enough and alert enough to identify danger to their personal good and danger to the public good. When such danger appears on the horizon, they should have the resources – in trusted relationships, in political parties and elected officials, in relationships to interest groups and other trustees of their concerns, in knowledge of and access to the courts as well as the electoral system, and in relevant information sources to jump into the political fray and make a lot of noise.

The role of the media in this context is to serve as a sophisticated fire alarm, with journalists ever-ready to alert citizens to personal and public dangers and point them towards trustworthy institutions capable of addressing their concerns. For such 'realists', e-democracy might be confined to the provision of a broad range of public information online; expanded opportunities to access government services at the click of a mouse; and perhaps even some limited ways of interacting with the powers that be through emails and online surveys. As a conception of citizenship-lite, this has the virtue of not raising expectations about anyone's contribution to democracy; it seems to assume that democratic norms can be realized while most citizens are busy getting on with their own lives, oblivious to the public sphere.

A second conception of citizenship is rooted in metaphors of the marketplace. The individual citizen is regarded here as a free agent, out to maximize personal gain. More like bargain-hunting consumers than Athenian-style members of a community, citizens so conceived are expected to steer clear of anything resembling a responsibility to be socially informed. Libertarian theorists (Berger and Neuhaus 1977; Saunders 1993) paint such civic self-serving as a precondition of liberty; rational choice theorists (Aldrich 1993; Mueller 2003) are less sanguine, contending that citizens are simply trapped within the systemic logic of collective action, doomed to seek low information costs and opportunities to freeload on the civic energies of others.

The role of the media in this civic context is utilitarian: to provide individual citizens with enough information to help them pursue their day-to-day personal interests. Democracy is played out in a sort of marketplace of ideas in which a combination of acute strategy and broad appeal raises some interests to the top of the political agenda, while dismissing others to the valueless margins. In this context, e-democracy would describe uses of the Internet by competing individuals and interest groups to secure their own information needs and social advantages at the expense of others. As in the more regulated and prohibitive spaces provided by broadcast media or the press, the objective of political advocacy is to outwit, discredit and nullify rival positions with a view to winning the game of politics.

From the perspective of most post-Schumpeterian versions of normative democratic theory, the above two models of citizenship are regarded as parsimonious and impoverishing. Without active participation by citizens in public affairs, democratic theorists have argued, the democratic project is something of a sham: rule by elites in the name of the people rather than rule by the people, who are capable of holding governing elites to account. Since the 1960s, the participatory citizen has been imagined, encouraged, and ultimately regarded as an indispensable actor within meaningful democracy. An acknowledgement on the part of governments and policy experts that they cannot be expected to know everything, especially in relation to the life of communities, has prompted a range of initiatives designed to promote participative citizenship. From public consultations, neighborhood councils, and Citizens' Juries to organized volunteering on local projects and attempts to bring civil-society organizations into the policy process, the ideal of participatory democracy has been regarded as the best safeguard against political alienation. Ensuring that citizens are up to the challenge of becoming active participators has led to civic skills being taught in schools through the citizenship/civics curriculum, while at the same time national and local governments have promoted a range of policies intended to 'engage the disengaged'. Of course, both participation and engagement are political and constructed notions, including a relatively narrow range of actions (voting, following the news, joining parties, movements and community associations, writing to elected representatives) and either ignoring or discouraging others (demonstrating, rioting, law-breaking, striking, ridiculing authority). While all of these activities might be regarded as participatory or engaged citizenship, discourses of official recognition are effective in differentiating between civic and uncivil participation. The media have played a major part in all of this, opening themselves up to public interaction through call-ins, studio discussions, outreach events, phone-votes, and emails from audience members. The rhetoric of media participation is replete with democratic claims, sometimes justifiable insofar as media interactivity does open up politics to citizens and citizens to one another. But there are also serious limitations: a populist vein runs through many of these participatory exercises, casting the media as ever-mobile ringleaders, ready to stoke up emotions around the latest reason for public anger. Used in such formats, active citizens can be reduced to one-line, vox pop caricatures, thrown into situations in which the image of the brawling mob displaces public discussion (Coleman and Ross 2010). Even when, as sometimes happens, media attempts to involve the public do lead to new ideas, revealed experiences and a sense that something needs to be done, there is a lack of any formal connection to institutions that can follow them up. Citizens experience the frustration of seeming to be talking to themselves and often give up, leaving the field even clearer for ranters who are not particularly bothered about constructive outcomes. All of this has led to a tragic paradox: there exist more opportunities than ever before for citizens wishing to have their say, via the media or directly to local and national governments, but there is a more pervasive sense of disappointment than ever before that citizens are outside the citadels of power and that those within do not know how to listen to them.

In the context of e-democracy, technologies of participation have mushroomed, with governments urging citizens to send them e-petitions, broadcasters inviting audiences to 'have your say', legislatures running online consultations about policies before them and elected representatives blogging away, often impervious to the feedback they receive (Coleman and Blumler 2009). Political elites have tended to make simplistic equations between interactive media and more inclusive decision-making, but there has been a colossal gulf between rhetoric and cultural change. Enthusiasm for participatory democracy still persists within governments and civil society, and new projects intended to exploit the Internet as a connecting channel between rulers and ruled are emerging across the globe, but there is a growing sense that inviting citizens to 'get involved', without offering them opportunities to determine and discuss the terms of their engagement, is something less than democratic.

The failings of participatory democracy in its populist form have given rise to a renewed interest in the deliberative idea of nurturing informed, thoughtful citizens, whose exposure to one another's experiences and arguments might equip them to perform a role as intelligent participants in their own governance. This transcends the traditional boundaries of indirect, representative democracy, positing the idea of democracy as a forum in which issues and policy proposals are debated and discussed on their merits rather than a game in which the attainment and retention of power is the principal goal (Habermas 1991; Dahlgren 2005).

However, the more that theorists call for such a multi-perspectival, rational, and consensual conception of citizenship, the more clearly its absence becomes apparent. With very few exceptions, the mass media, which are so good at delivering basic information and entertainment, seem to have given up any practical hope of serving as a critical forum for citizens' debate. In frustration, a number of political communication scholars have turned to the Internet as a promising space for inclusive and enlightened civic discourse. Such scholars argue that meaningful e-democracy entails e-deliberation: the opening up of the Internet as a popular *agora* in which positions can be exposed to public scrutiny and debate, and the force of the more reasoned argument might prevail (Dahlberg 2001; Coleman and Gotze 2001; Graham and Witschge 2003; Albrecht 2006; Delborne et al. 2011; Loveland and Popescu 2011)

But, like the other terms that we have discussed (citizenship, participation and engagement), the concept of deliberation has to be constructed before it can be applied. The deliberative citizen might be imagined as someone who is prepared to be open about her views, willing to spend time hearing and engaging with opposing positions, and prepared to talk relentlessly in search of compromise and consensus, but such an ideal is too vague and idealized to constitute a theory of citizenship. Deliberative scholars, who have been at the forefront of defining as well as observing the phenomenon of deliberation, have been under some pressure to explain what deliberation looks like when it occurs. But they are far from united in arriving at a clear-cut definition. Gonzalez-Bailon et al. (2010, 3) note that disagreement amongst researchers about the necessary and sufficient conditions for deliberation to take place makes it almost impossible to identify deliberative talk when it occurs:

> Without these conditions, deliberation is a moving target: it is difficult to match with any particular instance of public discussion, and it can always be argued that some crucial element is missing that disqualifies the entire empirical approach. The problem with this lack of conceptual clarity is not only that it goes against the basic principle of scientific refutability, hampering the development of the theory, but also that it blurs the boundaries between the definition of deliberation and its evaluation.

Muhlberger (2000, 2) observes that 'little agreement exists regarding what deliberation is and how it might be measured'. Parkinson (2003, 181) criticizes researchers, such as Button and Mattson (1999), for labeling as deliberative 'practices which exhibit none of the procedural conditions of genuine deliberation'. Gastil and Black (2008, 1) note that 'there exist varied theoretical conceptions of public deliberation and no clear—let alone widely-adopted—conceptual definition of the term' and proceed to make the rather grand claim that 'the study of deliberation is not so much a subfield within the larger body of political communication research, but, rather, can serve as a means of organizing and making sense of the political communication enterprise, as well as a means of revealing those spots that the field has overlooked'. Neblo (2005, 174) warns that 'no amount of conceptual maneuvering will allow the deliberative democrat to skirt the details of how deliberation will actually function in applied politics'. Two things are clear: there exists no scholarly consensus about what even the most basic characteristics of deliberation are; and scholars are leading players in the effort to construct a meaning that is sufficiently compelling to relate the notion of deliberative citizenship to the empirical world around them.

Online Deliberation Research

If, as we argue, deliberative citizenship is a construction, it follows that it is best understood by tracing how specific practices, both social and technical, have given rise to this particular way of imagining, designing, and evaluating citizenship. Top-down government strategies intended to promote 'responsible' citizenship are central to the shaping of civic behaviour. But more broadly, as Foucauldian governmentality scholars have emphasized, various other, non-state agencies and bodies of expertise are also implicated in efforts to shape citizen conduct through various 'technologies of citizenship' (Barnett 2003, 81–108; Cruikshank, 1999; Dean 2001). We argue here that online deliberation research is involved in cultivating a particular form of deliberative citizenship. Sometimes the links between deliberative research and practice are direct and explicit. For example, in their study of 58 European and US online policy consultations, Astrom and Gronlund (2012) observe that '44 percent of the researchers we considered had been practically involved in the cases they evaluated. They had been members of the project teams, planning the consultation, developing software and moderating debates'. Perhaps not surprisingly, Astrom and Gronlund (2012) found that projects that researchers were involved in running tended to be more positively evaluated than those that were observed independently. Their conclusion that 'The temptation for researchers examining the use of electronic forums is to jump into the struggle over defining what they are really for and to help forge new uses' Astrom and Gronlund (2012) accords with the findings of Macintosh, Coleman, and Schneeberger (2008) in their study of the unstable boundary between research and practice in European e-participation projects. But the links between online deliberation research and practice may also be less direct or explicit. Scholars researching online deliberation have also played, we argue, a significant part in constructing the object that they are studying insofar as they have identified deliberation's appearance online and have generated a body of detailed knowledge about the social and technical conditions under which it is most likely to be successful.

Most researchers, however, continue to speak and write as if deliberation and the capacities it presupposes are naturally occurring and universal rather than constructed and contingent. Holding on to an essentialist conception of liberal citizenship, they fail to consider the extent to which the deliberative citizen is 'formed and normed', in Ivison's (1997) evocative phrase, and to which they contribute to the construction of the object of their own research. In arguing that online deliberation researchers are deeply implicated in the construction of what they study is not to cast aspersions on their (our) integrity or suggest that such constructivism is an intellectual or ethical weakness. On the contrary, it is by coming to recognize how scholarly reflection contributes to the enactment of the social that we can (as we do in the final section of this chapter) face up to our responsibilities as knowledge producers.

We consider here two related ways in which researchers have contributed to the construction of online deliberation: ontologically, by naming certain forms of talk as deliberation and others as either mere chatter or insincere politicking; and socio-technically, by setting out the most appropriate ways for online deliberation to be made to happen.

Privileging Certain Forms of Talk

The Internet is replete with talk: billions of words, sentences, messages, sentiments. Much can be learned from studying how such talk is structured and the extent to which it influences civic behavior. But deliberation researchers ignore most online talk, regarding it as mere chatter; the casual noise of mundane sociability. Political talk fares rather better. Scholars have taken great interest in the various ways that citizens express themselves online, not only as potential voters during the heated periods of election campaigns, but also in day-to-day discussions amongst themselves and with elected officials about matters of public consequence. For deliberative purists, however, such verbal exchanges rarely meet the standards required for 'proper' deliberation. For them, the key features of deliberative talk, be it online or offline, are procedural and substantive rationality. And, of course, the terms of rationality are themselves highly constructed, often amounting to a westernized notion of politeness, fair play, and emotive repression (Min 2009). By the demanding standards of deliberative rationalism, most online discussion, even when it is about matters conventionally defined as political, falls short of the ideal norms operationalized by researchers in their normatively rather narrow content analyses (Davis 1999; Hill and Hughes 1999;

Wilhelm 2000). Online talk is routinely found to be uncivil, beset by affectively-charged contributors and not conducive to the sharing of arguments and shifting of preferences. Wilhelm (2000, 98), for example, concludes his content analysis of online discussion by noting that, 'the data support the conception of online political forums as facilitating self-expression and monologue, without in large measure the "listening", responsiveness, and dialogue that would promote communicative action, such as prioritizing issues, negotiating differences, reaching agreement'.

While early researchers, mainly focusing upon non-moderated newsgroups, failed to find deliberation online and bemoaned the poor quality of most political talk, it was not long before subsequent researchers began to 'discover' it. Interestingly, the appearance of online deliberation tended to coincide with experiments and pilot projects that were designed to bring it about (Price and Cappella 2002; Macintosh et al. 2003; Coleman 2004; Muhlberger and Weber 2006). In short, much of the optimism about online deliberation emanated from scholars researching spaces of civic talk that were constructed with a view to promoting the very norms that they were looking for. Indeed, in several cases researchers were involved in the design and management of projects intended to test the potential for online deliberation. The value of such exercises was that researchers were able to explore how particular tools and systems afforded observable deliberative outcomes. In establishing and scrutinizing online zones of well-regulated rational discourse, researchers were able to imagine what democratic citizenship might be like if it could be immunized against the messy incursions of everyday life. But findings based upon such experiments and pilot projects could not be generalized; there was a sense in which online deliberation was a creature of the laboratory.

The conflation between research and its object was compounded by researchers' normative obsession with rational argumentation modeled upon the Habermasian notion of discourse ethics, as if that were the only form of civic expression that deserved to be considered as deliberative. Some critics of the deliberative turn (Fraser 1990; Mouffe 2000; Sanders 1997; Young 2001, 2002) have argued that the straightjacket of rationalistic deliberation often serves to marginalize, undermine, and proscribe the expressive repertoires of subordinate groups, and act as a normalizing and conservative force against progressive social change. Sanders (1997, 347) argues that 'Appeals to deliberation ... have often been fraught with connotations of rationality, reserve, cautiousness, quietude, community, selflessness, and universalism, connotations which in fact probably undermine deliberation's democratic claims'. She goes on to suggest that the invitation to deliberate has strings attached. Deliberation is a request for a certain kind of talk: rational, contained, and orientated to a shared problem. Where antidemocrats have used the standards of expertise, moderation, and communal orientation as a way to exclude average citizens from political decision-making, modern democrats seem to adopt these standards as guides for what democratic politics should be like. And the exclusionary connotations of these standards persist. Arguing that democratic deliberation should be rational, moderate, and not selfish implicitly excludes public talk that is impassioned, extreme, and the product of particular interests (Sanders, 1997, 360).

Following on from this critique, Mouffe (2000) characterizes deliberative purists as being somewhat naïvely oblivious to the pervasiveness of social structure:

> One of the shortcomings of the deliberative approach is that, by postulating the availability of a public sphere where power would have been eliminated and where a rational consensus could be realized, this model of democratic politics is unable to acknowledge the dimension of antagonism that the pluralism of values entails and its ineradicable character ... In order to remedy this serious deficiency, we need a democratic model able to grasp the nature of the political. This requires developing an approach which places the question of power and antagonism at its very center.

In response to these doubts that have been raised about the cultural and political assumptions implicit in normative conceptions of deliberation, we argue that in some contexts reason-governed deliberation is unduly restrictive, discounting other important ways of making, receiving, and contesting public claims. In particular, we observe a tendency on the part of some proponents of the deliberative approach to civic discourse to celebrate its apolitical character, privileging the search for consensus above the profession of ideological candor and the contestation of values. Such perspectives are so normatively committed to a search for universally acceptable agreement that they have come to regard agonistic vigor as somehow antagonistic to the deliberative project. Not only is such depoliticized rationalism nothing more than an ideological position in itself (as Enlightenment Reason ever was), but it denies in the name of deliberative capacity-building some of the features of democratic citizenship that have proven historically to be most strategically advantageous to groups engaged in attempts to resist the forces of hegemonic authority.

It follows from this that we need to remain more open as researchers and practitioners to a catholic range of communicative practices and possibilities, including those that address naked power as well as sweet reason. Content analyses of online discussions that dismiss the expression of anecdotes, sentiments, reminiscences, calls to action, or casual observations as if they were a devalued currency, incomparable with the deliberative gold standard of the well-made argument, references to authoritative data and appeals to consensus, tell us no more than that researchers prefer certain modes of civic talk than others. They do not tell us which complex mix of expressive forms are most likely to explain antagonistic positions most clearly, inspire collective action, or generate feelings of solidarity.

Technologies of Discursive Order

Research on online deliberation has identified various online practices and architectures, including social as well as technical features, which make deliberation more likely to work. We refer to these as technologies of discursive order. They constitute techniques and strategies designed to produce forms of communicative interaction consistent with norms of deliberative quality. Upon investigation, most of the claims surrounding these techniques and strategies are highly contested. For example, some researchers have found that anonymity allows for a fluidity of identity so that citizens can present themselves in varied ways, without feeling judged or constrained by conventional cultural cues (Bowker 2003; Kim 2006). Others argue that anonymity contributes to a lack of civility and respect in online discussion and that compelling people to use their real names encourages them to take responsibility for what they say and be more thoughtful when contributing (Friedman et al. 2000; Polat and Pratchett 2009). Crucially for deliberation, knowing who is speaking also helps other interlocutors to check for performative contradictions and the sincerity of individual utterances (Habermas 1989). Several researchers have argued that the temporal aspects of discursive practices are highly significant. Asynchronous discussions, where participants have more time to reflect and more flexibility about when to participate, is often presented as being more likely to promote deliberation than real-time, synchronous interaction (Janssen 2005; Smith et al. 2009). Some deliberative sites take this logic further: the Local Issues Forums run by e-demcoracy.org, for example, limit the number of possible contributions to two per day. Rationing the number of posts prevents a few vociferous contributors from dominating discussions to the exclusion of others. It also encourages individuals to reflect more carefully before postings and to provide higher-quality contributions to the discussion.

Moderation practices can have a significant positive impact on the deliberative quality of discussion, whether it is in the form of pre-moderation (where contributions are screened and some contributions prohibited from reaching users) or post-moderation (the removal of posts after they have been posted). Online libertarians view moderation as an illegitimate form of censorship, which conflicts with the unrestricted expression that characterizes the Internet at its best. Other researchers, by contrast, have pointed to the important role that skilled individuals can play as moderators in promoting deliberation (Coleman and Gotze 2001; Edwards 2002; Wright 2009; Wright and Street 2007). In this view, moderators can help to maintain civility by warning participants of infractions of a site's rules of discussion, by removing offending posts, and by temporarily blocking repeat offenders from participating. The moderator also plays a broader role in facilitating deliberation, acting as a 'helper' and 'facilitator' not just a 'filter': they can recruit new participants to join deliberation, introduce new topics, encourage alternate viewpoints, and respond to participants' questions and complaints (Edwards 2002). As such, moderators may be viewed as important 'democratic intermediaries', in Edwards' (2003) terms, which promote and enhance the deliberative quality of discussion.

As well as formal design features such as these, the discursive and visual elements that surround particular online settings and practices also play a significant role in communicating their meaning and purpose to users. Various semiotic and discursive elements, from the name of particular sites to the visual images that are used, help to 'encode' and attach a 'preferred reading' and meaning to a practice that users 'decode' (Hall 1987). They can help, in Woolgar's (1991) words, to 'configure' a particular form of use of the technology. For example, they can encourage participants to adopt forms of civility and perhaps even restraint that are consistent with dominant understandings of deliberation.

By pointing to these and other features of online settings and practices, research on online deliberation has demonstrated how, under the 'right' conditions, deliberative discussion, as understood by scholars, can be promoted online. While some critics have questioned the feasibility of deliberation, defending more limited and 'realistic' notions of citizens' participation in public life (Chadwick 2009), online deliberation researchers have in recent years been able to point to successful examples of deliberative citizenship, as they understand it, and have been able to identify cases where online discussions have led to the positive effects predicted by deliberative theory: discussions have widened participants' repertoire of arguments, introduced them to new perspectives, and led to shifts in preferences (Price and Cappella 2002; Barabas 2004; Shane 2004; Janssen and Kies 2005; Iyengar, Luskin and Fishkin 2005; Monnoyer-Smith 2006; Min 2007; Coleman and Blumler 2009).

Current researchers in the field of online deliberation are seeking to build on this work by establishing online practices that are even more amenable to reason-governed deliberation. Some of the most inventive work is in the area of argument mapping and visualization. A common problem in large-scale discussions is cognitive overload, with important arguments getting lost amidst a mass of indecipherable noise. In the light of this, online deliberation researchers and practitioners have experimented with the use of maps that can visualize the logic of the various positions and arguments within a deliberative exchange. These maps make it supposedly easier for interlocutors to understand and chart their way through large and complex public discussions (IMPACT Project 2011; Buckingham-Shum 2006; Renton and Macintosh 2007). Visualization techniques are not limited to representing public discussions empirically. They also aim to increase the rationality of discussion by identifying and making explicit the premises, warrants, and validity claims behind different arguments. Reason can then be separated from other extraneous features of discussion: from rhetorical, expressive and emotional appeals; from the status of the speaker who is making an argument; or from the number of people who happen to support a particular proposal. The aim is to encourage reflection and ensure that the 'force of the better argument' prevails (Habermas 1991). As Hoffmann (2008) suggests, argument maps and visualizations are more than mere 'representations'; they should be understood, he argues, as tools that 'augment our natural abilities' and seek to stimulate our reasoning by 'challenging' and 'compelling' us to think deliberatively. By representing the logic of the better argument to us, argument visualization has a normative binding force: 'we as the users of an argumentation system have to accept the normative character of its rules as something that is beyond our own power' (Hoffmann 2008).

While these technologies of discursive ordering do not determine subjectivity, they do seek to 'elicit, promote, facilitate and attribute various capacities, qualities and statuses to particular agents' (Dean 2001, 32). Users, as Hoffmann (2008) implies above, must accept the practices of citizenship to which they are subject. By naming and identifying online deliberation's appearance and by generating ever more detailed knowledge about the social and technical practices and conditions under which it is most likely to succeed, online deliberation research has contributed to the enactment of a particular mode of citizenship in which people are prepared to submit to transparent and universal rationality. From this perspective, online deliberation research is not separate from its object of study, but is implicated in its construction, helping to create what it purports merely to discover (Law and Urry 2004). As such, we might say that online deliberation involves what Mol (1998) calls 'ontological politics': it involves making crucial decisions about which type of reality to recognize and promote, even if researchers typically deny this fact by continuing to assert mistakenly that deliberation is a natural and universal phenomenon rather than a constructed one.

In response to this assumption, we have been working recently with information scientists from the Open University to design a tool that can be used by citizens to interrogate information presented to them by political leaders in televised election debates. Rather than thinking of information needs as qualities that can be defined and evaluated for people by an external body, or information as something that is given to people by those in the know, we have sought to conceive of democratic information in terms of people's own sense of their entitlement to acquire knowledge that will enable them to act in and on the world as autonomous beings. Building on theoretical work on social justice, we explore citizens' reception and uses of televised election debates in terms of their capacity to recognise and realise democratic capabilities (Sen 1973, 1992; Nussbaum 1995, 2011; Garnham 1999). This approach begins by asking what sort of capabilities are needed by variously-situated people if they are to function in a particular kind of society. Unlike top-down notions of information, the capabilities' perspective insists that the utility of information must be defined from the actor's point of view, in terms of the extent to which such information enables her to realise her full potential within a particular social context. Information needs, in this sense, are self-defined and contextual; they cannot be satisfied on the basis of externally-determined criteria. This places individual citizens, as social actors in search of opportunities to live their lives freely and autonomously, as the judges of their information requirements – and, in the context of the present discussion, as framers of their own norms of deliberative competence.

Whereas earlier scholars pointed to the injustice of individuals and social groups having unequal access to information resources, the capabilities' approach goes further, suggesting that the determination of what constitutes necessary and valuable information should be just as much a matter of social equity as opportunities to access information which others deem to be necessary and valuable. In the context of the spectacle of televised deliberation involving party leaders, the capabilities' approach compels us to turn the usual effects questions on their head. Instead of asking whether debate-watching leads to outcomes that we (scholars and policy elites) have defined as being politically important, we are bound to ask what viewers feel entitled to gain from the debates and the extent to which these capabilities are enhanced, diminished or unaffected by debate-watching.

Conclusions: The Ontological Politics of Online Deliberation Research

In arguing that the concept of online deliberation is not only contingent and contested, but inevitably constructed by those who facilitate and evaluate it, we are not seeking to suggest that by eschewing constructivism researchers can gain privileged access to some less made- up and more authentic conception of civic discourse. In recent times social scientists have turned their attention to the foundational problematics of ontological politics, acknowledging the extent to which the object of their research is a product of their attempts to describe what is at stake. As Hay (2006, 78) has noted,

> Political scientists, for the most part, have tended to leave ontological issues to philosophers and to those social scientists less encumbered by substantive empirical concerns. Yet as the discipline has become more reflexive and perhaps rather less confident than once it was at the ease with which it might claim a scientific license for the knowledge it generates, so ontological issues have increasingly come to the fore.

The ontological status of public online deliberation is inseparable from the politics of determining who can speak for the public, what can be said in public, and what constitutes the public interest. As Ryfe (2007, 8) has rightly put it,

> When advocates of deliberation press to make public life more deliberative, they compete with others to set the "legitimate social vision" on the basis of which public life will be organized; they compete to name, classify, organize, and authorize public life. This work represents a politics of the most basic sort.

In the absence of metaphysical certainties, the aim of researchers should be to engage in critical reflection about the genealogies, meanings, and consequences of different discourses and practices of citizenship; to ask how best we might evaluate the particular constructions of deliberative citizenship that are enacted in online deliberation research and practice? Put more starkly, we might ask, if citizenship is a construction, what forms of citizenship should we, as researchers, be helping to enact? In setting out our own responses to that question, with a view to stimulating debate within the growing online deliberation research community and beyond, we are not seeking to impose a new normative framework, but to make explicit (and therefore accountable and debatable) what is too often only implicitly acknowledged by researchers.

A first response to the question of what forms of citizenship researchers should enact is to acknowledge that, while citizenship is always already a construction, not all processes of citizen formation are consistent with norms of democratic autonomy. Crucially, as Olson (2008) has argued, some processes of subject formation produce citizens with capacities of reflexivity and agency which enable them to influence and potentially contest the forces to which they are subject. Such citizens, he argues, 'would be more able to alter the range of practices and life possibilities they themselves are allowed' and be 'more able to participate in choosing the circumstances of their own self-government and freedom' (Olson 2008, 51). Citizen reflexivity and agency are not only significant consideration in the design and organization of online communicative practices. They are important in thinking about how to design and conduct research. Most researchers of online deliberation have opted to use content analysis as a means of measuring the quality of discussion, operationalizing their own conceptions of what 'good' communication looks like. Researchers have rarely given any significant role to citizens' own reflections upon, and evaluations of, the quality and experience of online communication—this tends to be true of political science and political communication more generally, with their fondness for survey research and rationalistic modeling (Markham and Couldry 2006). The dominant methods used in online deliberation research have tended to reproduce an inert and mute research subject. Using different methods, such as focus groups, interviews, or research diaries, we might be able to pay more attention in our research to the perceptions and reflections of participants themselves; to how they experience and evaluate the practices of citizen formation to which they are made subject. Renegotiating the established power relationship between expert researchers and the subjects of their research, the perceptions and reflections of research participants could then be used to inform the direction and shape of the research process itself.

Secondly, we propose that researchers should aim to align our research with the less powerful and not contribute to reproducing the power of the already dominant (Law and Urry 2004). Deliberative reasoning and publicity can help to discipline elites, encouraging those who usually dominate to account for themselves in public and to listen to the perspectives of others. Elster (1998, 111) refers here to the 'civilizing force of hypocrisy', where publicity is able to encourage speakers to 'replace the language of interest by the language of reason and to replace impartial motives by passionate ones'. At the same time, as we have already noted, overly formalized conception of deliberation can serve to subordinate individuals and groups by dismissing as 'non-deliberative' modes of expression, forms of position-stating, and demonstrations of affect. Many of these exclusionary and marginalizing practices are ethnocentric and gendered; most of them embody codes of class and status that work insidiously to filter out voices deemed to be vulgar, threatening, over-dependent, or unruly. Few researchers would knowingly support such norms on inequality, but spotting, describing, and challenging them is not always easy. Here again, there are implications for research methodology: perhaps, when it comes to analyzing deliberative quality, the more nuanced approach of discourse analysis would be better at identifying hesitations, put-downs, failures to be understood, or switches of communicative repertoire than the cruder counting mechanism of content analysis; perhaps, when it comes to evaluating practices of online moderation and facilitation, attention should be paid to who is not addressed, what is not said, and how rules might have been differently interpreted, rather than merely monitoring the catechistic principles of Habermasian discourse ethics.

As well as endeavoring to acknowledge and encourage voices that are too often unheard in formal deliberative situations, there may be much to be learned by researchers from seeking out spaces of unconventional political talk. In diverse modes and arenas of informal online communication people exchange opinions, stories, jokes, gossip, and desires, and these can sometimes assume a deliberative character, for attempts by people to persuade one another of the rightness of their preferences and values goes on all the time, interspersed amongst much else that is casual and mundane. Beyond the political bubble within which most policy formation, decision-making, and formally-structured deliberation take place, there exists a rich vein of public discussion from which researchers can gain an insight into what we might call street-level deliberation.

Thirdly, we would argue that online deliberation researchers need to become more attendant to outcomes; not simply in terms of whether participants trusted the process, learned anything new or would do it all again, but in terms of the political efficacy of citizens and of policy outputs. As Bang (2009) has suggested, new modes of governance have placed great emphasis upon the democratization of citizen input, but without outputs no form of collective action, including talk, amounts to much. While some policy scholars have written about the effects of interactive civic discourse upon policy (mainly the lack of it, it should be said), for most online deliberation researchers it seems as if the political process ends when civic talk stops. Online deliberation is not an alternative to political decision-making, but a means of enhancing it. And, in representative democracies, deliberation by the public or even elected parliamentarians is but one stage in the complex process of turning organized preferences into implementable policies. We know very little at the moment about how online deliberative talk relates in practice to institutional decision-making. Methodologically, investigating this would require researchers to become engaged with subjects being deliberated, and the ways in which they are structurally, politically, and linguistically inscribed, before turning to the ways in which citizens reflect upon them. Just as argument mapping and visualization (discussed above) are intended to summarize the range of positions within a deliberative exchange, there is a need for a broader mapping of the institutionally-embedded processes (including those entrenched within global, national, and local markets and their institutional offshoots) through which online deliberative talk must resonate if it is to become more than a political distraction and to increase the efficacy of citizens.

The study of online deliberation is still in its infancy. Much has been learned over more than a decade, during which the Internet has grown from being a minority tool to a socially-pervasive presence and deliberative theory has moved out of the rarefied environment of the departments of philosophy to influential departments of governments and grass-roots applications. Much has been learned, but much has been shaped at the same time, and often by the same researchers. We have been complicit in fashioning the object of our attention. Now might be a good time to reflect upon exactly what we have been trying to design.

References

Albrecht, Steffen. 2006. "Whose voice is heard in online deliberation? A study of participation and representation in political debates on the internet." *Information, Communication & Society* 9 (1): 62–82.

Aldrich, John H. 1993. "Rational choice and turnout." *American Political Science Review* 37 (1): 246–278.

Astrom, Joachim, and Ake Gronlund. 2012. "Online consultations in local government: What works, when and how." In *Connecting Democracy: Online Consultation and the Flow of Political Communication,* eds. Stephen Coleman and Peter Shane, 75–96. Cambridge, MA: MIT Press.

Bang, Henrik, and Anders Esmark. 2009. "Good governance in network society: Reconfiguring the political from politics to policy." *Administrative Theory and Praxis* 31 (1): 7–37.

Barabas, Jason. 2004. "How deliberation affects policy opinions." *American Political Science Review* 98: 687–701.

Barnett, Clive. 2003. *Culture and Democracy: Media, Space and Representation.* Edinburgh, Scotland: Edinburgh University Press.

Berger, Peter, and Richard Neuhaus. 1977. *To Empower People: The Role of Mediating Structures in Public Policy.* Washington, DC: American Enterprise Institute for Public Policy Research.

Bowker, Natilene, and Keith Tuffin. 2003. "Dicing with deception: People with disabilities' strategies for managing safety and identity online." *Journal of Computer-Mediated Communication,* 8 (2). http://jcmc.indiana.edu/vol8/issue2/bowker. html.

Buckingham-Shum, Simon. 2006, September. "Sensemaking on the pragmatic web: A hypermedia discourse perspective." Presented at the first International Pragmatic Web Conference, Stuttgart, Germany.

Button, Mark, and Kevin Mattson. 1999. "Deliberative democracy in practice: Challenges and prospects for civic deliberation." *Polity* 31 (4): 609–637.

Chadwick, Andrew. 2009. "Web 2.0: New challenges for the study of e-democracy in an era of informational exuberance." *I/S: A Journal of Law and Policy for the Information Society* 5 (1): 9–42.

Coleman, Stephen. 2004. "Connecting Parliament to the public via the Internet: Two case studies of online consultations." *Information, Communication & Society* 7 (1): 1–22.

Coleman, Stephen, and Jay G. Blumler. 2009. *The Internet and Democratic Citizenship: Theory, Practice, and Policy*. New York: Cambridge University Press.

Coleman, Stephen, and Jay G. Blumler. 2010. "The wisdom of which crowd? On the pathology of a listening government." *Political Quarterly* 82 (3): 355–364.

Coleman, Stephen, and John Gotze. 2001. *Bowling Together: Online Public Engagement in Policy Deliberation*. London: Hansard Society.

Coleman, Stephen, and Karen Ross. 2010. *The media and the Public: "Them" and "Us" in Media Discourse*. Oxford, England: Wiley-Blackwell.

Conover, Pamela, and Donald Searing. 1994. "Democracy, citizenship, and the study of political socialization." In *Developing Democracy: Comparative Research in Honour of J. F. P. Blondel*, eds. Ian Budge and David McKay, 24–55. London: Sage.

Cruikshank, Barbara. 1999. *The will to Empower: Democratic Citizens and Other Subjects*. Ithaca, NY: Cornell University Press.

Dahl, Robert. 1989. *Democracy and its Critics*. NewHaven, CT: Yale University Press.

Dahlberg, Lincoln. 2001. "The Internet and democratic discourse: Exploring the prospects of online deliberative forums extending the public sphere." *Information, Communication & Society* 4 (4): 615–633.

Dahlgren, Peter. 2005. "The Internet, public spheres, and political communication: Dispersion and deliberation." *Political Communication* 2 (22): 147–162.

Davis, Richard. 1999. *The Web of Politics: The Internet's Impact on the American Political System*. New York: Oxford University Press.

Dean, Mitchell. 1999. *Governmentality: Power and Rule in Modern Society*. Thousand Oaks, CA: SAGE.

Delborne, Jason, Ashley Anderson, Daniel Lee Kleinman, Mathilde Colin, and Maria Powell. 2011. "Virtual deliberation? Prospects and challenges for integrating the Internet in consensus' conferences." *Public Understanding of Science* 20 (3): 367–384.

Durose, Catherine, Stephen Greasley, and Liz Richardson (eds.). 2009. *Changing local governance, changing citizens*. Policy Press.

Easton, David, and Jack Dennis. 1967. "The child's acquisition of regime norms: Political efficacy." *The American Political Science Review* 61 (1): 25–38.

Edwards, Arthur. 2002. "The moderator as an emerging democratic intermediary: The role of the moderator in Internet discussions about public issues." *Information Polity* 7 (1): 3–20.

Elster, Jon. 1998. "Deliberation and constitution making." In *Deliberative Democracy*, ed. Jon Elster, 97–122. New York: Cambridge University Press.

Fraser, Nancy. 1990. "Rethinking the public sphere: A contribution to the critique of actually existing democracy." *Social Text* 25/26: 56–80.

Freeden, Michael. 2004. "Essential contestability and effective contestability." *Journal of Political Ideologies* 9 (1): 3–11.

Friedman, Batya, Peter Khan, and Daniel Howe. 2000. "Trust online." *Communications of the ACM* 43 (12): 34–40.

Garnham, Nicholas. 1999. "Amartya Sen's capabilities approach to the evaluation of welfare: Its application to communications." In *Communication, Citizenship and Social Policy: Rethinking the Limits of the Welfare State*, eds. Andrew Calabrese and Jean-Claude Burgelman, 113–124. Oxford and New York: Rowman & Littlefield.

Gastil, John, and Laura Black. 2008. "Public deliberation as the organizing principle of political communication research." *Journal of Deliberation* 4 (1): 1–47.

Gonzales-Bailon, Sandra, Andreas Kaltenbrunner, and Rafael Banchs. 2010. "The structure of political discussion networks: A model for the analysis of online deliberation." *Journal of Information Technology* 25 (2): 230–243.

Graham, Todd and Tamara Witschge. 2003. "In search of online deliberation: Towards a new method for examining the quality of online discussions." *Communications* 28 (2): 173–204.

Habermas, Jurgen. 1989. *The Theory of Communicative Action*. Boston: Beacon Press.

Habermas, Jurgen. 1991. *The Structural Transformation of the Public Sphere: An Inquiry into a Category of Bourgeois Society*. Cambridge, MA: MIT Press.

Hall, Stuart. 1980. "Encoding/decoding." In *Culture, Media, Language: Working Papers in Cultural Studies, 1972–79*, eds. Stuart Hall, Dorothy Hobson, Andy Lowe, and Paul Willis, 128–139. Abingdon, England: Hutchinson.

Hay, Colin. 2006. Political ontology. In *The Oxford Handbook of Contextual Political Analysis*, eds. Robert Goodin and Charles Tilly, 78–97. Oxford, England: Oxford University Press.

Hill, Kevin, and John Hughes. 1998. *Cyberpolitics: Citizen Activism in the Age of the Internet*. Lanham, MD: Rowman & Littlefield.

Hoffmann, Michael. 2008. "Requirements for reflective argument visualization tools: A case for using validity as a normative standard." In *Computational Models of Argument: Proceedings of COMMA 2008*, eds. Philippe Besnard, Sylvie Doutre and Anthony Hunter, 196–203. Amsterdam: IOS.

IMPACT Project. 2011. *Project summary: Integrated Method for Policy Making Using Argument Modelling and Computer Assisted Text Analysis* (European Framework 7 project: Grant Agreement No 247228). http://www.policy-impact. eu/projectsummary.

Ivison, Duncan. 1997. *The Self at Liberty: Political Argument and the Arts of Government.* Ithaca, NY: Cornell University Press.

Janssen, Davy, and Raphael Kies. 2005. "Online forums and political deliberation." *Acta Politica* 40 (3): 317–3.

Kim, Ji-Young. 2006. "The impact of internet use pattern on political engagement: A focus on on-line deliberation and virtual social capital." *Information Polity* 11 (1): 35–49.

Law, John, and John Urry. 2004. "Enacting the social." *Economy and Society* 33 (3): 390–410.

Loveland, Matthew, and Delia Popescu. 2011. "Democracy on the Web." *Information, Communication & Society* 14 (5): 684–703.

Luskin, Robert, James Fishkin, and Shanto Iyengar. 2003, August. "Considered opinions on U.S. foreign policy: Face-to-face versus online deliberative polling." Presented at the annual meeting of the American Political Science Association, Philadelphia, PA.

Macintosh, Ann, Stephen Coleman, and Agnes Schneeberger. 2009. "E-Participation: The research gaps." *Lecture Notes in Computer Science* 5694: 1–11.

Macintosh, Ann, Edmund Robson, Ella Smith, and Angus Whyte. 2003. "Electronic democracy and young people." *Social Science Computer Review* 21 (2): 43–54.

Markham, Tim, and Nick Couldry. 2007. "Tracking the reflexivity of the (dis) engaged citizen." *Qualitative Inquiry* 13 (5): 675–695.

Min, Seong-Jae. 2007. "Online vs. face-to-face deliberation: Effects on civic engagement." *Journal of Computer-Mediated-Communication* 12 (4): 1369–1387.

Min, Seong-Jae. 2009. *Deliberation, East Meets West: Exploring the Cultural Dimension of Citizen Deliberation.* Unpublished PhD thesis, The Graduate School of The Ohio State University, Columbus, OH.

Mol, Annemarie. 1998. "Ontological politics: A word and some questions." *The Sociological Review* 46 (2): 74–89.

Monnoyer-Smith, Laurence. 2006. "Citizen's deliberation on the Internet: An exploratory study." *International Journal of Electronic Government Research* 2 (3): 58–74.

Mouffe, Chantal. 2000. "Deliberative democracy or agonistic pluralism?" *Social Research* 66 (3): 745–758.

Mueller, Dennis. 2003. *Public Choice III*. Cambridge, England: Cambridge University Press.

Muhlberger, Peter. 2000, July. "Defining and measuring deliberative participation and potential: A theoretical analysis and operationalization." Paper presented at the International Society of Political Psychology Twenty-Third Annual Scientific Meeting, Seattle, WA.

Muhlberger, Peter, and Lori Weber. 2006. "Lessons from the Virtual Agora Project: The effects of agency, identity, information and deliberation on political knowledge." *Journal of Deliberation* 2 (1). http//services.bepress.com/jpd/vol2/iss1/art13.

Neblo, Michael. 2005. "Thinking through democracy: Between the theory and practice of deliberative politics." *Acta Politica* 40: 169–181.

Nussbaum, Martha C., and Jonathan Glover (eds.). *Women, Culture, and Development: A Study of Human Capabilities*. Oxford University Press, 1995.

Olson, Kevin. 2008. "Constructing citizens." *The Journal of Politics* 70 (1): 40–53.

Osborne, Thomas, and Nikolas Rose. 1999. "Do the social sciences create phenomena? The example of public opinion research." *British Journal of Sociology* 50 (3): 367–396.

Parkinson, John. 2003. "Legitimacy problems in deliberative democracy." *Political Studies* 51 (1): 180–196.

Polat, Rabia, and Lawrence Pratchett. 2009. "E-citizenship: Reconstructing the public online." In *Changing local governance, changing citizens*, eds. Catherine Durose, Stephen Greasley, and Liz Richardson, 193–210. Policy Press.

Price, Vincent, and Joseph N. Cappella. 2002. "Online deliberation and its influence: The electronic dialogue project in campaign 2000." *IT & Society* 1 (1): 303–329.

Pykett, Jessica, Michael Saward, and Anja Schaefer. 2010. "Framing the good citizen." *The British Journal of Politics & International Relations* 12 (4): 523–538.

Renton, Alastair, and Ann Macintosh. 2007. "Computer supported argument maps as a policy memory." *The Information Society* 23 (2): 125–133.

Ryfe, David. 2007. "Toward a sociology of deliberation." *Journal of Deliberation* 3 (1): 1–27.

Sanders, Lynn. 1997. "Against deliberation." *Political Theory* 25 (3): 347–376.

Saward, Michael. 2003. "Enacting democracy." *Political Studies* 51 (1): 161–179.

Schudson, Michael. 2000. "Good citizens and bad history: Today's political ideals in historical perspective." *The Communication Review* 4 (1): 1–20.

Schumpeter, Joseph. 1976. *Capitalism, Socialism and Democracy* (5th ed.). London: Allen & Unwin.

Sen, Amartya. 1992. *Inequality Reexamined*. Oxford University Press.

Shah, Dhavan, Jack McLeod, and Nam-Jin Lee. 2009. "Communication competence as a foundation for civic competence: Processes of socialization into citizenship." *Political Communication* 26 (1): 102–117.

Shane, Peter. 2004. *Democracy online: The Prospects for Political Renewal Through the Internet*. New York: Routledge.

Smith, Graham, Peter John, Patrick Sturgis, and Hisako Nomura. 2009, June. "Deliberation and internet engagement: initial findings from a randomised controlled trial evaluating the impact of facilitated internet forums." Paper presented at the European Consortium of Political Research General Conference, Potsdam, Germany.

Torney-Purta, Judith. 2000. "Comparative perspectives on political socialization and civic education." *Comparative Education Review* 44 (1): 88–95.

Wilhelm, Anthony. 2000. *Democracy in the Digital age: Challenges to Political Life in Cyberspace*. New York: Routledge.

Woolgar, Steve. 1991. "Configuring the user: The case of usability trials." In *A Sociology of Monsters Essays on Power Technology and Domination*, ed. John Law, 57–102. London: Routledge.

Wright, Scott. 2009. "The role of the moderator: Problems and possibilities for government-run online discussion forums." In *Online Deliberation: Design, Research, and Practice*, eds. Todd Davis and Seeta Peña Gangadharan, 233–242. Stanford, CA: CSLI Publications.

Wright, Scott and John Street. 2007. "Democracy, deliberation and design: The case of online discussion forums." *New Media & Society* 9 (5): 849–869.

Young, Iris Marion. 2001. "Activist challenges to deliberative democracy." *Political Theory* 29 (5): 670–690.

Young, Iris Marion. 2002. *Inclusion and Democracy*. New York: Oxford University Press.

Yves Sintomer

Chapter Fourteen. Random Selection, Republican Self-government, and Deliberative Democracy

Introduction

In 1439, the humanist Leonardo Bruni (1370–1444), Chancellor of the Florentine Republic and doubtless the most celebrated European intellectual of his time, published a short treaty in Greek: *On the Florentine Constitution.*[1] Florence was at the height of its splendor and power: during this period, it had seen the invention of perspective in art; it had also witnessed the development of new techniques in textile manufacturing and banking and, most important for our purpose, the rise of civic humanism. In this essay, Bruni positively valued Florence, in an Aristotelian vein, as a mixed constitution. The social composition of its citizenry, he claims, results from two exclusion principles: noble families (the magnates) are excluded from the most important offices (this is the anti-aristocratic principle), and manual workers are excluded from the political life (this is the anti-democratic principle). Three other main elements sustain the democratic dimension: the ideal of liberty (*vivere libero, vivere civile, vivere politico*) is at the core of its institutions and political system; offices are held for short-term periods, usually two to four months, including the most important of them, the *Signoria*; those who hold the offices are chosen through random selection (*tratta*). The executive, the legislative councils, and part of the judiciary are chosen in this manner (Bruni 1996).

On December 11, in 2004, after nearly 12 months of deliberation, a Citizen Assembly, selected by lot from the citizens of British Columbia in Canada, presented its *Final Report on Electoral Change* to the B.C. Legislature. It proposed to change the electoral system by introducing more proportionality (replacing the existing electoral system, the so-called First-Past-the-Post, with a new Single-Transferable

---

1   Previous versions of this chapter have been published in *Constellations*, 17/3, 2010, p. 472–487, and (with the title "Random Selection and Deliberative Democracy. Note for an Historical Comparison"), in G. Delannoi, O. Dowlen (eds.), *Sortition. Theory and Practice*, Imprint Academic, Exeter (UK), 2010, p. 31–51. A special thank to Oliver Dowlen, who has edited the previous English versions.

Vote system) (Herath 2007; Waren and Pearse 2008). This recommendation was then put to the electorate-at-large in a referendum held concurrently with the 2005 provincial election. Gordon Gibson, the creator of British Columbia's Citizen Assembly and councilor of the Prime Minister, justified the initiative in the following manner:

> "We are...adding new elements to both representative and direct democracy. These new elements differ in detail but all share one thing in common. They add to the mix a new set of representatives, different from those we elect. As things stand now, both streams of decision-making are highly influenced – almost captured – by experts and special interests. The idea of deliberative democracy is essentially to import the public interest, as represented by random panels, as a muscular third force. The traditional representatives we elect are chosen by majority consensus, for an extended period, as professionals, with unlimited jurisdiction to act in our name. The new kinds we are talking about are chosen at random, for a short period, as ordinary citizens for specified and limited purposes." (Gibson n.d.)

The decision seems only to have been the prelude to a larger wave of similar experiments. Ontario, the most populous Canadian State, followed British Columbia's example in 2005. One further example can be mentioned. In the autumn of 2006, the French presidential campaign was troubled for a few weeks by a proposal made by Ségolène Royal, the socialist candidate. Ms. Royal wanted to set up Citizens' Juries to evaluate politicians' actions. Ms. Royal, had promised that, if elected, she would reform the French Constitution through a process in which the Legislative Assembly and a Citizen Assembly selected by lot would work together to prepare a revised text that would then be put to a referendum. It is surprising to see how many different participatory and deliberative devices where random selection plays a role have been created in the last two decades, in very different contexts (Carson and Martin 1999; Sintomer 2007; Buchstein 2009).

It would be ridiculous to strictly compare Early Renaissance Florence and British Columbia: their contexts, institutions and political cultures are completely different. Nevertheless, two important questions arise. Can we claim that the recent interest in random selection marks the resurgence of a democratic tradition that was invented in Athens during the classical period and reinvented in the Italian city-states? What does this parallel teach us about deliberation, participation and representation? In what follows, I will proceed in two steps. First I will briefly describe the Republican self-government based on random selection that characterized the Florentine Republic and explore the ambiguous role that deliberation played in it. I will then contrast this polity with current experiments in deliberative democracy based on randomly selected mini-publics and will discuss what this reveals about deliberation, participation and decision-making.

Random Selection and Republican Self-Government in Early Renaissance Florence

As we know from the seminal works of Baron (1966; 1988; Blondiaux 1998), Pocock (2003), Skinner (1978), and Hankins (2000), the Florentine notion of *libertas* has been decisive in the formation of the modern political thought. Nicolai Rubinstein (1968; 1997) has shown that that the ideal of the *vivere libero* included not only independence from foreign powers, the rule of law, political equality among citizens (or at least among those who were full citizens) and the right to take an active part in public affairs, but also the right to participate directly in the government of the Republic.

Random Selection of Public Office Holders

In fact, most of the magistrates were randomly selected and held their offices for only a few months. This feature has been well documented by historians (Brucker 1977; 1990; Cadoni 1999, 19–100; Guidi 1981; Najemy 1982) and has recently raised interest in political theory (Manin 1997; Dowlen 2008; Buchstein 2009; McCormick 2006, 147–163). From 1282 onwards, the *Signoria*, which was similar to what we would now call an executive, was the most important power in the city. Its members represented the various corporations (the *arti*) through a complex system of quotas. It was in charge of foreign policy, controlled the administrative bodies and had the right to initiate the laws of the Republic. Up to 1494, when a Major Council was created following the Venetian model, the *Signoria* decided when the two legislative councils had to meet. Even though this institutional system was continually evolving, its basic features remained the same until the end of the fifteenth century. During this period, some of the most important political debates in the city concerned the repartition of political and administrative positions among the various corporations and the role of sortition in that process. From 1328 onwards the majority of official positions were attributed by lot (called *la tratta*). The candidate names were put in pouches (*borse*) and sortition provided the way of selecting those who would be in charge for a certain period. The members of the *Signoria* were selected by lot, and, during the republican period, most of the political and administrative offices were attributed according to a similar process.

The selection process actually took four steps (Najemy 1982, 169 ff). (1) In the first one, selection committees in each neighborhood had to choose those citizens who were considered apt enough to hold the office, according strict personal and political criteria. (2) During the second phase the list of those who had succeeded (the so-called *nominati*) was scrutinized by a city commission composed of preeminent citizens, the *arroti*. The names of those who achieved a qualified majority (two thirds of the ballots, in a process called *squittino*) were put in leather pouches (*imborsati*). For those offices that were attributed through quotas, there were different pouches for the major and the minor guilds. (3) Sortition itself only took place in the third step when the names were withdrawn from the pouches. *Ad hoc* officials, the *accopiatori*, were in charge at this crucial moment. The names of those who had not been selected were left in the pouches for the next sortition. After an unusual or important political event (such as a revolution or a drastic change within the regime) had taken place a new *squittino* would be organized before the old pouches were empty. (4) The last step consisted in eliminating the names of those who had been selected but who did not fit the necessary criteria for office (the so-called procedure of the *divieti*.) If any of those chosen still owed taxes, had served in a similar capacity in the recent past, had been sentenced in respect to certain crimes, had a parent in a similar position or already held an important office, they would not be allowed to take up their posts.

Sortition and Deliberation

What was the relation between sortition, election and deliberation in the Florentine Republic? It was very peculiar and very different both from how it operated in Athens and how it is used in our modern democracies. In the Attic city-state, offices where allocated either by random selection or, for the 10% most important, by election (Finley 1983; Hansen 1997). In the Florentine system, election and sortition were combined. In addition, we have to be aware of the different political values denoted by the term "election" in different historical periods and political cultures. Modern readers see elections as a process by which the grassroots select those who will then speak and act for them. Ancient Athenians would have had a similar understanding. Conversely, elections were a top-down process in Florence, a kind of co-option of worthy citizens by the political elite or "inner circle" where the political power of the state was concentrated. This only changed with the formation of the Major Council in 1494.

The meaning of the word "deliberation" also varies in respect to the language and context in which it is used. In English, it usually implies a careful discussion of all sides of a question. It is with reference to this meaning that the concept of "deliberative democracy" was created, and it is only in specific contexts that deliberation necessarily leads to a decision (most notably with the trial jury). In Early Renaissance Italy, the word had quite a different meaning. It implied the decision of a collective body, but not necessarily a collective discussion.[2] Francesco Guicciardini, a famous intellectual and politician who was Machiavelli's contemporary and one of the first theoreticians of representative government, wrote for example in 1512: "I easily accept that laws could be decided in the [Great] council (*che la deliberazione ne sia in consiglio*), because they are something quite universal and concern every city member; but I like the fact that it is impossible to discuss them publicly, or only following the orders of the *Signoria* and in favor of what it proposes – because if anybody were allowed the freedom to persuade or dissuade others, this would lead to great confusion." (Guicciardini 1932, 218–259, 230–231).

Discussions on public matters were very lively and quite important for the decision-making process in the Florentine Commune. Where did they take place? (a) There were political discussions in non-public places, for example in the big *palazzi* belonging to the most important families in the city. Such discussions also took place in spaces intermediately between the private and the public arenas: public meetings of a kind were regularly organized on the banks which existed at the bottom of the *palazzi*, and in the open shops and the *loggie* in front of them. In this respect the Florentine inner city was in some way similar to the Athenian agora or the Roman forum. (b) The general assembly of the people, called the *parlamento*, never had the role it had played in Athens. It had no regular meetings, was not an institution in which one could deliberate, and usually had a plebiscitary function. (c) A lot of discussions took place in the guilds, the *arti*, which were a basic feature of the medieval republican system. The *arti* could make decisions for themselves, had specific institutions, and could partly designate candidates for offices. Their meetings were only open to members. With the Early Renaissance, their importance strongly decreased and they gave place to a more unified political body. (d) Discussions leading to decisions also took place in the numerous electoral commissions that selected those whose names were to be put in the pouches. These were not open public affairs, as we previously noted, except during the short period at the end of the fifteenth century and the beginning of the

---

2   This meaning globally remains the same in contemporary Italian and Portuguese. French and Spanish are somewhere in between. In German, conversely, deliberation excludes decision and a "*deliberative Stimme*" (a deliberative voice) is only consultative. These semantic differences partly explain the difficult diffusion of the concept of "deliberative democracy" in West European languages other than English. On June, 5th, 2009, a brief comparison of the different national versions of Google came up with 208,000 findings for "deliberative democracy" in English, 21,000 for "*democracia deliberativa*" in Spanish, 17,000 for "*democrazia deliberativa*" in Italian, and only 8.000 for "*démocratie délibérative*" in French or "*deliberative Demokratie*" in German.

sixteenth when the Major Council (*consiglio maggiore*) was in place. (e) Most of the offices (including the most important, the *Signoria*) were collegial. This meant that although discussion took place, again, it was not in public. Executive decisions were taken in these offices. (f) The two legislative councils, selected by lot within much larger lists than the one which was used for the *Signoria*, had the power to pass or refuse the bills proposed by the executive; but they could not propose any bill by themselves and it was forbidden to criticize the proposals.[3] The only speeches allowed were in favor of the measure in hand and it is this arrangement that Guicciardini advocated in the above quotation. In addition, the sessions of the legislative councils were not public, i.e. open to all citizens. (g) A much deeper discussion took place in advisory bodies called *pratiche*, which the *Signoria* could call at will and which were selected by the most important political leaders. The quality of discussion was high in these bodies, they served to enlighten the public mind and forge a majority consensus, but they took no decisions and were not open to the public (Brucker 1977). Their role was a crucial factor in the progressive loss of republican substance from the Florentine institutions at the time of early Renaissance for they heralded the emergence of a political class that was dedicated to politics on a full-time basis, that was hegemonic in the electoral commissions and whose members could regularly pass from one public office to another.

Politics, Republican Self-Government and Democracy

In this complex system, deliberation, in the sense of public discussion that is used in most theories of deliberative democracy, was an essential dimension. Even though none were democracies, it is for this reason that we can claim that the Florentine Republic along with the other Italian communes that developed similar systems "reinvented politics." As Moses I. Finley (1983), Cornelius Castoriadis (1986) and Christian Meier (1990) suggest, politics is something very peculiar and has not existed in all societies and at all times; it implies not just the struggle for state power, which takes place in every state society, but also the existence of a public sphere (1991). The articulation of deliberation and decision-making in Florence was nevertheless very peculiar, and very different from what we find in

---

3 Along with the exclusion from citizenship of the working class, one the most important aristocratic features that Leonardo Bruni (1996) mentioned was precisely this point: that the legislative councils could not really discuss nor modify the bills proposed by the *Signoria*, but only approve or reject them. According to him, the other non-democratic elements were that the councils could not decide their own schedule, and that there was no more conscription but a professional mercenary army.

modern democracies.[4] The decision-making bodies were not open to the public; the deliberative institutions which were most open to the public did not take any decisions. The randomly selected legislature could take decisions but could not discuss the bills in question; the general assembly of the people could decide but not deliberate; and the body in which discussion was most lively, the *pratiche*, was co-opted by the inner-circle and was neither open to the wider public nor entitled to take decisions (Bruckner 1977, 251). Sortition in this context had therefore an ambiguous relation to deliberation.

In fact, its main function was to ensure an impartial resolution of conflicts between the different factions that deeply divided the Republic (Röcke 2005; Sintomer 2007; Buchstein 2009). However, this was not its only value for it also played a crucial role in establishing citizen self-government. Due to random selection and the rapid rotation of the offices (usually from two to six months), nearly all those who had the full citizenship were able, in theory, to have regular access to public office. Citizenship was essentially defined through the membership of one of the 21 officially recognized guilds. At the beginning of the fourteenth century this included between 7,000 and 8,000 persons from a population of about 90,000 people. In 1343, three quarters of the citizenry were nominated to take part in the *squittino* for the *Signoria*; around 800 passed the test and were *imborsati* – and were thus destined to hold one of the major offices in the years following the vote. In 1411, at the time of the birth of civic humanism, more than 5,000 citizens were *nominati* and more than 1,000 *imborsati*. The Major Council created in 1494 had around 3,000 members. Apart from the highest executive positions there were plenty of other offices that used sortition as a means of selection during this period. The rule was clear: the more important the office, the harder the competition (Guidi 1981, 43–44; Brucker 1977, 253).

Florentine citizenship was clearly restricted to a minority of the population. The ratio of full citizens to population was larger than that of Venice during the same period,[5] smaller than that of classical Athens,[6] and comparable with the

---

4   This explains the mixed feelings of familiarity and strangeness that we get when reading Machiavelli's *Istorie Fiorentine* (Machiavelli 1988).

5   Venetian citizenship was basically restricted to the Great Council members: around 1,100 persons for a population of 90,000 at the beginning of the XIVth Century, and 2,600 for a population of 250,000 before the 1575 plague (Lane 1978, 120, 295–297, 372).

6   Between 30,000 and 50,000 citizens, for a population of 250,000 to 300,000 people. In both cities, women were excluded from citizenship, but in addition, in Florence, manual workers (the *popolo minuto*) had only access to citizenship during the revolt of the Ciompi in 1378, when for a few months 13,000 new persons got access to citizenship

proportion of full citizens to the population of Great Britain at the end of the eighteenth century.[7] Florence was not a democracy in the meaning we presently give to the term. It was not self-government by all and, as we have seen previously, a large part of the power tended to be *de facto* in the hands of the inner-circle during much of this period. Despite this, it was more self-government than representative government and, compared to other regimes of its time, it embodied the ideal of self-government by the many - *governo largo*. The discrepancy between the constitutional ideal and the political practice in this matter, moreover, was probably no greater than in a modern democracy. The ideal of the *vivere libero*, which was at least partly embedded in the real life of the Republic of Florence, included the equal participation of the full citizen in public life and an equal - and real - opportunity to hold a public office. This ideal was realized through random selection and the rapid rotation of offices - techniques that were used in order to avoid or limit any division between state power and the citizenry. This polity was thus very different from the absolutist regimes that were emerging in the European countries at the same time, but also very different from the representative democracies that appeared two or three centuries later.

It was not a democracy but it was mixed regime, as Leonardo Bruni rightly concluded. The debate between the "democratic" and the "aristocratic" dimensions was explicit, and we find it both in the archives and in a large number of contemporary analytical works from this period. At the end of the fifteenth century, the old Aristotelian opposition between elections, considered as basically aristocratic, and sortition, that was seen as a democratic tool, seemed to revive in Florentine politics (Cadoni 1999), and was well synthesized in a dialogue by Francesco Guicciardini (1932a, 175–195). The main Tuscan city was a Republic, in the sense that it had a largely self-governed citizenry, and the republican ideal that was elaborated in this city-state helped to establish a radical tradition of self-government that can be found throughout the history of modern democracy.

Randomly Selected Mini-Publics and Deliberative Democracy

During the Early Renaissance, Florence was frequently compared with Athens, and it has played an important role in the development of the modern republican tradition (Baron 1966; Pocock 2003; Skinner 1978). Our analysis of its political

---

through the creation of three new guilds; Peasants from the neighborhood (the *contado*) remained totally excluded, together with the people living in territories under Florentine domination (the *dominio*).

7   338,000 persons within 8.5 million people (Gueniffey 1993, 97; Plumb 1969).

system provides a valuable viewpoint from which to understand the specific features of modern deliberative democracy and the challenges it might have to face.

According to most supporters of participatory instruments based on random selection, the return of this technique in politics, after centuries of eclipse, implies that some of the ideals of ancient democracies are coming back. A good example of this can be found in the writings of Lyn Carson and Brian Martin, two of the most coherent advocates of random selection. They write:

> "The assumption behind random selection in politics is that just about anyone who wishes to be involved in decision making is capable of making a useful contribution, and that the fairest way to ensure that everyone has such an opportunity is to give them an equal chance to be involved. Random selection worked in ancient Athens. It works today to select juries and has proved, through many practical experiments, that it can work well to deal with policy issues...For democracy...to be strong, it must contain the essential element of citizen participation, not just by a self-selected few but by ordinary people who rightly can determine their own futures. Given the difficulty of involving everyone in such a deliberative process, we argue that random selection is an ideal means by which a cross section of the population can be involved." (Carson and Martin 1999, 13–14)[8]

For sure, there are evident and huge differences in the social, political, economic and institutional contexts of modern democracies on the one hand, and of Athenian or Florentine Republics on the other. Nevertheless, can we speak of a partial resurgence of the ideal of self-government taking place in the contemporary experiments in deliberative democracy? These experiments might well be signs of a new democratic trend in the early twenty-first century, which could develop further or could remain trapped in a niche. The experiments themselves embody a larger critique of those paternalist traditions that tend to reduce democracy to representative government. Their supporters consider that civic participation in politics is crucial for the good health of our political system. They claim the political equality of all citizens in public discussion and, in some cases, in decision-making. They think that democratic legitimacy is closely linked to the expansion of deliberation in the sense of public debate: the more a decision comes from a lively and well organized public debate, the more it will be legitimate, both normatively and empirically (Habermas 1996; Manin 1997; Dryzek 1990; Elster

---

8   The "fair cross section of the community" is the notion that the U.S. Supreme Court referred to when it imposed the reform of the trial juries at the end of the nineteen-sixties in order to select them by lot among the all citizenship and not only among a particular group of it ("The Jury Selection and Service Act," 28 U.S.C., secs 1861–69 (quoted in Abramson 2003, 100).

1991; 1998). This line of thought is clearly a response to the growing distrust of the political system by the citizenry, which is a current and significant trend, at least in Europe. In the deliberative democracy corpus, sortition has a visible space (Fishkin 1996; Dienel 1997;Waren and Pearse 2008 among many others).

Nevertheless, it is important to stress the obvious differences between Florence and experiments like the British Columbia Citizen Assembly. In Canada, as in other Western countries, nearly all adults are full citizens. The technique of random selection is not a routine, nor part of the normal constitutional device; it is only used at particular moments, when a public authority freely decides to organize a Citizen Assembly, a Citizen Jury, a Consensus Conference or another kind of deliberative device. Up to 2010, no law has made sortition mandatory beyond the judicial domain. The political experiments based upon sortition usually operate on the margins of politics, and the British Columbia experiment is the exception rather than the norm.

Representative Sample and Descriptive Representation

A further, less evident but crucial, difference concerns the meaning of random selection. In Florence, as in Athens, sortition and a rapid rotation of the offices enabled citizens to govern and be governed in turn. This is why one can speak of self-government, and this is why, in the classical political thought from Aristotle to Guicciardini, random selection had been associated with democracy and elections with aristocracy (Rancière 2007). The contemporary use of random selection is quite different. The real chance to be selected in the British Columbia Citizen Assembly or in any other device of this type is very low. The idea, clearly expressed by Lyn Carson and Brian Martin, is to use sortition in order to select a microcosm of the citizenry, a group that has the same features and the same diversity as the citizenry, but at a smaller scale. This would form a "minipopulus," as Robert A. Dahl (1989, 340) first said, or a "mini-public," which is now the most common term. This possibility is statistically plausible when one takes a representative sample of the citizenry. A fair cross-section of the people tends, at a small scale, to be similar to the population at large.

The notion of representative sample is familiar to the twenty-first-century reader based on decades of its intensive use in statistics and opinion polls. This is why it seems "quite rational to see lotteries as a means to the end of descriptive representation." (Stone 2009, 375–397, 390) However, the representative sample is late 19th century invention. There could be no relation between random selection and descriptive representation in Athens or Florence, where the idea that random selection statistically leads to a cross section of the population was not scientifically available. At that time, chance had not yet been "tamed" in the political sphere (Hacking 1990).

The "microcosmic" reasoning that implied that political representatives had to be the social or cultural mirror of the people became important during the age of the French and North-American revolutions. For example, John Adams could write that the legislature "should be an exact portrait, in miniature, of the people at large." (Adams 1851, 4, 205) But because it was impossible to rely on the notion of a representative sample, its promoters ignored sortition and put forward other technical solutions (Sintomer 2007). The Anti-federalists proposed small constituencies in order to favor the lower middle-class – a proposal that was not particularly convincing and that was successfully criticized by the Federalists (Manin 1997). Another solution suggested the separate representation of different social groups through corporatist methods[9] – a proposal that was too closely identified with the Old Regime to convince radical democrats. In the nineteenth century, the higher classes' *de facto* hegemony among representatives regularly lead to the idea of the specific representation of subordinate groups, and particularly of the working class.[10] The representative sample was first introduced in politics with the opinion polls in the middle of the twentieth century (Blondiaux and Sintomer 2002) and it only became the instrument for selecting trial juries and various political juries and committees at the end of the nineteen-sixties and in the nineteen-seventies.[11]

Bernard Manin (1997) was the first to ask why selection by lot disappeared from the political scene with the modern revolutions. He gave an answer based on two elements. On the one hand, the founding fathers of the modern republics wanted an elective aristocracy rather than a democracy, and so it was logical that they should reject random selection. On the other hand, the theory of consent, deeply rooted in modern conceptions of natural law, had gained so much ground that it seemed difficult to legitimate a political authority not formally approved by the citizens of the state. These two arguments are important, but they cannot tell the whole story. In particular, they fail to explain why radical minority currents did not demand the use of selection by lot in politics, even though they campaigned for a mirror-like representation in which the representative body would

---

9   See among others Comte de Mirabeau, "Discours devant les états de Provence," January 30, 1789, *Œuvres de Mirabeau*, Paris 1825, t. VII, p. 7, quoted in Rosanvallon (1998).

10 See among others the "Manifeste des Soixante," *L'Opinion nationale*, February 17, 1764, quoted in Rosanvallon (1998).

11 The "fair cross section of the community" is an approximation of the representative sample when the group is too small to be truly representative.

resemble the people in its entirety. To understand these developments, one has to point to a number of other factors (Sintomer 2007). We have to abandon the realm of "pure" political ideas and look at the way in which they take material shape through techniques of rule and various tools and mechanisms. (In this respect, the history of political ideas would gain much from the lessons of the social history of science as it has developed in the last few decades.) The lack of a statistical concept of representative sampling, at the time of the French and American revolutions when probability calculus was already well developed, is a decisive reason why political selection by lot seemed doomed in modern democracies with their large populations – and why those who upheld a descriptive conception of representation inevitably had to choose other tools for the advance of their ideals.

Conversely, the question of the present comeback of random selection in a growing number of experiences also appears open to an answer largely centered on representative sampling. Random selection as it is practiced in politics today is inseparably bound up with that concept. In modern democracy, the deliberation of a cross section of the people is not the same as the self-government of the people. It gives everybody the same chance to be selected; but because this chance is very small, it does not allow all citizens to hold public office in turn. It leads instead to a mini-public counterfactual opinion that is representative of what the larger public opinion *could* be. John Adams could write that the microcosmic representation he was claiming for "should think, feel, reason, and act" like the people. For the contemporary politics of presence (Phillips 1995), the statistical similarity between "descriptive" representatives and the people is only a starting point. The mini-public has to deliberate, and in this process, it changes its mind. It begins to think somehow differently, and this is precisely the added value of deliberation. This is quite clear when we read James Fishkin, who invented the Deliberative Poll, one of the techniques of deliberative democracy that uses random selection:

> "Take a national random sample of the electorate and transport those people from all over the country to a single place. Immerse the sample in the issues, with carefully balanced briefing materials, with intensive discussions in small groups, and with the chance to question competing experts and politicians. At the end of several days of working through the issues face to face, poll the participants in detail. The resulting survey offers a representation of the considered judgments of the public" (Fishkin 1996, 162).

When traditional polls consist only in a "statistical aggregation of vague impressions formed mostly in ignorance of sharply competing arguments," Deliberative Polls allow us to know "what the public *would* think, had it a better opportunity to consider the questions at issue" (Fishkin 1996, 162).

Challenges of Deliberative Mini-Publics

Another difference between the Florentine Republic and contemporary randomly selected bodies is the relation between deliberation and decision-making. The modern schemes based on random selection tend to reveal a larger dynamic of deliberative democracy. In this chapter I will not discuss deliberative bodies such as supreme courts or administrative committees such as the Food and Drug Administration. I will focus instead on deliberative mini-publics. Schemes of this type offer a number of promises, such as to limit the distance between the political class and citizenry and to promote better communication between them. At the same time, however, they are confronted with three sets of challenges.

The first one is that *the counterfactual opinion can differ from the real opinion* of the people. When the proposal of British Columbia Citizen Assembly was put to the electorate-at-large in a referendum in 2005, it failed to pass the test: Because it was considered as a constitutional matter, the referendum required approval by 60% of votes and simple majorities in 60% of the districts in order to pass. Final results indicate that the referendum failed with only 57.7% of votes in favor, although it did have majority support in 77 of the 79 electoral districts. When the proposal was put again in a referendum in May 2009, the gap was even larger: only 38.7% of valid votes and 7 of 85 electoral districts were in favor of the proposal. In Ontario, the Citizen Assembly proposal convinced only a minority of voters and there will be no second chance. In Europe, the PASOK candidate selected by a cross section of Marousi citizens was not the one who won the elections some months later.

The tension between the counterfactual deliberation and the public debate at large seems to be inherent to deliberative democracy, as far as it takes an institutional form. It has not been widely addressed in political theory (Goodin and Dryzeck 2006, 219–244). This tension appears in several dimensions:

1. *Learning process.* The more the members of a representative sample learn in a Citizen Assembly, the more their knowledge and opinion will differ from the public opinion at large. The most interesting schemes, which lead to a real empowerment of the participants, tend to differ more from the average public opinion than the bad ones.
2. *Numbers.* When the number of participants grows, the deliberative quality of the discussions tends to decrease.
3. *Publicity.* Jon Elster (1991) and others have shown that the publicity of the debates does not necessarily leads to a better discussion. In some context at least, a discussion behind closed doors will be of a better quality. Most citizen juries discuss without any audience. In this context, it is more difficult

to involve the wider public and to increase its understanding of the case in question. Thus the meetings tend to be schools of democracy for the few, not for the many.

4. *Learning through discussion or through action.* The deliberative devices are conceived in order to foster and improve political education. However, they usually allow participants to meet only "for a short period, as ordinary citizens for specified and limited purposes," as Gordon Gibson (n.d.) puts it. In social movements or in NGOs, the deliberative quality is probably lower but the intensity and the emotional commitment of the participants is much higher. In some cases personal ambition, rather than the desire for democratic progress, could even become the main motivating factor.

Deliberative democracy also has to face another set of challenges. Because it focuses on the (deliberative) rule of the game, it often tends to forget or at least to underestimate power relations and the relationship between deliberative schemes and the broader democratic transformation of society at large. Those participatory devices that select individual by lot, without any tie between them, constitute an instrument that is not embedded in actual social relations. It therefore makes it difficult for these mechanisms to change existing power structures. This induces serious difficulties:

1. *Power in the deliberation itself.* One of the most discussed problems is the influence of power on the deliberative process itself. A formally equal procedure can leads to unequal outputs if it remains blind to the differences in social, economic or cultural capital that strongly influence the input side of the process. This has been widely discussed and techniques has arisen I order to reduce social inequalities in deliberation, such as the succession of plenary session and discussions in small groups.

2. *Top-down and bottom-up.* In addition, most deliberative mini-publics are top-down processes. It is therefore not very probable that radical changes will take place in which the power of those who have set up these instruments would be truly challenged.

3. *Individual vs. organized citizens.* A lot of deliberative designs, especially those that employ random selection, valorize individual citizens. They consider organized interests, including NGOs and community organization with some diffidence because they are supposed to defend particular interests. These deliberative instruments can even be used against the organized civil society, without which any progressive civic change is hardly conceivable.

4. *Consensus and dissent.* In Consensus Conferences, Citizens' Juries and may other devices (although not in Deliberative Polling), deliberative democracy is supposed to lead to a consensus. But do real changes usually come through consensual

arguments? Historically, the progress of justice and democracy has been imposed through huge social struggles, not through reasonable consensual discussions. The deliberative devices often tend to be inhospitable to politicization.

5. *Argumentation and passions*. As suggested by Jürgen Habermas (1991), a good deliberation is usually considered to favor the force of the better argument. However, in order to make real transformations in a world in which the structural resistances are huge, passions seem necessary; such transformations are hardly the product of mere rational argumentation. Rhetoric and emotions are crucial. In order to be strong enough to regulate the world markets, politics has to make people dream of another world. In this process arguing can only be one dimension among others.

6. *Deliberative democracy and social justice*. The relation between deliberative democracy and social justice remains unclear. Most of the instruments that deliberative theory has analyzed are linked with movements of emancipation of the subordinate classes or of outsiders groups. Experiments based on random selection barely address the critique of the new forms of inequality that are produced by contemporary capitalism. This has mostly been done in other participatory instruments such as the participatory budgeting in Porto Alegre (Abers 2000; Avritzer 2002; Sintomer 2004; Baiocchi 2005).

7. *Enlightened decision-making vs. counter-power*. Lastly, to summarize these points, deliberative democracy based upon mini-publics often tends to be a way of producing a more enlightened decision-making and a more enlightened consent. This is important but hardly enough – and if it does not contribute to the development of counter-powers (Fung and Wright 2001), interest in deliberative democracy will start to decline.

The Legitimacy of Random Selection

There is an apparent trade-off between deliberation in the English meaning (good discussion) and deliberation in the meaning found in Latin languages (decision of a collective body). The deliberative bodies open to ordinary citizens are not usually entitled to make decisions. Among the collective bodies that theorists tend to present as good examples of deliberative democracy, those that are entitled to take decisions, or whose advice is directly integrated with decision-making bodies, are mostly expert commissions such as supreme courts, ethics committees or neo-corporatist bodies. Among those open to "ordinary" citizens, most are only consultative or advisory boards: they are only "weak publics." (Fraser 1997) Why is this? Is it only a contingent phenomenon? Can we expect the situation to change in a next future?

The classical Athenian or Florentine Republics relied on a principle of self-government (combined with the rule of law). Representative democracy relies on another principle, the consent of the people expressed through elections (articulated within the rule of law and the human rights). Both strongly rely on the legitimacy of number, and especially on the majority principle. However, an important feature of our political regimes is that a lot of decisions are taken through expert committees. In some cases these committees apply the majority principle; in others they function by consensus. Their legitimacy has a strong epistemic dimension: it relies on expert knowledge and on well-designed procedures that favor good (non public) deliberation.

Mini-publics made up of ordinary citizens selected at random cannot rely on the legitimacy of number nor on the legitimacy of expert knowledge. This is why they are not usually entitled to take decisions. Nevertheless, they have their own kind of legitimacy. First of all, contemporary participatory devices are most often employed in order to enable an enlightened discussion to take place. One of their basic assumptions is that a careful deliberation will lead to reasonable results. This is why *the counterfactual opinion tends to be more reasonable than the wider public debate*. In fact, the epistemic quality of deliberative devices based on random selection is important.

In addition, deliberative participatory devices may have some epistemic advantages compared to representative government or expert committees. Most deliberative democrats rely on a negative argument, well expressed by John Dewey: "A class of experts is inevitably so removed from common interests as to become a class with private interests and private knowledge, which in social matters is not knowledge at all" (Dewey 1954, 207). This statement can be extended to the political class. Deliberative democrats also propose more positive arguments. One of the most common is that *good deliberation needs to include various points of view, so that the range of arguments can be enlarged, and the reasons better balanced*. In this line of thought, randomly selected mini-publics tend to be better than participatory devices based on voluntary involvement or on the organized civil society because they rest on a cross section of the people and maximize the epistemic diversity of their deliberation. This is why they can bring something valuable to what is, in fact, a context of increasing complexity.

A third argument for participatory deliberative devices is political. Their promise comes from the fact that discontent is growing against the actual functioning of representative democracies. There is a perceived need to counter the tendency to reduce politics to rhetorical shows, to limit the autonomy of the political class and to make it more accountable to the citizenry. *Participatory deliberative devices are instruments that promote better communication between the political class and the citizenry*. Those based on a representative sample of the population enable political communication to take place amongst ordinary people and not merely between "professional citizens."

The fourth argument is also political, but is more radical than the third one. Democratic theoreticians of representative government (as opposed to its elitist advocates) often concede that the best democratic system would be self-government, but add that, because self-government is impossible in the large communities typical of modern democracy, the second-best solution is representative government. One could however argue that: *since the best democratic system is self-government; and because self-government is impossible in the large communities typical of modern democracy, the second-best solution is actually to give a voice to counterfactual mini-publics selected by lot*. In this way at least it offers citizens an equal chance to participate in decision-making.

The fifth argument for participatory devices based on a representative sample of the population is *impartiality*. Elected representatives, experts, and organized interests tend to be moved by particular interests rather than by the notion of the common good. In contrast, random selection ensures that the large majority (or even nearly everybody, due to the possibility of recusal as in a trial jury) will judge according to what they consider the best for all without taking a partisan stance in any controversy. This advantage of impartiality may be strengthened when the advice or the decision has to be taken by a qualified majority or reached through consensus.

Advising, Controlling, Judging, Deciding

Taking into account these five types of legitimacy that participatory devices based on random selection can claim, what can be said about the potential of these contemporary experiments?

When the imperative of impartiality is high with respect to a particular topic, random selection offers a worthwhile method by which to select those who will deliberate. An important distinction has to be made, however. It is interesting to note how Hegel defends the institution of trial jury composed of laypersons. Their participation is justified, he writes, insofar, and only insofar, as what is at stake is not the universal, the right or the law, but a concrete and subjective judgment about a particular case (Hegel 1991, § 227–228). One can be less strict, but one has to recognize that it is not the same thing to deliberate on concrete particular cases and to enact a law. In particular cases, participatory instruments based on random selection have enough legitimacy to advise, but also, at least in some contexts, to control, to judge, as in trial juries (Abramson 2003), or even to decide – this has been the case in the Berlin Citizen Juries that, in 17 neighborhoods, have decided the attribution of half a million euros each to sustain local projects in the frame of the urban renewal policy (Röcke and Sintomer 2005). This could be developed much further.

On the other hand, in cases where impartiality is crucial but where a law is at stake, as in British Columbia, it would seems promising to couple a proposal made by a Citizen Assembly with a referendum, as was done in the Canadian Provinces – that is, to articulate the mini-pubic with the people at large.

It is undeniable that expert committees have an important role to play in cases that rest on highly technical questions. To ensure impartiality, however, it would be necessary to include laypersons in the decision-making, for example at particular moments in the proceedings, as in Consensus Conference on scientific issues invented in Denmark.

In cases where general political issues are at stake, participatory devices based on random selection do not have enough legitimacy to make the decision: the counterfactual opinion is not the same as an actual self-government. Two options could be considered. The first one is to give these devices a mere consultative function and then let elected representatives decide. The idea is to produce a more enlightened consent and a more enlightened government. This is the mainstream option, and we will probably see many experiences of this kind proposed and adopted in the next decades. An alternative would be to combine mini-publics with larger participatory processes. This would be a movement in the direction of a participatory democracy. It would combine representative government and deliberative democracy with forms of direct democracy. It could be worth making some steps forwards in this direction. For who could claim that the status quo is satisfactory?

Conclusion

The idea of deliberative democracy is an important contribution to the renewal of politics and could improve the efficiency and legitimacy of public policies. It is precisely because we live in a complex world that the need for public deliberation increases. Deliberative democracy is a good counter-tendency to populist tendencies, and to the domination of charismatic leaders.

Because of its inherent tensions, deliberative democracy cannot stand alone and has to be combined with participatory democracy, which is different and which has something to do with the principle of Republican self-government of Early Renaissance Florence. Participatory democracy implies the actual participation of a large proportion of the citizenry in politics, and in particular the involvement of dominated groups. It not only relies on institutional devices, but also on social movements. The good deliberation of the mini-public has to be linked with a better debate in the larger public sphere. The British Columbia scheme, which couples a Citizen Assembly with a referendum, indicates a path we could follow if we were to go in this direction.

Deliberative democracy and participatory democracy, even taken together, cannot stand alone. They are part of a broader evolution that modifies the meaning of political representation, and they are dimensions – until now, secondary dimensions – in the development of multi-level governance. The classical division of power between the executive, the legislative and the judiciary has always been an open process, rather than a stable equilibrium. By addressing the limits of representative government, some schemes of deliberative and participatory democracy propose to modify this supposed equilibrium by introducing a fourth power into the equation. While this makes the situation more complex, and a good equilibrium is not easy to find, this is a promising path.

Random selection has a role to play in this process. Coupled with the rapid rotation of the offices, it was crucial in the Early Renaissance Florence where it enabled a limited but real self-government to emerge. Contemporary schemes based on random selection rely on the notion of representative sample, which was unavailable before the end of the nineteenth century. These mini-publics embody a counterfactual opinion – what the larger public could think if it could truly deliberate. They are therefore closely linked to the ideal of deliberative democracy, which is something very different from the Florentine *vivere libero*. They offer sources of legitimacy that have to be combined with, rather than opposed to, the legitimacy of either representative or direct democracy.

References

Abers, Rebecca Neaera. 2000. *Inventing Local Democracy: Grassroots Politics in Brazil*. London: Lynne Rienner Publishers.

Abramson, Jeffrey. 2003. *We the Jury. The Jury System and the Ideal of Democracy*. Cambridge: Harvard University Press.

Adams, John. 1851. "Letter to John Penn." In *The Works of John Adams*, ed. John Adams. Boston: Little, Brown and Co.

Avritzer, Leonardo. 2002. *Democracy and the Public Space in Latin America*. Princeton: Princeton University Press.

Baiocchi, Gianpaolo. 2005. *Militants and Citizens. The Politics of Participatory Democracy in Porto Alegre*. Stanford: Stanford University Press.

Baron, Hans. 1966. *The Crisis of the Early Italian Renaissance*. Princeton: Princeton University Press.

Baron, Hans. 1988. *In Search of Florentine Civic Humanism*. Princeton: Princeton University Press.

Blondiaux, Loïc. 1998. *La fabrique de l'opinion. Une histoire sociale des sondages.* Paris: Le Seuil.

Blondiaux, Loïc, and Sintomer Yves. 2002. «Démocratie et déliberation.» *Politix* 15 (57) (First semester): 17–35.

Brucker, Gene A. 1977. *The Civic World of Early Renaissance Florence*. Princeton: Princeton University Press.

Brucker, Gene A. 1990. *Florence. The Golden Age, 1138–1737*. Berkeley: University of California Press.

Bruni, Leonardo. 1996. "Costituzione politica di Firenze." In *Opere*, ed. Paolo Viti. Torino: Utet.

Buchstein, Hubertus. 2009. *Demokratie und Lotterie. Das Los als politisches Entscheidungsinstrument von der Antike bis zur EU*. Frankfurt: Campus.

Cadoni, Giorgio. 1999. «Genesi e implicazioni dello scontro tra i fautori della «tratta» e i fautori delle «più fave». 1495–1499.» In *Lotte politiche e riforme istituzionali a Firenze tra il 1494 e il 1502*, ed. Istituto storico italiano per il medio evo, Fonti per la storia dell'Italia medevale, 19–100.

Carson, Lyn, and Brian Martin. 1999. *Random Selection in Politics*. Westport: Praeger Publishers.

Castoriadis, Cornelius. 1986. *Domaines de l'homme*. Paris: Seuil.

Dahl, Robert A. 1989. *Democracy and its Critics*. New Haven: Yale University Press.

Dewey, John. 1954. *The Public and Its Problems* [1927]. Athens OH: Swallow Press and Ohio University Press Books.

Dienel, Peter C. 1997. *Die Planungszelle*. Wiesbaden: Westdeutscher Verlag.

Dowlen, Olivier. 2008. *The Political Potential of Sortition. A Study of the Random Selection of Citizens for Public Office*. Exeter UK: Imprint Academic.

Dryzek, John S. 1990. *Discursive Democracy. Politics, Policy and Political Science*. Cambridge: Cambridge University Press.

Elster, Jon. 1991. *Arguing and Bargaining in the Federal Convention and the Assemblée Constituante*, Working Paper, 4. The University of Chicago, Center for the Study of Constitutionalism in Eastern Europe.

Elster, Jon. 1998. *Deliberative Democracy*. Cambridge: Cambridge University Press.

Finley, Moses I. 1983. *Politics in the Ancient World*. New York: Cambridge University Press.

Fishkin, James. 1996. *The Voice of the People. Public Opinion and Democracy*. New Haven: Yale University Press.

Fraser, Nancy. 1997. *Justice Interruptus. Critical Reflexion on the "Postsocialist" Condition.* London: Routledge.

Fung, Archon, and Erik Olin Wright. 2001. *Deepening Democracy. Institutional Innovations in Empowered Participatory Governance.* London: Verso.

Gibson, Gordon. 2007. "Deliberative Democracy and the B.C. Citizens' Assembly." Accessed February 23, 2007. http://www.ccfd.ca/index.php?option=com_cont ent&task=view&id=409&Itemid=284.

Goodin, Robert E., and John Dryzeck. 2006. "Deliberative Impacts: The Macro-Political Uptake of Mini-Publics." *Politics and Society* 34 (2) (June): 219–244.

Guicciardini, Francesco. 1932. "Del modo di eleggere gli uffici nel consiglio grande." In *Dialogo e discorsi del reggimento di Firenze*, ed. Roberto Palmarocchi, 175–195. Bari: Laterza.

Guicciardini, Francesco. 1932. "Del modo di ordinare il governo popolare" ["Discorso di Logrogno", 1512]. In *Dialogo e discorsi del reggimento di Firenze*, ed. Roberto Palmarocchi, 218–259. Laterza: Bari.

Guidi, Guidubaldo. 1981. *Il governo della città-repubblica di Firenze del primo quattrocento.* Firenze: Leo S. Olschki.

Habermas, Jürgen. 1991. *The Structural Transformation of the Public Sphere: An Inquiry into a Category of Bourgeois Society.* Cambridge MA: MIT Press.

Habermas, Jürgen. 1996. *Between Facts and Norms: Contributions to a Discourse Theory of Law and Democracy.* Cambridge, MA: MIT Press.

Hacking, Ian. 1990. *The Taming of Chance.* Cambridge: Cambridge University Press.

Hankins, James. 2000. *Renaissance Civic Humanism.* Cambridge: Cambridge University Press.

Hansen, Mogens Herman. 1997. *The Athenian Democracy in the Age of Demosthenes: Structure, Principles, and Ideology.* Norman OK: University of Oklahoma Press.

Hegel, Georg Wilhelm Friedrich. 1991. *Elements of the Philosophy of Right.* Cambridge: Cambridge University Press.

Herath, R. B. 2007. *Real Power to the People. A Novel Approach to Electoral Reform in British Columbia.* Lanham MD: University Press of America.

Lane, Frederic Chapin. 1978. *Storia di Venezia.* Torino: Einaudi.

Machiavelli, Niccolo. 1988. *Florentine Histories.* Princeton: Princeton University Press.

Manin, Bernard. 1997. *The Principles of Representative Government.* Cambridge: Cambridge University Press.

McCormick, John. 2006. "Contain the Wealthy and Patrol the Magistrates." *American Political Science Review* 100 (2) (May): 147–163.

Meier, Christian. 1990. *The Greek Discovery of Politics*. Cambridge MA: Harvard University Press.

Najemy, John. 1982. *Corporatism and Consensus in Florentine Electoral Politics, 1280–1400*. Chapel Hill: The University of North Carolina Press.

Phillips, Anne. 1995. *The Politics of Presence*. Oxford: Clarendon Press.

Plumb, John Harold. 1969. "The Growth of the Electorate in Enland from 1600 to 1715." *Past and Present* 45 (November): 90–116.

Pocock, John Greville Agard. 2003. *The Machiavellian Moment: Florentine Political Thought and the Atlantic Republican Tradition*. Princeton: Princeton University Press.

Rancière, Jacques. 2007. Hatred of Democracy. London: Verso.

Röcke, Anja. 2005. *Losverfahren und Demokratie. Historische und demokratietheoretische Perspektiven*. Münster: LIT.

Röcke, Anja, and Yves Sintomer. 2005. "Les jurys de citoyens berlinois et le tirage au sort: un nouveau modéle de démocratie participative?" In *Gestion de proximité et démocratie participative: les nouveaux paradigmes de l'action publique?*, ed. Marie-Hélène Bacqué, Henri Rey and Yves Sintomer, 139–160. Paris: La Découverte.

Rosanvallon, Pierre. 1998. *Le peuple introuvable. Histoire de la représentation démocratique en France*. Paris: Gallimard.

Rubinstein, Nicolai. 1968. "Florentine Constitutionalism and Medici Ascendancy in the Fifteenth Century." In *Florentines Studies. Politics and Society in Renaissance Florence*, ed. Nicolai Rubinstein, 442–462. Evanston IL: Northwestern University Press.

Rubinstein, Nicolai. 1997. *The Government of Florence Under the Medici (1434 to 1494)*. Oxford: Clarendon Press/Oxford University Press.

Sintomer, Yves. 2004. *The Porto Alegre Experiment: Learning Lessons for a Better Democracy*. New York: Zed Books.

Sintomer, Yves. 2007. *Le pouvoir au peuple. Jurys citoyens, tirage au sort et démocratie participative*. Paris: La Découverte.

Skinner, Quentin. 1978. *The Foundations of Modern Political Thought*, 2 Vol. Cambridge: Cambridge University Press.

Stone, Peter. 2009. "The Logic of Random Selection." *Political Theory* 37 (3) (June): 375–397.

Waren, Mark E., and Hilary Pearse. 2008. *Designing Deliberative Democracy. The British Columbia Citizens' Assembly*. Cambridge: Cambridge University Press.

Claus Offe

Chapter Fifteen. Crisis and Innovation of Liberal Democracy: Can Deliberation Be Institutionalized?[1]

Introduction: Diagnostics of Democratic Failure and the Need for Democratic Innovation

Liberal democracies, and certainly not only the new ones among them, are not functioning well. While there is no realistic and normatively respectable alternative to liberal democracy in sight, the widely observed decline of democratic politics, as well as state policies under democracy, provides reasons for concern. This concern is a challenge for sociologically informed political theorists to come up with designs for remedial innovations of liberal democracy. In this essay, I am going to review some institutional designs for democratic innovation. I shall proceed as follows. The first section will provide a very condensed summary of critical accounts concerning democracy's actual failures and symptoms of malfunctioning. In a second section, I distinguish two families of institutional innovations that are currently being proposed as remedies for some of the observed deficiencies of democracy, with an emphasis on "deliberative" methods of political preference formation.

Liberal democracy consists of four basic elements: *stateness* (is a regime form that – so far – is tied to states), *rule of law* (democratic states are states with a – mostly written – constitution which provides for – at least – two ways in which the exercise of state power is limited), *political competition* (democracies institutionalize the non-violent conduct of political conflict between contending groups – parties – aspiring to government office), and *accountability* (presence of mechanisms which serve to hold ruling elites accountable for what they do, including what they fail to do). These are very general features, which do not preclude historical changes. According to the diagnosis of prominent democratic theorists, we are in the midst of a second transformation of democracy (Dahl 2000, Warren 2003), with the first one being the transition from direct (agora, town hall) democracy

1   The chapter is a reprint of a part of the article under the same title that was published in *the Czech Sociological Review* 47 (3) 2011. The present version of this paper has greatly benefited from comments by Marek Skovajsa and Pieter Vanhuysse.

to party-dominated representative mass democracy. There is now a recent and abundant literature on the "crisis" of democracy (Crozier et al. 1975, Pharr and Putnam 2000, Rosanvallon 2008), even "the end" of democracy (Guéhenno 1993), the "end of politics", or the rise of "post-democracy" (Crouch 2004) and the para-statist making of public policies by transnational corporations and their in-house conversion of economic into political power (Crouch 2008). One of the context conditions that triggered these perceived challenges may have been the breakdown of state socialism. As long as state socialism existed, Western democracies could content themselves with claiming (and in my view rightly so) that they performed normatively as well as economically "better" than their authoritarian counterparts. Yet after that counterpart has become obsolete, they now have to demonstrate (and to provide compelling arguments) that they are "good", i.e. normatively sustain-able, on their *own* terms. What needs to be shown in a persuasive way is that the institutional structures and mechanisms of liberal democracy (as summarized above in section 2) are actually capable of delivering the functions (as discussed in section 1) for the performance of which liberal democracy is held to be the most desirable form of political rule. This demonstration is not an easy task, to put it mildly. Causal narratives on the crisis of democracy include economic globaliza-tion and the absence of effective supranational regulatory regimes, the exhaustion of left-of center political ideas and the hegemony of market-liberal public philoso-phies, together with their anti-statist implications, and the impact of financial and economic crises and the ensuing fiscal starvation of nation states which threatens to undermine their state capacity.

For reasons of limited space, I shall mention in a stenographical manner only some of the trends and symptoms that have lead authors to speak of the "crisis" – or creeping deconsolidation – of liberal democracy. In most liberal democracies there is a secular decline in electoral turnout. (Dalton 2004) Also, class-specific turnout rates in general elections are drifting apart, with the least well-to-do showing the lowest interest in *voting* in elections, and even more so in engaging in the more demanding participatory practices of *joining* (movements, political parties, associations) and *donating* (of money, expertise, time).[2] This trend is ac-companied by a sharp decline in citizens' trust in politicians. Both in new and in

---

2   In addition to my triplet of voting/joining/donating as modes of democratic partici-pation (see further below), one might think of "knowing" (i. e., having access to a reasonably correct picture of the collectively relevant situation and to methods that ensure the truth of the picture). But a discussion of the conditions of adequate – and unbiased – "cognitive participation" would have to focus on the media and their politi-cal function, a discussion I have to skip here for reasons of space.

old democracies, apathy, cynicism, and a sense of powerlessness is on the increase. Many of the terms that have been used to describe the situation of widespread political alienation start with a "dis": dissatisfaction, disenchantment, disappointment, the sense of the people being disempowered by elites, depoliticization, and disaffection (Torcal and Montero 2006). In sharp contrast to the decline of European democracies in the inter-war period, however, such alienation has not given rise to explicitly anti-democratic movements. People remain democrats, if "frustrated democrats". (Dalton 2004) Similar trends have been documented concerning all kinds of associations in general (again, with a class bias) and membership in political parties in particular. It has been argued that contemporary democracies are in fact "post-liberal" in that they are populated, at the level of the inputs of demands and preferences, by *two* categories of citizens: first, ordinary "natural" citizens – individuals who vote and participate in various ways – and second, a poorly legitimated class of "secondary citizens" which consists of associations, pressure groups, lobbies and similar agents of functional representation. (Schmitter 2000, Crouch 2008) By employing the organizational weapons of threats, warnings, and conditional promises, the latter can gain a measure of (highly intransparent) control over public policy that the multitude of individual citizens can hardly match.

Two Families of Remedies

Lipset's characterization of democracy as "democratic class struggle" emphasizes the essential aspect of contestation in the democratic process – the struggle for power among competing representative elites. Yet democratic politics does not just consist in the drama of competition, contestation, and open political conflict (a drama that is eventually to be decided at bargaining tables and by the casting of ballots in elections and the counting of votes). It also consists in the less conspicuous and less easily dramatized process in which citizens *form* judgments, interests, opinions, and preferences about the matters that affect them and the political community as a whole. The distinction between these two stages is important for democratic political theory; it is the same distinction as that between trying to *persuade* my opponent in a public exchange of information and argument and *outnumbering* my opponent through mobilizing support for "my" party or cause more effectively than the other side is able to. Democratic politics proceeds in cycles that involve *both* of these stages; we get a one-sided and defective picture of the democratic political process if we think of it only in terms of *expressing* preferences through voting and elections and not also in terms of the *formation* and *revision* of those preferences. (Goodin 2004) The two families of democratic innovations proposals focus on each of these two stages, the expression and the formation of the political will of citizens. The *conflict* of political wills and preferences as it is *expressed* in the voting booth is thus preceded by a process of will *formation* in which not numbers and the logic of aggregation, but well-informed interpretations of reality, arguments, and reasons *can* play a decisive role – but so can stereotypes, prejudice, resentments and the unthinking acceptance of strategically designed messages sent to mass constituencies by competing political elites.

The theoretical claim here is twofold. First, people do not "have" opinions and preferences (contrary to the reifying assumptions underlying much of survey research); instead, opinions and preferences are essentially in flux and constantly being *formed*, reproduced, validated, tested, abandoned, adapted, revised, upgraded, and reflectively enriched in the light of new information and experience. On most matters and issues, most people do not have an opinion and policy preference at all most of the time – until, that is, they are challenged to form one (for instance in spontaneous reaction to being asked a question in a survey, with the implicit expectation communicated being that one "should" or "normally does" have a view on the matter in question). Second, the process of opinion and preference *acquisition* is not exclusively an internal and monological one, but always takes place in communication and interactive dialogue with others. Opinions and preferences are thus social *constructs*, or the joint outcome of "my" own capacity and willingness to observe, to learn, to reason and the information and social relations, constraints, expectations, and opportunities in which such learning and reasoning is embedded. We might even argue that it is quite irrational to hold beliefs and preferences which are strictly "individual" ones, i.e. being formed under conditions of ignorance or disregard about what others, be they opposing "my" views or consenting with them, hold to be true and desirable. For I know my preferences only after I know the preferences of others on whose cooperation I depend (or whose preferences I need to defeat) in order to realize "our" preferences and interests. The external context of the ongoing internal process in which opinions and preferences are being formed can range from coercive, repressive, or manipulative control over the information that is accessible and the preferences that are sanctioned as permissible to, at the other end of a theoretical scale, egalitarian, open, encouraging, and challenging situations in which individuals are free to rationally consider, knowing and pondering the points of view of others (with whom they may end up agreeing or disagreeing), which beliefs and preferences they choose to form and adopt, and why. It is this latter set of qualities which is summarily referred to, in a broad current of democratic theory that has emerged since the early 1990s, as "deliberative".

Coming back to the two stages of democratic inputs – the stage of *formation* and the stage of *expression* of policy preferences – we must note two asymmetries between the two. First, before we can express an opinion or preference, it must have been passed through some formative stage (whatever its "deliberative" qualities), whereas there is no "must" in the opposite direction: a policy preference, once formed, may well be silenced when it comes to will expression, which may be due to the fact that there is no representative actor (political party, governing elite) who can be expected to "listen to" and to whom it would make subjective sense at all to address one's expression of will[3]. The other asymmetry is this: At the stage of *expression* of political will, the institutional framework of the process – political parties, elections, voting procedures – are all precisely defined and formally prescribed and monitored. In contrast, and while constitutional guarantees (freedoms of opinion, the media, assembly, association etc.) play an indispensable role as providers of possibilities and opportunities (as do civics curricula and other state-organized educational facilities), much of the actual formation of opinions and political preferences is (and must be according to liberal principles) an institutionally largely uncharted space in which powerful yet informal social processes of family life, work life, the experience within local faith-based and secular communities, neighborhoods, voluntary associations, consumption and life styles, media use etc. play a decisive role in the formation, validation, and change of political views and preferences and thus the "social realization" of those constitutionally guaranteed rights.

---

3   The widely documented finding that (a) electoral participation ("turnout") is low (i. e. abstention is high), (b) further declining in many "disaffected" liberal democracies, and (c) increasingly distorted in terms of socioeconomic and educational inequalities (which thus translate into inequalities of *political* representation) has led scholars to recommend the introduction of mandatory voting, thus eliminating citizens' option to abstain and hiding the gap between preferences and their expression (Lijphart 1997). Yet if voting were to be made mandatory, at least some voters would find themselves coerced to cast their ballot in favor of parties of whose merits and credibility they are not persuaded. This problem could be remedied by introducing the following rule: If n parties or candidates compete, the voter is given n+1 choices (boxes to mark on the ballot), the additional one standing for the option of NOTA ("none of the above"). - The perception of political elites' deficient responsivity, as suggested by the evidence of fiscal and institutional conditions constraining state capacity, can in turn contribute to a depoliticizing sense of political alienation and powerlessness which discourages the efforts to acquire political opinions and preferences in the first place.

The difference between the stages of *formation* and *expression* of political views and preferences consists in the gap concerning their degree of legal institutionalization. Statutory (and partly also constitutional) laws exist in all liberal democracies specifying the equal right to vote (i. e. express preferences) of all citizens, the right to stand in elections as a candidate, and the procedures according to which individual votes are aggregated in order to form operating representative institutions. These equal rights are, however, being made actual use of according to highly unequal patterns, namely according to inequalities of socio-economic and educational status, among others. In contrast, not even such nominal equality is institutionally provided for as it comes to the *formation* of preferences – the process in which citizens *find out* about the policy options that are available, each other's arguments and preferences, the composition of potential alliances, and what, in the light of such information, may be deemed as good (or better) for "all of us", and the remaining disagreements pertaining to this question. Again, prevailing patterns of social inequality seem to condition the highly unequal access to such opportunities of deliberative learning and clarification, with those cut off from relevant communicative and associational resources being not even able to indicate, with any measure of inter-temporal or substantive consistency, *where they stand*. Others in secure and privileged socio-economic positions have no doubt concerning this issue, as they are less affected by cognitive uncertainties and motivational cross pressures. It would not be implausible to assume that members of the former category, being confined to a condition of *structural uncertainty concerning their own interests and preferences* (Lukes 2005), are likely to abstain from participating in political life; only those who know what to say will raise their voices.

These are empirical questions that I cannot pursue here any further. What should have become clear in our discussion of the two stages of political will formation is that liberal democracies suffer from a condition of vast underutilization, both quantitative and qualitative, of the political resources that are nominally available to each citizen. By *quantitative* underutilization, I refer to the fact of increasing overall non-participation, increasingly patterned in line with social inequalities. By *qualitative* underutilization, I refer to the malfunctioning of the mechanisms (the media, the educational system, political mass parties) which supposedly can transform "raw" and unreflective political views and impulses into "refined" and more enlightened awareness and preferences. Current debates on democratic innovations focus upon either of them and try to devise appropriate remedies. After very briefly pointing to some proposals related to how participation and citizens' involvement can be enhanced in quantitative terms and at the stage of preference *expression*, the final part of the chapter will address some aspects of the hotly debated issue of how the quality of democratic participation might be improved through adopting deliberative procedures and institutions to upgrade the process of preference *formation*.

Strengthening the Voice of Citizens and the Expression of Their Will; Modes of Aggregation of "Given" Individual Preferences

Apart from the basic prerequisite of *knowing* about political issues, alternatives, and institutions, individual citizens can actively participate in politics through three main channels: *voting* (in general elections), *joining* (associations, parties, or movements; participating in political discussion), *donating* (money, time, expertise). All three are affected in contemporary democracies by either a manifest decline of their usage or/and an increasing class bias. That is to say, the middle class and those above it vote, join, and donate more often and more extensively than those below it in terms of income, wealth, socio-economic security, and education. In order to overcome those biases, a variety of measures have been proposed to facilitate, incentivize, and equalize the *expression* of political preferences. These include changing the electoral system to single transferable vote (STV); making voting mandatory (as in Australia, Belgium; Lijphart 1997); allowing for direct democratic and plebiscitary legislation (with practices of Switzerland and California serving as a model); enhancing devolution and increasing the autonomy of local governments; democratizing the funding of interest associations (Schmitter 2000); allowing for vicarious voting of parents (one extra vote for every mother per son and every father per daughter; Hinrichs 2002); introducing gender (and perhaps other, for instance birth cohort) quota in the operation of parties, parliaments, and governments (Phillips 1995); making the number of representatives contingent upon the turnout of constituencies (Participatory budgeting in Brazil, Santos 1998); opening the option for voicing dissent by introducing the NOTA option into the electoral process; making membership fees (more strongly) tax deductible; and reforming political and campaign finance according to the three principles of capping overall expenditures, making "plutocratic" donations either more anonymous to recipients or transparent to voters (and thus supposedly self-limiting), and financing campaign and political party expenditures out of public revenues (Nassmacher 2009; Ackerman and Ayres 2004)[4].

---

4   For overviews of these and similar proposals for innovation, see Fung and Wright (2003), Schmitter and Trechsel (2004), Smith (2005; 2009).

Improving Will Formation through Deliberation

There are two premises, or philosophical starting points, of any theory of deliberative democracy: First, the pursuit of *any* preference that is consistent with the law is legitimate under liberal principles. These principles deny the holders of state power the right (as it was claimed by the holders of power under state socialism) to denounce citizens holding certain (critical) preferences as suffering from "false consciousness", thus providing a pretext to repress allegedly hostile intentions deriving from it. At the same time we also need to keep in mind that preferences are not given and "natural", but *formed* and motivated through cognitive and moral considerations which in turn can be hampered by interests and passions, as well as by communicative conditions that hinder the reflective probing of one's preferences (Offe 1992). The institutional facilitation of such probing could contribute to the partial or full neutralization of what Steven Lukes (2005) has called the "third" – and least conspicuous – face of social power, namely the power to hinder others to find out what their interests are. Moreover, the prevalence of myth, resentment, ignorance, short-termism, the fetishization of personality and community, and aggressive impulses against elites or minorities can, if they become driving forces behind the perception of political realities and preference formation, seriously jeopardize the viability of liberal democracy. In this sense, political views, values, and preferences are not strictly a "private" affair of individual citizens, as their pursuit can generate negative externalities that affect the rights of others and ultimately those of "all of us". To the extent this is so, we may well claim a public interest in enhancing the overall quality of preferences, mediated through an improvement of the social contexts of preference formation as they demonstrably contribute to such enhancement.

A second premise is this: To repeat, the formation of political (as well as other) preferences is not just a matter of intra-personal, information-gathering, consideration and reflection alone, as in the monological process of "preference laundering" (Goodin 1982) taking place in some *forum internum*. Rather (and as argued above), it is a *social* process in which people *find out*, preferably in the course of a non-strategic exchange of information and practical reasoning, what other people consider true and desirable and fair for "all of us" – a process in the course of which the preferences with which people have entered the exchange may undergo *revisions*. (Whether or not such revisions will verge on consensus is bound to remain an open question for empirical observation.) The rule governing such deliberative exchange is something like this: You know what *you* want only after you know what *others* want, and after knowing and considering the reasons on which those others base their preferences. In practical terms, learning about other people's preferences and their reasons for holding them can encourage the formation and clarification of one's own preference on the matter under joint deliberation, provided the exchange takes place on a minimum level of respect and mutual assurance.

The institutional location in which preference formation as a social process takes place is the "life world" of everyday interaction or, more specifically, the "third sector" (Goodin 2003) as a residual sphere that is constrained yet not governed by the media of money and formal authority. The sociological distinctiveness of this "sector" consists in the fact that its organizational forms (foundations, movements, local initiatives and associations, faith-based organizations etc.) are at the same time non-governmental organizations (NGOs) and non-profit organizations (NPOs). That is to say, what they do is not predominantly guided by criteria of *legal* correctness (as in public administration) or the ambition to gain law-making powers (as in political parties); and neither is it primarily guided by an economic calculus of *profitability*. Instead, the activities of NGOs/NPOs are dominated by normative *intentions* and the values to which such intentions relate. Yet, while acting outside of the realms of market competition, political contestation, or hierarchies of authority such organizations can have a direct impact upon both economic and political processes. (Goodin and Dryzek 2006) The question by which methods such impact can be institutionalized in democratic polities (Offe 1997) has led to numerous experiments, institutional innovations, and empirical observation of the nature of deliberative preference formation and change. (Smith 2009; Warren and Pearse 2008)

Since the early 1990s, the philosopher James Fishkin (1991; 1995; 2009) has experimented in many countries and settings with the method of "Deliberative Polling". This method is designed to generate evidence of the "hypothetical", or counter-factual, will of the people, as opposed to empirical preferences of individuals as they are mirrored by conventional methods of survey research. It shows what people *would end up* believing and wanting *had they had* the opportunity to think about, with others, under conditions promoting "enlightened understanding" (Dahl 2000) and mutual respect, what they "really" want. The hypothesis, confirmed in many cases, is that the experience of informed deliberation enables participants to clarify, revise and upgrade their own preferences. Fishkin's method measures, in order to demonstrate the amount and the direction of preference revisions, the distribution of opinions and political preferences before and after a relatively short period of deliberation in which a randomly selected group of citizens is invited to participate. When institutionalized – for instance in the form of "National Issues Conferences" preceding national elections or even in the form of an annual "Deliberation Day" (Ackerman and Fishkin 2004), this would arguably have a major impact upon political elites: For as a result of Deliberative Polls, elites are provided with the opportunity to know what the well-considered, as opposed to the "raw" and unreflected, "will of the people" is.

Effects of Deliberation

We can distinguish four qualitative effects that the use of deliberative procedures can have upon political life. First, the experience of deliberation can have desirable consequences at the *individual* level of participants (Fishkin 2009, 133 *ff.*; Mutz 2008, 530). These include, among others, better information on the issue at hand, including the improved awareness of oppositional arguments; an increase of political tolerance and the willingness to compromise, as well as an increase in generalized social trust; increase in the willingness to participate through voting and civic engagement, and as a result, a greater sense of political efficacy; greater consistency of opinions.

A second effect can consist in the exercise of an *informal authority* (or a kind of "soft power") that originates from deliberative procedures once they are institutionalized as part of the political process. As (and to the extent that) media will report on consensual results and remaining disagreements of deliberating fora and mini-publics, outside observers, elite as well as non-elite, will be provided with the opportunity to learn from the difference (if any) between the "before" and "after" poll results in which direction and to what extent the post-deliberation ("refined") preferences will change relative to the "raw" pre-deliberation ones. The authority of people having passed through deliberation derives exactly (and somewhat paradoxically) from the fact that the participants of deliberative fora are randomly selected ordinary citizens who, representing only themselves rather than parties or interest groups, have neither the intention nor the organizational means to acquire political power themselves. It is exactly the absence of power ambitions of deliberators that can increase their "recommending force" (Fishkin 1995, 162; 2009, 134). The effect of spreading knowledge about policy preferences of deliberating (rather than power-seeking) ephemeral bodies will predictably make life more complex for political elites who are now, after such polls and the due publication of their outcomes in the media, publicly *known to know* that the so-called "will of the people" (as registered by ordinary opinion surveys to which they like to refer for legitimization purposes whenever it suits them) may in fact just be a mere *artefact* of prevailing non-deliberative conditions of preference formation. The public can thus learn that this "will of the people" is highly malleable and contingent upon contexts of communication. This learning is driven by a demonstration effect: if people actually *had* the time, expertise, and appropriate communicative framework to think seriously and competently about issues on the political agenda, chances are that they would change their original views and preferences.

Third, there are strong indications that deliberative institutions have not just the potential for widening the range of *substantive* policy options by bringing to evidence what people want once they have been put in the possession of pertinent information and after having debated arguments for and against the alternative policy options. They have also the potential of widening the *social inclusion* of participants (and contrary to so much of the anti-intellectual polemics of deliberation being an idiosyncratic leisure activity of the educated middle class that is *en vogue* among conservative academics). Such potential for greater social inclusiveness can be assumed on two grounds. First, to the extent the principle of *random selection* of participants can be implemented and self-selection reduced, participants will include categories of people who normally do not vote, join, donate, or even know much about political issues.[5] But, second – and in a perspective on such forms of non-participation that was first and classically stated by Schattschneider (1960; Offe 2006; Solt 2008) – there are theoretical arguments and empirical findings suggesting that non-participation and the associated waste of political resources is "endogenous to the failures of democracy" and of "normal politics" (Neblo et al. 2010, 566, 568) rather than being caused by individual characteristics such as a person's class membership or level of education. The implication of this perspective is of course that if different and additional forms of participation were available, non-participation might well be reduced. Neblo and his co-authors produce strong evidence that deliberation is in fact such an additional, participation-widening procedural device. "It is precisely people who are less likely to participate in traditional partisan politics who are most interested in deliberative participation". "Younger people, racial minorities and lower-income people expressed significantly *more* willingness to deliberate. ... The kinds of people attracted to the deliberative opportunities offered are fairly distinct from those drawn to partisan politics and interest group liberalism." (Neblo et al. 2010, 567, 571, 574)

Finally, there are also indications that while the composition of participants in deliberative procedures is designed to approximate randomness, the actual preference change that can be observed in the before/after surveys does interestingly

---

5   The random composition of deliberative fora would also increase the diversity of the points of view brought forward, which in itself can add to the informal authority claimed in the previous paragraph. The more diverse the members of a group are, the more immune are the results of deliberation from the suspicion of being biased by special interests.

not reflect a random alteration of opinions and attitudes. Instead, deliberative procedures, if conducted under conditions of randomness of participants' characteristics and thus of maximal diversity, generate qualitative outcomes concerning attitude changes and consensual policy recommendations which are *not* evenly distributed on a conservative-progressive (or "liberal" in the American sense) dimension of political views and preferences. This finding can be accounted for with a weak and a strong explanatory intuition. The weak one suggests that the very setting of deliberative fora – highly diverse individuals hitherto unknown to each other involved in an exchange of views and arguments on issues of public policy and trying to find solutions preferred by all participants – select against purely self-serving claims and propositions. As the statement "I am for policy X because it serves my interest" is unlikely to carry much persuasive power (and perhaps even discredits the speaker because of his or her undisguised selfishness), there is a built-in incentive to present policy preferences, even if they are driven by self-interest, as being adopted for the sake of values or reason – a rhetorical move that can subsequently trap the speaker in a dynamic of self-destructive hypocrisy: once you have started to present your interests as being congruent with *common* interests or *shared* values, you have started to force yourself to remain consistent and continue to argue in those terms, which may well lead to actually *betraying* (in either of the two senses of the word) the interests that were motivating the operation in the first place. Yet there is also reason to consider a strong explanation of how those deliberative procedures may translate into specific, non-random substantive outcomes. As Gastil et al. (2010) have shown in an analysis based on attitude changes generated in 65 Deliberative Polls, there is evidence supporting the presence of a conversion mechanism which translates the procedural equality of the deliberative setting into a general orientation toward equal social relations in policy solutions (Gastil et al. 2010, 8). The authors' main finding is that participants, while not re-describing themselves in overall ideological terms of "liberal" *vs.* "conservative", still undergo systematic shifts in preferences and beliefs; after participating in (single and relatively short) deliberative fora, participants were "more likely to support statements that promote cosmopolitanism [and to] oppose those that favor a more nationalist and parochial view of public affairs". As exposure to the hypothesized causal effect of participating in deliberation was just quite ephemeral, it does not come as a surprise that deliberation was found to "weakly" promote "agreement with egalitarian and collectivist worldviews" (Gastil et al. 2010, 20). Future research must provide us with more robust answers to the question of whether or not we can claim that the institutionalization of deliberative procedures would shift policy preferences and political views in sustainability-oriented, cosmopolitan and overall egalitarian and left liberal directions – directions that are marked by greater fact-regardingness, future-regardingness, and other-regardingness. To the extent this intuition can be further confirmed through rigorous analysis, the institutionalization and practical use of deliberative *will formation* (as a complement to the conventional channels of will *expression*, namely voting and bargaining) could itself become a promising *political* project rather than remaining a matter occupying political theorists and empirical researchers.

Structures of Deliberation

After having so far discussed some possible and desirable functions that delibera-tion can perform, let us, again, move on to the appropriate institutional structures in which these functions might be performed. Deliberative mini-publics (Goodin and Dryzek 2006; Fung and Wright 2003) must ideally conform to three criteria: they must be *democratic, deliberative*, and *consequential*.[6] The first of these criteria, the rights-egalitarian or *democratic* character, can be fulfilled in two ways. One is *open access to an assembly*: whoever wants to be present has the right to come and to presents his/her point of view. This applies, for instance, in the case of par-ticipatory budgeting or the "deliberation day" proposal of Ackerman and Fishkin (2004). The drawback of such self-selection is the presumably significant social selectivity that manifests itself in terms of (i) who shows up and (ii) who takes the floor and speaks for how long. The answer to both of these questions is likely to be: overwhelmingly members of the educated middle classes plus representa-tives of parties and interest groups. Moreover, if the assembly is large, delibera-tion according to the rules of a mini-public is hardly possible. Therefore, and as an alternative to open access, advocates of deliberative procedures have typically opted for the *random selection of participants* and the technique of (stratified) sampling which is intended to make the composition of the mini-public as much as possible a mirror image of the constituency. In this way, an inappropriate role of political party delegates and bearers of functional representation (i. e., interest associations) can be avoided. It must be said, however, that self-selection (and the biases contingent on it, for instance age, education, rhetorical skills) cannot be fully avoided; after all, before a random selection can take place, people must

---

6   Two additional criteria are discussed by Smith (2009): procedures must be *affordable* and *transferable* to a variety of political issues, i. e. not limited to the most basic issues having to do with electoral systems and the problem of "choosing how to choose", as in the famous case of electoral reform in the Canadian Province of British Columbia. (Warren and Pearse 2008).

declare their readiness – or else would have to be brought under the equivalent of jury duty or mandatory military service – to actually perform their role in the deliberative body should the lot decide that they are called upon to do so. Yet if the findings of Neblo et al. (2010), referred to above, turn out to be robust, deliberation would provide incentives for self-selection of participants to whom conventional channels of participation and representation do not appeal, thus neutralizing the distortions caused by middle class self-selection. Although both of these "democratic" methods of constituting a deliberative body – open access to assemblies and random selection of participants – clearly have their problems, the variety of experience, opinion, and points of view present in either of them is arguably still greater (and less affected by strategic interests in gaining and maintaining power) than it is the case in ordinary representative assemblies.

Secondly, and although *deliberative* settings will hardly ever achieve the criteria of an "ideal speech situation", there can be a considerable approximation to it through the role of facilitators, or *moderators*. Participants are asked and constantly reminded by the facilitator to speak out, to listen to others, to behave respectfully, to discipline their political passions, to declare their personal interests related to the issues under discussion, to learn about the issues and alternatives they are dealing with, to respond to the queries and arguments of others; to try to persuade others of their points of view through spelling out reasons; and to arrive at a policy recommendation which reflects, as far as possible, their shared understanding of what conforms to a notion of the common good. In that communicative process, the three virtues, referred to above, will typically be insisted upon by moderators and mutually appealed to by participants: *fact*-regardingness, *other*-regardingness, and *future*-regardingness. As to fact-regardingness, the typical question is: Do we know enough and do we make consistent and unbiased use of that knowledge, in order to develop an adequately informed recommendation on some policy question? Other-regardingness concerns the readiness to take into account the interests, values, and rights of others and issues of social justice pertaining to the way a proposed policy affects interests in favorable or unfavorable ways. And future-regardingness is the ability to look at and evaluate the long-term consequences of the solutions proposed and to deal with issues of their sustainability. In order for a group of deliberators to live up to these demanding standards (and usually under severe time constraints), the group must be *small* in order to allow for a full presentation of arguments and opinions of its members. Also, and in order to enforce the above rules of deliberation, the facilitator must assume the role of enforcing roughly equal participation and an adequate input of information (which is usually provided by a diverse group of experts who are made available for lectures and questioning).

Perhaps hardest to realize is the third criterion: Deliberations of mini-publics must be (known by participants beforehand to have a reasonable reliable prospect to be) *consequential*, i. e. are guaranteed to have some measure of political impact. This impact can be entirely informal, but even that presupposes that political elites and members of legislative assemblies take mini-publics seriously, and that the media report on the process and outcome (recommendations) of deliberation. "Planning Cells" (Dienel 1997) and "Citizen Juries" (Coote and Lenaghan 1997) are cases where the promised impact was to an extent formalized: sponsoring (local) governments made a formal commitment to provide reasons in public should they choose *not* to follow the recommendations given by deliberating mini-publics. Again the most far-reaching commitment was one that the government of British Columbia made, namely the commitment to hold a referendum on the Assembly's proposal (however one with strong super-majoritarian conditions which ultimately caused its failure by a narrow margin). At any rate, if the participants cannot rely on the expectation that what they do and come up with has at least some chance of "making a difference" in public policy, and that their common efforts are recognized as valuable (according to some proposals, also through the payment of a nominal fee paid to deliberators), their readiness to participate, to spend time on learning and understanding, and to properly deliberate will soon be exhausted.

Conclusion

I have introduced this essay by saying that contemporary liberal democracies are "not functioning well". Apart from the question of normative standards concerning characteristics and criteria of a "well-functioning" democracy that this proposition suggests, it can also be read as an empirical generalization: Many – and probably an increasing number and highly diverse sorts of – people converge on the belief, expressed in words and even more often in their patterns of behavior and (in)action, that the way democracies function and the political outcomes they generate are often frustrating, disappointing, short-sighted, unfair, and thus seriously deficient. Rather than this disappointment leading to widely advocated rejection of liberal democracy and its principles, there is an ongoing and vivid democratic meta-discourse on possible improvements, extensions, and innovations of the democratic mode of organizing political rule.

In this discourse, participants have focused on various stages of the overall democratic political process. One focus can be described by the question how ruling elites can be prevented from violating the limitations of their office through effective constraints that would make them act in more accountable ways. The proposal to strengthen the political role of courts and fiduciary institutions is sometimes made in response to this concern. Another focus is the institutional method by which the multitude of expressions of individual preferences of citizens is to be aggregated and condensed into a single (and time-limited) collective preference. Answers to this question emerge from debates on the pro's and con's of electoral systems and the virtues and vices of direct-democratic popular legislation. These two foci have remained almost entirely outside of the present discussion. Instead, I have concentrated on a third and a fourth issue. The former is the issue of actual political participation: how many people are entitled to make use of their democratic rights, how many do actually do so, how often, and concerning what categories of substantive matters. Here belong all democratic innovations that are intended to encourage more, and more evenly distributed, participation through voting and joining and other forms of *expressing* preferences and choices. Finally, there is the issue of how the preferences that are to be expressed and aggregated *come into being in the first place* – the formative phase of beliefs and preferences concerning political life. It at this stage where deliberative modes of *forming* and *revising* preferences can come to play a role.

I have argued that the practice of giving reasons, as well as the practice of listening to, respecting, and possibly adopting reasons that others give in an open-ended and disciplined face-to-face setting can be institutionalized. To that end, participation in such settings would have to be randomized and thereby changed according to egalitarian principles; time, place and topics of deliberation organized in formal ways; the mutual recognition of dissenting voices guaranteed; the civility of discourses and the availability of relevant information assured; and the public visibility of outcomes, consensual or otherwise, provided for. Institutional forms in which this happens are not a substitute for, but a complement to all those more familiar procedures of democratic politics which regulate the expression and aggregation of preferences and the accountability of office holders. Individual beliefs and preferences are logically prior to their expression and aggregation. Yet beliefs and preferences, the ultimate "raw material" of the political process, cannot be treated as individually "given" but are, as social constructs, in constant flux. Also, they are highly incomplete, as most people do simply not know what to believe and prefer on most collectively relevant matters most of the time. Deliberation is the process in which they find out; if properly conducted, it can also be a process in which the three virtues of taking the facts, the well-being of others, and future developments into consideration will be cultivated.

References

Ackerman, Bruce, and Ian Ayres. 2004. *Voting with Dollars: A New Paradigm for Campaign Finance.* New Haven: Yale University Press.

Ackerman, Bruce, and James S. Fishkin. 2004. *Deliberation Day.* New Haven: Yale University Press.

Coote, Anna, and Jo Lenaghan. 1997. *Citizens' Juries: Theory into Practice.* London: Institute for Public Policy Research.

Crouch, Colin. 2004. *Post-Democracy.* Cambridge: Polity.

Crouch, Colin. 2008. "What Will Follow the Demise of Privatised Keynesianism?" *The Political Quarterly* 79 (4): 476–487.

Crozier, Michel J., Samuel P. Huntington, and Joji Watanuki. 1975. *The Crisis of Democracy,* New York: NYU Press.

Dahl, Robert A. 2000. *On Democracy.* New Haven: Yale University Press.

Dalton, Russell J. 2004. *Democratic Challenges, Democratic Choices. The Erosion of Political Support in Advanced Industrial Democracies.* Oxford: Oxford University Press.

Dienel, Peter C. 1997. *Die Planungszelle. Eine Alternative zur Establishment-Demokratie.* Opladen: Westdeutscher Verlag.

Fishkin, James S. 1991. *Democracy and Deliberation. New Directions for Democratic Reform.* New Haven and London: Yale UP.

Fishkin, James S. 1995. *The Voice of the People. Public Opinion and Democracy.* New Haven: Yale University Press.

Fishkin, James. 2009. *When the People Speak. Deliberative Democracy and Public Consultation.* Oxford: Oxford University Press.

Fung, Archon and Erik Olin Wright (eds.). 2003. *Deepening Democracy. Institutional Innovations in Empowered Participatory Governance.* London: Verso.

Gastil, John, Chiara Bacci, and Michael Dollinger. 2010. "Is Deliberation Neutral? Patterns of Attitude Change during the Deliberative Polls" *Journal of Public Deliberation* 6/2. http://services.bepress.com/cgi/viewcontent.cgi?article=1128&context=jpd.

Goodin, Robert E. 1982. *Political Theory and Public Policy.* Chicago: University of Chicago Press.

Goodin, Robert E. 2003. "Democratic Accountability: The Distinctiveness of the Third Sector." *Archives Européennes de Sociologie* 44 (3): 359–369.

Goodin, Robert E. 2004. "Input Democracy." In *Power and Democracy,* eds. Frederik Engelstad and Oyvind Osterud, 79–100. Engelstad, Aldershot: Ashgate.

Goodin, Robert E., and John S. Dryzek. 2006. "Deliberative Impacts: The Macro-Political Uptake of Mini-Publics." *Politics and Society* 34 (2): 219–244.

Guéhenno, Jean Marie. 1993. *La Fin de la Démocratie*. Paris: Flammarion.

Heller, Hermann. 1983 [1933]. *Staatslehre*. Tübingen: Mohr 1983.

Hinrichs, Karl. 2002. "Do the Old Exploit the Young? Is Enfranchising Children a Good Idea?" *Archives Européennes Sociologiques* 43 (1): 35–58.

Kant, Immanuel. 2006 [1795]. "Toward perpetual peace." In *Toward Perpetual Peace and Other Writings on Politics, Peace, and History. Rethinking the Western Tradition*, ed. Pauline Kleingeld, 67–109. New Haven/London: Yale University Press.

Lijphart, Arend. 1997. "Unequal Participation. Democracy's Unresolved Dilemma." *American Political Science Review* 91 (1): 1–14.

Lipset, Seymor M. 1981. *Political Man*. Baltimore: John Hopkins University Press.

Lukes, Steven. 2005. *Power. A Radical View*. London: Palgrave.

Mill, John S. 1861. *Considerations on Representative Government*.

Mutz, Diana C. 2008. "Is Deliberative Democracy a Falsifiable Theory?" *Annual Review of Political Science* 11: 521–38.

Nassmacher, Karl Heinz. 2009. *Political Finance*. Baden-Baden: Nomos.

Neblo, Michael A., Kevin M. Esterling, Ryan P. Kennedy, David M. J. Lazer, and Anand E. Sokhey. 2010. "Who wants to deliberate- And Why?" *American Political Science Review* 104 (3): 566–583.

O'Connor, James. 1973. *The Fiscal Crisis of the State*. NY: Saint Martin's Press.

Offe, Claus. 1992. "Bindings, Shackles, Brakes: On Self-Limitation Strategies." In *Cultural-Political Interventions in the Unfinished Project of Enlightenment*, eds. Axel Honnth, Thomas McCarthy, Claus Offe and Albrecht Wellmer, 63–94. Cambridge, Mass., London: MIT-Press.

Offe, Claus. 1997. "Microaspects of Democratic Theory: what makes for the deliberative competence of citizens?" In *Democracy's Victory and Crisis*, ed. Axel Hadenius, 81–104. Cambridge: Cambridge University Press.

Offe, Claus. 2006. "Political disaffection as an outcome of institutional practices? Some post-Tocquevillean speculations." In *Political Disaffection in Contemporary Democracies. Social Capital, institutions, and politics*, eds. Mariano Torcal and José R. Montero, 23–45. London: Routledge.

Pharr, Susan J., and Robert D. Putnam (eds.). (2000). *Disaffected Democracies. What's troubling the trilateral countries?* Princeton: Princeton University Press.

Phillips, Anne. 1995. *The Politics of Presence: The Political Representation of Gender, Ethnicity, and Race*. Oxford: Oxford University Press.

Rosanvallon, Pierre. 2008. *Counter-Democracy: Politics in an Age of Distrust.* Cambridge: Cambridge University Press.

Santos, Bonaventura de S. 1998. "Participatory Budgeting in Porto Alegre: Toward a Redistributive Democracy." *Politics & Society* 26 (4): 461–510.

Schattschneider, Elmer Eric. 1960. *The Semi-Sovereign People.* New York: Holt, Rinehart and Winston.

Schmitter, Philippe C. 2000. "The Prospects of Post-Liberal Democracy." In *Kontingenz und Krise*, eds. Karl Hinrichs, Herbert Kitschelt and Helmut Wiesenthal, 25–40. Frankfurt: Campus.

Schmitter, Philippe C. and Alexander H. Trechsel (eds.). 2004. *The Future of Democracy in Europe. Trends, Analysis and Reforms.* Strasbourg: Council of Europe.

Sen, Armatya. 1999. *Development as Freedom.* New York: Knopf.

Smith, Graham. 2005. *Beyond the ballot: 57 democratic innovations from around the world.* http://www.soton.ac.uk/ccd/events/SuppMat/Beyond%20the%20 Ballot.pdf.

Smith, Graham. 2009. *Democratic Innovations: Designing Institutions for Citizen Participation.* Cambridge: Cambridge University Press.

Solt, Frederick. 2008. "Economic Inequality and Democratic Political Engagement." *American Journal of Political Science* 52 (1): 48–60.

Tocqueville, Alexis de. 1988 [1835, 1840]. *Democracy in America.* 2 vls. New York: Vintage.

Torcal, Mariano, and J. R. Montero (eds.). 2006. *Political Disaffection in Contemporary Democracies. Social Capital, Institutions, and Politics.* London: Routledge.

Warren, Mark E., and Hilary Pearse (eds.). 2008. *Designing Deliberative Democracy.* Cambridge: CUP.

Warren, Mark E. 2003. "A Second Transformation of Democracy?" In *Democracy Transformed?* eds. Bruce Cain, Russell Dalton and Susan Scarrow, 223–249. Oxford: Oxford University Press.

About the Authors

André Bächtiger is chair of Political Theory at the University of Stuttgart. His research focuses on the challenges of mapping and measuring deliberation and political communication as well as the preconditions and outcomes of high quality deliberation in the context of representative institutions and mini-publics. He is co-writing a book *Mapping and Measuring Deliberation* (with John Parkinson), Oxford University Press, 2016.

Kees Brants is honorary professor at the University of Amsterdam's School of Communication Research and professor emeritus in political communication at Leiden University.

Stephen Coleman is professor of political communication at the University of Leeds. His most recent book is 'How Voters Feel' and his most recent co-edited volume is *Can The Media Serve Democracy*? He is currently writing a book about how citizens experience talking about politics.

James S. Fishkin is professor and director of the Center for Deliberative Democracy at Stanford University. He holds the Janet M. Peck Chair in International Communication and teaches Communication and Political Science. He is the author of *When the People Speak: Deliberative Democracy and Public Consultation* (Oxford, 2009).

John Gastil is professor and head of the Department of Communication Arts and Sciences at Pennsylvania State University, where he directs the McCourtney Institute for Democracy. He specializes in public deliberation and group decision making, with a current focus on the Citizens' Initiative Review. His recent book include *Democracy in Small Groups* (2nd ed.).

Thomas Gautschi received his PhD from Utrecht University and is professor of social research at Mannheim University in Germany.

Borbála Göncz is research fellow at the Institute of Sociology and Social Policy at the Corvinus University of Budapest where she earned her PhD. Her research focuses on attitudes towards the European integration and European identity, some aspects of migration and deliberative methods. She has participated in research projects that used deliberative methods.

Katherine R. Knobloch is assistant professor and the associate director of the Center for Public Deliberation in the Department of Communication Studies at

Colorado State University. Her research focuses on deliberative democracy and community engagement. Specifically, she explores the development, evaluation, and impact of deliberative public processes.

György Lengyel is professor of sociology at the Corvinus University of Budapest. His research interests lie mostly in elites and institutions. Among his recent publications are *Elites in hard times* (Comparative Sociology, 2014/1) and *Europe of Elites* (ed. with H. Best and L. Verzichelli, Oxford U.P., 2012).

Giles Moss is lecturer in media policy. He obtained his PhD at the University of Oxford. His research focuses on the relationship between new media and politics. A common theme in much of his work is the role of public engagement and deliberation in politics and policy-making.

Claus Offe was professor of political science at Humboldt University, Berlin, where he has held a chair of Political Sociology and Social Policy. Since 2006 he is Professor of Political Science at Hertie School of Governance, Berlin. His fields of research are democratic theory, transition studies, EU integration, and welfare state and labor market studies.

Seraina Pedrini received her PhD from the University of Bern and works at the Swiss Statistical Office.

Anna Przybylska is assistant professor as well as founder and head of the Centre for Deliberation at the Institute of Sociology, University of Warsaw. She is a manager of the project "In Dialogue": www.wdialogu.uw.edu.pl/en.

Tyrone Reitman is co-founder and executive director of Healthy Democracy, the organization that developed and now promotes the Citizens' Initiative Review. His professional background includes advocacy for increased transparency and accountability in government and politics. He holds an Master's in public affairs from the University of Oregon.

Tatsuro Sakano is doctor of engineering and a professor at Department of Value and Decision Science of Tokyo Institute of Technology in Tokyo. Scientific interest in behavioral aspect of collective will formation and institutional design.

Yves Sintomer is senior fellow at the French University Institute and professor of political science at Paris 8 University. He is author of *Participatory Budgeting in Europe; Democracy and Public Governance* (with C. Herzberg and A. Röcke), Ashgate, London, 2015; *Local participation in Southern Europe: Causes, Characteristics and Consequences* (with J. Font and D. della Porta), Rowman & Littlefield, Washington D.C., 2014.

Alice Siu is associate director of the Center for Deliberative Democracy at Stanford University. She received her PhD from the Department of Communication at Stanford University. Her research interests are in deliberation, including the effects of socio-economic class on deliberation, the quality of deliberation, and the quality of arguments in deliberation.

Marco R. Steenbergen received his PhD from Stony Brook University and is professor of political methodology at the University of Zurich in Switzerland.

Jürg Steiner is professor emeritus of political science at both the the Universitry of Bern and the University of North Carolina at Chapel Hill. His latest book is *The Foundations of Deliberative Democracy. Empirical Research and Normative Implications*, Cambridge University Press, 2012.

Éva Vépy-Schlemmer is Ph.D. candidate at the Institute of Sociology and Social Policy at the Corvinus University of Budapest. She has participated in various research including deliberative methods. Her research focus on discourse quality analysis.

Elżbieta Wesołowska is psychologist, associate professor at Social Science Department of Warmia and Mazury University in Olsztyn (Poland). Her scientific interest are in social psychology, dynamics of group processes and social interaction in deliberative debate conditions.

Marcin Zgiep is PhD candidate in the Institute for Social Studies, University of Warsaw. His main research interests lie in political philosophy and theory with particular emphasis on modern democratic governance within multi-level, network environment. His doctoral thesis focuses on the interplay between normative theory of public deliberation and contemporary, real-world democratic practices.

Fan Yang is member of the Collaborative Innovation Center of Judicial Civilization (Jilin University), and also post-doctoral fellow in KoGuan Law School of Shanghai Jiao Tong University. He received his Ph.D degree at Institute des Sciences sociales du Politique (ISP) of Ecole Normale Supérieure de Cachan in France. His studies focus on sociology of law and legal philosophy.

Weiyu Zhang is associate professor at the Department of Communication and New Media, National University of Singapore. Her research focuses on civic engagement and ICTs, with an emphasis on Asia. Her published works appeared in Journal of Communication, Communication Theory, Communication Research, and many others.

Warsaw Studies in Politics and Society

Edited by Radosław Markowski

www.peterlang.com